Quantum Computing Models for Cybersecurity and Wireless Communications

Scrivener Publishing
100 Cummings Center, Suite 541J
Beverly, MA 01915-6106

Sustainable Computing and Optimization

Series Editors: Dr. Prasenjit Chatterjee (dr.prasenjitchatterjee6@gmail.com), Morteza Yazdani and Dilbagh Panchal

The objective of the series is to bring together global research scholars, experts, and scientists in the research areas of sustainable computing and optimization to share their knowledge and experiences on current research achievements in these fields. Since the series was launched in 2021, it has provided a golden opportunity for the research community to share their novel research results, findings, and innovations to a wide range of topics and applications. The series promotes sustainable computing and optimization methodologies to solve real-life problems mainly from engineering and management systems domains.

Publishers at Scrivener
Martin Scrivener (martin@scrivenerpublishing.com)
Phillip Carmical (pcarmical@scrivenerpublishing.com)

Quantum Computing Models for Cybersecurity and Wireless Communications

Edited by

Budati Anil Kumar

Faculty of Electronics & Communication Engineering, Koneru Lakshmaiah Education Foundation (Deemed University), Aziz Nagar Campus, Hyderabad, Telangana, India

Singamaneni Kranthi Kumar

Faculty of Computer Engineering and Technology, Chaitanya Bharathi Institute of Technology, Gandipet, Hyderabad, Telangana, India

and

Li Xingwang

School of Physics and Electronic Information Engineering, Henan Polytechnic University, Jiaozuo, China

Scrivener Publishing

WILEY

This edition first published 2025 by John Wiley & Sons, Inc., 111 River Street, Hoboken, NJ 07030, USA and Scrivener Publishing LLC, 100 Cummings Center, Suite 541J, Beverly, MA 01915, USA

For more information about Scrivener publications please visit www.scrivenerpublishing.com.

Wiley Global Headquarters
111 River Street, Hoboken, NJ 07030, USA

For details of our global editorial offices, customer services, and more information about Wiley products visit us at www.wiley.com.

Library of Congress Cataloging-in-Publication Data

ISBN 978-1-394-27139-9

Front cover images courtesy of Wikimedia Commons
Cover design by Russell Richardson

Set in size of 11pt and Minion Pro by Manila Typesetting Company, Makati, Philippines

Printed in the USA

10 9 8 7 6 5 4 3 2 1

Contents

Preface

Artificial intelligence, cybersecurity, and practical cryptography are just a few of the areas where quantum machine learning has the most potential. Advanced data encryption techniques are urgently needed as our growing reliance on the internet exposes us to threats brought on by cyber-attacks. Although many current encryption standards may not be breakable by current quantum-based machines, it is vital to keep ahead of the impending threats and prepare for sophisticated cyberattacks using quantum-proof solutions. The difficult issues that classical computers are unable to address, such as the techniques employed in data encryption, can be solved by quantum computers. Modern encryption techniques are based on mathematical formulas that would be impractically difficult for traditional computers to decrypt. Working tirelessly to create quantum-secure encryption techniques is the research goal. One possible method is for securely transferring a quantum key between two endpoints that makes use of the quantum physics qualities known as quantum key distribution (QKD). Before recent developments, this technique could only be used with fiber optic connections, but now quantum key transfer is also possible over the Internet. Although there are still many unsolved problems concerning quantum computing, it is evident that present methods of cybersecurity and encryption are at risk. We need to adapt the way we safeguard our data and take a defense-intensive strategy characterized by many layers of quantum-secure security to lessen the threat. To protect themselves from potential quantum threats, security-conscious organizations are actively looking for quantum-ready encryption solutions, including those provided by Quantum Exchange.

Future quantum machines will exponentially boost computing power, creating new opportunities for improving cybersecurity. Both classical and quantum-based cyberattacks can be proactively identified and stopped by quantum-based cybersecurity before they harm. Complex math-based problems that support several encryption standards could be quickly solved using quantum machine learning. The traditional cryptography standards on classical computers, which rely on difficult mathematical calculations like prime factorization, would take millennia or more. However, these issues might be resolved by quantum machines in a manageable amount of time. Despite the lack of widespread commercial quantum devices, it is wise to plan for quantum-based cybersecurity difficulties and deal with present restrictions. The security and privacy of commercial organizations will greatly increase as a result of this preparation. For instance, today's adversaries could penetrate private networks. When large-scale quantum machines are made commercially available in the future, this enormous computational capacity could be used to undermine networks and infrastructures by decrypting critical data. Quantum machine learning-based cybersecurity, especially in the context of quantum computing and quantum chaotic characteristics, presents stronger and more exciting chances for protecting important and sensitive information by outpacing these possible attacks. Through book chapters, academics, researchers, and scientists have contributed their ideas, concepts, and use cases on cutting-edge technologies like blockchain, quantum machine learning, cybersecurity, IoT, and SDN. The main purpose of this book is to publish the latest research papers focusing on problems and challenges in the areas of data transmission technology, computer algorithms, artificial intelligence (AI) based devices, computer technology, and their solutions to motivate researchers.

This book serves as a ready reference for researchers and professionals working in the area of quantum computing models in communications, machine learning techniques, the healthcare industry, and IoT-enabled technologies.

Acknowledgment

We, the editors of the *Quantum Computing Models for Cybersecurity & Wireless Communications,* wish to acknowledge the hard work, commitment and dedication of the authors who have contributed their wonderful chapters to our edited volume in the stipulated time.

Further, we would like to convey our special gratitude to Dr Prasenjit Chatterjee, Dean (Research and Consultancy), MCKV Institute of Engineering, West Bengal, India for his consistent support and guidance at each stage of the book's development.

We wish to bestow our best regards to all referees for providing productive comments to the authors to improve their chapters to meet the required standard. A successful book publication is the integrated result of everyone's contribution and not just those named as editors or authors.

Finally, the editors acknowledge everyone who helped us directly and indirectly.

Budati Anil Kumar
Singamaneni Kranthi Kumar
Li Xingwang

1

Performance Evaluation of Avionics System Under Hardware-In-Loop Simulation Framework with Implementation of an AS9100 Quality Management System

Rajesh Shankar Karvande[1*] and Tatineni Madhavi[2]

[1]'F' RCI, DRDO, Hyderabad, TS, India
[2]EECE, GITAM, Hyderabad, TS, India

Abstract
Performance evaluation of avionics subsystem is mandatory before the deployment of the system. In the aerospace and defense industry it is critical to validate the embedded system software along with the flight subsystem in real time before real launch. The launch of the flight vehicle is single shot operation and involves so many factors. To avoid the catastrophic failures due to errors in algorithms, subsystems integrated working under real time, it is essential and mandatory to validate the software using Hardware-In-Loop Simulation (HILS) platform. This is unique platform that evaluate the performance of mission software i.e. control and guidance software using different criteria and conditions. This is cost effective tool to evaluate the performance for the expensive flight trial and using its rapid prototyping technique designer can validate their software in early stage of development. Development of AS9100 Quality Management System (QMS) in the HILS process is essential and inevitable part of avionics design to improve the process. This paper focus on the embedded system testing, validation, and certification area. The HILS test-bed designed as part of performance evaluation, different configuration of the HILS for centralized and distributed architecture, test plan for all software test cases with different perturbation cases. The lifecycle of the HILS process is explained in details with respect to AS9100 QMS requirements and implementation. Development of HILS test-bed for centralized and distributed

**Corresponding author*: rajeshkarvande@rediffmail.com

Budati Anil Kumar, Singamaneni Kranthi Kumar and Li Xingwang (eds.) Quantum Computing Models for Cybersecurity and Wireless Communications, (1–12) © 2025 Scrivener Publishing LLC

architecture configuration is explained in details. The results are discussed and the conclusion and suggestions for future improvement are discussed in last section.

Keywords: 6Dof plant model, hardware-in-loop simulation, inertial navigation system, on board computer, OBC-in-loop, quality management system

1.1 Introduction

Performance Evaluation of avionics system specially used in aerospace vehicle is essential and critical task that ensure the success rate of developmental flight trial. The evaluation of the On-Board Computer (OBC) mission software along with the integrated flight hardware is carried out using the unique Hardware In Loop Simulation Test-bed [1, 2]. There are number of steps involved in testing phase of HILS. Design of the test-bed, development of the simulation software, testing of the OBC software. All the errors or deficiency related with mission software has been validated in HILS with number of test cases. Unit level testing carried out by the developer is not sufficient to test system completely. This unit testing only verifies the system independently working as per design. The integrated level testing and user acceptance testing is performed at HILS as shown in Figure 1.1. This testing highlights the design issues like lags, communication delay, bandwidth etc. for the individual system when it is integrated with other sub-systems.

In the total product life cycle of software development HILS is important phase for the validation and testing of avionics system is shown in Figure 1.1. HILS consists of both Hardware and Software parts: Simulation computer based on the configuration of the avionics system that is helpful to select the I/O cards of the system like MIL-STD 1553 cards, ADC cards, DAC cards and RS-422 cards [7]. The second part is the 6Dof software development part based on the Real Time Operating Systems. The problem is that the HILS process has many branches and there is no process control. It has been experienced the delay and ineffectiveness in the early stages of the HILS. It was highly essential to establish a stepwise process with the effectiveness

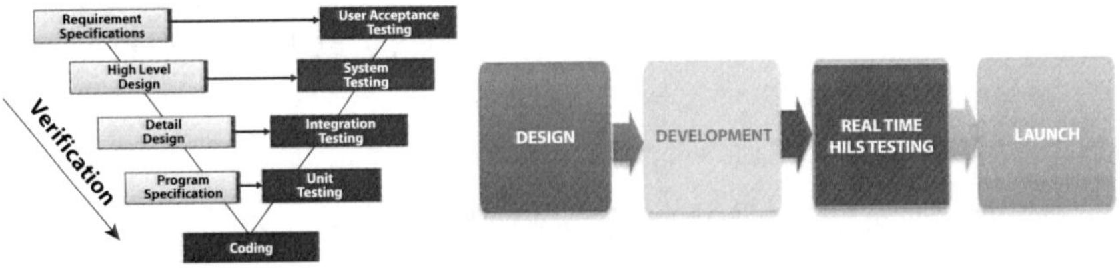

Figure 1.1 Testing phases of software and the avionics product lifecycle.

and timely delivery of the product from HILS. So more focus and effort has been given to develop unified HILS process that will be stepwise process with the effectiveness of the Quality Management System for ensuring the timely completion of the process. The process of HILS is covered under the Aerospace Standard AS9100. The problem is to develop the methodology that defines the scope of the HILS process that is critical part of the project cycle to evaluate the performance of the software and flight hardware in integrated mode. This paper has given the detail explanation about the development of HILS process and the development of AS9100 QMS standard that is adopted for this process that has been bonded together first time to achieve the quality objective for the HILS as well as at the laboratory level to be recognized as global level. First the concept of the performance evaluation is explained with HILS Configuration, then the development of control i.e. Test plan, Test cases, Test results followed by induction of AS9100 quality absorption to HILS activities. The Key Performance Indicator (KPI) that shows the effectiveness of the concept of development of QMS at process level and the performance of the HILS according to that is discussed at the end with conclusion and suggestion at the end.

There are White Box Testing and Black Box Testing. White Box testing only verify the algorithm by visual inspection or flow chats. Performance evaluation is also called as the Black Box testing methodology that execute the algorithm and evaluate that the development is meeting the goals of design. This uses the input design specifications and parameters and measure output generated after execution of the software in real time. Hardware-In-Loop Simulation Framework is unique setup that is used for the performance evaluation of the Avionics system for both centralized architecture as well as distributed architecture.

Centralized Architecture

In this scheme all the algorithms are built using single processor with On Board Computer is shown in Figure 1.2. All the required interfaces are controlled by the processor. The sub systems are mainly electro mechanical that do not have any processing or computing unit inside the subsystem.

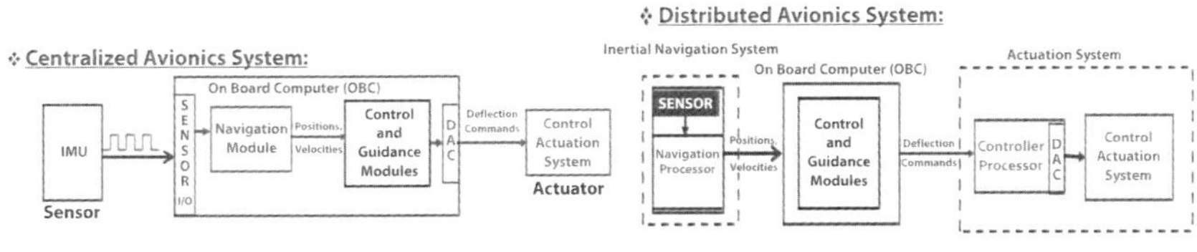

Figure 1.2 Centralized and distributed architecture of the avionics system.

Distributed Architecture

There is processor available in each subsystem and the data processed inside the subsystem itself is shown in Figure 1.2, e.g. in the case of Inertial Navigation System, the raw data gyros and accelerometers samples are processed inside the INS unit and the processed data i.e. positions, velocities, rates, accelerations, quaternions are posted to the OBC at regular interval. Similarly actuator setup has their own processor to process the deflection commands and send back the feedback information about the actuator at regular interval.

The challenge is to establish testing methodology for both architecture and the develop the uniform methodology in this area. The recent research paper has been studied for the development of the process effectiveness. Paper title "Development of Hardware-In-Loop Simulation Test-bed for testing of Navigation System-INS" by Rajesh K & B Ramesh Kumar explain the testing methodology for INS. It is limited for INS system only. Another paper titled "On joint hardware-in-the-loop simulation of aircraft control system and propulsion system" by Yao Zhao explains about the HILS system of the aircraft system. The development of the process for timely completion of the HILS activities and control for the effectiveness monitoring of the process paper is essential to help the researcher and engineers to have a layout of methodology for future experiments in this area.

1.2 HILS Process and Quality Management System

There are many AS9100 is Quality Management system for Aviation, Space and Defence industry released by International Aerospace Quality Group (IAQG). AS9100 Quality Management System goes hand to hand with each process of the Aerospace Research and Development Laboratory. After the Design and Development phase is finalized then the simulation and testing of the subsystem in integrated mode has been initiated. HILS process is the part of testing of the product and covered under QMS. Four Major processes has been defined and covered under QMS.

- HILS Planning and Configuration Management.
- Development of the HILS Setup
- OBC Software Validation
- Hardware In Loop Simulation.

A. HILS Planning and Configuration Management

Planning is crucial as all the schedule of the further testing and real launch depends on the HILS planning as shown in Figure 1.3. In parallel with the

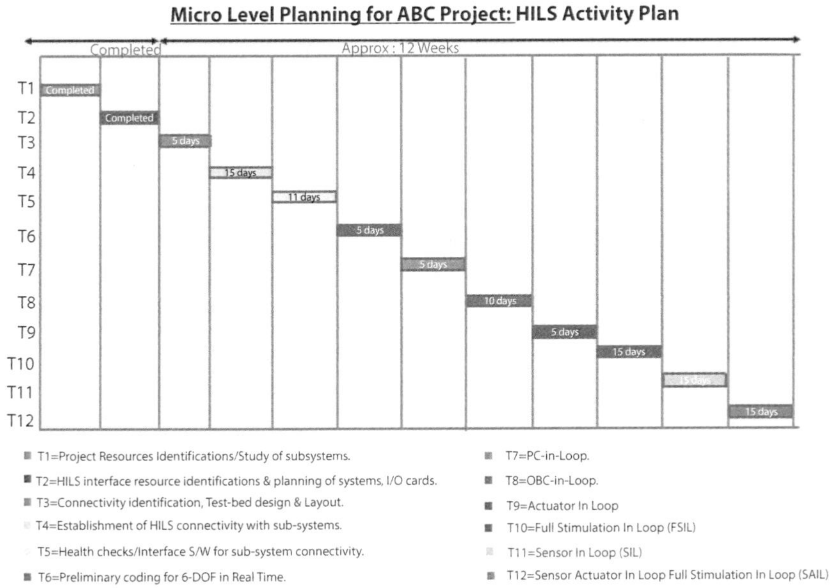

Figure 1.3 Planning of HILS activities of the project.

development cycle, development of HILS testbed, planning of test cases and HILS testing is established. Test-bed development focuses on the configuration, Timeline required and the HILS test cases for the mission software validation. Development of HILS testbed and development of simulation software mainly depend on the avionics configuration, Interface Control Document (ICD) of each sub-system and interface communication protocol of different sub-systems. This all together is covered under the HILS configuration and planning.

B. Development of HILS Test-Bed

Generally, the design and configuration of the HILS Setup is based on the avionics system used for the aerospace vehicle. The process block diagram is shown in Figure 1.4. The data acquisition system based on popular communication protocols, MIL-STD 1553, RS-422, ADC, DAC, and Digital Input/Output. These all the I/O systems are integrated with the HILS System for the configuration of Simulation System. Application layer of the simulation computer is plant model algorithms. Two different configurations have been designed and developed for Centralized architecture of avionics system and distributed architecture of the avionics system. The 6Dof equation that is part of simulation system is developed using the mathematical model [4] and under the real time operating system [7].

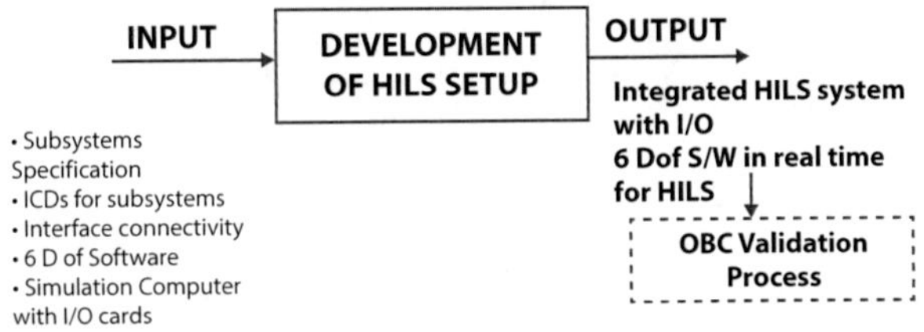

Figure 1.4 Development of HILS setup" HILS QMS process.

The other supporting modules like thrust, aero, interpolation computational algorithm has been developed using real time operating system and high-level software language. This integrated plant software is tested using the input data provided by the designer. The output data that is generated after execution of the HILS run that is controlled process. Mainly the 6Dof parameters i.e. three rates and accelerations are compared with the designer data. Here, the process coverage focuses on the coding standard, white box testing as a part of algorithm verification and the output parameters.

C. OBC Software Validation

The Second process is the OBC software validation. The Control and Guidance (C&G) algorithm are developed with On-Board Computer [8]. The execution time, lags, transportation delay issues get addressed in HILS by execution of OBC software [5]. The water fall methodology as per the software engineering is followed for the testing of the OBC software is shown in Figure 1.5. The iterative software is tested and the observation has been given to the developer to improve the code. This in the iterative

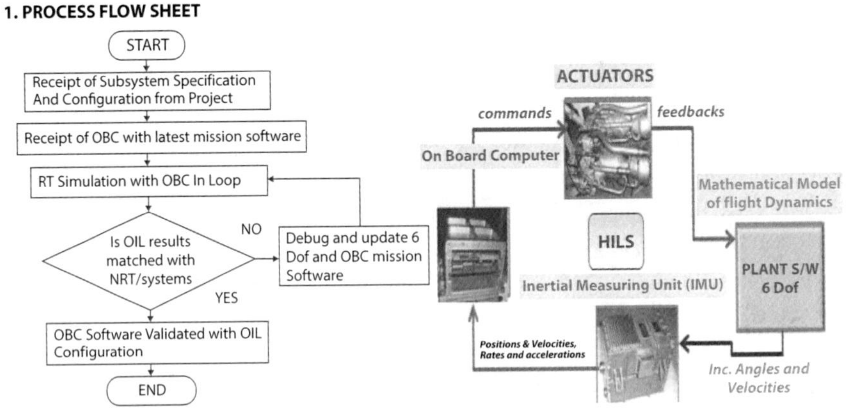

Figure 1.5 "OBC software validation" process flow.

process this testing has been carried out. Only OBC software and hardware is validated in OBC-In-Loop in initial phase of HILS process. Other flight subsystems i.e. INS and actuators are simulated in plat model. Plant model execute the INC and Actuator simulator based on mathematical model of the sensor and the actuator model. The HILS simulation is developed under Real Time Linux operating system [14].

1.3 HILS Testing Phase

Final phase of HILS testing is carried out in step-wise manner. After the validation of OBC-In-Loop, in stepwise manner flight hardware is introduced in HILS for their hardware and software validation [11].

- *Actuator-In-Loop (AIL)*: In the case real actuators are integrated and the performance of the actuator dynamics is validated [3]. The parameters like lags, bandwidth and the dead zone related with Actuator is validated and rectified in AIL [9, 10].
- *Full-Stimulation-In-Loop (FSIL)*: INS consists of two parts: sensors and Navigation algorithm. In FSIL only navigation algorithm of INS is validated. This is type of static test with bypassing the real sensor and only stimulated data is sent to INS to validate the navigation algorithm [6].
- *Sensor-In-Loop (SIL)*: INS sensor performance is validated. The INS/IMU experience three directional rotation by the HILS Flight Motion Simulator (FMS). According to the trajectory dynamics, rotations by 6Dof plant model has been sent to FMS with the three directions simultaneously. This Gyros rotate and send the information to OBC for the validation of C&G algorithm [6].
- *Sensor-Actuator-In-Loop (SAIL)*: This is the final stage of the HILS validation process. Flight hardware Actuators as well as INS are integrated in HILS as per the communication interfaces. Both subsystems are executing their algorithm simultaneously. The integrated performance in real time is validated [10].

Number of test cases has been generated to test the robustness of the software as well as system is tabulated as per Table 1.1. These test cases has been performed in different conditions and in different configurations.

Table 1.1 Test cases of HILS for OBC software.

	Non Real Time Runs (NRT)	OBC In Loop (OIL)	Full Stimulation In Loop (FSIL)	Sensor In Loop (SIL)	Sensor Actuator in Loop (SAIL)
Case-1	OK	OK	OK	OK	OK
Case-2	OK	OK	OK	OK	OK
Case-3	OK	OK	OK	OK	OK
Case-4	OK	OK	OK	OK	OK
Case-5	OK	OK	OK	OK	OK

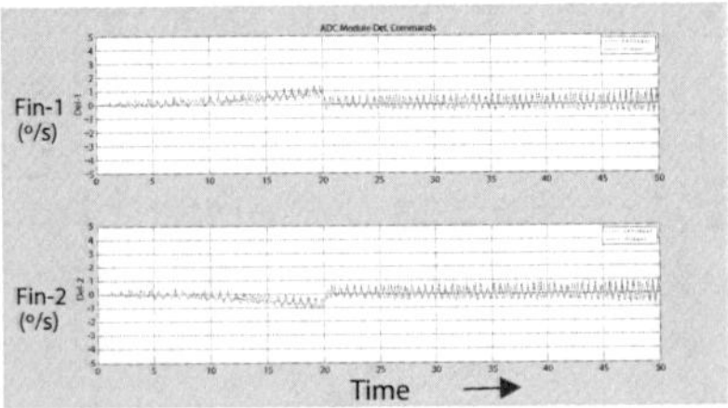

Input data like Thrust profile, stability related parameters changed to see the impact on the simulation. These cases are tabulated in Table 1.1. These perturbation cases are defined as Case-2 to Case-5 with variation in input conditions. Nominal case is as per design and called Case-1.

Embedded system testing has been performed under HILS platform to test the hardware and software. After the extensive testing the flight subsystem and final software integrated with the aerospace vehicle. Simulation runs generates the output data and that has to be validated with the designer parameters/results. This is required to confirm the proper execution and software of the control and guidance algorithm. The standard deviation from the design results should not be more than the tolerance limit with all the factors like delays, bandwidth, and bias taken into account

After the results found to be satisfactory, the software is integrated with flight vehicle and proceeded for the real test.

1.4 AS9100 QMS Integrated with HILS Process

HILS testing is final clearance after the software development phase. This is iterative process that means the software errors or improvements has been modified and in the next release version software treated as final one. For every software version, all the test cases are performed in HILS and the data is captured for the analysis.

During the total span of HILS testing, if there is no controlled procedure or layout with plan and configuration then there is huge impact on the further schedule. Hence development of stepwise HILS methodology with the development of AS9100 QMS procedures cover all the aspect of the HILS process. This enables the on time delivery of the tested mission software for deployment that is real launch for user acceptance.

At the AS9100 certified Research and Development Laboratory level, Apex manual is the reference for the QMS standard. At every process level,

Function Manual is the main reference document that explains all the aspect of process. All the process, responsibilities for the process, input required for the process/activity, output of the process, KPI of every activity is covered in the systematic form in function manual. The calibration of the equipment used for measurement is required and done at regular interval. The major critical machinery and equipment installed in HILS have to be maintained with all the records and logbooks [12]. QMS with HILS process integrated with each step/activity in such a way that the effect of the implementation of QMS only resulted in better and timely output. Different records are maintained for the functionality and traceability of HILS process.

Version Control and change control Management: Software version control is mandatory. Software undergoes many changes based on the requirement of the configuration. Many times, software change has also been done due to HILS observations. The software version with checksum and release date is maintained in HILS along with the change note. In the case of distributed architecture, version control is maintained for each and every subsystem and the HILS runs are carried out with final software version.

Configuration Management: Different configuration is used for HILS like OIL, AIL, FSIL, SIL, and SAIL etc. All the details are controlled under configuration Management [7, 6].

HILS planning, Reports, and Logbook: HILS planning document is available at the initial level of the project to brief about the configuration, planning, and test cases.

Key Performance Indicator and customer Feedback: KPI is defined milestone of each HILS process achieved during the total cycle of HILS testing of the project. The KPI in the below graph showing the data analysis

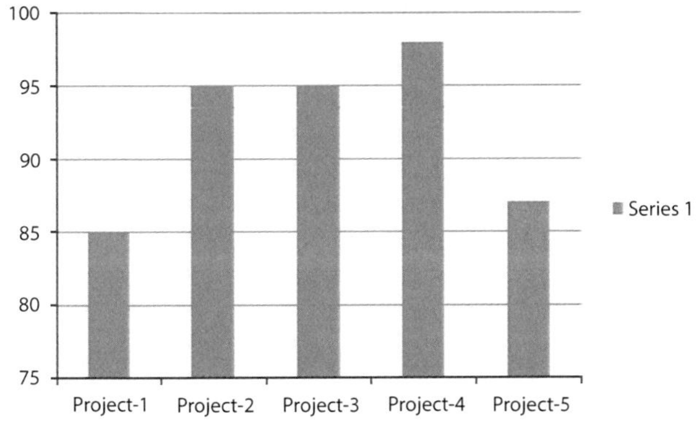

Figure 1.6 KPI and Customer satisfaction index for different projects.

of projects running in HILS based on the customer i.e. project and the KPI achieved during the process. It is shown in the Figure 1.6 that for every project almost HILS process performance is more than 85 % that shows the QMS importance and implementation level.

1.5 Conclusion and Suggestions

Embedded System testing, validation, and certification process has been carried out systematically in HILS and explained in detail in this paper. Performance evaluation in the real time is carried out using HILS in real time that is unique facility for aerospace applications. It is cost effective and rapid prototype test setup that is used to address any design issues before real launch and improve success rate of real launch. The significance of this paper is to explain about the Embedded system's testing, validation and QMS process developed during HILS as scope of the HILS is more border with software and hardware are involved in HILS process. The systematic approach after QMS has improved HILS process significantly and the HILS runs are done in short span of project time cycle. AS 9100 QMS development and implementation for aerospace industry goes hand to hand during project cycle for effective completion of the project. This paper focused on HILS process and the development and implementation of the AS9100 QMS for HILS. The paper covered all the HILS processes, development of HILS Test-bed to validation and testing of mission software and implementation of QMS to each of these sub process. The adoption of QMS in the HILS process improved the performance of the HILS process in recent years and the data shown in this paper shows that the objective of HILS process has been met by development of AS9100. In future the QMS standard specifically developed for HILS will be developed specifically focus on HILS for the significant improvement and global recognition of HILS Laboratory.

References

1. Lauss, G. *et al.*, A Frame Work for Sensitivity Analysis of Real-Time Power Hardware In Loop Systems. *IEEE Access*, 10, 101305–101318, 2022, DOI: 10.1109/ACCESS.2022.3206780.
2. Xu, H. *et al.*, A General Platform of Hardware-In-Loop Simulation for Integrated Design. *Proceeding of the 40th Chinese Control Conferende*, pp. 6766–6771, July 2021.

3. Prasad, M.V.K.S., Rao, P.S., Nayak, J., Aeroload Simulator of Interceptor Missile using Fin Loader Simulator. *Def. Sci. J.*, 71, 1, 102–107, January 2021, DOI : 10.14429/dsj.71.16045, 2021.
4. Lee, J.S. and Choi, G., Modeling and Hardware-In-Loop Simulaion System Realization of Electrical Machine Drive. *CES Trans. Electr. Mach. Syst.*, 5, 3, 194–201, Sep. 2021.
5. Li, Y. *et al.*, Design of General Hardware-In-Loop underwater communication Emulation System. *IEEE Access*, 9, 37685–37696, 2021, DOI: 10.1109/ACCESS.2021.3058290.
6. Karvande, R. and Ramesh Kumar, B., Development of Hardware-In-Loop Simulation Test-bed for testing of Navigation System-INS. *Proceeding of International conference on Machine Intelligence Research and Advancement*, 2013. DOI: 10.1109/ICMIRA.2013.112.
7. Karvande, R., cPCI based Hardware-In-Loop Simulation System development under Real Time Operating System. *Proceeding of International conference on Advances in computing, Communications and informatics*, 2014. DOI: 10.1109/ICACCI.2014.6968563.
8. Li, D., Fu, L., Wang, L., Fan, W., Li, Y., Cable-Driven Parallel Robot in the Hardware-in-the-Loop Simulation for GNC System. *Advances in Guidance, Navigation and Control*, vol. 644, p. 3393, 2022.
9. Zhao, Y., Zhang, W., Sang, D., Yu, S., On joint hardware-in-the-loop simulation of aircraft control system and propulsion system. *2017 36th Chinese Control Conference (CCC)*, pp. 10387–10391, 2017.
10. Fang, K., Zhou, Y., Ma, P., Yang, M., Credibility evaluation of hardware-in-the-loop simulation systems. *2018 Chinese Control And Decision Conference (CCDC)*, pp. 3794–3799, 2018.
11. Karvande, R.S., Sobhan Kumar, L., Raman, M., Multi-node MIL-STD-1553 Avionics Bus-Monitor Development Under Linux Platform, in: *Advances in Decision Sciences, Image Processing, Security and Computer Vision*, vol. 3, p. 245, 2020. DOI:10.1007/978-3-030-24322-7_32.
12. Qian, X., Xiaodong, L. *et al.*, A Servo Simulation Test Calibration and Compensation Method for Hardware-In-Loop Simulation of Aerocraft Control System. *4th Chinese Control and Decision Conference (CCDC)*, 2022, DOI: 10.1109/CCDC55256.2022.10033579.
13. Lv, H. *et al.*, Impact of Wireless on Robot Control: The network Hardware-In-Loop-Simulation FrameWork and Real Life Comparision. *IEEE Trans. Ind. Inform.*, 19, 10, 9255–9265, Sep 2023, DOI: 10.1109/TII.2022.3227639.
14. Sargar, P., Agarwal, H. *et al.*, Implementation of Real Time Operating System based 6-degree-of-freedom Missile Trajectory. *Glob. J. Pure Appl. Math.*, 13, 3321–3143, Jan 2017.

2

YouTube Comment Summarizer and Time-Based Analysis

Preeti Bailke, Rugved Junghare*, Prajakta Kumbhare, Pratik Mandalkar, Pratik Mane and Netra Mohekar

VIT Pune, Maharashtra, India

Abstract
With the explosive growth of YouTube as a platform for sharing videos and fostering online communities, the comments section has become a vital arena for discourse and interaction. The YouTube Comment Analyzer is a powerful tool designed to delve into this vast repository of user-generated comments, offering invaluable insights and analytics. This innovative tool employs cutting-edge Natural Language Processing (NLP) techniques dissect and understand wealth of information contained within YouTube comments. Its primary functionalities include sentiment analysis, comment extraction, real-time monitoring, and summary generation.

Keywords: Extractive summarization, comment extraction, sentiment analysis

2.1 Introduction

The prevalence of short attention spans and the corresponding demand for concise, summarized content underscore a fundamental shift in how individuals consume information in the digital age. This phenomenon is particularly pronounced in online environments, where users are inundated with an abundance of information vying for their attention.

In the digital era, individuals are exposed to an unprecedented volume of information daily. This abundance has led to a heightened sense of information overload, wherein users confront a deluge of content that exceeds

**Corresponding author*: rugved.junghare221@vit.edu

Budati Anil Kumar, Singamaneni Kranthi Kumar and Li Xingwang (eds.) Quantum Computing Models for Cybersecurity and Wireless Communications, (13–32) © 2025 Scrivener Publishing LLC

their cognitive processing capacities. The prevalence of multitasking, often facilitated by the use of multiple devices, contributes to shortened attention spans. Users engage with content amidst a myriad of distractions, necessitating information to be concise and easily digestible. YouTube has become primary source of the information consumption. The rapid-scrolling nature of these platforms encourages brevity in communication, with users expecting to grasp the essence of content within a matter of seconds.

The rise of visual content, such as videos and images, has further accentuated the demand for concise information. Users are drawn to visually stimulating and quickly consumable content, favoring formats that convey messages without requiring prolonged attention. The ubiquity of smartphones and the ability to access content on-the-go contribute to shorter attention spans. Users engage with content in fragmented time intervals, prompting the need for information to be presented succinctly.

FOMO culture, driven by the fear of missing out on the latest information or trends, compels users to seek information efficiently. This fear amplifies the desire for content that can be quickly scanned and comprehended to stay abreast of rapidly changing narratives. In the attention economy, where attention is considered a valuable currency, content creators and platforms compete for users' limited attention. To capture and retain this attention, content must be condensed, impactful, and immediately relevant.

Short attention spans also arise from the constant barrage of notifications, advertisements, and competing stimuli. Users, faced with an array of distractions, gravitate toward content that offers a quick and meaningful engagement. Some studies suggest that prolonged exposure to digital environments may contribute to neuroplastic changes, impacting attention spans. The brain adapts to rapid stimuli, potentially making individuals more adept at processing condensed information.

Both educational and professional environments increasingly value the ability to convey complex information concisely. This emphasis on brevity has permeated various facets of online communication, including comment sections on platforms like YouTube.

Understanding and navigating this landscape of short attention spans is pivotal for content creators, platforms, and tool developers. It requires a strategic approach that not only acknowledges the evolving nature of digital consumption but actively embraces it through innovations like efficient summarization tools to meet the demands of today's fast-paced information ecosystem.

This research paper introduces an innovative tool designed to address this challenge: the "YouTube Comment Analyser." Unlike existing tools, this analyzer not only examines sentiment but also allows for time-based analysis, categorizing comments into the latest, recent, and old, providing valuable context to the sentiments expressed. Additionally, it offers a summarization feature to distill the most important insights from a plethora of comments.

In this paper, we will delve into the methodology behind the YouTube Comment Analyser, exploring how it extracts, processes, and analyzes YouTube comments.

In an age where data-driven decisions are paramount, the YouTube Comment Analyser represents a significant step towards harnessing the power of user-generated content for actionable insights. As we progress through this paper, we will uncover the inner workings of this tool, its impact on content creators and marketers, and the ethical considerations that ensure its responsible use in the digital landscape.

Key Features of the Project

This study embarks on a trailblazing journey, where a series of meticulously crafted key features unfold, reshaping the landscape of conventional methodologies. The key features of the project are as follows:

1. Sentiment Analysis: The tool employs NLP techniques to perform sentiment-analysis, on YouTube comments. It assesses the emotional tone of comments, allowing users to gauge the sentiment of viewers towards a particular video or topic.
2. Comment Extraction: The tool is capable of efficiently extracting comments from YouTube videos. It can gather a large volume of comments, making it a valuable resource for content creators, researchers, and marketers looking to understand audience engagement.
3. Real-Time Monitoring: This tool offers real-time monitoring capabilities, providing users with up-to-the-minute insights into comment sentiment. It enables users to track changes in sentiment over time and react promptly to emerging trends or issues.
4. Summary Generation: The tool employs extractive summarization techniques to condense the vast amount of comments into concise summaries. This feature allows users to quickly grasp the key points and sentiments expressed in the comments without having to read each one individually.
5. Advanced NLP Techniques: Highlight the utilization of advanced NLP techniques such as tokenization, named

Actual Text:

"In recent years, technological innovations have reshaped the way we live and work. The rapid evolution of artificial intelligence, augmented reality, and other cutting-edge technologies has not only transformed industries but has also influenced our daily lives. From smart homes that adapt to our preferences to breakthroughs in medical science, the continuous march of technology promises a future that was once only imaginable in science fiction."

Summary:

"From smart homes that adapt to our preferences to breakthroughs in medical science, the continuous march of technology promises a future that was once only imaginable in science fiction."

Accuracy:

100%

Figure 2.1 Example evaluation - accurate summary generation by ChatGPT 3.5

entity recognition, and part-of-speech tagging to enhance the accuracy and depth of comment analysis.

6. User-Friendly Interface: Discuss the user-friendly interface of the tool, making it accessible to a wide range of users, including non-technical individuals, content creators, and marketers.

The Figure 2.1 demonstrates the successful summarization of a given text by ChatGPT 3.5, with the generated summary achieving 100% accuracy in capturing the essential content and nuances of the original passage.

2.2 Literature Review

The literature review encompasses a comprehensive exploration of sentiment analysis, machine learning, and natural language processing as applied to YouTube comments. Expanding beyond sentiment analysis, the papers also address text summarization and keyword extraction. For instance, text summarization using Natural Language Processing (NLP) techniques, providing insights into approaches for condensing textual information [1]. In the realm of sentiment analysis, one paper stands out by exploring sentiment analysis through the lens of machine learning algorithms. Utilizing the NLTK dataset and employing text mining techniques, their study contributes to the construction of a machine learning classifier for sentiment prediction in comments, showcasing advancements in precision compared to previous works. This reflects the ongoing evolution and refinement of sentiment analysis methodologies [2]. The review also includes studies that concentrate on specific algorithms, such as exploration of sentiment analysis using the Naive Bayes classifier, highlighting the importance of data labeling and tokenization [3]. One study introduces recent advances in the representation and recognition of Arabic text, such as the ArCAR system, demonstrate the ability of deep learning techniques to accurately classify and understand Arabic content based on habits [4]. Research using simulation software such as Ansoft HFSS demonstrates the potential of this model to provide new ways to improve machine learning algorithms in YouTube comments and reviews [5]. The inclusion of studies such as on Malayalam text summarization illustrates a diverse range of summarization techniques, including recurrent neural network-based models and graph reduction approaches [6]. Another paper adds to this diversity by exploring textual keyword extraction and summarization, showcasing the multifaceted nature of text analysis techniques [7]. Moving to medical applications, a study focuses on breast cancer detection using artificial neural networks (ANN) and Naive Bayes algorithms. This research sheds light on the potential of machine learning for medical purposes, emphasizing the classification of biomarker data to aid in cancer diagnosis [8]. This research addresses the differences between sentiment analysis and language recognition by focusing on mixed data. It uses machine learning and deep learning like BERT and RoBERTa and is designed to detect emotions and negative expressions in negative content of different languages, primarily Tamil and English. This study highlights the importance of advances in NLP for managing online conversations, especially on social media platforms [9]. Research proposes a model predicting YouTube video like proportions based on sentiment analysis, achieving an 80% accuracy rate. These studies collectively showcase the versatility of sentiment analysis in understanding user-generated content on YouTube, employing diverse methodologies and algorithms to extract meaningful insights. Overall, the literature review contributes to the evolving field of sentiment analysis by highlighting advancements in methodology, language application, and real-world implications [10]. Together, these papers collectively contribute to the rich tapestry of advancements in text analysis, demonstrating varied applications and methodologies within the field. YouTube comment sentiment analysis is a recurrent theme in the literature, with the study exploring various machine learning algorithms and correlating sentiment trends with real-world events [11]. The research uses machine learning to identify hate speech and hate speech in online content, particularly on social media platforms such as Twitter and Facebook. They developed a research model using deep learning technology and emphasized the need for a comprehensive strategy that includes government policies and individual responsibility to combat online abuse [12]. Additionally, one study investigates the use of the Naive Bayes algorithm for spam and non-spam message detection, emphasizing its capability to handle a large number of features [13]. The study explores both reinforced learning with an attention layer and a deep learning-based model for text summarization, achieving promising results with BLEU and ROUGE scores of 0.4 and 0.6, respectively, on a standard dataset. These findings suggest significant advancements in generating accurate and concise summaries compared to existing methods [14].

2.3 Methodology

Due to the wide range of user-generated content on YouTube, many comments can be seen representing different ideas, idiosyncrasies, or even sarcasm. This project uses various techniques to evaluate and understand YouTube comments, including sentiment analysis, sarcasm detection, slang identification, extraction and abstraction summarization method, and data collection from the YouTube Data API. The analysis was improved by adding the appropriate dictionary and new words, sarcastic, linguistic, and emotional, were added. This article provides an in-depth look at the workflow that involves using advanced programming languages such as Pegasus to abstract and render specific functions for API interactions. Graphical representation of emotions, sarcasm, and slang frequency makes the text easier to read. Through this comprehensive study, we aim to contribute valuable insights into the intricate tapestry of user interactions on the YouTube platform, bridging the gap between raw data and meaningful analysis.

The workflow for the project can be easily understood by the Figure 2.2.

2.3.1 YouTube Comments Data Collection

2.3.1.1 YouTube Data API Integration

https://www.googleapis.com/youtube/v3/commentThreads: This is the base URL for the YouTube Data API endpoint for comment threads.

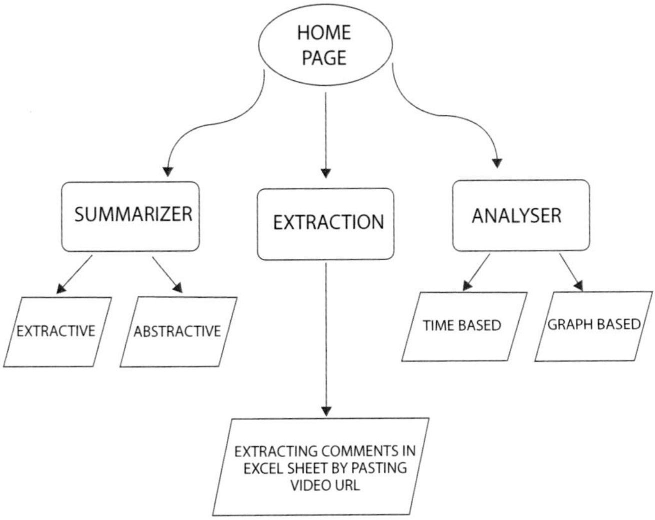

Figure 2.2 System architecture (To understand the workflow of the project).

The data collection process initiated with the integration of the YouTube Data API. An API key (YOUTUBE_API_KEY) was obtained and utilized for authentication, allowing access to YouTube's extensive data. The API key played a crucial role in authorizing requests to the API and facilitating the retrieval of comments from specific videos (Figure 2.3).

2.3.1.2 *get_video_comments Function*

A custom function, get_video_comments, was developed to interact with the YouTube Data API and retrieve comments associated with a given video. This function constructed a URL, incorporating the video ID and additional parameters such as the API key and the maximum number of results per page (set to 100). Upon making a GET request to the constructed URL using the requests library, the function processed the JSON response, extracting relevant information.

2.3.1.3 *Comment Processing*

The process_comments function was implemented to extract pertinent information from the JSON response obtained through the YouTube Data API. This included details such as the publication date and the text content

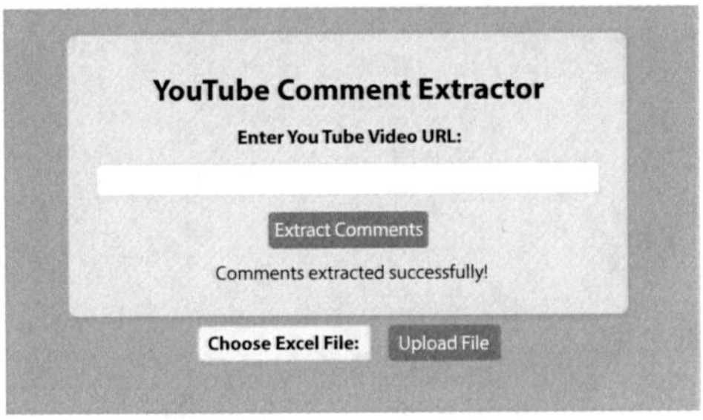

Figure 2.3 This page show the comment extraction part in the project will the help of YouTube API comment threads.

of each comment. The extracted information was organized into a structured format, specifically a list of dictionaries.

2.3.1.4 Handling Pagination with get_all_video_comments

Recognizing the potential pagination of comments, the get_all_video_comments function was devised. This higher-level function iteratively called the get_video_comments function, considering the presence of a nextPageToken in the API response. This iterative process ensured the comprehensive retrieval of all comments associated with a particular video.

2.3.1.5 Excel File Creation with save_to_excel

To facilitate further analysis and provide users with accessible data, the save_to_excel function was introduced. This function transformed the list of processed comments into a Pandas DataFrame, subsequently saving it as an Excel file named "comments.xlsx." This step contributed to data consistency and usability.

2.3.2 Datasets

This methodology involves integrating manually created lexicons, including emotion.txt for sentiment, sarcasm_lexicon.txt for sarcasm detection, sentimentDataSet.txt for sentiment analysis over time, and slang_lexicon.txt for identifying slang. In sentiment analysis, words from emotion.txt are used to assign emotional labels to comments, and sentiment distribution is visualized. The sarcasm_lexicon.txt is employed to identify potential sarcastic remarks, with a graph illustrating the frequency of sarcasm. For sentiment analysis over time, the lexicon in sentimentDataSet.txt is integrated, comments are grouped by time frames, and sentiments are visualized on a timeline. The slang_lexicon.txt aids in detecting slang, and a graph showcases the frequency of slang usage in the comments. These analyses collectively provide insights into the emotional, sarcastic, and linguistic characteristics of the comment's dataset.

2.3.3 Extractive Summarization

Formula and Steps:

1. Word Frequency Calculation:
Formula:

$$\boldsymbol{word\_freq[word] = (word\_freq[word]) / (\max\_freq)} \quad (2.1)$$

Iterate through each word in the document.

If the word is not a stop word or punctuation, increment its count in the word_freq dictionary.

Normalize word frequencies by dividing each word's count by the maximum frequency.

2. Sentence Importance Score Calculation:
Formula:

$$\boldsymbol{sent\_scores\left[sent\right] = \sum_{word\ in\ sent} word\_freq[word.text])} \quad (2.2)$$

Tokenize the document into sentences.

For each sentence, calculate the importance score based on the sum of normalized word frequencies within that sentence.

Store the sentence scores in the sent_scores dictionary.

3. Sentence Selection:
Formula:

$$\boldsymbol{select\_len = int(0.3 \times len(sent\_tokens))} \quad (2.3)$$

Determine how many numbers of sentences to be added in summary based on a percentage (30%) of total number of sentences which will be included in the final summary.

Select top sentences with highest importance scores using the nlargest function.

4. Summary Generation:
Formula:

$$\begin{aligned} \textit{summary} &= \textit{nlargest}\,(\textit{select\_le}, \textbf{sent\_scores}, \\ \textbf{key} &= \textbf{sent\_scores.get}) \end{aligned} \tag{2.4}$$

Create the final summary by joining the selected sentences.

Return the summary along with the original raw text, the word count of the raw text, and the word count of the summary.

The methodology involves assigning importance scores to sentences based on the normalized frequencies of words they contain. Sentences with higher aggregated word frequencies are considered more important. The final summary is generated by selecting the top sentences with the highest importance scores. This approach is designed to capture the most significant information from the original text and create a concise extractive summary (Figure 2.4).

4. Abstractive Summarization

Abstract summarization is a way to create beautiful words that capture the essence and meaning of the sentence, going beyond simple sentences and creating essence and meaning. Unlike subtractive summarization, which selects and combines key sentences, abstract summarization requires understanding the semantics of the original text and creatively constructing new sentences to better convey the key message. This approach often uses deep learning techniques and advanced language models to evaluate and rewrite data. As a result, content can become more useful, intelligent, and context-rich, enabling a human understanding of the material.

The methodology initiates with user interaction, where an Excel file containing comments, extracted using the previous YouTube API, is uploaded to the Flask web application. Subsequently, the Pegasus tokenizer and PegasusForConditionalGeneration model are loaded from the "google/pegasus-xsum" pretrained model using the Hugging Face Transformers library. Through the application of pandas, the process extracts comments from the specified column in the Excel file, which was generated through interactions with the YouTube API. The pivotal generate_summary_for_set function orchestrates tokenization using the Pegasus tokenizer and generates abstractive summaries, ensuring that the summary length conforms

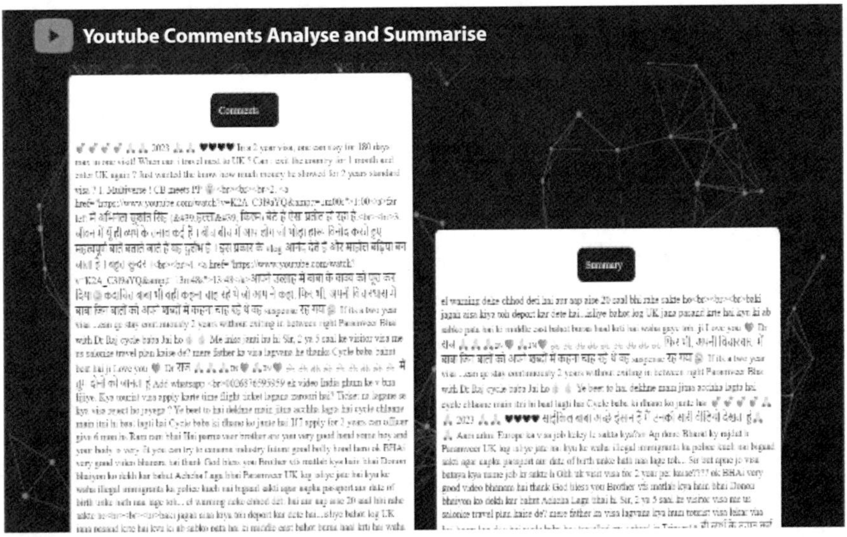

Figure 2.4 Generated extractive summary by the methods such as word frequency calculation, sentence importance score calculation, and sentence selection described in the paper.

to the model's maximum token limit. Tokenization, a critical step, involves converting comments into numerical tokens, enhancing the model's comprehension. The control over summary length is paramount for model efficiency, and the methodology dynamically adapts its approach based on the comment count: a single summary for 100 or fewer comments and sets of summaries for larger datasets. Strategically placed debugging statements aid in the analysis, printing the original comment length and generated summaries (Figure 2.7). The template rendering in summary.html furnishes users with a clear presentation of essential information. Robust exception handling, addressing scenarios like PermissionError, ensures that users receive informative error messages for a seamless experience. For instance, tokenization involves converting text into tokens, and controlling the summary length is achieved by dynamically adjusting the methodology based on the comment count, as exemplified in the generation of sets for more than 100 comments.

5. Sentiment Analysis:

The sentiment analysis process begins with the user uploading a Google Sheet file containing comments to the Flask web application. Leveraging the Pandas library, the application extracts comments from the specified column. Sentiment analysis is facilitated by a custom sentiment lexicon stored in the "sentimentDataSet.txt" file, associating words with positive, negative, or neutral sentiments. Each comment undergoes tokenization, with subsequent analysis checking if individual words match entries in the sentiment lexicon, thereby determining the sentiment of the comment. The sentiment analysis results are then visualized through a Matplotlib-generated bar graph, displaying the frequency of positive, negative, and neutral comments.

Let C represent the set of comments extracted from the Google Sheet. The sentiment lexicon is defined as,

$$L_{sentiment} = \{(w, s) \mid w \in words, s \in \{positive, negative, neutral\}\} \tag{2.5}$$

The sentiment analysis function S can be expressed as:

$$S(C) = \{s(w) \mid w \in C\} \tag{2.6}$$

6. Sarcasm Detection:

To identify sarcastic expressions, the application refers to a predefined sarcasm lexicon stored in the "sarcasm_lexicon.txt" file. Following a process similar to sentiment analysis, tokenized words from the comments are cross-referenced with the sarcasm lexicon to pinpoint words indicative of sarcasm. The count of detected sarcasm instances is integrated into the sentiment analysis bar graph for a comprehensive view of sentiment and sarcasm frequencies.

$L_{sarcasm}$ be the sarcasm lexicon, and the sarcasm detection function D is as follows:

$$D(C) = \{d(w) \mid w \in C\} \tag{2.7}$$

where d(w) is a binary function indicating whether word w is sarcastic based on the sarcasm lexicon.

7. Slang Words Detection:

The detection of slang words involves comparing tokenized comments against a predefined slang lexicon stored in the "slang_lexicon.txt" file. Similar to sentiment and sarcasm analysis, the presence of slang words is determined by checking if tokenized words match entries in the slang lexicon. The count of detected slang instances is then integrated into the sentiment and sarcasm analysis bar graph for a comprehensive view of sentiment, sarcasm, and slang frequencies.

For slang words detection with a lexicon L_{slang}, the function W is:

$$\mathbf{W(C) = \{w(w)|w \in C\}} \tag{2.8}$$

where w(w) is a binary function indicating whether word w is slang based on the slang lexicon.

8. Graphical Representation:

To offer a graphical representation of sentiment, sarcasm, and slang frequencies, the application employs Matplotlib to generate a bar graph. Counters are generated for sentiment, sarcasm, and slang instances in the comments. These counters are then combined to obtain an overall count of sentiment, sarcasm, and slang instances, providing users with a holistic view of the language characteristics within the comments. The resulting bar graph is presented within the web application, allowing users to visually interpret sentiment, sarcasm, and slang distributions.

The frequency of sentiment, sarcasm, and slang instances can be represented as:

$$f_{sentiment} = Frequency(S(C)) \tag{2.9}$$

$$f_{sarcasm} = Frequency(D(C)) \tag{2.10}$$

$$f_{slang} = Frequency(W(C)) \tag{2.11}$$

The combined counter $f_{combined}$ is the sum of sentiment, sarcasm, and slang frequencies.

$$f_{combined} = f_{sentiment} + f_{sarcasm} + f_{slang} \tag{2.12}$$

These frequencies are then used to generate a bar graph for visualization.

9. Technology Used

The web application is built on a foundation of HTML and CSS, where HTML provides the structural framework of the pages, and CSS is employed for styling, ensuring an aesthetically pleasing and user-friendly layout. Python, specifically the Flask framework, serves as the backend technology, handling server-side logic and managing HTTP requests. The Jinja templating engine is used for dynamic content generation, allowing seamless integration of backend data into the HTML views.

Client-side interactions and dynamic content updates are facilitated through JavaScript and jQuery, providing users with a smooth and responsive experience without requiring page reloads. The Particle.js library enhances the visual appeal of the website by creating an animated particle background. Images are embedded directly into the HTML using Base64 encoding, minimizing the need for additional HTTP requests.

The design follows responsive principles, adapting to various device screen sizes, thanks to viewport meta tags. Data visualization is implemented using charts or graphs, presenting analysis results in a visually informative manner. Additionally, a UI/UX methodology section has been incorporated into the project, detailing design principles (Figures 2.5 and 2.6), user interactions, and considerations for an optimal user experience. This comprehensive set of technologies ensures a modern, interactive, and user-centric web application.

A. Data Collection:
Novelty: The project stands out in data collection by dynamically fetching comments in real-time using the YouTube API. This ensures a live and constantly updated dataset, a feature not commonly found in static comment analysis tools. The real-time nature of data collection adds a dynamic and responsive element to the analysis, setting it apart from traditional batch processing methods.

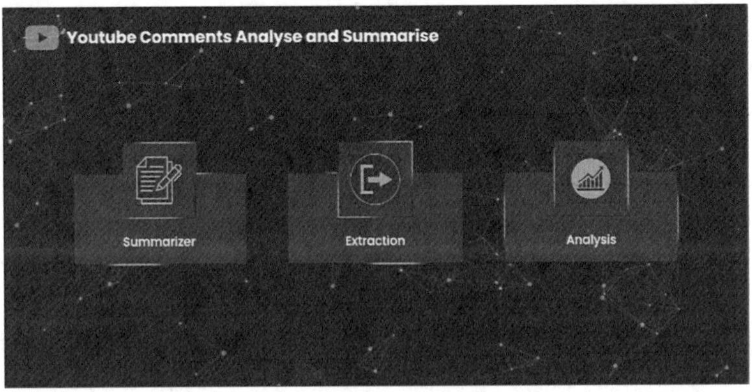

Figure 2.5 The above images show the homepage of the project.

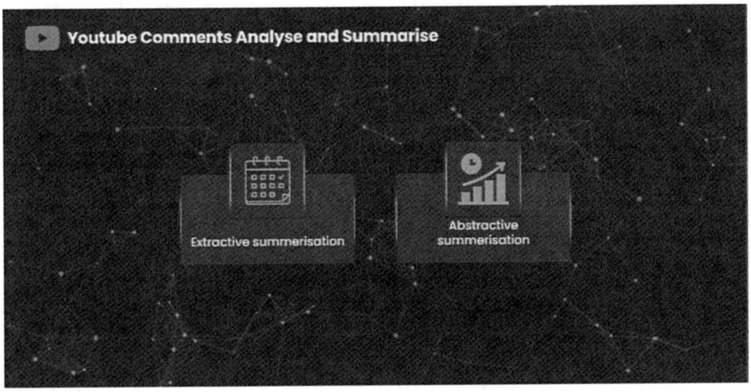

Figure 2.6 Summarization age of the project. User may choose action what he/she wants to perform.

B. API Integration:
Novelty: The seamless integration of the YouTube API distinguishes this project by providing a direct and efficient channel for retrieving comments. Unlike many projects that rely on manual data input or periodic batch updates, this real-time API integration ensures the project's agility and adaptability to the dynamic nature of online content.

C. Extractive Summarizer:

1. Advanced Sentence Ranking Mechanism:
   Unlike traditional extractive summarization tools that often rely on basic methods like TF-IDF for keyword extraction, this project innovates by implementing a sophisticated sentence ranking mechanism. The algorithm employs advanced natural language processing (NLP) techniques, such as word embeddings and semantic similarity analysis, to determine the relevance and importance of each sentence within the user comments.
2. Context-Aware Sentence Selection:
   The Extractive Summarizer innovates by identifying and prioritizing sentences that encapsulate the essence of user comments. This goes beyond mere keyword relevance; it focuses on selecting sentences that collectively represent the core ideas, sentiments, and discussions present in the comments. The prioritization is based on the semantic richness and informativeness of each sentence.

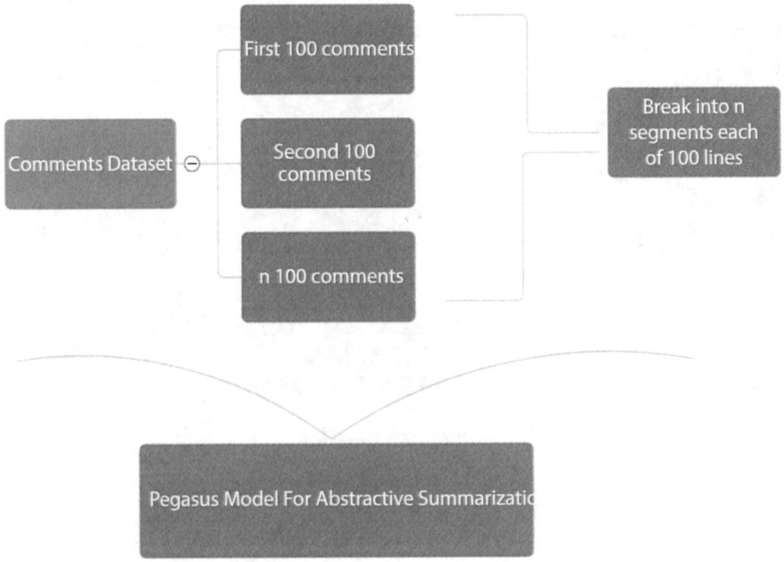

Figure 2.7 Flowchart for understanding abstractive summarization using PEGASUS.

D. Abstractive Summarization:
The innovative aspects in this summarizer include the integration of a summarization model, specifically the Pegasus model from the transformer's library. This model is pre-trained for conditional text generation and is capable of summarizing sets of user comments (Figure 2.7). The code demonstrates a dynamic approach to summarization, adapting to different comment set sizes. It handles the scenario where there are more than 100 comments by generating summaries for sets of 100 comments each, allowing scalability (Figure 2.8).

E. Sentiment Analysis

1. Custom Sentiment Dataset: The code incorporates a custom sentiment dataset loaded from "summarizer/sentimentDataSet.txt". This dataset presumably contains sentiment labels associated with specific words. This approach allows for a more tailored and nuanced sentiment analysis, as it considers sentiments beyond the basic positive, negative, or neutral categories.

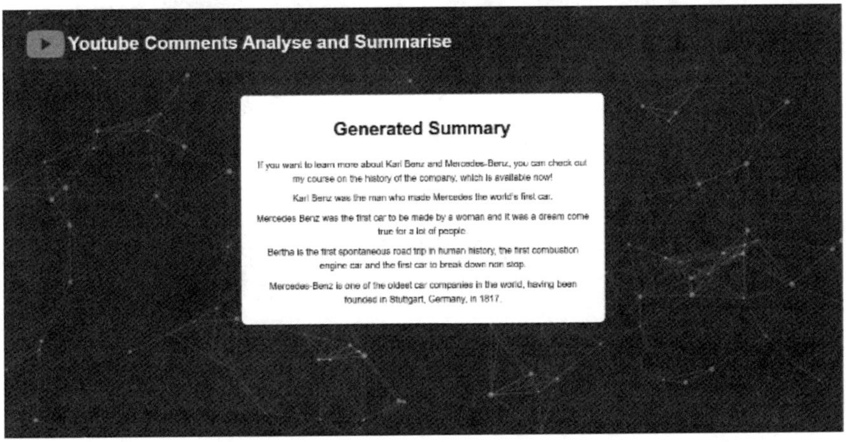

Figure 2.8 Generated abstractive summary by integrating Pegasus model into the project.

2. Context-Aware Analysis: The sentiment analysis module appears to analyze comments in a context-aware manner. Instead of merely assigning sentiments to individual words, it considers the sentiment of the entire comment, taking into account the relationships between words. This can lead to a more accurate representation of the overall sentiment expressed in user comments.
3. Integration of External Lexicons: The code utilizes external lexicons, such as "summarizer/sarcasm_lexicon.txt" and "summarizer/slang_lexicon.txt", to detect sarcasm and slang in the comments. Integrating external resources enhances the sentiment analysis by capturing nuances like sarcasm and slang, which are often missed by standard sentiment analysis models.
4. Visualization of Sentiment Analysis Results: The code generates a bar graph that visually represents the distribution of emotions, sarcasm, and slang in the comments (Figure 2.9). This graphical representation provides a clear and intuitive overview of the sentiment analysis results, making it easier for users to interpret and analyze the sentiment patterns in the dataset.

This project includes sarcasm and slang detection which provide us the counts of these words in graphical format.

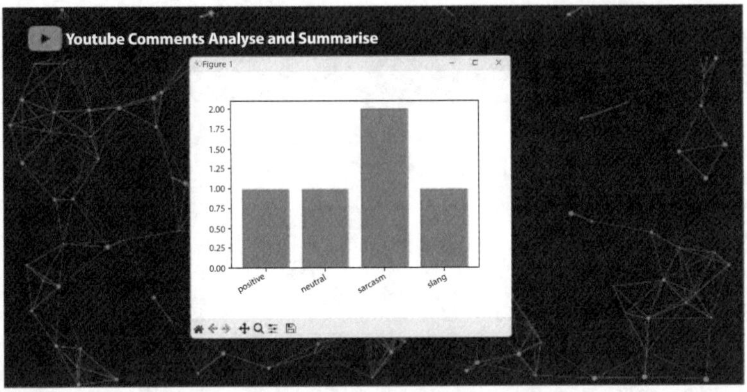

Figure 2.9 Result of sentiment analysis performed by the project in graphical format.

2.4 Result

Our utilization of a time-based framework provides a novel perspective on comment analysis, allowing us to observe and interpret sentiment fluctuations in real-time. This approach enhances the temporal dimension of our analysis and offers valuable insights into viewer engagement and sentiment dynamics.

Furthermore, the incorporation of cutting-edge summarization techniques ensures that the generated summaries are not only up-to-date but also highly informative, assisting content creators, marketers, and researchers in quickly grasping the key sentiments and trends within the comment data.

2.5 Performance

In referencing the human evaluation methodology employed by Google's PEGASUS model, as documented in the research paper 'PEGASUS: Pre-training with Extracted Gap-sentences for Abstractive Summarization,' the evaluation approach for our summarization model closely mirrors the one outlined in their study. The evaluation task directed workers to rate four summaries per document on a scale ranging from 1 (poor summary) to 5 (great summary). To ensure objectivity, the order of summary presentation was randomized for each task. Three separate workers independently performed each evaluation task, with the median score across workers retained for each summary. Refer https://arxiv.org/abs/1912.08777.

For quality assurance in our evaluations, specific criteria were set for workers, including the following:

- Location: Workers from the United States
- Minimum approval rate: 95%
- Minimum HITs completed: 1000

Compensation of 1 USD per task was provided to workers adhering to these criteria. This meticulous approach not only aimed at ensuring high-quality evaluations but also contributed to the reproducibility of our results. Notably, multiple iterations of the same experiment with different workers meeting the defined criteria consistently yielded similar outcomes. The HIT template utilized in our experiments is openly accessible at https://github.com/google-research/pegasus, aligning with the transparency and reproducibility standards established by the PEGASUS model.

2.6 Conclusion

In conclusion, this research paper introduces a pioneering approach to YouTube comment analysis that combines a time-based framework with advanced summarization techniques. By leveraging the latest methods and technologies, we offer a more dynamic and insightful perspective on comment sentiment analysis, contributing to the evolving field of NLP and data analysis.

References

1. Balaji, N., Megha, N., Kumari, D., Sunil Kumar, P., Bhavatarini, N., Shikah Rai, A., Text Summarization using NLP Technique, in: *2022 IEEE International Conference on Distributed Computing, VLSI, Electrical Circuits and Robotics, DISCOVER 2022 - Proceedings*, Institute of Electrical and Electronics Engineers Inc., pp. 30–35, 2022, doi: 10.1109/DISCOVER55800.2022.9974823.
2. Jemai, F., Hayouni, M., Baccar, S., Sentiment Analysis Using Machine Learning Algorithms, in: *2021 International Wireless Communications and Mobile Computing, IWCMC 2021*, Institute of Electrical and Electronics Engineers Inc., pp. 775–779, 2021, doi: 10.1109/IWCMC51323.2021.9498965.
3. Juliane, C., Implementation of Naive Bayes Algorithm on Sentiment Analysis Application, 2021.
4. Muaad, A.Y., Jayappa, H., Al-Antari, M.A., Lee, S., Arcar: A novel deep learning computer-aided recognition for character-level arabic text representation

and recognition. *Algorithms*, 14, 7, article no. 216, Jul. 2021, doi: 10.3390/a14070216.
5. Mujawar, M., Dommeti, V., Naz, M., Muduli, A., Design and performance comparison of arrays of circular, square and hexagonal meta-material structures for wearable applications. *J. Magn. Magn. Mater.*, 553, 169235, Mar. 2022, doi: 10.1016/j.jmmm.2022.169235.
6. Nallapati, R., Zhai, F., Zhou, B., SummaRuNNer: A Recurrent Neural Network based Sequence Model for Extractive Summarization of Documents, Nov. 2016, [Online]. Available: http://arxiv.org/abs/1611.04230.
7. Nasar, Z., Jaffry, S.W., Malik, M.K., Textual keyword extraction and summarization: State-of-the-art. *Inf. Process. Manage.*, 56, 6, 88–91, Nov. 2019, doi: 10.1016/j.ipm.2019.102088.
8. Saritas, M.M. and Yasar, A., International Journal of Intelligent Systems and Applications in Engineering Performance Analysis of ANN and Naive Bayes Classification Algorithm for Data Classification. Original Research Paper. *Int. J. Intell. Syst. Appl. Eng. IJISAE*, 7, 2, 88–91, 2019, doi: 10.1039/b000000x.
9. Shanmugavadivel, K., Sathishkumar, V.E., Raja, S., Lingaiah, T.B., Neelakandan, S., Subramanian, M., Deep learning based sentiment analysis and offensive language identification on multilingual code-mixed data. *Sci. Rep.*, 12, 1, article no. 21557, Dec. 2022, doi: 10.1038/s41598-022-26092-3.
10. Singh, G., Sentiment Analysis on Youtube Comments to Predict Youtube Video Like Proportions ISAC LORENTZ.
11. Singh, R. and Tiwari, A., Youtube comments sentiment analysis. *Int. J. Sci. Res. Eng. Manag. (IJSREM)*, 5, 2021, [Online]. Available: https://www.researchgate.net/publication/351351202.
12. Sinyangwe, C. and Kunda, D., Article in *Zambia ICT J.*, 7, 1, 2023, doi: 10.33260/zictjournal.v7i1.
13. Thanuja Nishadi, A.S., Text Analysis: Naïve Bayes Algorithm using Python JupyterLab. *Int. J. Sci. Res. Publ. (IJSRP)*, 9, 11, 9515, Nov. 2019, doi: 10.29322/ijsrp.9.11.2019.p9515.
14. Yadav, A.K. *et al.*, Extractive text summarization using deep learning approach. *Int. J. Inf. Technol.*, 14, Mar. 2022, doi: 10.1007/s41870-022-00863-7.

3

Enhancing Gait Recognition Using YOLOv8 and Robust Video Matting for Low-Light and Adverse Conditions

Premanand Ghadekar, Aadesh Chawla, Sakshi Bodhe*, Sharvari Bawane and Dhruv Kshirsagar

Department of Information Technology, Vishwakarma Institute of Technology, Pune, India

Abstract

In the domain of computer vision and biometric identification, gait recognition presents a significant yet complex challenge due to factors such as variations in attire, lighting conditions, and occlusions. The proposed paper introduces a significant advancement in gait recognition by leveraging the capabilities of YOLOv8 object detection combined with robust video matting (RVM) techniques. Through the fusion of YOLOv8's object detection and RVM's matting methods, a substantial improvement of about 93% in accuracy and dependability in gait recognition is achieved. The proposed paper provides a distinctive contribution that centers on advancing gait recognition in these adverse conditions. The recognition is implemented such that the YOLOv8 detection model detects human subjects within video frames, and the RVM technique further enhances the segmentation of these subjects, facilitating more accurate feature extraction and creating the silhouettes that are further used for the classification. A key aspect of our work is the fine-tuning of threshold parameters in the frame extraction formulae of the RVM technique. This achieved an accuracy of 95% in low-light conditions, 95.2% in foggy conditions, 94.1% in hazed environments, and 95% in rainy conditions. Empirical results demonstrate the effectiveness of this fusion, resulting in noteworthy enhancements in both gait recognition accuracy and resilience against adverse conditions such as haze, fog, low visibility, and rain.

**Corresponding author*: sakshi.bodhe21@vit.edu

Budati Anil Kumar, Singamaneni Kranthi Kumar and Li Xingwang (eds.) Quantum Computing Models for Cybersecurity and Wireless Communications, (33–50) © 2025 Scrivener Publishing LLC

Keywords: Computer vision, gait recognition, object detection, robust video matting, YOLOv8

3.1 Introduction

In recent years, the field of computer vision has witnessed remarkable progress, ushering in a new era of possibilities in various domains, including biometric identification. Among the challenges in this realm, gait recognition has emerged as a significant area of interest due to its potential applications in surveillance, security, and authentication systems. However, the intricacies of gait recognition, influenced by diverse factors such as clothing variations, lighting conditions, and occlusions, have posed persistent challenges.

This research paper presents a novel approach that addresses the complexities of gait recognition by harnessing the combined potential of two cutting-edge technologies: YOLOv8 object detection and robust video matting (RVM). YOLOv8, a member of the renowned YOLO series, offers state-of-the-art object detection capabilities, enabling the precise identification of human subjects within video frames. Complementing this, integrating robust video matting techniques refines subject segmentation, contributing to enhanced feature extraction and accurate representation. By synergistically leveraging YOLOv8's object detection and RVM's matting prowess, this research aims to advance the accuracy, reliability, and robustness of gait recognition. The fusion of these methodologies promises to mitigate the challenges posed by varying environmental conditions and provide a more comprehensive understanding of gait patterns. Through empirical evaluations and performance analyses, the proposed work will illuminate the efficacy of the proposed approach, highlighting its potential to transcend traditional gait recognition limitations and pave the way for improved practical applications.

3.2 Related Works

Gait recognition, a field at the intersection of computer vision and biometrics, has witnessed substantial growth in recent years, driven by innovative methodologies and applications across domains such as security, healthcare, and human-computer interaction. This literature review explores a collection of research papers that have contributed significantly to the evolution of gait recognition.

In the realm of representation learning for Gait recognition, the authors introduced the concept of contrastive predictive coding (CPC), a powerful technique for unsupervised learning. CPC finds applications in gait recognition, enabling the extraction of meaningful representations from gait data without requiring labeled data [1].

B. Lin *et al.* explored gait recognition methods that leverage global and local features in combination with temporal aggregation. These techniques significantly enhance the accuracy and robustness of gait recognition systems, providing a more comprehensive representation of an individual's walking pattern [2]. C. Fan *et al.* introduced Gaitpart which is a novel approach to gait recognition by segmenting the gait cycle into temporal parts, allowing for the capture of finer-grained details in gait patterns, and ultimately leading to more accurate recognition [3, 4]. Meng *et al.* in their work, present FastPoseGait, an open-source toolbox for efficient pose-based gait recognition. FastPoseGait, built on PyTorch, offers support for cutting-edge pose-based gait recognition algorithms and related benchmarks. This toolbox integrates state-of-the- art algorithms under a unified framework, making it easier to assess the effectiveness and efficiency of different approaches. This contribution significantly aids researchers in comparing and developing gait recognition methodologies [5]. Sokolova *et al.* introduce a novel gait representation called Gait Parsing Sequence (GPS). GPS sequences consist of fine-grained human segmentation data extracted from video frames. This innovative approach provides higher information entropy for encoding the shapes and dynamics of fine-grained human body parts during walking. GPS has the potential to enhance gait recognition accuracy, particularly in real-world scenarios where subjects exhibit complex movements [6, 7].

Pinyoanuntapong, Ekkasit, *et al.* introduce the Condition-Adaptive Graph (CAG) convolution network for gait recognition based on skeleton data. The CAG network dynamically adjusts to the specific attributes and viewing angles of skeleton sequences and incorporates a Joint-Specific Filter Learning (JSFL) module that generates sequence-adaptive filters at the joint level. This research underscores the importance of adapting to varying conditions in the context of gait recognition [8]. A previous work on Gait included combining of silhouettes and skeletons to refine joint predictions for gait recognition. By incorporating temporal information from silhouette sequences, the authors demonstrate improved gait recognition performance without requiring extra annotation [9]. Fan, Chao, *et al.* presented GPGait, which introduces the Human-Oriented Transformation (HOT) and Human-Oriented Descriptors (HOD).The primary goal is to create a unified and discriminative pose representation with multiple features, ultimately improving the adaptability of pose-based gait recognition methods to various datasets and scenarios [7].

The Additive Margin Softmax (AMSoftmax) loss function introduces an interpretable angular margin to improve face verification by minimizing intra-class variance and maximizing inter-class separation, enhancing performance over prior margin-based Softmax methods [10]. Matteo Gadaleta *et al.* proposed identification of the user through template matching and different analysis methods [11]. Hanqing Chao *et al.* proposed the Horizontal Pyramid Mapping that is used for discriminative representation. GaitSet approach outperforms the existing methods in gait recognition accuracy [12]. Studies on gait biometrics indicate that mimicking gait for authentication attacks is challenging due to inherent physiological limitations, with attempts at imitation often resulting in decreased success over time, suggesting a natural resistance plateau against such attacks [13]. Ting Chen *et al.* proposed that composition of data augmentations is crucial for the effective predictive tasks in gait recognition [14]. Kaiming He *et al.* proposed that the Momentum contrast is used for unsupervised visual representation learning with dynamic dictionary [15]. Shanchuan Lin *et al.* proposed that recurrent architecture improves the matting quality and consistency of the model [17].

3.3 Methodology

To enhance gait recognition capabilities, this research employs a novel approach that combines the power of YOLOv8 object detection and robust video matting (RVM). The proposed methodology involves several key steps as shown in Figure 3.1.

A. Data Collection and Preparation

B. The dataset includes various video sources like surveillance footage, publicly available gait databases, and controlled environments to cover both controlled and uncontrolled scenarios, replicating real-world complexity. The CASIA dataset has four subsets: Dataset A with 19,139 images, Dataset B with 124 subjects recorded in silhouette from 11 perspectives capturing various angles, clothing styles, and traits, Dataset C with infrared recordings of four walking styles from 153 subjects, and Dataset D with gait data and footprints from 88 subjects. This research paper focuses on CASIA Dataset B, analyzing variations in clothing and viewing angles across 11 perspectives from 0° to 180° [14–18].

C. Frame extraction and silhouette generation
The initial step in the gait recognition data preprocessing pipeline involves frame extraction, decomposing video sequences into static images for subsequent analysis, feature extraction, and model training. This enables frame-level gait information analysis using computer vision techniques.

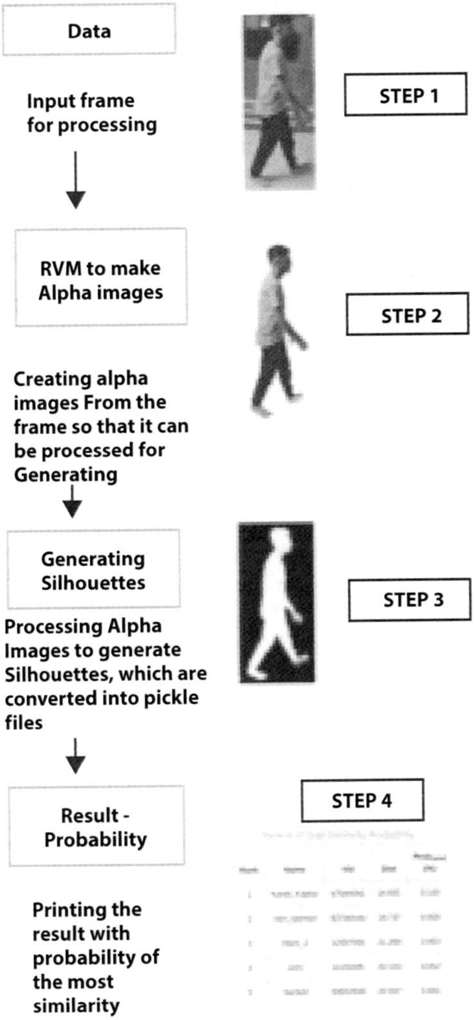

Figure 3.1 The proposed project flow diagram of the Gait Recognition system.

Silhouette Extraction using Robust Video Matting (RVM) isolates individuals within frames with precise matte extraction, even in complex backgrounds. Background Subtraction removes backgrounds, leaving only the subject or object of interest, suitable for static background scenarios but challenging with dynamic backgrounds or changing lighting conditions. The frame representation concept assigns alpha coefficients to linearly combine foreground subjects and backgrounds in video frames.

$$I=\alpha F + (1-\alpha)B \tag{3.1}$$

- I symbolize the frame itself.
- α signifies the alpha matte, which characterizes the transparency of the foreground.
- F represents the foreground subject.
- B stands for the background against which the subject is moving.

The primary aim of equation (i) is to effectively distinguish the subject (foreground) from its surroundings (background), thereby isolating the subject with precision. This process is central to the improvement of gait recognition systems. A key innovation of the research involves the application of a Convolutional Gated Recurrent Unit (ConvGRU). We use the ConvGRU to preserve and utilize temporal information within the video frames.

The ConvGRU is comprised of four essential components:

- Z_t: The update gate.
- R_t: The reset gate.
- O_t: The new state proposal.
- H_t: The hidden state, which encapsulates information passed from the previous time step.

These components are mathematically represented in the ConvGRU equations. The update gate (Z_t) determines what information to retain from the previous state. The reset gate (R_t) regulates which information should be discarded. The new state proposal (O_t) provides the updated information, and the hidden state (H_t) retains the current state. The research builds upon the concept of Robust Video Matting (RVM) for gait recognition, with a particular focus on the enhancement of recognition accuracy and robustness. The incorporation of ConvGRU for temporal information and the Deep Guided Filter (DGF) for high-resolution processing make the system well-equipped for real-world gait recognition, yielding improved accuracy and robustness.

Validation through Experimental Assessments: The pretreatment strategy's effectiveness is comprehensively validated through a series of experimental evaluations conducted on benchmark datasets such as CASIA-B and OutdoorGait. As from Figure 3.2, the results obtained underscore the strategy's impactful contribution by yielding a substantial average enhancement ranging from 2.8% to 6.4% in the accuracy of existing gait recognition model.

Frame extraction is essential for several reasons:

- Temporal Coherence: It maintains the temporal coherence of the video data, ensuring that the order and timing of

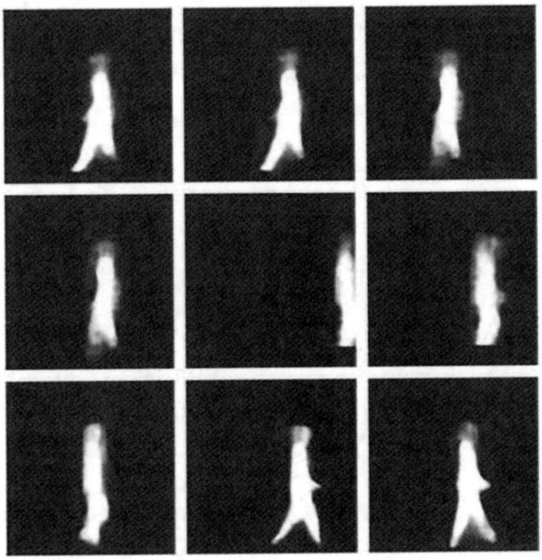

Figure 3.2 Depicting the silhouette generated using the robust video matting technique.

frames are preserved, which is crucial for analyzing dynamic movements like gait.

- Isolation of Gait Information: Each frame encapsulates a specific moment in time, containing valuable gait-related information that can be analyzed independently.
- Standardization: Frame extraction standardizes the data, ensuring that all frames have consistent dimensions and can be easily processed by subsequent algorithms and models.

In the data preprocessing pipeline for gait recognition as shown in Figure 3.3, the initial step involves the conversion of videos into individual frames, enabling a frame-by-frame analysis. Subsequently, precise matte

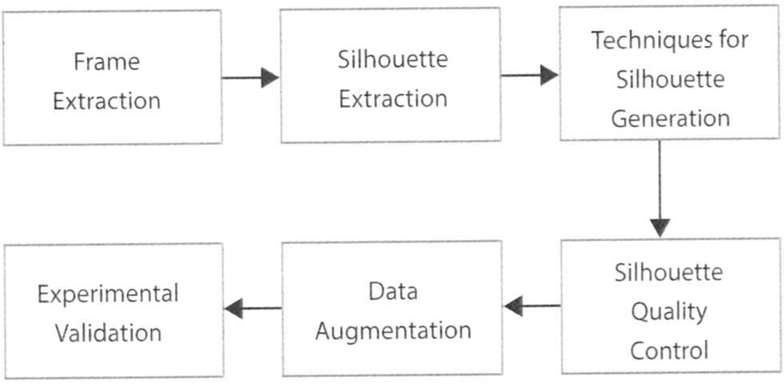

Figure 3.3 Gait pretreatment process.

Figure 3.4 Indicating the generated images on a frame from the video input frame.

extraction is carried out using Robust Video Matting (RVM), isolating individuals within video frames accurately. Two techniques, background subtraction and RVM are employed for silhouette generation, depending on the complexity of the background as shown in Figure 3.4.

A crucial stage follows, where a dedicated silhouette classification model is used for quality control, retaining frames with substantial gait information. Experimental validation on benchmark datasets like CASIA-B and OutdoorGait underscores the strategy's effectiveness, yielding notable improvements in gait recognition accuracy, particularly in real-world surveillance scenarios.

D. Subject Identification

Subject identification plays a pivotal role within the domain of computer vision, particularly when the objective is to track or analyze human subjects. In the context of the research, this method has harnessed the formidable capabilities of YOLOv8, which stands as a cutting-edge object detection model.

$$C = \Pr(\text{object}) * \text{IoU} \tag{3.2}$$

In YOLOv8, an object detection algorithm, the confidence score (C) for each detected object is determined by the product of two elements: Pr(object), representing the likelihood of an object's presence within a specific image cell, and IoU (Intersection over Union), which measures the correspondence between the predicted and true bounding boxes. Pr(object) assesses the model's confidence in object presence, with values ranging from 0 to 1, while IoU gauges the overlap between the predicted and ground truth bounding boxes. When an image or a frame from a video is subjected to YOLOv8, the model undertakes a holistic scan of the entire image in a single pass as depicted in Fu. This process harnesses the power of a convolutional neural network (CNN), a specialized deep learning model proficient in processing image data.

E. Saving data for recognition

Within the realm of gait recognition research, the data preservation phase stands as a pivotal element within the project pipeline, particularly after an array of preprocessing procedures like resizing, augmentation, subject

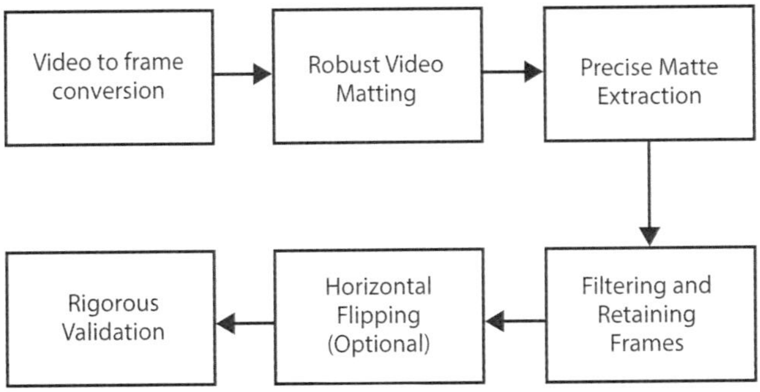

Figure 3.5 Depicting the methodology followed at each stage of the process for pre-processing.

identification, and silhouette refinement. This section delves deeper into the methodology employed for data preservation: A glimpse of this can be seen in Figure 3.5: Depicting the methodology followed at each stage of the process for pre- processing. Data storage embraces flexibility with the utilization of various formats tailored to meet specific project requisites. For instance, silhouettes might be archived as image files, such as JPEG or PNG, while matte data may find its place within text files or opt for a binary format.

The complete process flow can be seen in Figure 3.6. The user can interact with the system via a front end. The Registration section marks the identity of the person alongside the data, which in this case is the video of the person walking. The other section of Recognition uses the information recorded from the registration section and compares it with the data provided, which is the video of the person who has to be identified. If the probability is higher than a level, then the person is recognized by the name which was registered in the registration section and thus the result is achieved.

3.4 Comparision with Existing Systems

In the realm of gait recognition under challenging environmental conditions, our project stands as a beacon of innovation and uniqueness. Adverse conditions such as haze, rain, storms, blurry videos, and low-light scenarios have long posed significant hurdles to accurate gait recognition. Unlike traditional approaches, the project harnesses the power of YOLOv8, a state-of-the-art deep learning model, to navigate these difficulties. One of the key differentiators of our work is the manipulation of pixel thresholds within the Robust Video Matting (RVM) technique.

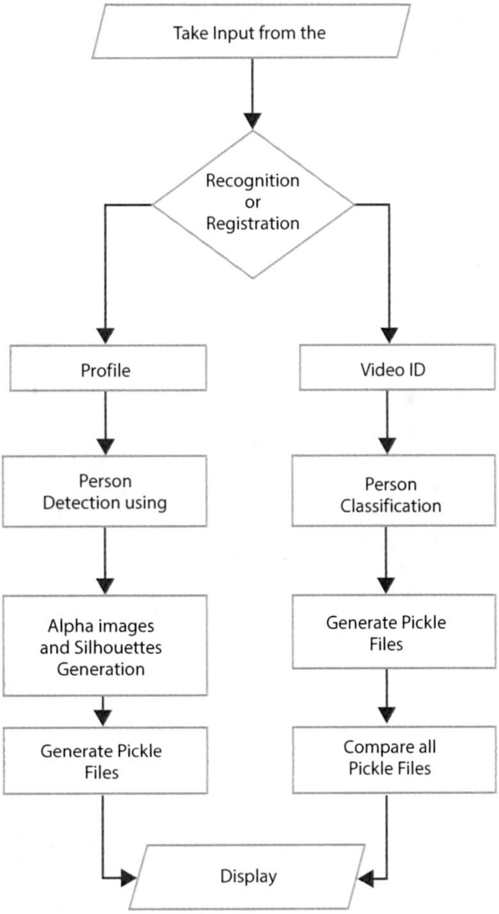

Figure 3.6 Overall flow diagram of the system.

- For a dataset size of 10, the YOLOv8 approach attains an accuracy rate of 93.2%, while the GAN-based approach reports a slightly higher figure of 95.3%.
- As dataset sizes increase, the YOLOv8 approach maintains its lead in accuracy. For instance, at a dataset size of 70, it achieves an accuracy of 92.03%, whereas the GAN- based approach slightly lags at 92.73%.

Classification models compared:
Figure 3.7 compares the performance of YOLOv5 and YOLOv8 across different dataset sizes. Both models start with high accuracy at 94%, maintaining levels above 91% even with larger datasets, showing consistency.

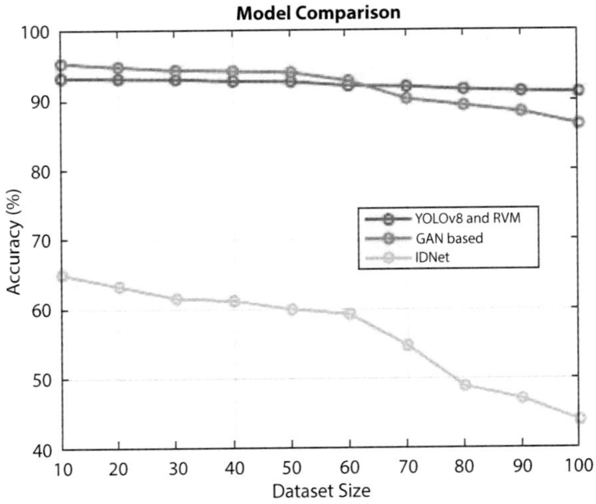

Figure 3.7 GAN based approach [9].

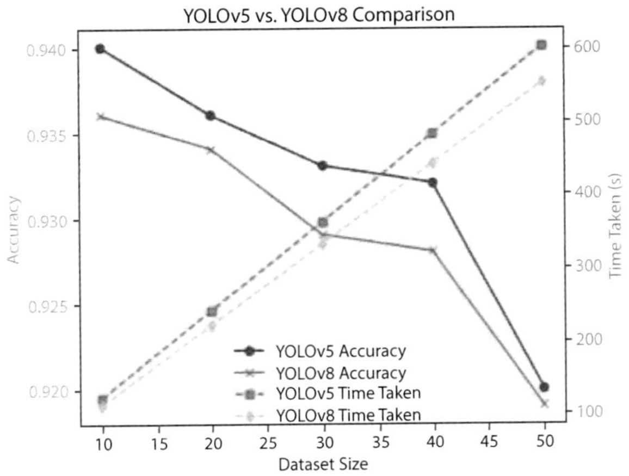

Figure 3.8 Indicating the comparison between accuracy and time taken by each YOLOv8 and YOLOv5 model [19].

The figure also shows processing times increasing from 2 to 10 minutes as dataset size grows, aiding in understanding model efficiency (Figure 3.8).

Adverse weather impact:
Adverse weather significantly affects visibility and operational effectiveness of computer vision systems like gait recognition. Each weather condition's impact is analyzed.

Low light:
The accuracy matrix shows gait recognition precision under different ext_frame_size_threshold and cut_img_pixel_threshold values. In low light, the system achieves 95% accuracy with ext_frame_size_threshold set to 800 and cut_img_pixel_threshold also at 800.

Conversely, the nadir of performance is observed at an accuracy level of 87% as shown in Figure 3.9. This nadir is reached when both ext_frame_size_threshold and cut_img_pixel_threshold is elevated to 1000. From a vantage of optimization, it becomes evident that the pixel values attaining the apex of accuracy in this scenario are those represented by the tuple (800, 800). In essence, when operating under low light conditions, the most effective gait recognition outcomes are achieved when both the ext_frame_size_threshold and the cut_img_pixel_threshold are meticulously calibrated to a value of 800. Predicated upon the provided dataset, it becomes discernible that the harmonious configuration of ext_frame_size_threshold and cut_img_pixel_threshold, each calibrated to 800, emerges as the optimal approach for achieving peak accuracy in the domain of gait recognition when confronted with "Low Light" conditions.

FoggyCondition

We conducted a thorough analysis across different "ext_frame_size_threshold" and "cut_img_pixel_threshold" values from 800 to 1100. This allowed us to assess system performance accurately under varying conditions. The gait recognition system's accuracy under the "Foggy" condition

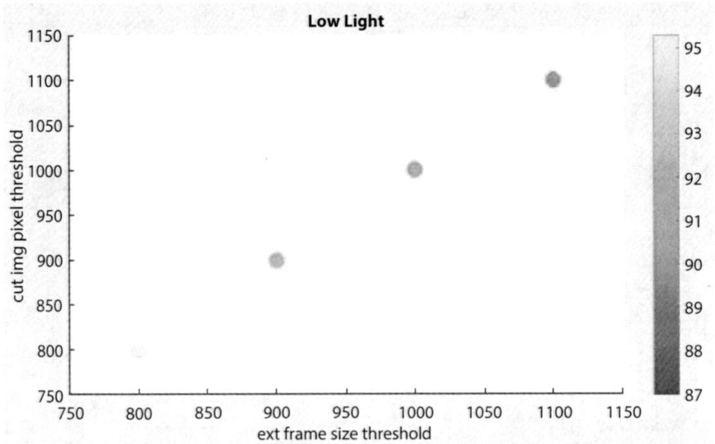

Figure 3.9 Indicating the comparison between accuracy and different pixel threshold values for low light condition.

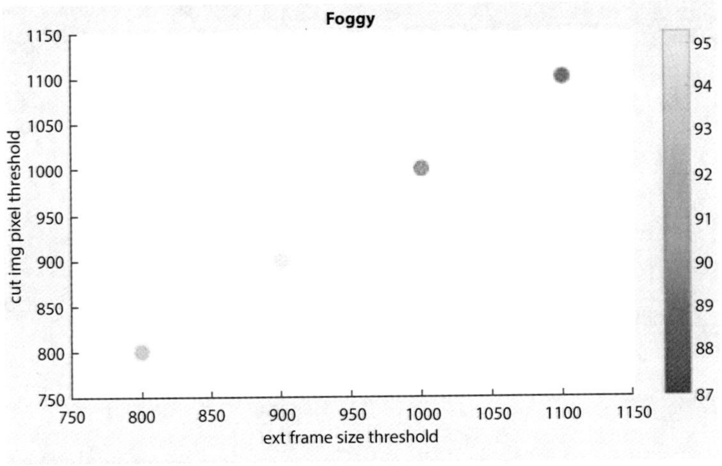

Figure 3.10 Pixel threshold values for low light condition.

is summarized in a matrix, with rows representing different weather conditions and columns representing threshold combinations as shown in Figure 3.10. Here are the accuracy values for the "Foggy" condition:

- "ext_frame_size_threshold" 800, "cut_img_pixel_threshold" 800: 93%
- "ext_frame_size_threshold" 900, "cut_img_pixel_threshold" 900: 95.3%
- "ext_frame_size_threshold" 1000, "cut_img_pixel_threshold" 1000: 90%
- "ext_frame_size_threshold" 1100, "cut_img_pixel_threshold" 1100: 89%

Haze-
The "Haze" condition yields the following accuracy values corresponding to various threshold settings: For an "ext_frame_size_threshold" of 800 and a "cut_img_pixel_threshold" of 800, the accuracy is recorded at 94.2. With "ext_frame_size_threshold" and "cut_img_pixel_threshold" both set to 900, the accuracy stands at 90. At "ext_frame_size_threshold" and "cut_img_pixel_threshold" values of 1000, the accuracy is registered at 88. When "ext_frame_size_threshold" and "cut_img_pixel_threshold" are both set to 1100, the accuracy decreases to 87. The highest accuracy, measuring 94.2, is achieved when threshold values are set at their lower bounds. In contrast, when both "ext_frame_size_threshold" and "cut_img_pixel_threshold"

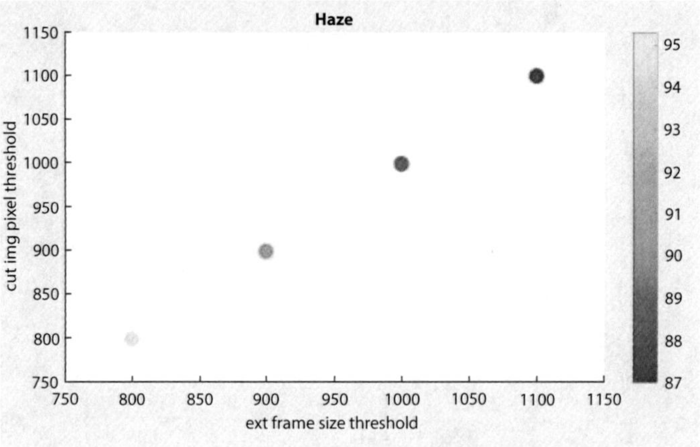

Figure 3.11 Indicating the comparison between accuracy and different pixel threshold values for low light condition.

reach their upper limits, the accuracy diminishes to 87. In sum, the data and graphical representation for the "Haze" condition distinctly highlight the reciprocal relationship between threshold values and accuracy as shown in Figure 3.11.

Rainy

Within the provided graphical representation, the segment dedicated to the "Rainy" condition (as shown in Figure 3.12) offers insight into the

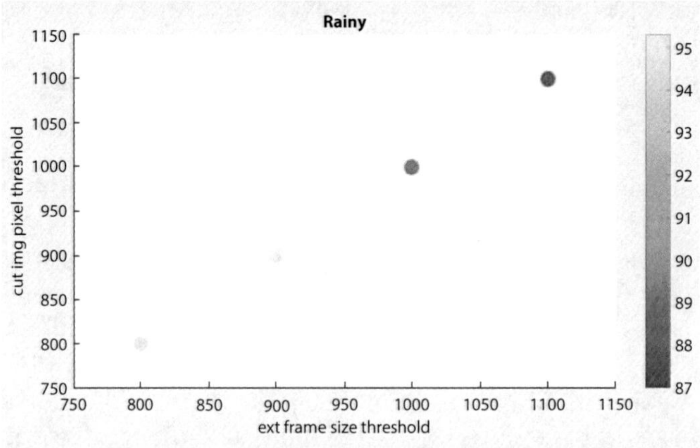

Figure 3.12 Indicating the comparison between accuracy and different pixel threshold values for low light condition.

performance of a gait recognition methodology in the presence of rainy weather conditions as shown in Figure 3.12.

Notably, an increase in both "ext_frame_size_threshold" and "cut_img_pixel_threshold" appears to be associated with a diminishing accuracy. The system attains its highest accuracy of 95% when both threshold values are set at 900 which can be observed from Table 3.1. However, when these values reach the upper bound of 1000, the accuracy experiences a notable decline, dropping to 89%. Furthermore, the highest permissible thresholds, each set at 1100, result in an accuracy of 88%. In conclusion, the "Rainy" section of the graph plays a pivotal role in elucidating the interplay between threshold values and accuracy within the gait recognition system when operating in rainy conditions.

From Table 3.2, as presented below is intended to demonstrate the substantial differences in processing time between two distinct approaches to gait recognition: the GAN-based method and the RVM & YOLOv8-based approach.

Table 3.1 Indicating the comparison of different threshold values for weather condition.

Weather condition	Threshold combination	Accuracy
Low Light	(ext_frame_size, cut_img_pixel) = (800, 800)	95.0%
	(ext_frame_size, cut_img_pixel) = (1000, 1000)	87.0%
Foggy	(ext_frame_size, cut_img_pixel) = (900, 900)	95.3%
	(ext_frame_size, cut_img_pixel) = (1100, 1100)	89.0%
Haze	(ext_frame_size, cut_img_pixel) = (800, 800)	94.2%
	(ext_frame_size, cut_img_pixel) = (1100, 1100)	87.0%
Rainy	(ext_frame_size, cut_img_pixel) = (900, 900)	95.0%
	(ext_frame_size, cut_img_pixel) = (1000, 1000)	89.0%
	(ext_frame_size, cut_img_pixel) = (1100, 1100)	88.0%

Table 3.2 Comparison of the proposed approach with GAN based approach.

Dataset size	GAN-based approach [11]	RVM & YOLOv8 approach (proposed approach)
Small	5 minutes	2 minutes
Medium	30 minutes	5 minutes
Large	6 hours	35 minutes
Very Large	2 days	8 hours (estimated)

3.5 Future Scope

The future prospects for advancing gait recognition through the integration of YOLOv8 and Robust Video Matting (RVM) hold significant promise and opportunities. As technological advancements continue to shape the landscape of computer vision and deep learning, these models stand to benefit from further refinements and optimizations to enhance their performance. For instance, YOLOv8's object detection capabilities can undergo refinement by incorporating advanced features such as attention mechanisms or transformer architectures. These innovations have demonstrated notable achievements in various computer vision domains and may offer substantial improvements in gait recognition. Additionally, expanding the training datasets for YOLOv8 to encompass more extensive and diverse scenarios and environments can enhance the model's adaptability and robustness.

3.6 Conclusion

In conclusion, the fusion of YOLOv8 and Robust Video Matting (RVM) presents a significant stride forward in the realm of gait recognition. This research has unfolded a comprehensive pretreatment strategy that encompasses frame extraction, silhouette generation with RVM, silhouette quality control, and optional data augmentation through horizontal flipping. The experimental results on benchmark datasets have unequivocally demonstrated the efficacy of this approach, yielding substantial improvements in gait recognition accuracy, particularly in complex real-world scenarios. Beyond the scope of this research, the future holds promising prospects. Continuous advancements in deep learning techniques, coupled with the refinement of YOLOv8 and RVM, stand to further optimize the fusion of object detection and matte extraction. The incorporation of larger and more diverse datasets will enhance the models' adaptability to a wide array of environmental conditions and gait variations.

Acknowledgment

The authors would like to express their genuine gratitude to Vishwakarma Institute of Technology, Pune, for their generous provision of access to their GPU Node. This resource has been instrumental in enabling the successful completion of the research initiatives. The GPU computing facility at VIT Pune has substantially bolstered the research capabilities, affording us the capability to perform intricate computations and simulations with exceptional swiftness and effectiveness.

References

1. van den Oord, A., Li, Y., Vinyals, O., Representation learning with contrastive predictive coding, 2018, ArXiv, vol. abs/1807.03748.
2. Lin, B., Zhang, S., Yu, X., Gait recognition via effective global local feature representation and local temporal aggregation. *ICCV*, pp. 14 628–14 636, 2020.
3. Fan, C., Peng, Y., Cao, C., Liu, X., Hou, S., Chi, J., Huang, Y., Li, Q., He, Z., Gaitpart: Temporal part-based model for gait recognition, in: *CVPR*, 2020.
4. Pinyoanuntapong, E., Ali, A., Wang, P., Lee, M., Chen, C., Gaitmixer: Skeleton-based gait representation learning via wide-spectrum multi axial mixer, 2022, ArXiv, vol. abs/2210.15491.
5. Meng, S. *et al.*, FastPoseGait: A Toolbox and Benchmark for Efficient Pose-based Gait Recognition, 2023, arXiv preprint arXiv:2309.00794.
6. Sokolova, A. and Konushin, A., Pose-based deep gait recognition. *IET Biom.*, 8, 2, 134–143, 2019.
7. Fan, C. *et al.*, Exploring Deep Models for Practical Gait Recognition, 2023, arXiv preprint arXiv:2303.03301.
8. Pinyoanuntapong, E. *et al.*, GaitSADA: Self-Aligned Domain Adaptation for mmWave Gait Recognition, 2023, arXiv preprint arXiv:2301.13384.
9. Fan, C. *et al.*, OpenGait: Revisiting Gait Recognition Towards Better Practicality. *Proceedings of the IEEE/CVF Conference on Computer Vision and Pattern Recognition*, 2023.
10. Wang, F., Cheng, J., Liu, W., Liu, H., Additive margin softmax for face verification. *IEEE Signal Process Lett.*, 25, 926–930, 2018.

11. Gadaleta, M. and Rossi, M., Idnet: Smartphone-based gait recognition with convolutional neural networks. *Pattern Recognit.*, 74, 25–37, 2018.
12. Chao, H., He, Y., Zhang, J., Feng, J., Gaitset: Regarding gait as a set for cross-view gait recognition, 2018, ArXiv, vol. abs/1811.06186.
13. Wang, S., Zhang, J., Tong, L., Walk the walk: Attacking gait biometrics by imitation, in: *ISC*, 2010.
14. Chen, T., Kornblith, S., Norouzi, M., Hinton, G.E., A simple framework for contrastive learning of visual representations, 2020, ArXiv, vol. abs/2002.05709.
15. He, K., Fan, H., Wu, Y., Xie, S., Girshick, R.B., Momentum contrast for unsupervised visual representation learning. *CVPR*, 2019.
16. He, K., Zhang, X., Ren, S., Sun, J., Deep residual learning for image recognition. *CVPR*, 2015.
17. Lin, S. *et al.*, Robust high-resolution video matting with temporal guidance. *Proceedings of the IEEE/CVF Winter Conference on Applications of Computer Vision*, 2022.
18. Han, Y., Wang, Z., Han, X., Fan, X., GaitPretreatment: Robust Pretreatment Strategy for Gait Recognition. *2022 International Conference on Communications, Computing, Cybersecurity, and Informatics (CCCI)*, Dalian, China, pp. 1–6, 2022, doi: 10.1109/CCCI55352.2022.9926541.
19. Selcuk, B. and Serif, T., A Comparison of YOLOv5 and YOLOv8 in the Context of Mobile UI Detection, in: *International Conference on Mobile Web and Intelligent Information Systems*, pp. 161–174, Springer Nature Switzerland, Cham, 2023, August.

4

An Ensemble-Based Machine Learning Framework for Breast Cancer Prediction

Ramya Palaniappan*, **Maha Lakshmi, Namitha, Nirmala Devi and Naga Phani**

Department of Computer Science & Engineering, Madanapalle Institute of Technology & Science, Andhra Pradesh, India

Abstract

Breast cancer is a category of disease defined by aberrant cell proliferation in the breast, which depending on the features of the cells may be benign or malignant. It rarely affects men and primarily affects women. Clinical scientists are increasingly concentrating on applying Artificial Diagnosis methods to identify, classify, and diagnose cancer cells. The broadly utilized Wisconsin Bosom Malignant growth Dataset from the College of California, Irvine AI storehouse is utilized in this work. This data, encompassing 32 parameters like mean, radius, compactness, and texture, allows for the evaluation of the proposed structure's effectiveness in characterizing breast cancer, a superior troupe classifier is assembled, and the best model among a few standard models — including Choice Tree, Irregular Woodland, and Backing Vector Machine — is picked. The performance of selected model is then enhanced via the Ada Boosting technique. To gauge the proposed model's performance, various metrics like the confusion matrix, F1-Score, accuracy, recall, and precision are employed. The experimental findings demonstrate that the suggested ensemble model outperforms prior literature research, achieving an accuracy of 98.06%. The review features how AI calculations and computerized reasoning procedures can further develop bosom disease analysis and expectation. It offers likely bearings for progressing clinical judgment and, in the long run, bettering patient results.

Keywords: Breast cancer prediction, artificial intelligence, machine learning, predictive analysis, boosting technique

**Corresponding author*: ramyap@mits.ac.in

Budati Anil Kumar, Singamaneni Kranthi Kumar and Li Xingwang (eds.) Quantum Computing Models for Cybersecurity and Wireless Communications, (51–72) © 2025 Scrivener Publishing LLC

4.1 Introduction

All around the world, there have been 6,85,000 bosom malignant growth-related passings and 2.3 million new occasions of the disease in females in 2023. Bosom disease is the most widely recognized threat across the world, consisting of 7.8 million women living at the end of 2023 who have taken a clinical analysis within the past five years. Ladies with no specific gamble factors as opposed to sex or mature record for close to half of all instances of bosom malignant growth. Worldwide, this cancer is there in almost all the nations. The highest risk factor for breast related cancer in female gender. Breast cancer affects approximately 0.5-1% of males. Breast cancer incidence among females has risen globally, affecting individuals at any point after puberty.

According to global statistics, cancer related to breast, is one of the most common malignant among females globally and counts for the majority of up-to-date cancer cases and cancer-related deaths. Breast cancer poses a significant public health challenge in contemporary society. Prompt diagnosis of the disease dramatically improves a patient's prognosis and chances of endurance by working with prompt restorative treatment. Patients may abstain from helpless treatments whether the benign tumors are further accurately classified. Therefore, a lot of research is focused on accurately diagnosing breast cancer and classifying people into categories that are malignant or benign. Machine learning is usually known as the taken methodology in breast related cancer pattern separation and forecast modeling due to its different uses in detecting key characteristics from intricate datasets.

The above presented in Figure 4.1, is a graph that depicts how frequently breast cancer occurs, as it is so important to get to know how it affects the other various populations. In the above graph, incidence and mortality rate of 100,000 women as per the races due to breast cancer is visualized. Such that, the light pink bar addresses the frequency or event of bosom malignant growth in a specific race of ladies and the dim pink bar addresses the death pace of the specific race of ladies. In this diagram they portrayed races White, Dark, Asian/Pacific Islander, Native American/Alaskan local, Hispanic.

It got difficult for the doctors to diagnose many instances at once as a result of the rise in breast cancer patients. Therefore, it is crucial to have an automated device or system that provides accurate diagnosis findings quickly. This helps medical professionals in prescribing the right medication and beginning the patient's treatment as soon as possible. In this

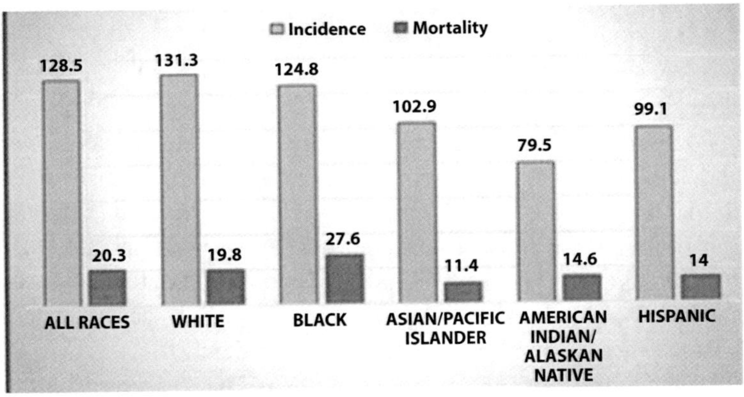

Figure 4.1 Incidence and mortality rate by race per 1,00,000 women [NIH Surveillance, Epidemiology, and End Results Programs, U.S. 2013-2017, Age-Adjusted].

examination work, we propose an original system to distinguish bosom disease and analyzing the clinical and demographics data of the patient on applying machine learning (ML) algorithms.

The excess piece of the paper is coordinated as follows. The partnered writing audit examining the different AI calculations for recognizing bosom disease and its exhibition measure is talked about in Section 4.2. The AI calculations utilized for malignant growth recognition are advised in segment Section 4.3. The proposed framework including the model selection, ablation study, proposed ensemble model, experimental setup is detailed in Section 4.4. Experimental results and its differentiation related works are made sense of in segment Sections 4.4 and 4.5 and 4.6. The end and future extension is revealed in area Section 4.7.

4.2 Related Works

In a study by Gaurav Singh and *et al.* [1] developed a breast cancer prediction model employing machine learning techniques such as Gaussian Naive Bayes, Support Vector Machine, K-Nearest Neighbors, and Logistic Regression. Using the bosom disease dataset from the UCI AI Vault, the dataset was parted with 80% for preparing and 20% for different purposes. Execution assessment measurements including review, exactness, accuracy, F1 score, and Jaccard list were utilized to think about the models. The results revealed that KNN achieved superior performance across all metrics with an exactness of 0.99, trailed by logistic regression at 0.97, SVM at 0.96, and Naive Bayes at 0.97. This study [9, 10] underscores the effectiveness of KNN over SVM, Logistic Regression, and Naive Bayes in breast cancer prediction.

Ramik Rawal's and *et al.* [2] aimed to devise a method to minimize errors and enhance accuracy in bosom malignant growth analysis. The review employed a range of classification algorithms, including Support Vector Machines, Naive Bayes, K-Nearest Neighbors, and C4.5, for its analysis. Multiple datasets were compared, and the analysis was conducted on the Jupyter platform in a simulated environment. The bosom disease [11, 12] dataset was obtained from the UCI Repository, with specific attributes selected using the Wrapper Method for feature selection. The study also evaluated the model development time, noting that KNN required only 0.01 seconds, while SVM took the longest at 0.07 seconds. Despite its longer development time, SVM exhibited the highest accuracy at 97.13%. Following SVM, C4.5, Naive Bayes, and KNN achieved accuracies ranging from 95.12% to 95.28%.

In 2019, a research team comprised of computer science students from VES Institute of Technology, Mumbai, released a paper on SSRN [3]. Their study centered on the application of machine learning for breast cancer prediction, utilizing the Breast Cancer Wisconsin dataset (UCI repository). The team [13, 14] explored various classification algorithms including logistic regression, random forest, K-nearest neighbor, decision tree, and Naive Bayes. Employing a 75%/25% split for training and testing data respectively, they assessed each model's performance using metrics like accuracy, precision, specificity, and sensitivity. Ultimately, the Decision Tree algorithm [15] demonstrated superior performance with an average accuracy of 95.90% across both datasets, suggesting its potential efficacy within this specific prediction task.

Vanlal hmangaihsanga, P.C. and *et al.* [4] a study investigated the optimal algorithm for breast cancer prediction. After testing multiple techniques (Support Vector Machines, Logistic Regression, K-Nearest Neighbors, Decision Trees, and Random Forest) on World Breast Cancer datasets, the Random Forest Classifier and Logistic Regression yielded the highest accuracy (97%), followed by Decision Tree (93%), and K Nearest Neighbor (94%). Despite Logistic Regression and the Random Forest Classifier having similar accuracy values [16–18], considering efficiency, sensitivity, and specificity, Random Forest Classifier outperformed. Their contribution lies in developing a novel breast cancer prediction model, with Random Forest Classifier showing superior performance.

Harshada Trimukhe's *et al.* [5] aimed Researchers explored the use of machine learning techniques, including K-Nearest Neighbors, Logistic Regression, Decision Trees, Naive Bayes, and Support Vector Machines, for breast cancer detection. They utilized datasets from the UCI Machine

Learning Repository, particularly the Wisconsin Diagnostic Breast Cancer dataset, which contained 570 data entries. The algorithms were developed using frameworks like scikit-learn and TensorFlow. The study reported 95% accuracy for KNN, 93% for SVM, 92% for Naive Bayes, and 90% for Logistic Regression. Through systematic comparison, KNN emerged as the most reliable algorithm for predicting breast cancer.

Kumar Shubham *et al.* [6] This research investigated the application of machine learning to improve breast cancer diagnosis accuracy. They utilized a dataset comprising information on 699 patients with malignant breast growths from clinics in Wisconsin. Attributes such as class, mitoses, and bunch width were considered. The study [19] employed machine learning algorithms such as K-Nearest Neighbors, Decision Trees, and Support Vector Machines., and Decision Tree to produce graphs to differentiate between benign and malignant cases, obtaining two benign and four malignant results. After evaluating the accuracy of each algorithm, they found SVM to have the highest accuracy at 96%. Precision values were also determined, with SVM achieving the highest accuracy for both benign and malignant cases. KNN and DT achieved accuracies of 95% and 93%, respectively. Based on their findings, their analysis revealed that Support Vector Machines (SVM) achieved the highest effectiveness in predicting breast cancer.

Karthikeyan B. *et al.* [7] The study utilized the Wisconsin Breast Cancer dataset available from the UCI Machine Learning Repository, which consisted of 569 rows and 32 columns. An investigation compared the performance of three supervised machine learning algorithms - logistic regression, random forest classifier, and decision tree classifier - for breast cancer detection. The results indicated that logistic regression achieved the highest accuracy (99.3%), followed by the random forest classifier (96.5%) and the decision tree classifier (93.7%), outperforming others not only in accuracy but also in criteria such as precision, specificity, sensitivity, and f1-score.

Ahmed Hamza Osman *et al.* [8] employed the Wisconsin Breast Cancer Diagnostic dataset to identify the most effective machine learning algorithm for breast cancer detection. The study will compare the performance of Support Vector Machines, Random Forests, Logistic Regression, Decision Tree (C4.5), and K-Nearest Neighbors. Python code for each algorithm was implemented using the scikit-learn module in Anaconda. The study [20] assessed model performance using metrics including the Confusion Matrix, Accuracy, Precision, Sensitivity, F1 Score, and AUC. Results revealed that the Support Vector Machine outperformed other methods, achieving an accuracy of 97.2%, a precision of 97.5%, and an AUC of 96.6%. The study found that Support Vector Machines are the best at properly predicting and detecting breast cancer.

Our contribution in building a novel breast cancer prediction model is summarized as follows.

- Train the ML models on large dataset to help in building a prediction model.
- Build various ML models to predict breast cancer and perform ablation studies to select the best parameters for the models selected.
- Employing standard evaluation metrics like accuracy, precision, sensitivity and recall, the study assessed the models' performance.
- Refine the model on applying AdaBoosting procedure and record the results.

Show how the suggested model outperforms related models in the topic of research.

4.3 Proposed Framework

This section, is covered by the process of the suggested technology for detecting breast cancer. And also gives the information about the ablation study conducted to identify the parameters of the baseline models that gave better performance. The ensembling procedure used for improving the evaluation of the chosen ML model is also included in the summary.

Figure 4.2 shows the recommended framework for predicting breast cancer. Leveraged a dataset from the UCI Machine Learning collection. After analyzing correlation among the attributes in the dataset through visualization procedures like heat map, box plot between related attributes, and removed the outliers. Then performed data pre-processing procedures like standardization, normalization to prepare the data for effective machine learning analysis, and employed Principal Component Analysis (PCA) to reduce its dimensionality and extract hidden features. Subsequently, the data was divided into a 75:15 split for training and testing purposes, respectively.

4.3.1 ML Models and Ablation Study

Later on, selected six baseline ML models were trained with the preprocessed & dimensionality reduced training data. Performed an ablation study to understand the contribution of parameters of each model towards making effective predictions. For example, in the K-NN classifier, and

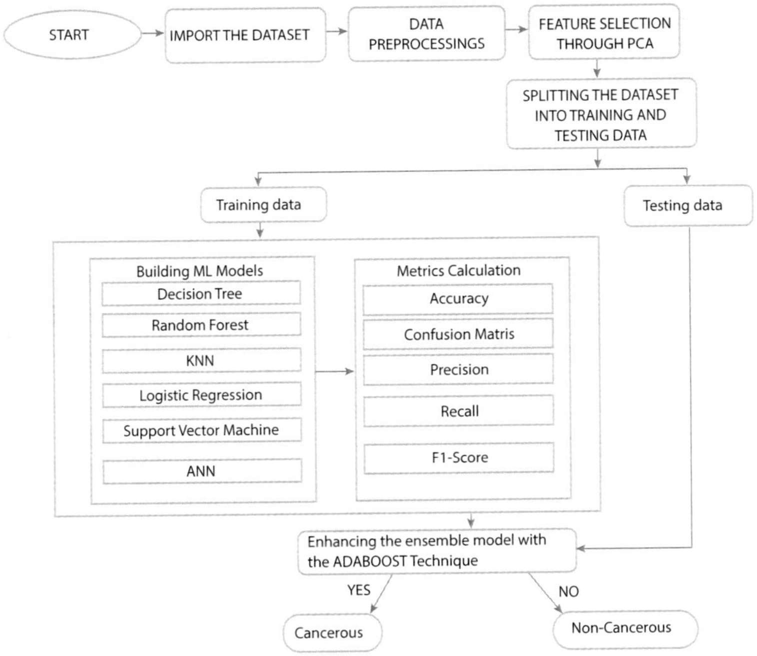

Figure 4.2 Proposed framework for breast cancer detection.

experimented with varying values for the number of clusters (k) and the distance calculation method (d), subsequently analyzing the outcomes to delve deeper into the model's performance. In the Decision Tree algorithm, we adjusted parameters such as the splitting criteria (c) and this investigation analyzes the tree's maximum depth. (d), after which a thorough examination of the resultant changes in performance is done to derive meaningful insights.

4.3.2 Building Ensemble Model Using AdaBoost

Thought to, construct a high-performing Adaboosting ensemble, this study investigates the optimal baseline model based on testing accuracy. This ensures the ensemble surpasses the individual model's performance. We investigated numerous factors to improve accuracy in our Boosted Ensemble model. For AdaBoost, we experimented with various n_estimator values ranging from 2000. Finally, compared the proposed model's performance to baseline learners and other breast cancer prediction models.

Suppose we are given training data $\{(x_i, y_i)\}_{i=1}^{N} \cdots$, where $x_i \in \mathbb{R}^k$ and $y_i \epsilon \{-1,1\}$.

The algorithm of introduced ensemble framework for breast cancer prediction is described in Algorithm 1.

Algorithm 1. Ada Boost algorithm for breast cancer detection

```
for each data point i:
   Initialize weight: w_i = 1/N
for each weak classifier m in a pre-defined set, where m belongs to 1 to M :
   ε_m = Sum (w_i * I(fm(xi) ≠ yi)) / Sum(w_i) *Train weak classifier m
   to minimize
weighted error:
   α_m = ln ((1 - ε_m) / ε_m) * Calculate importance of weak classifier
   for each data point i: * Update of weights
         w_i = w_i * e^ (α_m * I(fm(xi) ≠ yi)) *Increase weight for misclassi-
         fied points
For each data point x_i:
   For each weak classifier m:
         Make prediction based on weak classifier:
            ŷ_i_m = f_m(xi)
         Weight prediction based on classifier importance:
            weighted_prediction = α_m * ŷ_i, m
Combine weighted predictions to make final classification decision
```

4.4 Experimental Setup

4.4.1 Dataset

The UCI Machine Learning Repository offers the Wisconsin Breast Cancer dataset, specifically intended for classification problems that contain measurements of breast cancer malignant growth. It describes every notional attribute of the dataset. Tumors are divided into two categories: benign and malignant. The collection has 569 instances, with 32. In this dataset all features like compactness (To assess the size and shape characteristics), smoothness (uniformity or regularity of contour), radius (to mean distance from center to points on perimeter), symmetry (similarity in shape and size), Fractal dimension (To quantify the irregularity and complexity), area (define the area of the Nucleus) and many more. The categorical features of the dataset are partially showcased in Table 4.1.

Table 4.1 Attributes of wisconsin dataset.

Attributes	Description
Diagnosis	There are two categories for it: B for benign and M for malignant.
area	Specifies the size of the masses and the nucleus's area.
ID	It is used to track medical histories and serves as a unique identifier for every patient in a dataset.
Concavity	It offers important details regarding the irregularity or smoothness of the margins surrounding the lesion.
Fractal dimension	It is useful for measuring the intricacy and irregularity of borders or textures seen in mammograms.
Smoothness	It speaks about the regularity or consistency of contour.
radius	It is used to determine the size and extent of a tumor and represents the mean distance from the center to locations on the periphery.
Symmetry	It describes how the Corresponding areas are comparable in terms of shape, size, and appearance.
Compactness	To evaluate the features of shape and size.

4.4.2 Data Visualization

In this section, visualization of data is done, which is the important work while building a ML model. A heat map is a data visualization approach that displays the association between attributes. And also generated the heat map for the collected data, to know about their correlation and it is depicted in Figure 4.3.

The data is visualized using many visualization plots, one among them is boxplot. It represents a set of numerical data arranged in quartiles. It is a basic method for visualizing the form of our data. It simplifies the comparison of data features across categories. And also learnt that boxplots are useful when there is a need to quickly compare two or more distributions. Here the graph depicted in Figure 4.4 plots between the diagnosis and perimeter mean. X-axis denotes the diagnosis, and Y-axis denotes the perimeter mean. The midline of the box represents the median, which is the data's midpoint value when ranked from least to greatest. The boxplot depicts the central 50% of the data, represented by the range between the first and third quartiles. The whiskers extend outwards, encompassing the most extreme data points excluding outliers. Outliers, defined as points falling outside a specific range

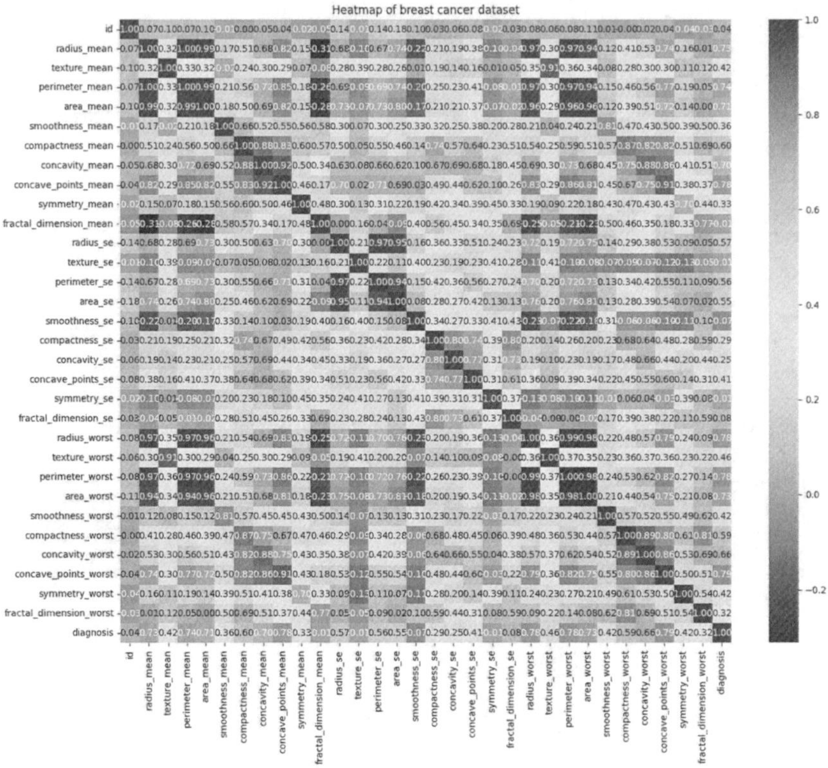

Figure 4.3 Correlation among the attributes of Wisconsin Dataset (X-Axis: Features & Y-Axis: Features).

(often 1.5 times the interquartile range above or below the third and first quartiles, respectively), are not included within the boxplot visualization.

4.4.3 Data Pre-Processing Phase

After checking the null values and Prior to employing Principal Component Analysis (PCA) for feature selection, we analyzed the data types of all dataset attributes, at first calculated the covariance ratio of all the attributes with respect to the target variable/attribute. And then after calculating covariance ratio, and then plotted a graph that visualizes between the covariance ratio and the number of principal components as shown below in Figure 4.5. With the help of the below graph, then decided to take 17 principal components. If we observe the below mentioned graph, the cumulative variance ratio reaches its saturation point in between 15 to 20. So, we finally decided to go with the 17 principal components to give as input to the ML model.

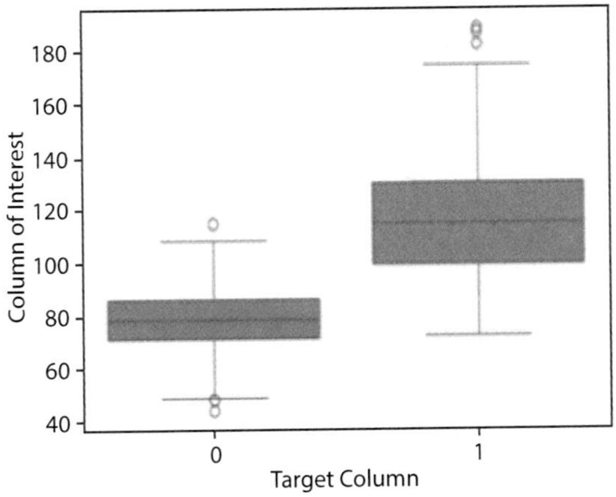

Figure 4.4 Box plot of attributes (X-Axis: Diagnosis, Y-Axis: Perimeter mean).

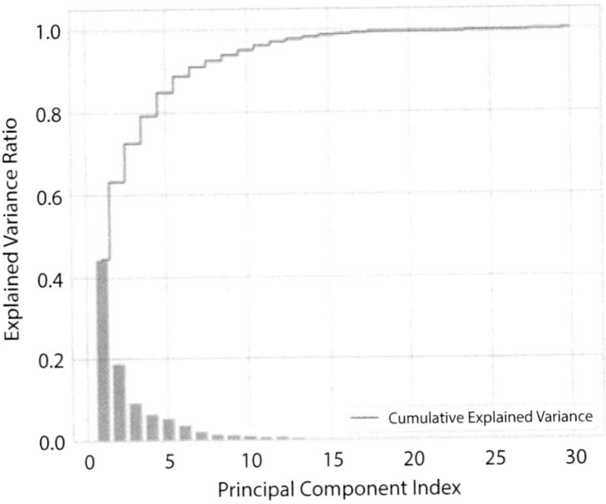

Figure 4.5 Principal component analysis for feature selection.

4.4.4 Proposed Methodology

Now, to evaluate the models' performance, the pre-processed data was split into a 75:25 training-testing ratio. This means 75% of the data was used to train seven baseline machine learning models: Support Vector Machine, K-Nearest Neighbors, Decision Tree, Random Forest, Artificial Neural Network (ANN), and Logistic Regression. After building and training the models, we calculate all the required metrics namely-confusion matrix, F1-score, recall, precision, accuracy. By comparing all the metrics for every model, acknowledged that, the efficient model of all the models and for that efficient model the boosting technique is performed. So that helps in improving or giving more accurate predictions for breast cancer prediction.

4.4.5 Performance Metrics

- **Accuracy:**

$$\text{Accuracy} = \frac{\text{x}}{\text{y}} \tag{4.1}$$

x- Points properly classified
y- Total points in the test set

- **Confusion Matrix:**

TRUE POSITIVE	FALSE POSITIVE
FALSE NEGATIVE	TRUE NEGATIVE

- **Precision:**

$$Precision = \frac{TP}{TP + FP} \tag{4.2}$$

- **Recall:**

$$Recall = \frac{TP}{TP + FN} \tag{4.3}$$

TP- True Positive
FP- False Positive
FN- False Negative

- **F1-Score:**

$$\boldsymbol{F1 - Score} = \frac{\boldsymbol{2 \times x \times y}}{\boldsymbol{x + y}} \tag{4.4}$$

x- Precision
y- Recall

4.5 Results and Discussion

4.5.1 Comparison with Baseline Models

In this section, we examined the findings and analysis of the proposed framework for breast cancer detection. Performed ablation study on SVC algorithm by varying the values for regularization parameter, c and degree for polynomial kernel, using grid search cross validation with a polynomial kernel set. The accuracy achieved with the hyper-parameter tuning is shown in Table 4.2. Additionally, performed an ablation study on a decision tree algorithm on varying the values for the parameters max_depth, max-sample leaf, criteria and the results are tabulated in Table 4.3.

For Random Forest Classifier, hyper-parameter tuning is performed by modifying the values for the parameters like Min_sample_split, estimator's, max_depth and Table 4.4 presents the accuracy scores achieved by the various models.

For ANN Classifier, hyper-parameter tuning is performed by modifying the values for the parameters like mlp alpha, mlp hidden layers, pca n components the achieved accuracy scores for the compared methods are presented in Table 4.5.

Table 4.2 Ablation study with SVC algorithm.

SVC Model with polynomial kernel	Regularization parameter	Degree of poly kernel	Accuracy
Variant 1	10	3	95.90%
Variant 2	1000	5	92.98%
Variant 3	1000	15	77.19%
Variant 4	**10**	**1**	**97.07%**

Table 4.3 Ablation study with Decision Tree algorithm.

Decision Tree Model	Max_depth	Max_samples_leaf	Criterion	Accuracy
Variant 1	**20**	**100**	**Gini**	**90.14%**
Variant 2	10	50	Gini	89.02%
Variant 3	5	150	Gini	86.24%

Table 4.4 Ablation study with Random Forest algorithm.

Random forest classifier	Max_ features	Min_sample_ split	N_estimators	Max_ depth	Accuracy
Variant 1	**Auto**	**5**	**100**	**20**	**96.50%**
Variant 2	auto	5	50	10	94.61%

Table 4.5 Ablation study with ANN algorithm.

ANN model	MLP alpha	MLP hidden layers	PCA n components	Accuracy
Variant 1	**0.0001**	**100**	**17**	**96.50%**
Variant 2	0.001	50	16	94.21%
Variant 3	0.01	25	15	93.04%

For KNN Classifier, hyper-parameter tuning is done by modifying the values for the parameters like n_neighbors, metric and Table 4.6 similarly presents the accuracy results for the evaluated models.

The confusion matrix score for SVC model, Decision Tree model, Random Forest model, Logistic Regression model, KNN model & ANN model with best set of parameters is shown in Figure 4.6. Figure 4.7 shows the accuracies achieved by different algorithms..

Visualized confusion matrices for every algorithm; the results vary depending on the algorithm. Obtained false negative values of 6 and 2, for decision trees and random forests. False negative values for KNN and logistic regression are 2 and 1. Got false negative values of 5 and 7, for

Table 4.6 Ablation study with KNN algorithm.

KNN classifier model	n_neighbors	metric	Accuracy
Variant 1	3	Minkowski	95.8%
Variant 2	5	Minkowski	95.8%
Variant 3	**9**	**Minkowski**	**97.2%**
Variant 4	3	Manhattan	94.4%
Variant 5	5	Manhattan	95.8%
Variant 6	9	Manhattan	96.5%

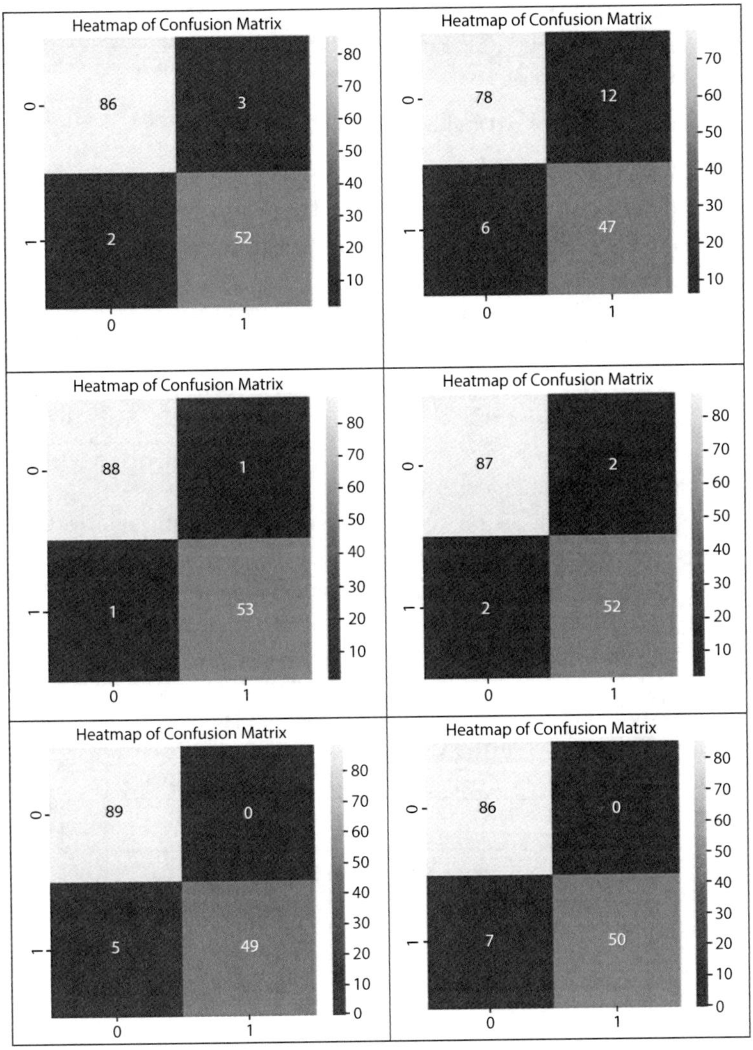

Figure 4.6 Confusion matrix for all algorithms (Random Forest, Decision Tree, Logistic Regression, KNN, ANN, SVM respectively).

ANN and SVM. In comparison to other algorithms, found that logistic regression has the lowest negative value, or 1, while random forest and KNN have the second-lowest negative value, or 2.

Here, by adjusting the settings of n_estimators, our approach achieved an accuracy of 98.60% using KNN boosting with a logistic regression classifier. Then obtained the maximum accuracy for KNN boosting by varying the estimator value starting from 50 to 600.After first using estimators with values of 50, 100, and 150, obtained an accuracy of 97.20. Then verified this result with estimators with values of 200, 250, and 300.Upon final verification using estimators 350, 400, 450, and 500, 550, 600.

4.5.2 Comparison with Existing Literature Works

Table 4.8 gives the information about algorithms that are used in our research work and their accuracy after performing the parameter tuning, which helps in understanding and comparing the accuracy with respect to the parameters.

After building all the models, accuracy for ANN- 96.50%, Decision Tree- 96%, The employed models achieved the following accuracies: K-Nearest Neighbors (97.20%), Logistic Regression (97.90%), Random Forest (96.00%), and Support Vector Machine (98.80%). And then after getting all the results for the models, finally thought of performing the boosting for the efficient algorithms- KNN.

After applying the boosting technique on the specific algorithms, the results are as shown in the Table 4.9, that is, for SVM- 96.50%, KNN- 98.60% and for the Random Forest- 89.60%. These are the highest values of accuracy that we got for each algorithm by checking each estimator from 50 to 2000.

Table 4.7 Ablation study of Adaboosting with KNN.

KNN+Ada boosting model	**n_estimators**	**Accuracy**
Variant 1	(50,100,150)	97.20%
Variant 2	(200,250,300)	97.20%
Variant 3	**(350,400,450)**	**98.60%**
Variant 4	(500,550,600)	98.60%

Table 4.8 Accuracies of all algorithms after parameter tuning.

Algorithm	**Accuracy (after parameter tuning)**
Random Forest	96.50%
Decision Tree	90.14%
Support Vector Machine	97.90%
ANN	96.50%
K-Nearest Neighbor	97.20%

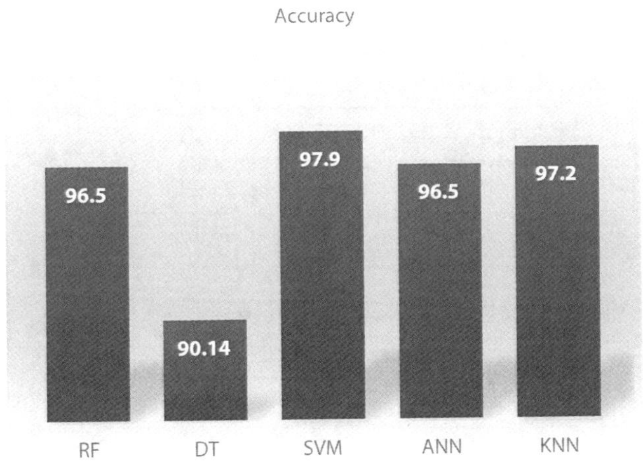

Figure 4.7 Graph representing the accuracies.

Table 4.9 After Adaboosting.

Algorithm	Accuracy (after boosting)
KNN	98.60%

4.6 Existing Works

Coming to the existing works we have two different existing works that have used the same dataset as ours. By which we can compare and check the progress of our work.

Table 4.10, shows the results of the related/existing works-I which have used the same dataset as ours, that is, Wisconsin Breast Cancer Dataset. Compared to their results proposed system got the highest results for the algorithms- Decision tree, SVM and KNN. By which we can understand that, we have achieved more progress than the existing paper-I.

Table 4.11 shows the results of the related/existing works-II which have used the same dataset as ours, that is, Wisconsin Breast Cancer Dataset. Comparing to their results as depicted in Figure 4.8, proposed system got the highest results for the algorithms- Decision tree, SVM, Random Forest and KNN. By which we can understand that, we have achieved more progress than the existing paper-II.

Table 4.10 Results of existing paper-I.

Algorithm	Accuracy
Decision Tree (C4.5)	95.13%
Support Vector Machine	97.13%
Navie Bayes	95.99%
K-Nearest Neighbor	95.27%

Table 4.11 Results of existing paper-II.

Algorithm	Accuracy
Decision Tree	94.71%
Gaussian NB	92.10%
MLP	97.57%
K Nearest Neighbor	95.32%
Support Vector Machine	91.88%
Random Forest	96%
Sophistic Gradient Descent	85.32%

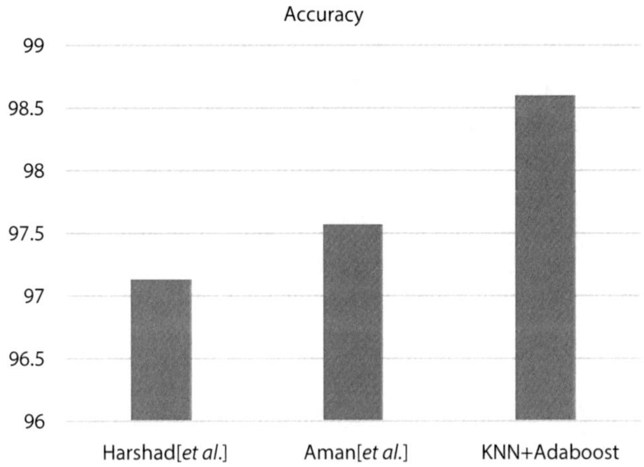

Figure 4.8 Comparison of accuracies between existing and proposed systems.

4.7 Conclusion and Future Work

This article delves into the use of machine learning, deep learning, and data mining techniques for breast cancer prediction. Our core aim is to identify the most effective algorithm for accurate breast cancer prognosis. To achieve this, a comprehensive review of existing research in this domain, aiming to synthesize and present this knowledge in a way that is accessible to even those new to the field of machine learning algorithms., laying the groundwork for a solid foundation in deep learning. In the process of evaluating this article, fourteen research papers were looked at to obtain a greater understanding of the basic types and indicators, and causes of breast cancer. Once more, the most important machine, group, and deep learning techniques were covered.

These methods significantly improve the algorithms used to forecast breast cancer. A few issues that still exist will need to be addressed in future development. Strategies to overcome the challenge of limited datasets in breast cancer prediction involve researchers using a variety of data augmentation techniques. Because it might lead to bias towards either a positive or negative prediction, Researchers must carefully address the challenge of imbalanced datasets, where the disparity between positive and negative breast cancer cases can significantly hinder model performance, pictures against affected patches must be corrected in order to provide reliable diagnostic and breast cancer prognosis.

Dataset

The well-known Wisconsin Breast Cancer Dataset (WBCD) resides within the UCI Machine Learning Repository.

References

1. Nemade, V. and Fegade, V., Machine Learning Techniques for Breast Cancer Prediction. *Procedia Comput. Sci.*, 218, 1314–1320, 2023, ISSN 1877-0509.
2. Sharma, A., Goyal, D., Mohana, R., An ensemble learning-based framework for breast cancer prediction. *Decis. Anal. J.*, 10, 100372, 2024, ISSN 2772-6622.
3. Singh, G., Breast Cancer Prediction Using Machine Learning. *Int. J. Sci. Res. Comput. Sci. Eng. Inf. Technol. (IJSRCSEIT)*, 6, 4, 278–284, July-August-2020, ISSN : 2456-3307.

4. Mehta, D., Mohite, A., Shinde, V., Khatri, R., Dokare, I., Detection of Breast Cancer using Machine Learning Algorithms. *Proceedings of the 7th International Conference on Innovations and Research in Technology and Engineering (ICIRTE-2022)*, VPPCOE & VA, Mumbai-22, INDIA, 2022.
5. Khalid, A., Mehmood, A., Alabrah, A., Alkhamees, B.F., Amin, F., AlSalman, H., Choi, G.S., Breast Cancer Detection and Prevention Using Machine Learning. *Diagnostics*, 13, 19, 3113, 2023.
6. Naji, M.A., El Filali, S., Aarika, K., Benlahmar, E.H., Abdelouhahid, R.A., Debauche, O., Machine Learning Algorithms For Breast Cancer Prediction And Diagnosis. *Procedia Comput. Sci.*, 191, 487–492, 2021, ISSN 1877-0509.
7. Bhise, S., Gadekar, S., Gaur, A.S., Bepari, S., Deepmala Kale, D.S.A., Breast cancer detection using machine learning techniques. *Int. J. Eng. Res. Technol.*, *10*, 7, 2278–0181, 2021.
8. Amethiya, Y., Pipariya, P., Patel, S., Shah, M., Comparative analysis of breast cancer detection using machine learning and biosensors. *Intell. Med.*, 2, 2, 69–81, 2022, ISSN 2667-1026.
9. Thongkam, J., Xu, G., Zhang, Y., AdaBoost algorithm with random forests for predicting breast cancer survivability. *2008 IEEE International Joint Conference on Neural Networks (IEEE World Congress on Computational Intelligence)*, pp. 3062–3069, Hong Kong, China, 2008.
10. Hambali, M., Saheed, Y., Oladele, T., Gbolagade, M., ADABOOST Ensemble Algorithms for Breast Cancer Classification. *J. Adv. Comput. Res.*, *10*, 2, 31–52, 2019.
11. Zizaan, A. and Idri, A., Evaluating and comparing bagging and boosting of hybrid learning for breast cancer screening. *Sci. Afr.*, 23, e01989, 2024, ISSN24682276.
12. Kabiraj, S., Akter, L., Raihan, M., Diba, N.J., Podder, E., Hassan, M.M., Prediction of Recurrence and Non-recurrence Events of Breast Cancer using Bagging Algorithm. *2020 11th International Conference on Computing, Communication and Networking Technologies (ICCCNT)*, pp. 1–5, Kharagpur, India, 2020.
13. Chaurasia, V. and Pal, S., Stacking-Based Ensemble Framework and Feature Selection Technique for the Detection of Breast Cancer. *SN Comput. Sci.*, 2, 67, 2021.
14. Dhanya, R., Paul, I.R., Akula, S.S., Sivakumar, M., Nair, J.J., F-test feature selection in Stacking ensemble model for breast cancer prediction. *Procedia Comput. Sci.*, 171, 1561–1570, 2020, ISSN 1877-0509.
15. Liu, L., Research on Logistic Regression Algorithm of Breast Cancer Diagnose Data by Machine Learning. *2018 International Conference on Robots & Intelligent System (ICRIS)*, pp. 157–160, Changsha, China, 2018.
16. Al-Hadidi, M.R., Alarabeyyat, A., Alhanahnah, M., Breast Cancer Detection Using K-Nearest Neighbor Machine Learning Algorithm. *9th International Conference on Developments in eSystems Engineering (DeSE)*, pp. 35–39, Liverpool, UK, 2016.

17. Maglogiannis, I., Zafiropoulos, E., Anagnostopoulos, I., An intelligent system for automated breast cancer diagnosis and prognosis using SVM based classifiers. *Appl. Intell.*, 30, 24–36, 2009.
18. Janghel, R.R., Shukla, A., Tiwari, R., Kala, R., Breast cancer diagnosis using Artificial Neural Network models. *The 3rd International Conference on Information Sciences and Interaction Sciences*, pp. 89–94, Chengdu, China, 2010.
19. Al-Salihy, N.K. and Ibrikci, T., Classifying breast cancer by using decision tree algorithms, in: *Proceedings of the 6th International Conference on Software and Computer Applications (ICSCA '17)*, pp. 144–148, Association for Computing Machinery, New York, NY, USA, 2017.
20. Dai, B., Chen, R.-C., Zhu, S.-Z., Zhang, W.-W., Using Random Forest Algorithm for Breast Cancer Diagnosis. *2018 International Symposium on Computer, Consumer and Control (IS3C)*, pp. 449–452, Taichung, Taiwan, 2018.

5

Proactive Fault Detection in Weather Forecast Control Systems Through Heartbeat Monitoring and Cloud-Based Analytics

Shelly Prakash* **and Vaibhav Vyas**

Banasthali Vidyapith, Tonk, Rajasthan, India

Abstract

Weather forecast control systems play a pivotal role in providing accurate and timely weather predictions, contributing to various sectors such as agriculture, transportation, and emergency management. Ensuring the reliability and performance of these systems is crucial for delivering accurate data. This paper introduces a novel approach to proactive fault detection in weather forecast control systems through the integration of advanced heartbeat monitoring mechanisms and latest cloud technologies.

The proposed system implements modified heartbeat monitoring techniques to continuously assess the health and performance of individual sensors within the forecast control system. The heartbeat alerting system is introduced with a threshold counter which rechecks the system if there is a gap in the heartbeat stream travelling through kafka. Along with this, during threshold inspection, reports are generated and sent to the handlers. These reports serve two purposes, firstly they are used to monitor the physical parameters of the system when the heartbeat was missed, so that the handlers can identify the root cause of the potential error. Secondly these reports serve as a feed for machine learning algorithms which learn about the patterns of causes and failure occurrences through this data. The rechecking method also eliminates the possibility of false positives when a heartbeat is missed. This proactive approach minimizes downtime and improves the overall reliability of weather forecast control systems by enabling preemptive maintenance actions. The effectiveness of the proposed framework is

**Corresponding author*: shellyprakash.mpsi@gmail.com

Budati Anil Kumar, Singamaneni Kranthi Kumar and Li Xingwang (eds.) Quantum Computing Models for Cybersecurity and Wireless Communications, (73–98) © 2025 Scrivener Publishing LLC

then compared with the existing fault tolerance models. Through the utilization of machine learning algorithms and predictive analytics in the cloud environment, the system can detect patterns and trends indicative of emerging faults before they turn down the system in future.

Keywords: Cloud computing, proactive fault detection, heartbeat monitoring, predictive maintenance, fault tolerance

5.1 Introduction

Any cloud-based application is a complex system prone to faults and failures which can occur in the sensors, controllers, and networks that severely disrupt the operation of any system. Cloud computing has emerged as a transformation in new technologies, offering scalable and flexible infrastructure for processing vast amounts of data. However, this shift to cloud based architectures introduces new challenges in terms of system monitoring and fault detection. Also, during the research it is observed that there is usually a correlation between failure and energy use. Greater infrastructure and equipment will be required to address the problems if we require robust fault tolerance, which will further increase power consumption [33].

Currently, the predominant approach for detecting such faults relies on reactive methods that identify issues only after a complete failure has already happened. For instance, failures are detected based on citizen complaints or system alerts when a system is not functioning. To minimize such disruptions, more proactive techniques are needed that can accurately predict failures before they occur, enabling preventative maintenance.

Heartbeat technology is although not a new term for cloud users but it serves as a real time monitoring mechanism, providing insights about the operational health of individual components and specially sensors. The integration of IoT sensors is crucial in weather forecasting to read real time data. The sensors dispersed across geographical locations contribute to the understanding of weather pattern. But every device in a network requires a fault tolerant communication network.

Therefore, we integrated Apache Kafka- a distributed streaming platform that excels in handling real time data with high throughput and fault tolerance. It provides reliable and scalable data pipeline. It ensures the continuous flow of information(heartbeat messages here) from server to the cloud, facilitating the fast, congestion free access to data. It is also responsible for transmitting failure prediction alerts to operators.

5.1.1 Cloud Computing

Cloud computing refers to the delivery of computing services, including storage, processing power, networking, and various applications, over the internet. Instead of relying on local servers or personal devices to handle computing tasks, users can access and use computing resources provided by remote data centers. The main characteristics of cloud are: scalability, reliability, on-demand service, flexibility, rapid elasticity, resource pooling, etc. [18, 19].

5.1.1.1 Fault, Error, Failure

In cloud computing, managing faults, handling errors, and designing systems with built-in robustness are essential for ensuring high availability and reliability of services [2, 6]. In the context of cloud computing, "failure," "fault," and "error" are related concepts, but they have distinct meanings.

5.1.1.1.1 Failure

It refers to the inability of a system, component, or service to perform its intended functions. A failure can occur at different levels, including hardware, software, network, or even the entire data center. It results in a breakdown of normal operations and may lead to service disruptions.

5.1.1.1.2 Fault

It is an undesirable or unexpected event that can cause a failure. It is a defect or problem in the system or its components that, if triggered, may lead to a failure. Faults can manifest as hardware malfunctions, software bugs, network disruptions, or other issues within the cloud infrastructure. Identifying and addressing faults proactively is crucial to preventing failures.

5.1.1.1.3 Error

It is a deviation from the expected behavior or a mistake in the execution of a program or process. It is often the result of a fault and may lead to a failure if not handled properly. Errors can occur due to bugs in software, misconfigurations, or other issues. In the cloud, errors may affect the performance, reliability, or security of services.

Fault Tolerance and Its Types

Fault tolerance is a characteristic of a system or process that enables it to continue functioning and providing services even in the presence of faults or failures [1]. The primary goal of fault tolerance is to ensure that the system remains operational, reliable, and available, despite the occurrence of unexpected events such as hardware failures, software bugs, network disruptions, or other types of faults [3, 28]. Fault tolerance is thus categorized into two broad types: Proactive and Reactive Table 5.1 [8].

Kafka Streams

We used Apache Kafka, a distributed streaming platform, for both ingesting real-time IoT sensor data into the cloud as well as publishing model predictions to downstream alerting systems. Kafka provides high-throughput, low-latency pipelines by partitioning streams across clusters [25].

Internet of Things (IoT) Sensors

In weather forecasting model, Internet of Things (IoT) sensors must be installed at various locations to capture and transmit the heartbeat signals

Table 5.1 Difference between Proactive and Reactive fault tolerance.

Proactive fault tolerance	**Reactive fault tolerance**
Focused on preventing faults in advance by using predictive techniques and preventive measures.	Focusses on responding to faults as they occur, by relying on backup systems and recovery processes.
Its aim is to minimize the occurrence of faults.	Its aim is to minimize the impact of faults.
It may involve additional computational overhead for predictive analytics, monitoring, and preventive actions.	It may require resources for backup systems, recovery procedures, and fault isolation.
Proactive Fault Tolerance Techniques: • Pre-emptive migration • Load Balancing • Self-healing • Software rejuvenation	*Reactive Fault Tolerance Techniques:* • S-Guard • Replication • Task resubmission • Job migration • Check pointing • Retry

from sensors into the cloud platform. The sensors connect to the external ports of the controllers to continuously record for heartbeats. IoT standards like MQTT handle device communication and management.

5.2 Related Work

Prior research has explored applying heartbeat or ping monitoring concepts to infrastructure systems including computer networks and industrial assets. Network administrators have long used pings to probe system availability [16]. Prior work has also applied heartbeat monitoring to cloud server systems. However, the use of heartbeats specifically for proactive and predictive fault detection in intelligent transportation systems remains relatively unexplored [4]. Our paper focuses on this promising but understudied application domain.

[35] introduces a hybrid fault-tolerance approach utilizing the replication impact heuristic, incorporating both reactive and proactive policies. The primary objective is to enhance resource efficiency by reducing resource consumption. The key is to assign different tasks to different replicas. They have considered four scenarios: replication and resubmission without improvement, replication, and resubmission with reliability-based assessment, hybrid approach based on replication impact heuristic without fault injection, and hybrid approach with fault injection. The results indicate that the proposed approach enhances VM efficiency and ensures that tasks are not paused in cases of faults.

[36] introduces a three-phase approach to enhance the reliability of cloud services through a fault-based mechanism. In the first phase, virtual machine (VM) failures are detected, including those due to high response time, Byzantine faults, and performance faults. The second phase involves an optimized checkpoint algorithm, determining suitable intervals for marking checkpoints during task execution. Finally, in the checkpoint and recovery phase, a backup and recovery algorithm identifies the optimal global checkpoint for restarting failed tasks. Evaluation results using real-time data demonstrate that the proposed method offers a superior fault-tolerant solution, reducing execution time and energy consumption while increasing overall reliability compared to non-optimized methods.

Most existing work on failure detection relies on reactive approaches based on manual inspections or automatic alerts when total outages occur [7, 9]. In general, current techniques suffer from long delays between fault onset and detection. They fail to provide any early warning. Our proactive heartbeat approach provides a paradigm shift capable of failure prediction rather than just reaction.

Cloud Computing and Machine Learning

[22–26] The cloud facilitates both real time analytics on streaming heartbeat data as well as deep learning on historical data. Long Short-Term Memory (LSTM) Networks is one of the time series analysis algorithms. LSTMs are a type of recurrent neural network (RNN) specifically designed for sequence data. They are well-suited for capturing long-term dependencies in time series data, making them effective for analyzing the temporal patterns in meteorological data. Although its results are not used to evaluate energy efficiency of this proposed model. Extensive deep learning algorithms are to be incorporated along with this process. The first feed is a constant stream of heartbeat data from the Kafka pipeline; the second feed is a periodic report that includes physical & environmental readings like CPU temperature [31].

To implement an LSTM model for proactive fault detection, the process began with data preprocessing by organizing the time series data into sequences suitable for LSTM learning. Training and testing sets were created, and then the LSTM model was built using TensorFlow/Keras, with experimentation on architecture and hyperparameters. The model was trained with the training data and then evaluated on the test set to assess its performance. Predictions were made using the trained model. A threshold for fault detection was established based on the predicted values, considering deviations from expected behavior as potential anomalies [28]. The model and preprocessing steps were fine-tuned based on the specific characteristics of the dataset and objectives, while focusing on integrating other machine learning components for a robust fault detection system. The model is to be regularly monitored and updated to adapt to changing weather patterns and system dynamics.

Cloud Computing and Internet of Things (IoT)

[13] emphasizes that fully integrated IoT-cloud solutions hold the potential for transformative applications but necessitate ongoing innovation across multiple domains, including system architecture, communication networks, security, and standards. The paper delves into various architectural approaches, outlining three primary integration models: direct connectivity of IoT devices to the cloud, connections through cloud gateways, and hybrid methods. The analysis extends to prominent IoT cloud platforms, such as AWS IoT, Microsoft Azure, and IBM Watson, scrutinizing their integrated services for device connectivity, data handling, and storage. Security considerations, including authentication, access control,

trust management, and potential vulnerabilities, are thoroughly examined, with a review of encryption, access policies, and anomaly detection methods [10].

[14] The paper explores security concerns and defense mechanisms in the realm of Internet of Things (IoT) systems, offering insights into the unique challenges posed by IoT architectures, applications, and communication models compared to traditional IT systems. It delves into common vulnerabilities like insufficient authorization, lack of transport encryption, privacy threats, insecure web interfaces, and denial of service attacks. A proposed IoT security framework introduces layers focusing on confidentiality, integrity, availability, authentication, access control, and non-repudiation. Cryptographic mechanisms, both symmetric and asymmetric encryption, key establishment protocols, hash functions, and digital signatures, are discussed in the context of IoT. The examination of security controls spans sensor security, encryption, and access control at various layers. The necessity for robust network architecture, scalable access control and authentication, data provenance tracing, lightweight cryptography for Internet of Things devices, and standardized security frameworks is highlighted.

[15] The paper presents an up-to-date survey on the integration of Internet of Things (IoT) and cloud computing platforms, exploring various architectural approaches such as direct integration, middleware-based integration, cloud-based middleware, and service-oriented architecture. It meticulously examines commercial solutions like Amazon Web Services IoT, Microsoft Azure IoT Suite, and IBM Watson IoT Platform. Identifying key technical challenges like massive scale, heterogeneity, security, and quality of service, the paper delves into open issues in IoT-cloud integration, such as semantic interoperability, fog computing, data abstraction, self-management, and context-aware computing. Standardization efforts across multiple bodies are reviewed, emphasizing the crucial need for convergence. Future research directions suggest adaptive security models, energy-aware integration, machine learning capabilities, and testing mechanisms to further advance IoT-cloud systems [33].

Recent work has adopted IoT sensors, cloud analytics and Kafka streams for smart city applications [11, 12]. We build on these technologies but apply them in a novel integrated architecture specifically designed for predictive weather forecasting based on heartbeats. Table 5.2 discusses key features of some of the popular fault tolerance models.

Table 5.2 Related work on fault tolerance in Cloud computing applications.

Fault tolerance architectures	Technique	Applications/ characteristics	Limitations
PCFT [8]	Preemptive migration	Focusing on Cloud service reliability in applications where multiple VM's are coordinating.	Computational complexity and operational overhead
Hybrid meta heuristic approach [21]	Preemptive migration & load balancing	Combines Modified Harris Hanks Optimization (MHHO) & Ant Colony optimization	Adaptability concerns, computational overhead, sensitivity towards parameter setting & scalability issues.
Sequential codelet PXM [20]	Fault Prevention	Parallel computing	Complex control mechanisms
Enhanced FTA [17]	Proactive & Reactive both	Trustworthy VM model, fault isolation, elimination & recovery	Not energy efficient, complex design
ACFT [7]	Proactive & Reactive both	Job migration, checkpointing & recovery is focused	Job migration is limited to 3 chances, sequential calling by decision maker, which should be dynamic, there should be Parallel invoking all modules based on faults
Aggressive AFT [5]	Checkpointing, resubmission & replication	Focusses on transient faults, smart decision agent is introduced.	Increased resource overhead.
FTMSFIS [26]	Fuzzy logic, replication, checkpointing	Fuzzy logic based adaptable fault tolerant method	It compares the two methods: replication & checkpointing.

5.3 Proposed Proactive Fault Detection Architecture

In this section, we describe the complete architecture for proactive weather forecasting control system using heartbeat data. Figure 5.1 provides an overview of the key components.

The proposed architecture consists of the following key stages:

1. *IoT Sensors*: A network of sensors captures heartbeat messages from controllers across the city.
2. *Kafka Ingestion*: A Kafka topic ingests the real-time heartbeat streams into the cloud platform.
3. *Advanced Heartbeat Failure detection*: This module collects heartbeats and physical parameters periodically, if a

Figure 5.1 Relationship between fault, error, and failure.

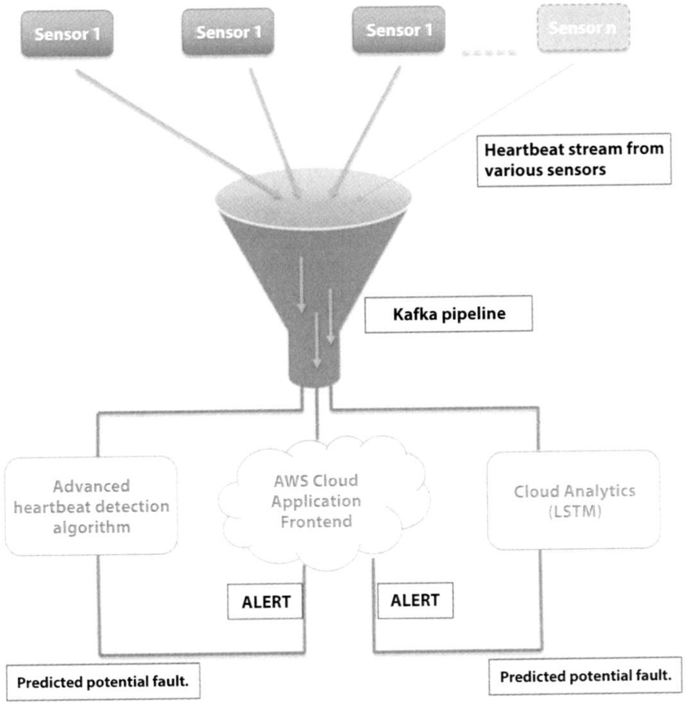

Figure 5.2 System architecture for proactive weather monitoring using heartbeat data.

heartbeat is missed then an algorithm is triggered to detect the fault. The algorithm is discussed in further section.

4. *Cloud Analytics*: Machine learning models detect anomalies in heartbeat patterns indicating likely failures.
5. *Prediction*: The analytics module predicts impending faults based on detected abnormalities.
6. *Kafka Alerting*: Predictions are published via Kafka to alert frontend dashboards.

From Figure 5.2, the stream of heartbeat signals collected from sensors across the city is fed into the cloud platform, where machine learning algorithms running on scalable cloud infrastructure analyze the data in real-time to detect anomalies.

Advanced Heartbeat Failure Detection Algorithm

Create Confidence factor (α):

- To enhance the current strategy, it is proposed to maintain a simple tracking counter, denoted as the confidence factor (α). This counter will be incremented whenever a node fails to transmit the heartbeat message, effectively keeping track of the node's accessibility and reliability within the network.

Confidence Testing:

- If the confidence factor (α) surpasses a predefined threshold, the node is flagged for confidence testing.
- During confidence testing, the node is prompted to resend heartbeat messages with alternating frequencies, collecting critical details (such as CPU temperature, network details) to maintain a log report.

Detect False Positives:

- This approach aims to address false positive cases, where a node may not have failed, but heartbeat messages were not received due to slow software response or congestion.

Fault Localization:

- Additionally, it facilitates fault localization. If the node continues to be unresponsive, it is marked as a failed node, triggering an alert to the master node.

Reactive Fault Techniques are administered:

- Critical services are then migrated, and fault recovery procedures are initiated to restore proper functioning.

Fault Negatives:

- Log report can be downloaded at any time weather a fault is detected or not. This log report also identifies False negatives i.e. a case when the system is not giving accurate results and is about to fail but since it is working fine and sending continuous heartbeats, the potential failure is getting undetected. But the log report contains information of reliability value of sensors and their continuous temperature feeds, along with their CPU utilization and some physical parameters. The abnormality in this data, will avoid the failure that might occur to that sensor.

Figures 5.16–5.19 shows code snippets from the system that demonstrate some of the functionalities of our proposed model.

Heartbeat data stream is used to train LSTM neural network models to learn expected periodic heartbeat patterns for each monitored sensor location. The LSTM models encode a range of normal heartbeat intervals based on parameters like minimum, maximum, mean, variance, etc. Cloud GPUs accelerate model training by parallelizing deep learning computations.

Subsequently, live heartbeat readings are continuously ingested from the Kafka topic and fed through the trained LSTM models. The models compare the real-time intervals against the expected periodicity distributions. If current durations deviate beyond thresholds, the algorithms raise an anomaly flag signaling potential equipment failure.

In addition, a rules-based engine supplements the LSTM models with hard-coded rules for heartbeat intervals. For example, if no heartbeats are received for a duration exceeding 5 minutes, a critical alert is triggered irrespective of model predictions. This rule provides robustness.

Fault Prediction

When the analytics layer detects abnormal heartbeats through either the LSTM neural networks or the rules engine, it signifies a high likelihood of impending failure. For instance, highly irregular heartbeat intervals from a specific sensor imply a defective embedded controller or sensor malfunction.

Rather than waiting for a catastrophic outage, the algorithms automatically predict the existence of a fault preemptively based on the anomalies. This enables generating actionable alerts to repair issues preventatively before any disruption occurs, which is a key benefit of the proactive approach.

Internally, the predictions are published as MQTT messages containing the anomalous sensor ID, sensor location coordinates, model confidence scores, failure probability, and other metadata. These events are streamed asynchronously to the next stage for downstream consumption [27–31].

Evaluation Metrics

The evaluation in the proactive heartbeat monitoring approach is based on using several key performance metrics:

Fault Detection Latency: Measured as the time duration between the onset of a fault and when it was successfully detected by the system.
Application Uptime: Percentage of total time that the sensors were operational and functioning normally. The goal is to maximize uptime as close to 100% as possible. Heartbeat monitoring increased uptime by detecting faults before downtime.
Application Downtime: The total amount of time sensors were non-operational due to failures.
False Positive Rate: Percentage of fault alerts generated that turned out to be incorrect.
False Negative Rate: Percentage of actual faults that were missed and not detected by the system.
Throughput: No. of tasks completed/specified time interval
Success Rate: No. of Tasks completed/Total no. of tasks.
Availability: Application Uptime/Specified time interval []

Proposed Model Application/Technologies in AWS

1. AWS EC2: Amazon Elastic Compute Cloud (EC2) is a core AWS service that provides resizable virtual machines (instances) in the cloud. These instances can be configured with

the desired operating system, memory, storage, and networking options.

Key Advantages:

Flexibility: Customize your compute environment to match your application's specific needs.

Scalability: Easily increase or decrease instance capacity based on changing resource demands.

Reliability: AWS offers robust infrastructure with built-in redundancy and fault tolerance for your instances.

Cost-Effectiveness: Pay-as-you-go pricing model helps you manage costs effectively.

2. Docker: Docker is a software platform that simplifies the process of building, shipping, and running applications using containers. A container packages your application code, its dependencies, and a lightweight operating system into a self-contained unit.

   Key Advantages:

   Portability: Docker images run consistently across different environments (development, test, production), minimizing compatibility issues.

   Efficiency: Containers are lightweight and share the host operating system, leading to efficient resource usage.

   Versioning and Reproducibility: Dockerfiles track changes, allowing you to roll back or share specific versions of your application environment.

3. PM2 (Optional): PM2 is a powerful process manager for Node.js applications, providing tools to keep your application running, monitor its performance, and manage multiple instances.

   Key Advantages:

   Enhanced Uptime: Can automatically restart your application in case of crashes or unexpected downtime.

   Load Balancing: PM2 distributes incoming traffic across multiple instances of your application for improved performance.

   Simplified Monitoring: Provides key metrics on your application's resource usage, helping identify bottlenecks.

4. Nginx: Nginx is a high-performance web server, reverse proxy, and load balancer known for its speed, efficiency, and scalability.

Key Advantages:

Handles High Concurrency: Nginx excels at managing large volumes of simultaneous web requests with minimal overhead.

Reverse Proxy: Acts as an intermediary between users and your application, offering security and performance benefits.

Load Balancing: Can distribute traffic across multiple backend servers, improving scalability and reducing downtime.

Content Caching: Can store frequently requested content, speeding up your website's response times [30].

Although we can use Kaka in place of Nginx, both have separate application base.

Stepwise Modeling of the Proposed Application

- Step 1: Creation of an Amazon EC2 instance: We launched an EC2 instance from the AWS Management Console depending on requirements and workload.
- Step 2: Set up of Docker and containers: We Installed Docker on our EC2 instance by following the official Docker documentation. After that, we started the creation and deployment of containers on the EC2 instance using Docker.
- Step 3: Performing container live migration: To demonstrate container live migration, we used a container orchestration tool called Amazon Elastic Kubernetes Service (EKS) that supports live migration. We set up an EKS cluster, configured the necessary resources, and performed live migration of containers between nodes in the cluster.
- Step 4: Monitoring and measuring the impact: We utilized AWS CloudWatch to collect performance metrics such as CPU utilization, memory usage, network traffic, and latency. We monitored these metrics before, during, and after the live migration process to observe the impact on the application's performance.
- Step 5: Cost analysis: We monitored and tracked the cost of running our containers during the live migration process. AWS provides a billing dashboard where we can view cost breakdowns.
- Step 6: Documenting and analyzing the results: We recorded our findings and observations regarding the impact and cost

of container live migration, the analysis of the performance metrics, and cost data to conclude the effectiveness and efficiency of container live migration.

Backend Works

Firebase(database):

Firebase Realtime Database, is a powerful tool for building web applications with real-time data updates.

- Cloud-hosted NoSQL database provided by Google Firebase.
- Data is stored as JSON and synchronized in real time across all connected clients.
- Designed for low-latency, highly responsive applications

Key Benefits

- Real-time Updates: Changes to the database are instantaneously pushed to all connected clients.
- Offline Support: Firebase Realtime Database can function offline, synchronizing data when a connection is re-established.
- Ease of Use: Simple API, great integration with other Firebase services.
- Scalability: Handles large numbers of concurrent users.
- Cost-Effective: Offers a generous free tier, and paid plans are based on usage.

Firebase is used for real-time tracking of log messages sent by the sensor and getting real-time updates of faults and health status updates by the sensor.

The following are the screenshots of the application based on our proposed model.

Figure 5.3 shows the front end screenshot of weather forecasting app, with a dropdown for injecting types of faults only for demonstration purposes. No fault, temperature, weather fault, Sensor fault and False positive are the crucial ones' here.

Figure 5.4 shows the normal operation of an application with sensors sending heartbeat messages at 10s intervals. This is a message log entry window.

Figure 5.5 shows the series of message logs reported after sensor fault is injected. Also note the time taken to retry and to be confident that this is not false positive case because retrying also shows no response from sensor. Also a message is prompted to download the error report which

Figure 5.3 FrontEnd: Types of fault injection (including false positive case).

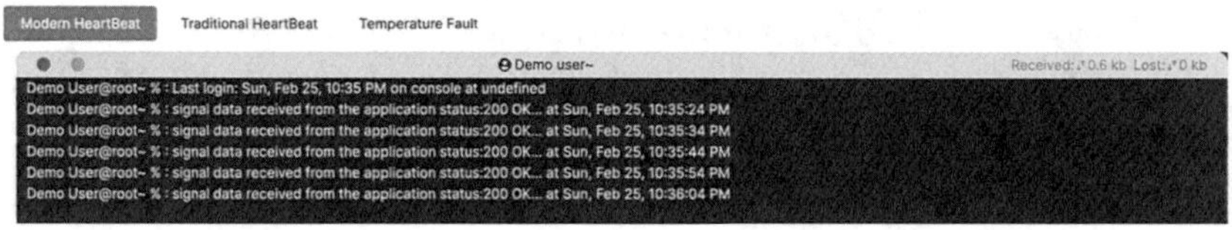

Figure 5.4 Heartbeat received at equal time intervals (10s).

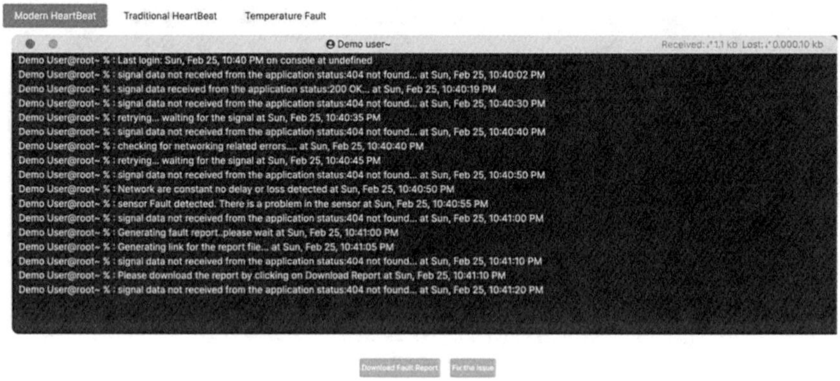

Figure 5.5 Message log entry in case of sensor fault.

will display the details of environmental parameters and possible failure conditions. This will help in fault localization and fault recovery on time to avoid No Service. The time duration between time of missed heartbeat and confirming sensor fault is 25s, the heartbeat is requested/retried at 5 sec intervals for 5 times before confirming sensor failure.

Figure 5.6 shows message entry logs when sudden hike or decrees in fault is detected. This will be done through machine learning algorithms which will detect that in given geographical conditions this hike in temperature or sudden weather change is impossible and will send an alert for possible sensor malfunction and possible failure.

Figure 5.7 suggests a series of events when heartbeat is missed but only due to network lag and not due to any type of fault, and so it recovers quickly. The time duration between time of missed heartbeat and recovering is 12s, the heartbeat is requested/retried at 5 sec intervals for two times and then the heartbeat is received again, confirming that the sensor has not failed.

Following are the graphs of the existing models [34] VFT, PRP-FRC, AFTRC, which display reliability and execution time comparison between them.

The three existing models compared shows following results in the Figure 5.8.

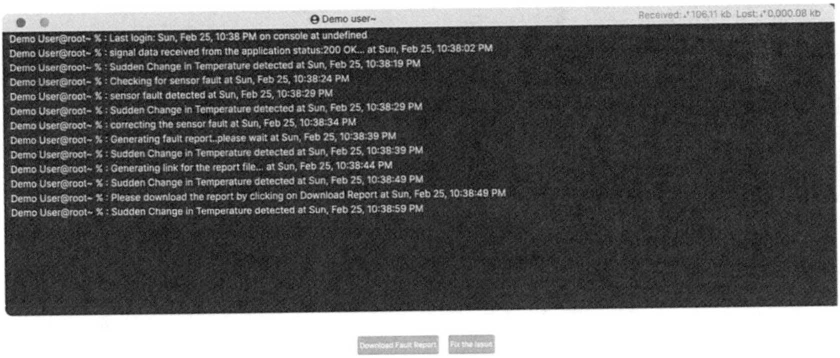

Figure 5.6 Message log entry in case of temperature/weather fault.

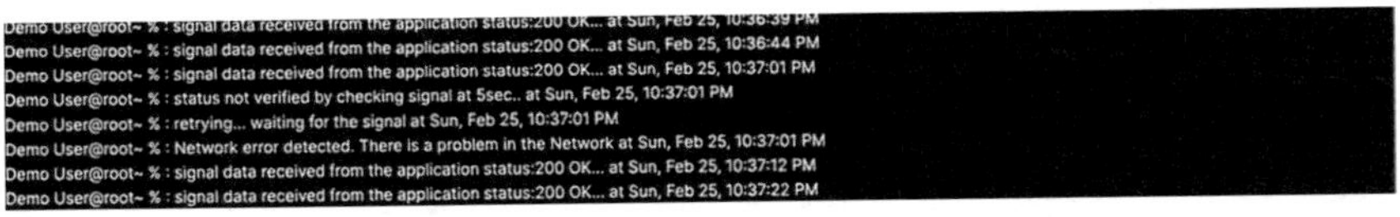

Figure 5.7 Message log entry in case of false positive.

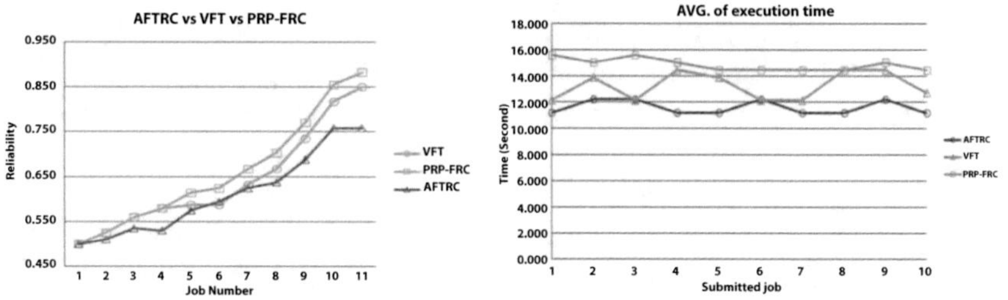

Figure 5.8 Reliability and execution time graph comparing AFTRC, VFT & PRP-FRC [34].

(Figure 5.9) Heartbeat requests are also consuming very less data i.e. 166KB in 160 requests made. Resource utilization at this point is just 12%. (Figure 5.10) Network In data is max 12MB and Network Out data is max 22MB which is consumed by our algorithm. The CPU utilization as shown in Figures 5.11 & 5.12 is just 20% even at the time when advanced heartbeat fault detection algorithm is running and when the log report is downloaded. Figures 5.13 & 5.14 display average read/write latency and message count during this time. In Figure 5.15, log report of sensor 01 is shown which shows that during the time period of fault injection, all its heartbeats, fault messages is recorded, CPU & RAM usage (collected from Cloudwatch), sensor details and average recovery time is also recorded which is 25 sec in this case.

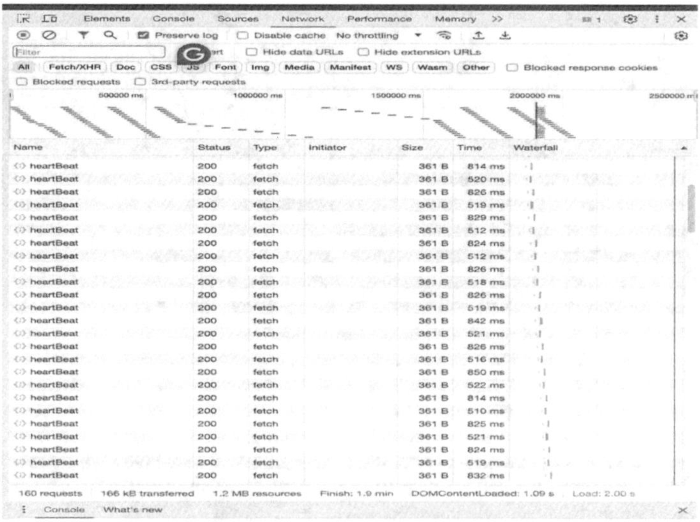

Figure 5.9 Log of continuous heartbeat messages stream received by the sensors.

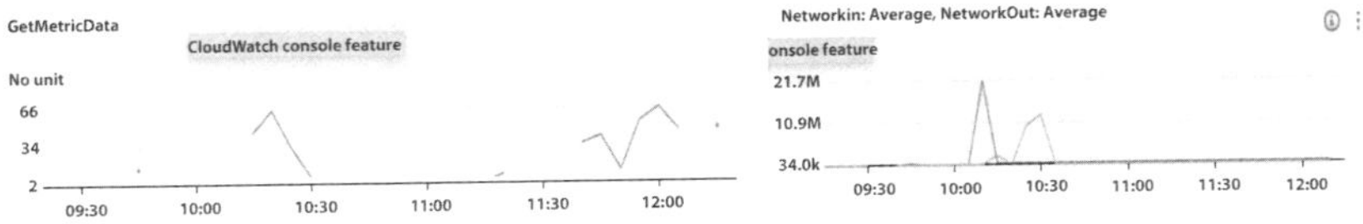

Figure 5.10 Get API data and Network IN/OUT data in the monitoring time period.

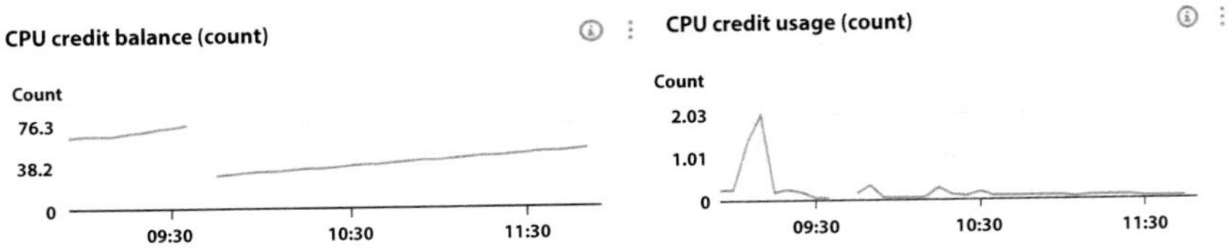

Figure 5.11 CPU credit balance and CPU credit usage in the monitoring time period.

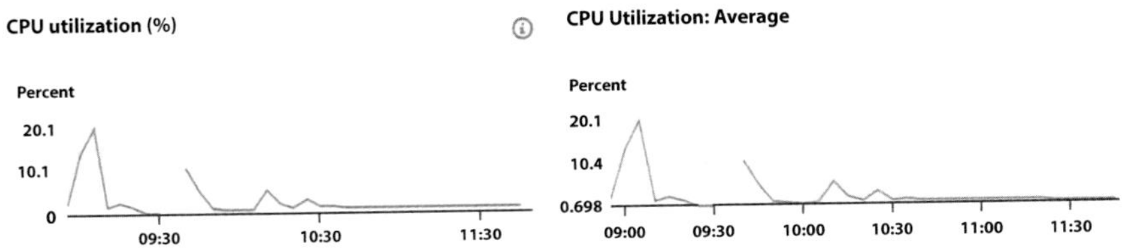

Figure 5.12 CPU Utilization in the monitoring time period.

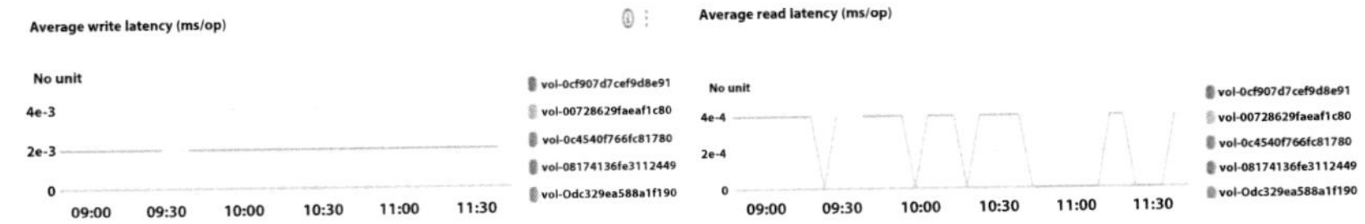

Figure 5.13 Average read/write latency in the monitoring time period.

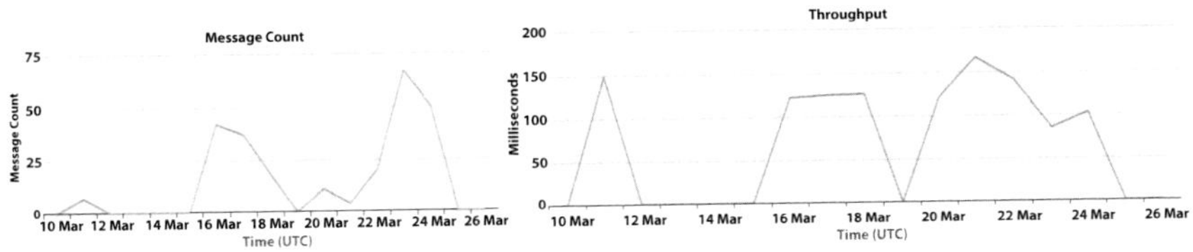

Figure 5.14 Message count & throughput in the monitoring time period.

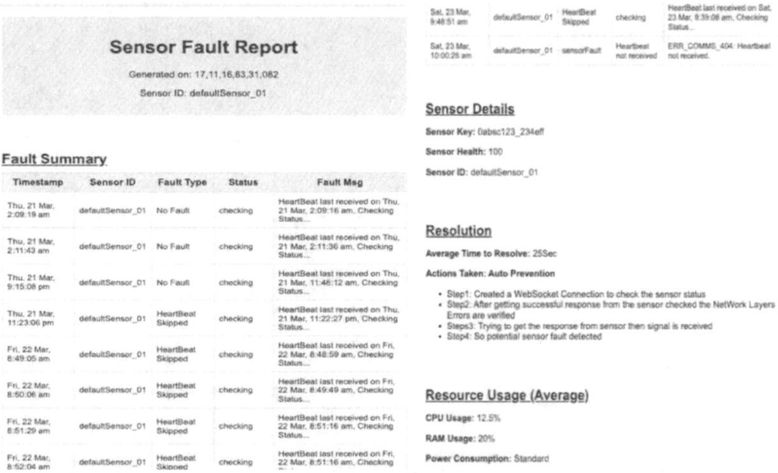

Sensor Fault Report

Generated on: 17,11,16,83,31,082

Sensor ID: defaultSensor_01

Fault Summary

Timestamp	Sensor ID	Fault Type	Status	Fault Msg
Thu, 21 Mar, 2:09:19 am	defaultSensor_01	No Fault	checking	HeartBeat last received on Thu, 21 Mar, 2:09:16 am, Checking Status...
Thu, 21 Mar, 2:11:43 am	defaultSensor_01	No Fault	checking	HeartBeat last received on Thu, 21 Mar, 2:11:36 am, Checking Status...
Thu, 21 Mar, 9:15:08 pm	defaultSensor_01	No Fault	checking	HeartBeat last received on Thu, 21 Mar, 11:46:12 am, Checking Status...
Thu, 21 Mar, 11:23:06 pm	defaultSensor_01	HeartBeat Skipped	checking	HeartBeat last received on Thu, 21 Mar, 11:22:27 pm, Checking Status...
Fri, 22 Mar, 8:49:05 am	defaultSensor_01	HeartBeat Skipped	checking	HeartBeat last received on Fri, 22 Mar, 8:48:59 am, Checking Status...
Fri, 22 Mar, 8:50:06 am	defaultSensor_01	HeartBeat Skipped	checking	HeartBeat last received on Fri, 22 Mar, 8:49:49 am, Checking Status...
Fri, 22 Mar, 8:51:29 am	defaultSensor_01	HeartBeat Skipped	checking	HeartBeat last received on Fri, 22 Mar, 8:51:16 am, Checking Status...
Fri, 22 Mar, 8:52:04 am	defaultSensor_01	HeartBeat Skipped	checking	HeartBeat last received on Fri, 22 Mar, 8:51:16 am, Checking
Sat, 23 Mar, 9:48:51 am	defaultSensor_01	HeartBeat Skipped	checking	HeartBeat last received on Sat, 23 Mar, 9:39:08 am, Checking Status...
Sat, 23 Mar, 10:00:28 am	defaultSensor_01	sensorFault	Heartbeat not received	ERR_COMMS_404: Heartbeat not received.

Sensor Details

Sensor Key: 0absc123_234eff

Sensor Health: 100

Sensor ID: defaultSensor_01

Resolution

Average Time to Resolve: 25Sec

Actions Taken: Auto Prevention

- Step1: Created a WebSocket Connection to check the sensor status
- Step2: After getting successful response from the sensor checked the NetWork Layers Errors are verified
- Steps3: Trying to get the response from sensor then signal is received
- Step4: So potential sensor fault detected

Resource Usage (Average)

CPU Usage: 12.5%

RAM Usage: 20%

Power Consumption: Standard

Figure 5.15 Log report of sensor 1, displaying heartbeat status, sensor details, recovery time, resolution actions, CPU and RAM usage in the monitoring time period.

Following are some code snippets from our running proposed model, which partially displays the functioning of some parts of the mentioned steps the codes are used to generate the Figures 5.16, 5.17, 5.18 and 5.19 respectively.

Table 5.3 displays 4 types of faults injected into the system to mirror the fault types that may occur in a physical sensor. In each type of fault, each sensor (which is played by a VM in the background) has to either recover (RT, i.e. Recovery time), alert for failure (MHbR, i.e. Missed heartbeat rate), or do nothing (False negative, FN). Thus, each time a VM recovers to the normal state, using our approach, the recovery time is noted and is declared passed. Each time VM fails to recover or declares faults falsely, then it is declared as failed and its time is noted in seconds. The VM with highest pass ratio overall is declared as best and the one with lowest MHbR will be declared as lowest reliable.

Overall, in our approach, results concluded that false negatives were hard to detect and resulted in failure. This will be solved when the machine learning algorithm is incorporated and when a system is devised to periodically check the log report to detect any anomalies in the sensors. This will eliminate the case of false negatives.

```
else if (logIndex === newLog.length) {
onlyOnceSetTimerRef.current = true;
setTimerValue(timerRef, {
  timer: 5,
  reqStatus: true,
  msg: "Close Req",
});
```

Figure 5.16 Code snippet for retrying heartbeat request at 5 sec interval.

```
let logIndex = 0;
if (checkStatus === "sensorFault") {
  faultIntervalRef.current = setInterval(() => {
    const now = new Date();
    const options = {
      weekday: "short",
      month: "short",
      day: "numeric",
      hour: "numeric",
      minute: "numeric",
      second: "numeric",
    };
```

Figure 5.17 Code snippet for shifting fault injection value from "No Fault" to "Sensor Fault."

```
if (logIndex === 1 || logIndex === 3 || logIndex === 5) {
  const dataReceive = new TextEncoder().encode(
    JSON.stringify(newLog[logIndex])
  ).length;
  const dataSizeInKB = (dataReceive / 1024).toFixed(2);
  setDataSizeN(
    (prevTotalSize) =>
      parseFloat(prevTotalSize).toFixed(2) +
      parseFloat(dataSizeInKB).toFixed(2)
  );
```

Figure 5.18 Code snippet for displaying data packet received and sent.

```
// Set the initial value of the timer database to 10
setTimerValue(timerRef, {
  timer: 10,
  reqStatus: false,

  msg: "open req",
});
```

Figure 5.19 Code snippet for setting heartbeat request at normal 10 s interval.

Table 5.3 Results obtained after various faults injected in the application and their recovery times.

Fault injection type	Sensor 1 (S1)				Sensor 2 (S2)				Best (high MhbR)	Worst (low MhbR)
	RT	FP	FN	MHbR	RT	FP	FN	MHbR		
Temperature Fault (Pass1)	Pass (76s)	Pass (18s)	Fail (23 s)	2	Pass (32 s)	Pass (22s)	Pass (13s)	3	S2	S1
Sensor Fault (Pass 2)	Pass (64s)	Pass (13s)	Pass (14 s)	3	Pass (91s)	Pass (17s)	Pass (14s)	3	S2	S1
False Positive (Pass 3)	Pass (12s)	Pass (42s)	Pass (12 s)	3	Pass (34s)	Pass (12s)	Pass (23s)	3	S2	S1
Network Fault (Pass 3)	Pass (12s)	Pass (32s)	Fail (45 s)	2	Pass (32s)	Pass (12s)	Fail (34s)	2	S2	S1

5.4 Conclusion

In this paper, we presented a novel proactive fault detection architecture for weather forecasting control systems using heartbeat monitoring. The continuous analysis of heartbeat signals from distributed sensors enables early identification of anomalies predictive of failures. [17, 32] This allows preventative maintenance to be scheduled before any operational disruption. There are however technology and research limitations that pose opportunities for further work. Some of the results mentioned in this paper present a view that this method consumes less resources, less CPU is utilized on an average and lesser network data is consumed. Thus making it very energy efficient. The proactive model is implemented on AWS EC2 instance using UBUNTU server and firebase database. Reactive techniques applied in alliance with this proactive model will make it more robust in future.

References

1. Amin, Z., Singh, H., Ahluwalia, N., Review on Fault Tolerance Techniques in Cloud Computing. *Int. J. Comput. Appl.*, 116, 11–17, 2015, 10.5120/20435-2768.
2. Bala, A. and Chana, I., Fault Tolerance-Challenges, Techniques and Implementation in Cloud Computing. *Int. J. Comput. Sci.*, 9, 9, 1812–1820, 2012.
3. Engelmann, C., Vallee, G., Naughton, T., Scott, S., Proactive Fault Tolerance Using Preemptive Migration, pp. 252–257, 2009, 10.1109/PDP.2009.31.
4. Litvinova, A., Engelmann, C., Scott, S., A proactive fault tolerance framework for high-performance computing. *Proceedings of the 9th IASTED International Conference on Parallel and Distributed Computing and Networks, PDCN*, 2010.
5. Rahman, M.M. and Rouf, M.A., Aggressive Fault Tolerance in Cloud Computing using Smart Decision Agent, 2021.
6. Kumar, A. and Malhotra, D., Study of Various Proactive Fault Tolerance Techniques in Cloud Computing. *Int. J. Comput. Sci. Eng.*, 06, 81–87, 2018, 10.26438/ijcse/v6si3.8187.
7. Sumangali, K. and Benny, N., Advanced cloud fault tolerance system. *IOP Conf. Ser.: Mater. Sci. Eng.*, 263, 042060, 2017, 10.1088/1757-899X/263/4/042060.
8. Liu, J., Wang, S., Zhou, A., Kumar, S., Yang, F., Buyya, R., Using Proactive Fault-Tolerance Approach to Enhance Cloud Service Reliability. *IEEE Trans. Cloud Comput.*, 6, 1191–1202, 2018, 10.1109/TCC.2016.2567392.
9. Rehman, A.U., Aguiar, R., Barraca, J., Fault-Tolerance in the Scope of Cloud Computing. *IEEE Access*, 10, 1–21, 2022, 10.1109/ACCESS.2022.3182211.

10. Tamilvzhi, T. and Parvathavarthini, B., A novel method for adaptive fault tolerance during load balancing in cloud computing. *Cluster Comput.*, 22, 5, 10425–10438, 2019.
11. Atlam, H., Alenezi, A., Alshdadi, A., Walters, R., Wills, G., Integration of Cloud Computing with Internet of Things: Challenges and Open Issues, 2017, 10.1109/iThings-GreenCom-CPSCom-SmartData.2017.105.
12. Ansari, M., Ali, S., Alam, M., Internet of things (IoT) fusion with cloud computing: current research and future direction. *IJATEE,* 9, 1812–1845, 2023, 10.19101/IJATEE.2021.876002.
13. Botta, A., De Donato, W., Persico, V., Pescapé, A., Integration of cloud computing and internet of things: a survey. *Future Gener. Comput. Syst.*, 56, 684–700, 2016.
14. Alaba, F.A., Othman, M., Hashem, I.A.T. *et al.*, Internet of Things security: A survey. *J. Netw. Comput. Appl.*, 88, 10–28, 2017.
15. Díaz, M., Martín, C., Li, S., State-of-the-art, challenges, and open issues in the integration of internet of things and cloud computing. *J. Netw. Comput. Appl.*, 67, 2, 99–117, 2016, Available at: https://www.sciencedirect.com/science/article/abs/pii/S108480451600028X?via%3Dihub.
16. Jhawar, R., Piuri, V., Santambrogio, M., A Comprehensive Conceptual System-Level Approach to Fault Tolerance in Cloud Computing. *Systems Conference (SysCon), 2012 IEEE International*, 2012, 10.1109/SysCon.2012.6189503.
17. Veerapandi, S., Surendiran, R., Alagarsamy, K., Enhanced Fault Tolerant Cloud Architecture to Cloud based Computing using Both Proactive and Reactive Mechanisms. *DS J. Digital Sci. Technol.*, 1, 32–40, 2023, 10.59232/DST-V1I1P105.
18. Nazeer, K. and Banu, N., Fault Tolerance For Energy Efficient Green Cloud Computing-A Study, 2014.
19. Bharany, S., Badotra, S., Rani, S., Alazab, M., Jhaveri, R., Gadekallu, T., Energy efficient fault tolerance techniques in green cloud computing: A systematic survey and taxonomy. *Sustain. Energy Technol. Assess.*, 53, 102613, 2022, 10.1016/j.seta.2022.102613.
20. Roa Perdomo, D., Herrera Guaitero, R., Fox, D., Yviquel, H., Raskar, S., Li, X., Monsalve Diaz, J.M., Towards Fault Tolerance and Resilience in the Sequential Codelet Model, 2024, 10.1007/978-3-031-52186-7_6.
21. Kashyap, V., Ahuja, R., Kumar, A., A hybrid approach for fault-tolerance aware load balancing in fog computing. *Cluster Comput.*, 27, 3, 1–17, 2024, 10.1007/s10586-023-04219-z.
22. Kalaskar, C. and Thangam, S., Fault Tolerance of Cloud Infrastructure with Machine Learning. *Cybern. Inf. Technol.*, 23, 26–50, 2023, 10.2478/cait-2023-0034.
23. Tamilvizhi, T. and Surendran, R., Time and cost-effective recovery mechanism for unhealthy resources in proactive fault tolerance framework, pp. 444–449, 2021, 10.1049/icp.2021.0756.

24. Theodoropoulos, T., Violos, J., Tsanakas, S., Leivadeas, A., Tserpes, K., Varvarigou, T., Intelligent Proactive Fault Tolerance at the Edge through Resource Usage Prediction, 2023, 10.48550/arXiv.2302.05336.
25. Li, J., Stones, R., Luo, J., Random Versus Copyset Placement: Data-Loss Models for Proactive-Tolerance Replica-Based Data Storage. *IEEE Trans. Reliab.*, 9, 2, 1–12, 2021, 10.1109/TR.2021.3105675.
26. Kumari, P. and Kaur, P., An Adaptable Approach to Fault Tolerance in Cloud Computing. *Int. J. Cloud Appl. Comput.*, 13, 1–24, 2023, 10.4018/IJCAC.319032.
27. Theodoropoulos, T., Violos, J., Tsanakas, S., Leivadeas, A., Tserpes, K., Varvarigou, T., Intelligent proactive fault tolerance at the edge through resource usage prediction. *ITU J. Future Evol. Technol.*, 3, 761–778, 2022, 10.52953/EHJP3291.
28. Haneef, S. and Venkataraman, N., Proactive Fault Prediction of Fog Devices Using LSTM-CRP Conceptual Framework for IoT Applications. *Sensors*, 23, 2913, 2023, 10.3390/s23062913.
29. Mulu, A., Gemeda, K., Ramulu, P., Prediction and classification of IoT sensor faults using hybrid deep learning model. *SN Appl. Sci.*, 6, 21, 2024, 10.1007/s42452-024-05633-7.
30. Khosravi, Garg, S. K., Buyya, R., Energy and carbon-efficient placement of virtual machines in distributed cloud data centers. *Euro-Par 2013 Parallel Processing*, 8097, 317–328, 2013.
31. Sharma, Y., Javadi, B., Si, W., Sun, D., Reliability and Energy Efficiency in Cloud Computing Systems: Survey and Taxonomy. *J. Netw. Comput. Appl.* 74, 2016, 10.1016/j.jnca.2016.08.010.
32. Kumari, P. and Kaur, P., A Survey of Fault Tolerance in Cloud Computing. *J. King Saud Univ. Comput. Inf. Sci.*, 33, 1–10, 2018, 10.1016/j.jksuci.2018.09.021.
33. Patel, S. and Singh, A., Fault Tolerance Mechanisms and its Implementation in Cloud Computing – A Review, 3, 1–7, 2014.
34. Nazari Cheraghlou, M., Khadem-Zadeh, A., Haghparast, M., A New Hybrid Fault Tolerance Approach for Internet of Things. *Electronics*, 8, 518, 2019, 10.3390/electronics8050518.
35. Abdelfattah, E., Elkawkagy, M., El-Sisi, A., Hybrid Fault Tolerance Approach Based on Replication Impact Heuristic for Cloud Computing, 2020.
36. Satish, T., Madhusudhan, S., Mustapha, S., Gupta, P., Tripathi, R., Intelligent Fault-Tolerant Mechanism for Data Centers of Cloud Infrastructure. *Math. Probl. Eng.*, 1, 1, 1–12, 2022, 10.1155/2022/2379643.

6

FlowGuard: Efficient Traffic Monitoring System

Varsha Dange, Atharva Bonde, Om Borse, Harshal Chaudhari* and Sanskar Chaudhari

Vishwakarma Institute of Technology, Pune, Maharashtra, India

Abstract
The FlowGuard Traffic Monitoring project is briefed here, with a focus on how cutting-edge technology is used. It describes the system's objectives, which include instantly adjusting traffic lights to improve flow and save fuel usage. The introduction emphasizes how important it is to alleviate traffic congestion and support environmentally friendly modes of travel as essential components of the system's goal. This introduction also highlights the pressing necessity to confront modern urban issues and the pressing need for creative solutions considering the escalating traffic jams. The study explains how the dynamic adjustment mechanism of the FlowGuard Traffic Monitoring System constitutes a paradigm leap in traffic signal optimization by exploring its inner workings. The Sustain FlowGuard system has the potential to revolutionize intelligent traffic management by promoting a harmonic combination of innovation and sustainability. This will usher in a new era in which cities may prosper with less environmental impact and optimized mobility.

Keywords: Deep learning, computer vision, real-time traffic data

6.1 Introduction

This section introduces the FlowGuard System, a technological marvel designed to revolutionize urban traffic management. At its core, the system harnesses cutting-edge technology to address the perennial challenges

**Corresponding author*: harshal.chaudhari22@vit.edu

Budati Anil Kumar, Singamaneni Kranthi Kumar and Li Xingwang (eds.) Quantum Computing Models for Cybersecurity and Wireless Communications, (99–124) © 2025 Scrivener Publishing LLC

associated with traffic congestion and inefficient traffic flow. The primary focus is on seamlessly integrating advanced solutions, particularly in the form of dynamic traffic signal optimization, to create a more responsive and adaptive traffic control infrastructure.

The system's objectives are multifaceted, with a key emphasis on the instantaneous adjustment of traffic lights. This feature serves a dual purpose: optimizing traffic flow and contributing to fuel conservation, aligning with broader sustainability goals. By strategically deploying state-of-the-art mechanisms, the Sustain flow system aims to alleviate the bottlenecks that often plague urban road networks.

Importantly, the introduction underscores the pivotal role of the FlowGuard System in promoting environmentally friendly modes of travel. Beyond mere traffic management, the system is positioned as an essential component in fostering sustainable urban development. It's not just about making traffic more efficient; it's about integrating technology to drive positive, eco-conscious changes in the urban landscape.

Delving into the technical intricacies, the study elucidates the dynamic adjustment mechanism of the Sustain flow system, portraying it as a paradigm leap in traffic signal optimization. This mechanism is explored in detail, unveiling the inner workings that differentiate it from conventional systems. The incorporation of modern technology is not limited to enhancing traffic flow; it's a strategic move to establish the system as a transformative force propelling wider urban development initiatives.

This introductory section lays the foundation for a comprehensive examination of the complex strategy underpinning the Sustain flow system. It is an invitation to explore how this innovative approach has the potential to redefine the dynamics of urban mobility and sustainability. By seamlessly blending cutting-edge technology with a holistic urban development perspective, the FlowGuard System emerges as a catalyst for positive change in the intricate tapestry of urban life.

6.2 Literature Review

[1] The escalating issue of urban traffic congestion because of the sudden escalation in population and vehicles has prompted a critical need for innovative traffic management solutions. In the paper "Vehicle Detection and Counting of a Vehicle Using OpenCV" by Karthik Srivathsa D S and Dr. Kamalraj R, the authors stress how important vehicle detection and counting are to the management of urban traffic. Using OpenCV to analyze images and videos, particularly in the context of computer vision

applications, the paper underscores its significance in addressing traffic challenges. The real-time insights provided by OpenCV, including vehicle speed and traffic density, enable informed decision-making for both road users and traffic organizations. This paper helps with smart traffic control systems. It shows how OpenCV can make traffic flow better, ease congestion, and improve city transportation.

[2] In their paper titled "Smart Traffic Monitoring System based on Vehicle Counts for Traffic Management in Smart City," Geethika Boddu, Viswasri Ankamreddi, Narsipuram Shyamkumar, and Yogesh Kumar address the pressing issue of traffic congestion, particularly prevalent in cities like Mumbai, Bangalore, and New Delhi in India. Recognizing the adverse health effects of air pollution due to traffic, the authors propose an innovative solution leveraging computer vision for real-time traffic monitoring. They identify the limitations of fixed-time traffic signals and introduce a dynamic system that utilizes live streaming from public surveillance cameras. This proposed system employs cloud-based processing, employing OpenCV filters to distinguish between vehicles, animals, and pedestrians, calculating traffic density. The on-board vehicle manager, in conjunction with a traffic management algorithm, then optimizes traffic light sequences in response to current traffic conditions, offering a promising approach to enhance urban traffic management in smart cities. This paper contributes to the literature by providing a comprehensive solution that combines computer vision, real-time data processing, and adaptive traffic signal control to address the challenges of traditional fixed-timer traffic lights.

[3] In the paper titled "Vehicle Counting Module Design in Small Scale for Traffic Management in Smart City" by Janak Trivedi, Dr. Mandalapu Sarada Devi, and Dave Dhara, the authors delve into the research-oriented domain of automatic object counting and classification within image and video processing systems. Recognizing and classifying objects through various methods are central to this investigation, where both offline (stored) and real-time video sequences are considered. The paper particularly emphasizes on the development of smart cities in India, with a performance evaluation using recorded videos from major cities like Bangalore, Ahmedabad, Chennai, and Mumbai. Section II highlights the significance of car parking utility and its necessity, emphasizing how the proposed car counting method contributes to the successful implementation of an automatic car parking system. A motivating case study is presented to underscore the relevance of this work. Section III reviews existing methods, discusses their limitations, and introduces proposed techniques and algorithms. Simulation results, including tabular representations for different threshold values, are provided, with

a thorough discussion on Standard Recall, Precision, and F1 Parameters. The application of these methods is exemplified using traffic videos from Ahmedabad. This paper not only contributes to the understanding of small-scale vehicle counting but also offers insights for effective traffic management in the context of developing smart cities.

[4] The paper "Automatic Vehicle Detection and Counting System" authored by Kritika Ranjan *et al.* introduces a novel approach for detecting and classifying vehicles on two-lane roads. Their work involves the development of a Python program, 'vehicle.py,' housing user-defined functions for efficient vehicle detection and classification. Employing the BackgroundSubtractorMOG2 algorithm, grounded in Gaussian Mixture for Foreground/Background Segmentation, and utilizing the OpenCV library in Python for real-time computer vision, the authors present a practical and effective solution. The proposed workflow, outlined in 'main.py,' demonstrates the system's functionality. In the broader context of automatic vehicle detection literature, this paper contributes to the growing emphasis on real-time computer vision applications, showcasing the adaptability of contemporary techniques for accurate vehicle counting on roads. The integration of OpenCV underscores the significance of leveraging robust and accessible libraries, presenting a balanced and effective solution for two-lane road scenarios.

[5] In their paper, "Moving Vehicle Detection for Measuring Traffic Count Using OpenCV," Nilesh J Uke and Ravindra C Thool underscore the significance of accurate traffic data, including counts, speed, and vehicle classification, in transportation projects. While traditional methods often rely on sensors like magnetic loop detectors, the authors advocate for vision-based video monitoring systems. These systems use one camera fixed on a vertical support, such as a pole which offer advantages such as comprehensive traffic parameter measurement, including vehicle classifications, lane changes, and parking areas. The proposed approach, leveraging OpenCV, aligns with the contemporary trend of employing computer vision for efficient traffic monitoring. This paper contributes to the literature by presenting a practical and adaptable solution for moving vehicle detection and traffic measurement, addressing the increasing demand for intelligent transportation systems in urban areas. The authors' focus on a single-camera setup for multi-lane and bidirectional traffic flow classification further enhances the system's versatility and cost-effectiveness.

[6] The paper "Density-based Traffic Control System using Arduino" by Chanda Jyoshna addresses the prevalent issue of traffic congestion in cities. The writers offer a plan using Arduino Uno ATMega 328P to make a traffic signal based on how many vehicles are there. The plan uses four infrared

cameras, eight LEDs, eight 220 ohm resistors, and an Arduino Uno microcontroller. The infrared sensors measure traffic by counting vehicles, and the Arduino Uno processes the data. The system uses red, yellow, and green LEDs to show traffic, giving green to the busiest path and red to the rest. The microcontroller employs a 1000 ms delay to track and respond to traffic conditions based on sensor outputs. This project aims to contribute to effective traffic control strategies using technology.

[7] The paper titled "Traffic Monitoring System: A Review" by Amogh Sanjeev Sinai Karapurkar and Sonia Kuwelkar addresses the inefficiencies in traditional traffic signal systems in India, where signals have predefined static timings. The problem arises when vehicles have to wait unnecessarily due to red signals, even if there is no traffic on the other side. The paper proposes a dynamic timing system based on real-time vehicle detection, aiming to improve traffic flow and reduce time wastage. The authors review various research studies in the domain of traffic systems using image processing techniques and aim to identify the most efficient systems. The paper is organized with sections describing the need for a Traffic Monitoring System, guidelines for incorporation, enhancements to existing systems, classification based on hardware and software tools, and the proposed methodology. The review and comparison of different research studies are presented, leading to conclusions towards the final section of the paper.

[8] The paper titled "Smart Traffic Monitoring and Controlling" by Rohit Prasad, Himanshu Yadav, Devarsh Kumar, Sachin Pandey, Abhimanyu Yadav addresses the growing challenge of traffic congestion with an Internet of Things (IoT) based solution. The conventional manual traffic control has proven inefficient, especially with predefined signal timings. The proposed model utilizes IoT and cloud computing to create an intelligent traffic management system. A network of sensors monitors vehicle density at intersections, and the system reroutes traffic based on real-time congestion data. The aim is to create a traffic monitoring and control system based on IoT. where a traffic manager, using an Android phone, connects to the system through IoT to set paths and control traffic lights accordingly. The system dynamically adjusts traffic lights based on sensed traffic density, providing an innovative solution to enhance traffic flow and respond to emergencies such as ambulance passage. The central unit employs an ATmega16 microcontroller, and the communication between the controller and the system is encrypted with a password. This IoT-based approach aims to optimize traffic management, lessen traffic and raise the general effectiveness of urban transportation.

[9] The paper titled "Intelligent Traffic Control System Using Arduino" by L. David William Raj, N. Ranjani Priya Bai, C. Pooja, M. Padmini Bai,

D. Nandika addresses the growing challenges in traffic management in metropolitan cities. Recognizing the inefficiencies in current traffic control systems and the significant time people spend waiting at signals, the paper proposes an advanced system that focuses on traffic density rather than fixed time slots for signal control. The system employs IR sensors for vehicle detection, with Arduino UNO analyzing scenarios and controlling LEDs based on predefined code. The goal is to dynamically manage traffic based on density, aiming to alleviate congestion issues caused by rigid signal timing. The project scope emphasizes the need for a system that adapts to varying traffic conditions rather than relying on fixed programming.

[10] The paper "Road Traffic Monitoring System" by G. Shobana and M. Suguna addresses the challenges of increasing road traffic, emphasizing the inefficiencies in current traffic signal control systems. The authors propose an Internet of Things (IoT)-based solution to dynamically manage traffic signals in real-time, aiming to reduce congestion, fuel wastage, and waiting times. The paper advocates for the use of sensors and Arduino microcontrollers to gather and process transportation data, enabling intelligent decision-making based on traffic density. The proposed system seeks to optimize signal timing and improve overall traffic flow. The paper includes a literature survey, details on the proposed system, a simulation model, hardware setup, and concludes with potential avenues for. Future research.

[11] The paper "Research on Urban Intelligent Traffic Monitoring System Based on Video Image Processing" by Jiandong Cao looks into the enhancing of emerging technologies, such as the Internet of Things (IoT), sensor technology, network transmission technology, computer technology, and artificial intelligence, into urban traffic monitoring systems. The author notes the widespread application of these technologies in various domains to enhance intelligence and efficiency. The paper focuses on intelligent traffic, where the use of cutting-edge technologies attempts to boost safety, reduce traffic congestion, and improve management. The current state of IoT technology in intelligent transportation is acknowledged as mature, with video surveillance technology based on image processing playing a crucial role. The author emphasizes the significance of optimizing and transforming this technology to align with the evolving landscape of intelligent video surveillance in the IoT era. The paper sets out to address this by leveraging IoT video sensor technology, computer technology, and other high-tech solutions to develop an intelligent traffic monitoring system. The system is designed to cater to the specific needs of public security traffic management departments, aiming to provide robust support for their operations. The research is positioned at the intersection of IoT, video image processing, and traffic management, with the ultimate

goal of enhancing the intelligence and efficiency of urban traffic monitoring systems.

[12] The paper "Arduino-Based Traffic Monitoring and Controlling System" by L Srinivas, J Bhavani, K Janakiram, M Rupasri, and A B Chandrika addresses the escalating issue of traffic congestion in modern life, attributing it to factors such as the excessive number of automobiles, the poor infrastructure, and the uneven distribution of development. The negative effects of traffic congestion are emphasized by the writers, including slower travel times, longer trip times, and longer lines of cars. In order to address this issue, the paper suggests a dynamic and automated traffic light control system. To make hardware implementation easier, it presents a simulation model with Arduino-based codes. The conventional fixed green signal times for each traffic light on an intersection are challenged, and the authors propose dynamic, time-based coordination schemes that adapt to present traffic conditions. The microcontroller, aided by sensors and a programmed algorithm, intelligently manages traffic flow, aiming to replicate the decision-making process of a traffic inspector. The proposed system offers a technological solution to address traffic congestion by dynamically modifying the timing of traffic lights in response to current circumstances, potentially contributing to more efficient and adaptive traffic management.

[13] The paper "Development of an IoT-based Real-time Traffic Monitoring System for City Governance" by Mohammed Sarrab, Supriya Pulparambil, and Medhat Awadalla addresses the significance of smart city governance in enhancing the standard of living for citizens. The authors emphasize the role of various smart services, including healthcare, building management, traffic management, and transportation, in generating public value. With the advent of the physical infrastructure of smart cities is outfitted with smart devices thanks to the Internet of Things (IoT), continuously generating multidimensional data for intelligent infrastructure. The focus is on smart traffic infrastructure, a critical component of smart cities, given the escalating issue of traffic congestion. The paper discusses intelligent transport systems, encompassing adaptive traffic signal controls, freeway management, emergency services, and roadside units, which collect real-time traffic data to minimize road congestions and improve socio-economic activities. While existing applications like Google Maps offer real-time updates for urban roads, the authors argue for the significance of keeping an eye on collector routes that are used by cyclists, walkers, and other types of vehicles. In order to save drivers time while driving by sending early warning signals, the study suggests an Internet of Things (IoT)-based system model with layered architecture to deliver real-time traffic updates through roadside message units and improve overall city mobility. The

proposed system's features include estimating traffic congestions on collector roads, updating residents via roadside display devices, keeping an eye on the density of traffic on smart campuses, helping the authorities transmit crucial warnings about traffic incidents, and offering a real-time dashboard for traffic updates. The paper concludes with sections on related work, research methodology, system model and technologies, experiments, evaluation, discussion, limitations, and future work.

[14] In the paper "A Review of Different Components of the Intelligent Traffic Management System (ITMS)" by Nikhil Nigam, Dhirendra Pratap Singh, and Jaytrilok Choudhary, the authors address the escalating issue of urban traffic congestion driven by rapid urban growth. Understanding of the detrimental consequences on the environment and public health, they stress the necessity of intelligent systems to reduce traffic by taking into account the growing number of automobiles. This research investigates how to improve traffic control in complicated scenarios by integrating cutting-edge technology including fuzzy logic (FL), microcontrollers, wireless sensor networks (WSNs), machine learning (ML), and the Internet of Things (IoT). Environmental impact assessment, electronic toll collection, anomaly detection, unlawful activity identification, security monitoring, and traffic signal control systems are just a few of the applications of ITMS that the authors highlight. As these applications gradually become integral to human life, the paper outlines challenges associated with ITMS development, providing a foundation for robust solutions. The authors contribute to the discourse on traffic management by elucidating the multifaceted aspects of ITMS and its potential to improve overall human...quality of life.

[15] The paper "Efficient and Effective Traffic Management System" by Engr. Chijioke C.C. and Ugwuanyi S.E addresses the challenges and risks associated with traffic control, emphasizing the demanding and hazardous nature of the job, including long hours, adverse weather conditions, and the constant threat of being struck by passing vehicles. The authors underscore the importance of safety equipment for traffic controllers and highlight issues such as fatigue and driver behavior, including aggression towards traffic controllers. The paper details the typical setup of a worksite, incorporating warning signage, temporary speed restrictions, and lane closure indicators to manage traffic flow. The worksite design varies based on road type, and the paper discusses strategies for multi-lane roads, wide roads, and intersections, emphasizing the need for effective communication and detour planning. Furthermore, the authors examine the challenges associated with roundabouts and 4-way intersections, presenting findings on accident causes and the effectiveness of traffic control measures such as the

"give way to the vehicle from the right" rule and the use of "YEILD" signs at low-volume intersections. This paper contributes valuable insights into the complexities of traffic management, offering considerations for safety, efficiency, and accident reduction strategies.

[16] This paper delves into the multifaceted challenges posed by escalating populations and insufficient road infrastructure, specifically honing in on the pervasive issue of traffic congestion in urban areas. The repercussions are broad, encompassing heightened government expenditure, environmental degradation, and the strain experienced by residents. To address these challenges, the paper meticulously scrutinizes the intricate realm of real-time traffic data analysis and the application of algorithms. The primary objective is to unravel energy-efficient and optimal routes within the framework of a Smart Urban Traffic Management System (SUTMS), with a keen eye on enhancing system efficiency and curbing travel time. Additionally, the paper conducts a thorough examination of contemporary studies that explore the pros and cons of these methods when integrated into the intricate tapestry of SUTMS.

[17] Within the literature review of this paper, an exhaustive exploration is undertaken to dissect the myriad factors that converge to exacerbate the issue of traffic congestion. Delving into its significant impacts, such as accidents, time loss, and escalated costs, the review underscores the imperative for resilient and intelligent solutions tailored to the distinctive challenges of Nigeria's bustling mega cities. A pronounced emphasis is placed on the transformative potential of Vehicle-to-Infrastructure (V2I) technology, heralding a paradigm shift in traffic management and accident mitigation. This sets the conceptual stage for the envisaged system, intricately designed to harness V2I communication intricacies and leverage the innovative Safe-to-Pass-First (SPF) algorithm. The ultimate objective is to elevate intersection control precision and amplify vehicular throughput in a holistic bid to ameliorate the prevailing traffic quandaries.

[18] As urban areas grapple with escalating traffic congestion, the imperative for intelligent traffic control systems is underscored in a paper that systematically investigates and analyzes various architectural frameworks. Published in the 2021 XXIV International Conference on Soft Computing and Measurements (SCM), the research not only delves into the complexities of existing intelligent transport systems but also proposes a refined architecture tailored specifically for intelligent traffic control. Positioned as a strategic response to modern traffic management challenges, the paper contributes significantly to the discourse on leveraging advanced technological solutions to alleviate congestion and enhance overall efficiency in urban transportation.

[19] Urban areas face growing challenges related to traffic congestion, primarily stemming from the exponential rise in population and insufficient

road infrastructure. This surge in urbanization has resulted in multifaceted issues, including heightened government expenditure, environmental degradation, and increased stress levels among residents. Recognizing the critical need for effective solutions, the paper concentrates on exploring the complexities of algorithm implementation and real-time traffic data analysis within the framework of a Smart Urban Traffic Management System (SUTMS). The overarching goal is to enhance the overall efficiency of the transportation system and curtail travel time. The paper critically examines contemporary studies focused on these methodologies, shedding light on their advantages and constraints when integrated into the dynamic landscape of SUTMS. Through this comprehensive exploration, the paper contributes to the ongoing discourse on developing sustainable and intelligent solutions to address the complex issue of urban traffic congestion. Published in 17th International Symposium on Distributed Computing and Applications for Business Engineering and Science (DCABES), this research represents a valuable addition to the body of knowledge aimed at fostering smarter and more efficient urban traffic management.

[20] This literature review extensively explores the multifaceted challenges confronting smart cities in the context of escalating vehicle types, inadequate control of traffic on the roads and malfunctions in the traffic light systems. Together, these issues exacerbate traffic jams, raise emissions, and amplify noise pollution, all of which pose serious risks to the sustainability of metropolitan areas. The inadequacies of traditional fixed time-based traffic control systems become apparent, particularly in their inability to effectively manage intricate traffic flows at junctions. This review underscores the imperative for a paradigm shift towards real-time traffic management systems capable of dynamically regulating traffic patterns. It advocates for the incorporation of sophisticated image processing techniques, exemplified by the Canny Edge detection method, to enhance responsiveness and overall system efficiency. Furthermore, the review critically addresses the pressing need to integrate features that specifically cater to emergency vehicle situations, ensuring heightened resilience and reliability of the traffic management system. By scrutinizing the limitations of existing approaches and proposing innovative solutions, this literature review significantly contributes to the discourse on developing intelligent and adaptive traffic management systems. Published in Published in 7th International Conference on Computer and Communication Engineering (ICCCE), this research represents a substantial advancement in the pursuit of enhancing urban traffic management in the context of smart cities.

[21] With the growing need for smarter urban infrastructure, IoT-based solutions have become critical for optimizing city management processes.

A 2018 study published in the Asian Journal of Science and Applied Technology explores the implementation of IoT technologies for garbage monitoring and street light control. The research provides a detailed examination of how sensors can be used to automate waste collection schedules and control streetlights based on real-time data, resulting in more efficient waste management systems and reduced energy consumption in public lighting. This dual approach not only cuts costs but also improves the environmental sustainability of urban services.

[22] The complexities of modern traffic systems demand advanced technological solutions, as demonstrated in the 2021 XXIV International Conference on Soft Computing and Measurements (SCM). The paper investigates various architectural frameworks for intelligent traffic management systems, proposing an architecture that leverages soft computing techniques to optimize traffic flow in real-time. By integrating advanced algorithms and adaptive models, the proposed system can dynamically respond to fluctuating traffic conditions, reducing congestion and improving overall urban mobility. This contribution is significant in the ongoing discourse around smart city development, offering a framework tailored to the challenges of 21st-century urban traffic.

[23] A recent paper presented at the 2023 Third International Conference on Artificial Intelligence and Smart Energy (ICAIS) introduced an energy-efficient smart urban traffic management system. The researchers proposed an optimized path discovery algorithm, which leverages AI to significantly reduce energy consumption and traffic congestion, marking an important advancement in sustainable traffic solutions.

[24] Traffic congestion remains one of the most pressing issues in urban areas, and the 2019 study presented at the 15th International Conference on Electronics, Computer, and Computation (ICECCO) offers a smart traffic management system as a solution. By utilizing advanced computation and real-time data processing, the system dynamically adjusts traffic light timings to optimize traffic flow, reduce wait times, and minimize traffic jams. This approach not only improves the overall efficiency of road networks but also enhances road safety by reducing the likelihood of accidents due to erratic traffic patterns. The research underscores the potential of computational technologies in tackling the evolving challenges of urban transportation.

[25] Big data analytics have become integral to modern traffic management, as detailed in the 2020 IEEE 9th Global Conference on Consumer Electronics (GCCE). The paper investigates how machine learning techniques can be applied to traffic data, leading to more intelligent and adaptive traffic systems capable of addressing the evolving challenges of urban transportation networks.

Serial number	Paper title & author	Technology used	Description & comparisons
1	Vehicle Detection and Counting of a Vehicle Using OpenCV by Karthik Srivathsa, Dr. Kamalraj	OpenCV	Counting of vehicles using OpenCV.
2	A Review of Different Components of the Intelligent Traffic Management System (ITMS) by Nikhil Nigam, Dhirendra Pratap Singh, Jaytrilok Choudhary	ITMS	Overview of ITMS components.
3	A Case Study Towards Efficient And Effective Traffic Management System by Engr. Chijioke C.C., Ugwuanyi S.E.	Embedded System	Case study on efficient traffic management.
4	Moving Vehicle Detection for Measuring Traffic Count Using OpenCV by Nilesh J Uke, Ravindra Thool	OpenCV	Traffic count measurement using OpenCV.
5	Automatic Vehicle Detection and Counting System by Kritika Ranjan, K.Suneetha, Ishika, Hari Priya, Riyal Chandrakar, Akash Biswas	Embedded System	Automatic vehicle detection and counting.
6	Smart Traffic Monitoring System based on Vehicle Counts by Geethika Boddu, Viswasri Ankamreddi, Narsipuram Shyamkumar, Yogesh Kumar	OpenCV	Smart traffic monitoring based on vehicle counts.
7	Vehicle Counting Module Design in Small Scale for Traffic Management in Smart City by Janak Trived, Dr. Mandalapu Sarada Devi, Dave Dhara	Embedded System	Creation of a traffic management module for vehicle counting.
8	Intelligent Traffic Signal Control System Using Embedded System by Dinesh Rotake, Prof. Swapnili Karmore	Embedded System	Traffic signal control using embedded system.

(*Continued*)

(*Continued*)

Serial number	Paper title & author	Technology used	Description & comparisons
9	Traffic Monitoring System: A Review by Amogh Sanjeev, Sinai Karapurkar, Sonia Kuwelkar	N.A.	Review of a traffic monitoring system.
10	Smart Traffic Monitoring and Controlling by Rohit Prasad, Himanshu Yadav, Devarsh Kumar, Sachin Pandey, Abhimanyu Yadav	Embedded System	Smart traffic monitoring and controlling system.
11	Intelligent Traffic Control System Using Arduino by L. David William Raj, N. Ranjani Priya Bai, C. Pooja, M. Padmini Bai, D. Nandika	Arduino	Traffic control system using Arduino.
12	Road Traffic Monitoring System by G. Shobana, M. Suguna	Machine Learning Techniques	Road traffic monitoring system.
13	Research on Urban Intelligent Traffic Monitoring System Based on Video Image Processing by Jiandong Cao	Video Image Processing	Urban intelligent traffic monitoring system.
14	Arduino Based Traffic Monitoring and Controlling System by L Srinivas, J Bhavani, K Janakiram, M Rupasri, A B Chandrika	Arduino	Traffic monitoring and controlling using Arduino.
15	An Adaptive Approach: Smart Traffic Congestion Control System by A. Atta, S. Abbas, M.A. Khan, G. Ahmed, U. Farooq	OpenCV	Smart traffic congestion control system.
16	Development of the Intelligent Traffic Management System Architecture by Svyatoslav A. Seliverstov, Arseny M. Sazanov, Yaroslav A. Seliverstov, Elena N. Benderskaya, Kirill V. Nikitin	Machine Learning Techniques	Establishment of the Intelligent Traffic Management System Architecture.

(*Continued*)

(*Continued*)

Serial number	Paper title & author	Technology used	Description & comparisons
17	Smart Urban Traffic Management System using Energy Efficient Optimized Path Discovery by Piyush Agarwal, Sachin Sharma	Machine Learning Techniques	Smart urban traffic management system with energy-efficient optimized path discovery.
18	Smart Traffic Management System by Abubakar M. Miyim, Mansur A. Muhammed	Embedded System	Smart Traffic Management System.
19	Big Traffic Data Analytics For Smart Urban Intelligent Traffic System Using Machine Learning Techniques by Su Hlaing, Mie Tin, Mie Khin, Phyo Wai, G R Sinha	Machine Learning Techniques	The application of machine learning techniques to big traffic data analytics for a smart urban intelligent traffic system.
20	Image Processing Based Smart Traffic Control System for Smart City by Vedansh Bhardwaj, Yaswanth Rasamsetti, Vipina Valsan	Image Processing	Image processing-based intelligent traffic management system for a smart city.
-	FlowGuard System - Literature Review	OpenCV, Embedded System	The FlowGuard System is introduced as a revolutionary solution to urban traffic challenges, leveraging cutting-edge technology for dynamic traffic signal optimization. Emphasizing multifaceted objectives, the system aims for instant traffic light adjustments, optimizing traffic flow, and contributing to fuel conservation. Beyond traffic management, it positions itself as a key player in fostering sustainable urban development, intertwining eco-conscious changes in the urban landscape. Technical intricacies reveal a paradigm leap in traffic signal optimization, with modern technology strategically propelling the system as a transformative force for wider urban development initiatives. Seamlessly blending innovation with a holistic urban perspective, the FlowGuard System emerges as a catalyst for positive change in the intricate tapestry of urban life.

6.3 Methodology

6.3.1 Theory

The "FlowGuard System" employs a combination of Arduino IDE, Jumper wires, Servo Motor, LEDs, and software tools like Arduino IDE and Pyfirmata with the OpenCV Library. This dynamic system functions through a sequence of steps: it begins by accurately counting vehicles, configuring initial signal timings for optimal traffic flow, and adjusting timings dynamically based on vehicle counts. The transition from a green to red signal initiates a physical barrier using a servo motor, temporarily halting traffic. During red signal phases, the vehicle counter resets, preparing for the next cycle.

Figure 6.1 illustrates the interfacing of an Arduino UNO with a Servo Motor and LEDs, using jumper wires to establish connections between the components. The integration of PyFirmata and Arduino boards enables real-time adjustments to traffic signals based on live vehicle count data. This not only optimizes traffic flow but also enhances safety and reduces congestion. As urban areas expand, effective traffic management becomes paramount for sustainable urban planning. Figure 6.2 demonstrates the smart traffic system's architecture, utilizing Arduino, OpenCV, and Python for real-time traffic signal adjustments to optimize vehicle flow and enhance safety.

This innovative system exemplifies the potential of technology to address real-world challenges, showcasing the role of such solutions in creating safer and more efficient transportation networks within growing urban environments. Figure 6.3 presents the Arduino Uno, a microcontroller board used in various electronics projects, essential for processing and controlling the connected components.

Figure 6.1 Arduino UNO interfaced with Servo Motor and LEDs using Jumper wires to connect Arduino UNO with servo motor and the LEDs.

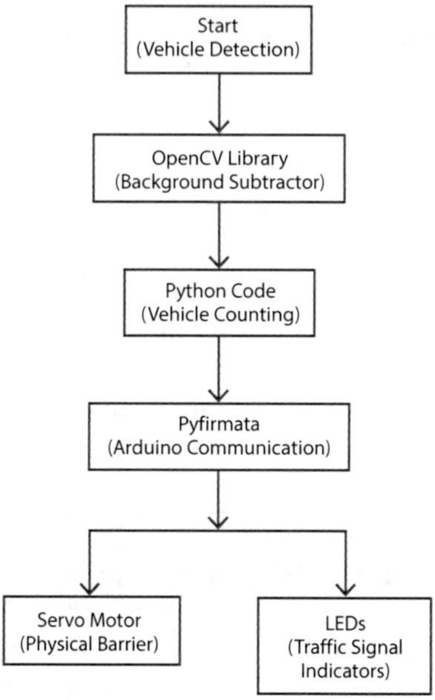

Figure 6.2 Smart traffic system uses Arduino, OpenCV, and Python for real-time signal adjustments, optimizing flow, enhancing safety, and reducing congestion in urban areas.

Figure 6.3 Arduino Uno.

6.3.2 Requirement

6.3.2.1 Hardware Requirements

This Provides an easy-to-use platform for connecting various sensors, LEDs, motors, and other components. Includes digital and analog input/output pins, a USB port for programming, and a power jack. Popular among beginners and experienced makers alike.

Figure 6.4 showcases a Servo Motor, which is commonly used in automation projects for precise control of angular position. Precise angle control makes them ideal for tasks like steering, opening doors, or mimicking animal movements.

The LEDs depicted here in Figure 6.5 are used as indicators in the traffic system, signaling different traffic states based on the control logic. Energy-efficient and long-lasting alternative to traditional incandescent bulbs. Used for indication, illumination, and decorative purposes. Available in various colors and intensities.

The Jumper Wire in this Figure 6.6 represents the physical connectors used to establish connections between electronic components on a breadboard. Insulated wires with male connectors at each end. Different lengths and colors available for flexibility and organization.

Figure 6.4 Servo motor.

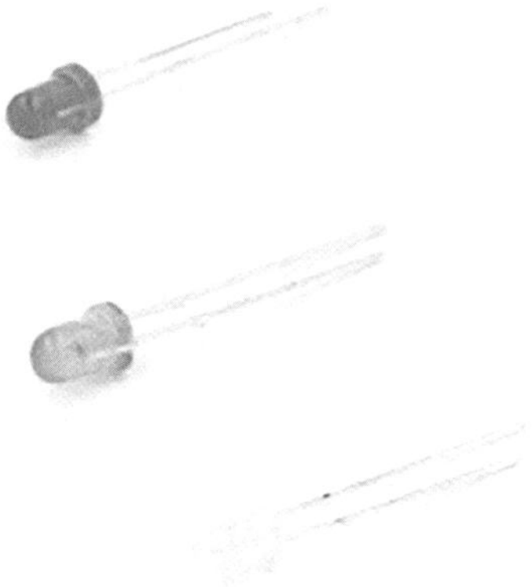

Figure 6.5 LED.

Figure 6.6 Jumper wire.

6.3.2.2 *Software Requirements*

Software used to write and upload code to Arduino boards. Allows for control of connected hardware components like LEDs, motors, and sensors. Figure 6.7 the Standard PyFirmata sketch in the Arduino IDE highlights the setup used for communication between the Arduino and external devices through the PyFirmata library. The Arduino IDE displayed in the Figure 6.8 is the primary development environment for writing and uploading code to Arduino boards.

Python library that allows Python programs to send and receive data to/from Arduino boards. Simplifies interfacing Arduino with Python for various applications like data acquisition, robotics control, and interactive projects.

Figure 6.7 Arduino IDE.

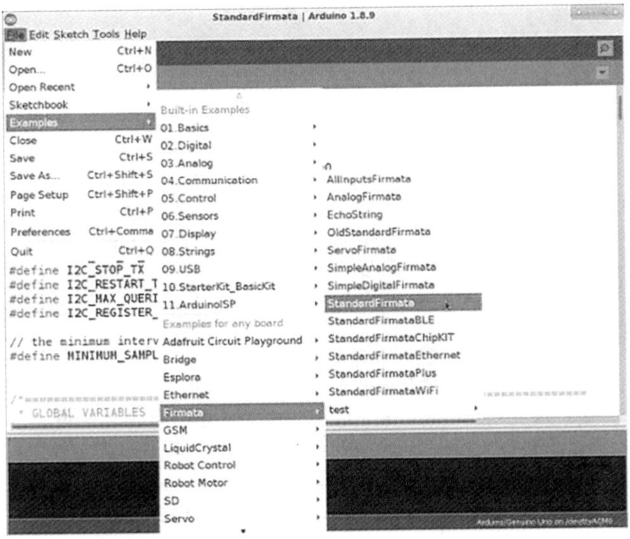

Figure 6.8 Pyfirmata.

6.3.3 Workflow

The methodology for implementing the "FlowGuard System" unfolds through a series of carefully orchestrated steps. The initial phase involves the development of a vehicle counting mechanism employing a Background Subtractor from the OpenCV Library. This innovative technique allows for the extraction of moving objects, forming the foundation for accurate vehicle detection and counting.

Subsequently, a seamless integration process takes place, harmonizing the Python code responsible for vehicle counting with the Arduino IDE using Pyfirmata. This integration establishes a vital communication link between the Python environment and the Arduino board, enabling the real-time transfer of crucial vehicle count data.

The major portion of our system depends on coding the Arduino UNO, intricately designed to interpret the incoming vehicle count data and respond dynamically. The code orchestrates adjustments to traffic signal timings based on the received information, ensuring the system operates optimally in response to changing traffic conditions. Additionally, the inclusion of a servo motor plays a pivotal role, acting as a physical barrier during the transition from a green to red signal and contributing significantly to effective traffic management.

6.3.4 Flowchart

The provided diagram illustrates a traffic light control system integrated with a real-time vehicle detection system utilizing the OpenCV computer vision (CV) module. The CV system processes the live feed for continuous vehicle detection at the intersection. If the count surpasses 8, the Timing block dynamically adjusts the traffic light phases. In this scenario, the red light extends to nine seconds, the green light to seven seconds, and the yellow light to a single second, prioritizing the direction with heightened traffic. Conversely, when the count is eight or below, the red light lasts five seconds, the green light three seconds, and the yellow light a single second. This adaptive approach aims to alleviate congestion by leveraging real-time CV-based vehicle detection to accurately count vehicles, optimizing traffic light timings, and enhancing overall intersection efficiency. Figure 6.9 below shows an adaptive traffic signal timing flowchart, which adjusts the signal duration based on real-time traffic analysis, enhancing the efficiency of the traffic management system.

6.4 Results and Discussions

The system's real-time responsiveness to changing conditions, facilitated by Python-Arduino integration, showcased its adaptability. The inclusion of a servo motor as a traffic barrier during signal transitions effectively contributed to the overall system efficiency. These results underscore the

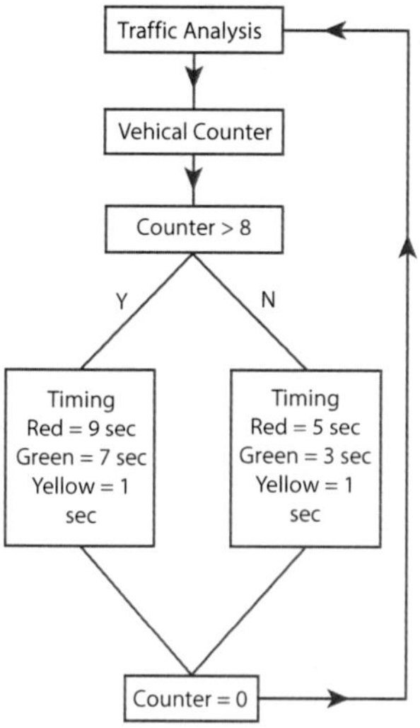

Figure 6.9 Adaptive traffic signal timing flowchart.

potential of technology-driven solutions in optimizing urban traffic management and promoting safer, more efficient transportation networks.

Figure 6.10 illustrates the prototype design of our FlowGuard Traffic Monitoring System, showcasing how vehicles are managed across multiple traffic signals. The counters for each signal indicate the number of vehicles detected, optimizing the flow of traffic in real-time.

Figure 6.11 above depicts the vehicle counter in action, displaying the number of vehicles passing through the monitored area. It also indicates the status of the traffic signals, providing an overview of traffic management efficiency.

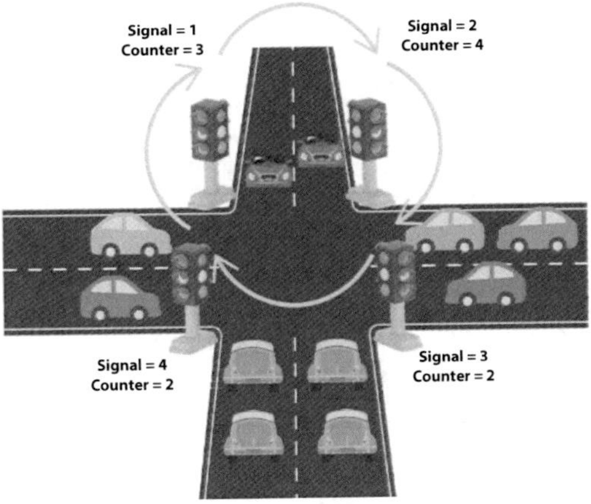

Figure 6.10 This image contains the prototype of our FlowGuard System.

Figure 6.11 This image shows the Vehicle counter and the indication of the traffic signals.

Figure 6.12 above demonstrates the operation of the servo motor when the traffic signal turns red. The image shows the system's response to stop vehicle movement, as indicated by the red light.

Figure 6.13 illustrates the functioning of the servo motor when the traffic signal turns yellow. The system prepares for a transition in vehicle movement, ensuring a smooth flow of traffic.

Figure 6.14 above showcases the servo motor's operation when the traffic signal turns green. The system allows vehicles to move forward, demonstrating the effectiveness of automated traffic control.

Figure 6.12 This image shows the working of servo motor when the signal turns Red.

Figure 6.13 This image shows the working of servo motor when the signal turns Yellow.

Figure 6.14 This image shows the working of servo motor when the signal turns Green.

6.5 Conclusion

The FlowGuard System not only signifies a technological breakthrough in traffic management but embodies a transformative force shaping the urban landscape. Its ability to reduce traffic and encourage environmentally friendly forms of mobility emphasizes how important it is to creating eco-aware urban areas. The system's ability to innovate and adapt puts it in a prime position to be a pillar in the continued development of intelligent urban mobility systems. The Sustain flow system illuminates a road towards efficient, harmonious, and sustainable communities by combining state-of-the-art technology with a dedication to environmental well-being. It is a beacon of innovation. The sustain flow system serves as a model for the future of intelligent traffic solutions, and this article advocates for further research and use of urban development.

6.6 Future Scope

FlowGuard System's future scope predicts a path characterized by ongoing innovation and expansion. The incorporation of state-of-the-art technology, such as I.O.T. and A.I. present intriguing potential to raise the system's overall effectiveness and capacity for forecasting. The system's national and international expansion has the potential to handle a variety of traffic issues and customize solutions for unique city dynamics.

Additionally, a crucial area for further research and development is how to modify the sustain flow system to accommodate new developments in transportation, such as the popularity of shared mobility services and driverless cars. The system's innate flexibility puts it in a leading position to influence how intelligent transportation is shaped in the future. As cities evolve, the FlowGuard System stands poised to play a pivotal role in ushering in a new era of sustainable, resilient, and technologically advanced urban mobility solutions.

Acknowledgment

Our sincere gratitude is extended to our project guide and professors for their invaluable guidance and wisdom throughout our project. Their continuous support has been a vital motivator, keeping us focused and determined. We would also like to express our heartfelt appreciation to both the internal and external examiners for their insightful feedback, which significantly contributed to refining and enhancing the quality of our project.

Our collaborative success is a result of the combined efforts of these mentors, whose expertise and encouragement have been instrumental in overcoming challenges and transforming our vision into reality. This project stands as a collective achievement, and we are genuinely grateful to everyone who played a role in its creation.

References

1. Srivathsa, K. and Kamalraj, D., Vehicle Detection and Counting of a Vehicle using OpenCV. *Int. Res. J. Mod. Eng. Technol. Sci.*, , 3, 5, 1264–1268, 2021.
2. Nigam, N., Singh, D.P., Choudhary, J., A Review of Different Components of the Intelligent Traffic Management System (ITMS). *Symmetry*, 15, 583, 2023.
3. Chijioke, C.C. and Ugwuanyi, S.E., A Case Study Towards Efficient And Effective Traffic Management System. *J. Archit. Civ. Eng.*, 2, 4, 01–06, 2014.
4. Uke, N.J. and Thool, R., Moving Vehicle Detection for Measuring Traffic Count Using OpenCV. *J. Autom. Control Eng.*, 1, 4, 349–352, December 2013.
5. Ranjan, K., Suneetha, K., Ishika, Priya, H., Chandrakar, R., Biswas, A., Automatic Vehicle Detection and Counting System. *J. Emerg. Technol. Innov. Res. (JETIR)*, ISSN-2349-5162, 8, 5, 1201–1208, May 2021.
6. Boddu, G., Ankamreddi, V., Shyamkumar, N., Kumar, Y., Smart Traffic Monitoring System based on vehicle counts. *Int. Res. J. Eng. Technol. (IRJET)*, 6, 7, 1087–1090, July 2019, e-ISSN: 2395-0056.
7. Trived, J., Devi, M.S., Dhara, D., Vehicle Counting Module Design in Small Scale for Traffic Management in Smart City. *3rd International Conference for Convergence in Technology (I2CT)*, 2018.
8. Rotake, D. and Karmore, S., Intelligent Traffic Signal Control System Using Embedded System. *Innov. Syst. Des. Eng.*, 3, 5, 11–20, 2012.

9. Sanjeev, A., Karapurkar, S., Kuwelkar, S., Traffic Monitoring System: A Review. *Int. J. Sci. Res. (IJSR)*, ISSN: 2319-7064, 10, 8, 787-790, August 2021.
10. Prasad, R., Yadav, H., Kumar, D., Pandey, S., Yadav, A., Smart Traffic Monitoring and Controlling. *J. Emerg. Technol. Innov. Res. (JETIR)*, ISSN-2349-5162, 8, 6, 744–748, 2021.
11. David William Raj, L., Ranjani Priya Bai, N., Pooja, C., Padmini Bai, M., Nandika, D., Intelligent Traffic Control System Using Arduino. *Int. Res. J. Eng. Technol. (IRJET)*, e-ISSN: 2395-0056, 8, 5, 2021.
12. Shobana, G. and Suguna, M., Road Traffic Monitoring System. *Int. J. Eng. Adv. Technol. (IJEAT)*, ISSN: 2249-8958, 8, 6S3, 1249–1251, 2019.
13. Cao, J., Research on Urban Intelligent Traffic Monitoring System Based on Video Image Processing. *Int. J. Signal Process. Image Process. Pattern Recognit.*, 9, 6, 393–406, 2016.
14. Srinivas, L., Bhavani, J., Janakiram, K., Rupasri, M., Chandrika, A.B., Arduino Based Traffic Monitoring and Controlling System. *Int. J. Mod. Trends Sci. Technol.*, 6, 6, 50–53, 2020, ISSN: 2455-3778.
15. Atta, A., Abbas, S., Khan, M.A., Ahmed, G., Farooq, U., An adaptive approach: smart traffic congestion control system. *J. King Saud Univ. Comput. Inf. Sci.*, 30, 3, 269–276, 2018.
16. Shahzad, G., Won, H., Lee, C., Ahmad, A.W., Yang, H., Energy-Efficient Intelligent Street Lighting System Using Traffic-Adaptive Control. *IEEE Sens. J.*, 16, 13, 5397–5405, July 2016.
17. Rudrawar, O., Daga, S., Chadha, J.R., Kulkami, P.S., Smart street lighting system with light intensity control using power electronics. *Technologies for Smart-City Energy Security and Power (ICSESP)*, March 2018.
18. He, J., Zhu, Z., Wang, F., Li, J., Illumination Control of Intelligent Street Lamps Based on Fuzzy Decision. *International Conference on Intelligent Transportation, Big Data & Smart City (ICITBS)*, 12-13 Jan. 2019.
19. Zeng, J., Ni, W., Zhang, R., Shi, L., Guo, C., Chen, Y., Intelligent Street Lamp Control System with Dynamic Light Control Function. *17th International Symposium on Distributed Computing and Applications for Business Engineering and Science (DCABES)*, Oct. 2018.
20. Abdullah, A., Yusoff, S.H., Zaini, S.A., Midi, N.S., Mohamad, S.Y., Smart Street Light Using Intensity Controller. *2018 7th International Conference on Computer and Communication Engineering (ICCCE)*, Sept. 2018.
21. Bagya Lakshmi, K., Suresh Kumar, M., Sindhuja, S., Padmavathy, R., Jayabharathi, P., IoT Based Garbage Monitoring and Street Light Control. *Asian J. Sci. Appl. Technol.*, 7, 2, 33–37, 2018.
22. Seliverstov, S.A., Sazanov, A.M., Seliverstov, Y.A., Benderskaya, E.N., Nikitin, K.V., Development of the Intelligent Traffic Management System Architecture, in: *Proceedings of the XXIV International Conference on Soft Computing and Measurements (SCM)*, pp. 1–4, IEEE, 2021.
23. Agarwal, P. and Sharma, S., Smart Urban Traffic Management System using Energy Efficient Optimized Path Discovery, in: *Proceedings of the Third*

International Conference on Artificial Intelligence and Smart Energy (ICAIS), pp. 1–5, IEEE, 2023.
24. Miyim, A.M. and Muhammed, M.A., Smart Traffic Management System, in: *Proceedings of the 15th International Conference on Electronics. Computer, and Computation (ICECCO)*, pp. 1–5, IEEE, 2019.
25. Hlaing, S.S., Tin, M.M., Khin, M.M., Wai, P.P., Sinha, G.R., Big Traffic Data Analytics For Smart Urban Intelligent Traffic System Using Machine Learning Techniques, in: *IEEE 9th Global Conference on Consumer Electronics (GCCE)*, pp. 1–4, IEEE, 2020.

References for Pictures of Components Used

1. Arduino Uno – https://docs.arduino.cc/hardware/uno-rev3
2. Servo Motor - https://stock.adobe.com/in/search?k=servo%20motor
3. LED - https://www.amazon.com/Baomain-Green-Yellow-Emitting-iodes/dp/B01MDOBZCZ
4. Jumper wires – https://www.amazon.com/Foxnovo-Breadboard-Jumper-Wires-Female/dp/B00PBZMN7C
5. Arduino IDE - https://docs.arduino.cc/learn/starting-guide/the-arduino-software-ide
6. Pyfirmata - https://realpython.com/arduino-python/

7

A Survey on Heart Disease Prediction Using Ensemble Techniques in ML

Sudhakar Vecha[1]* and M.V.P. Chandra Sekhara Rao[2]

[1]*Dr. YSR A.N.U. College of Engineering & Technology, Acharya Nagarjuna University, Guntur, A.P., India*
[2]*Department of CSBS, R.V.R & J.C College of Engineering, Affiliated ANU, Guntur, A.P., India*

Abstract
Heart disease ranks among the leading causes of death worldwide. Heart diseases, also known as cardiovascular diseases, can be categorized into four groups: heart failure, cardiomyopathy, coronary heart disease and congenital heart disease. Heart disease must be diagnosed correctly and quick in order to stop further damage and protect life. Therefore, a predictive system that can detect cardiovascular disease before it gets to a serious stage required. For preventative healthcare to be effective, heart disease risk must be promptly and accurately predicted. Because ensemble learning techniques can increase prediction resilience and accuracy, their significance in the field of heart disease prediction has expanded. This review present an ample overview of ensemble learning methods used in heart disease prediction and summarizes their strengths, weaknesses, and recent advances.

Keywords: Heart disease prediction, ensemble learning

7.1 Introduction

Heart disease and other cardiovascular diseases continue to be serious global public health issues [1]. Timely intervention and prevention of heart disease depend strongly on early detection and prediction of the condition [2]. Ensemble learning, a machine learning technique [4] that merge multiple models to increase prediction performance, has turn into more

**Corresponding author*: vsksudhakar@gmail.com

Budati Anil Kumar, Singamaneni Kranthi Kumar and Li Xingwang (eds.) Quantum Computing Models for Cybersecurity and Wireless Communications, (125–138) © 2025 Scrivener Publishing LLC

accepted in the field of heart disease prediction. This paper explores different ensemble learning models used in this context.

Ensemble Learning Techniques in Machine Learning (ML)

The goal of machine learning (ML), a branch of artificial intelligence, is to develop models and methods that let computers learn from data and predictor make decisions without the need for explicit programming. It entails creating and training computer programs to automatically recognize, analyze, and interpret data patterns, then use those patterns to generate predictions or conclusions.

ML is based on the fundamental principle of assisting computers learn from history and acquire new information. ML algorithms are not explicitly coded with predetermined rules or instructions; rather they are made to learn from data and modify their behavior as necessary.

Ensemble Learning

Ensemble learning techniques are algorithms [17] that combine the predictions of multiple base models to achieve better performance than individual models. The main objective of ensemble learning is to reduce bias, variance, and overfitting [18]. Common ensemble methods used in heart disease prediction include:

a) Bagging (bootstrap aggregation): Algorithms such as Random Forest build different subsets of the training data by bootstrapping and then train distinct decision trees on these separations. The final prediction is a combination of these tree predictions. The step-by-step process of machine learning is illustrated in Figure 7.1.

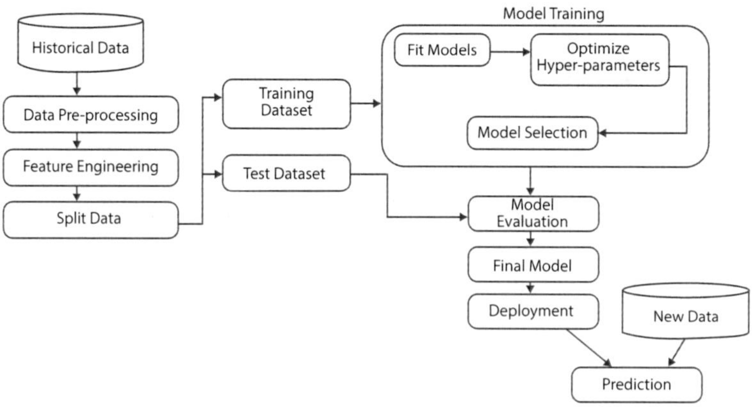

Figure 7.1 Illustration of the machine learning process.

b) Boosting: Algorithms such as AdaBoost, Gradient Boosting, and XGBoost [20] iteratively train weak learners and assign higher weights to them is classified instances. This process continues until a strong learner is achieved.
c) Stacking: By learning a meta-learner on the predictions of many base models, stacking aggregates the predictions from those base models.
d) Voting: Voting methods combine the predictions of multiple models by performing a majority voting (for classification) or averaging (for regression) [21].

7.2 Literature Survey

The number of researchers who have worked on various ML algorithms for Heart disease identification is discussed in this section. Researchers have recognized that machine-learning

Algorithms work effectively in identifying heart disease. The Studies that have been discovered are as follows:

G. Sugendran *et al.* [5] proposed an EGA-based FWSVM algorithm. Classifiers for machine learning that estimate the risk of heart disease acquired knowledge from UCI dataset.

Mert Ozcan *et al.* [6], using Classification and Regression Tree (CART) model, to forecast heart disease and derive recommendations for decision-making for explaining the associations between input and output factors.

This paper [7], an ensemble structure based on stacking model fusion such as LR, RF, SVM, K-NN, ET, GBDT, XGBoost, LightGBM, Cat Boost, and MLP.

Authors in [9] provided an effective strategy based on six different machine learning classifiers that recognize status of patients, the SMOTE to deal with the issue of un even distribution, and HPO to identify the optimal parameters for ML classifiers conjunction with SMOTE. SMOTE and ExtraTrees (ET), which were optimized with hyper band optimized, produced improved results.

The study in [10] proposed the AdaBoost Ensemble model for heart disease prediction, which is based on recognized feature designs. Heterogeneous classifiers were the similar and ensemble classifiers created by integrating several techniques. When it comes to classifiers with good accuracy, AdaBoost-RF is the best.

This paper [11] developed two algorithms, RVC and SCC. The classifier that functions as the basis estimator for a bagging technique is derived using the random analysis of distance sequence. Spectf and Statlog datasets from UCI data were used to prediction of heart disease.

Works in [12] used ML techniques- LR, AdaBoost, RF, Gradient Boosting Classifier (GBM), Gaussian-NB and SVM. SMOTE is performed to issue of class imbalance. The dataset Heart-Failure-clinical-records-dataset is used in prediction of heart disease.

Pronab Ghosh *et al.* [13] developed new hybrid classifiers like DBTM, RFBM, KNNBM, ABBM and GBBM by combining the conventional classifiers with bagging and boosting methods.

In paper [14] there were six distinct heart related datasets used. Using Random Forest and MOPSO, a novel method for heart disease prediction is proposed. Random selection on training sets and feature selection in random forests.

A Stacking Ensemble Model to predict Cardiovascular Diseases in [15] through the use of machine learning models, such as gradient boosting DT, RF, extreme gradient boosting, linear regression and SVM. Different errors of evaluation measures were utilized.

C. Beulah Christalin Latha *et al.* [16] to forecast heart disease using six machine learning algorithms – Bayes net, NB, RF, C4.5, MLP, PART and attempted to improve the accuracy using ensemble methods like Boosting, Bagging, Stacking and Majority vote.

7.3 Datasets

The Selection of the dataset is an important factor in heart disease prediction. Data sets commonly used in heart disease prediction research include the Cleveland [5, 9, 10, 13, 16] Heart Disease dataset, Statlog Heart dataset [9, 11, 13], SPECT [14], SPECTF (Singe Photon Emission Computed Tomography of Heart with filters) [14] and Framingham heart disease data set. These dataset contains different clinical and demographic characteristics that make them suitable for different prediction models.

Cleveland Heart Disease Dataset

- Number of Instances: The original dataset contains 303 instances (patient records). Number of Features: There are 76 attributes in the dataset, but only 14 of the mare used in most machine learning studies. These 14 attributes are typically used as the input features for classification tasks. Target variable: Predicting the existence or absence of cardiac disease is the primary objective of utilizing this dataset.

Statlog Heart Dataset

- This dataset is used for classification tasks related to prediction of heart disease. It contains set of features that describe various medical and demographic characteristics of patients. There are 14 attributes in the dataset and number of samples in the dataset can vary depending on the source and version of the dataset.

Framingham Heart Disease Dataset

- The dataset contains above 4,240 records. There are 16 columns and 15 features. Target variable: Determining the patient's 10-year risk of developing coronary heart disease is the aim of the dataset..

SPECT (Singe Photon Emission Computed Tomography of Heart)

- It contains data from SPECT imaging of the heart, and the primary objective is to classify the images as indicative of a heart condition or as normal. The dataset includes attributes that represent information extracted from SPECT images.

7.4 Ensemble Learning in Heart Disease

Ensemble learning methods have been applied to heart disease prediction with remarkable success. They offer several advantages:

a) Improved prediction accuracy: ensemble methods often outperform individual models and provide more accurate predictions.
b) Robustness: ensembles are less prone to overfitting and provide stable predictions across different datasets.
c) Feature importance: Ensemble methods can evaluate the importance of input features, to help identify critical risk factors.
d) Model Interpretability: Some ensemble methods such as Random forest, provide ratings of feature importance and can be better interpreted than complex Deep Learning models

Table 7.1 describes the survey papers for heart disease classification and prediction with accuracies.

Table 7.1 Comprehensive view of machine learning with accuracy for heart disease prediction.

Year	Author	Data set resource	ML techniques with accuracy (in percentage)	
2022	V.K. Gnanavel *et al.* [3]	A Hospital dataset		LR-98.10 DT-95.86 **RF-98.11** **SVM-98.11** NB-96.34 K-N-98.09
2023	G Sugendran *et al.* [5]	UCI Dataset		K-NN-83.54 RF-87.25 **EGA-FWSVM-91.68**
2022	Muhammad Haseeb Aslam *et al.* [19]	A UCI dataset containing statlog and Cleveland heart disease is used		SVM-64.9 **RF-97.2** DT-74.91 LR-66.99 KNN-89.99 GB-92.49 Bagging-92.7 Ensemble-54.7 NN-66.85

(Continued)

Table 7.1 Comprehensive view of machine learning with accuracy for heart disease prediction. (*Continued*)

Year	Author	Data set resource	ML techniques with accuracy (in percentage)	
2022	Liu J *et al.* [7]	AUCI Heart Dataset		KNN-71.74 SVM-72.46 LR-88.41 RF-87.68 ET-88.04 GBDT-87.68 XGBoost-82.97 LightGBM-87.32 CatBoost-89.49 MLP-87.32 **Stacking-89.86**
2022	Jafar Abdollahi *et al.* [8]	UCI repository	RF, KNN, MLP, DTREE, NB, LR, SVM, Suggest Method (ST-GA)	RF-94 KNN-89, MLP-94 DTREE-94 NB-86 LR-87 SVM-89.05 **ST-GA-97.57**

(*Continued*)

Table 7.1 Comprehensive view of machine learning with accuracy for heart disease prediction. (*Continued*)

Year	Author	Data set resource	ML techniques with accuracy (in percentage)	
2022	Abdallahabdellatif *et al.* [9]	Cleveland and Statlog heart data sets in UCI	LR, SGD, ET, XGBoost, kNN, SVM	LR-70.39 SGD-71.73 **ET-95.73** XgBoost-94.44 kNN-89.86 SVM-91.11
2022	T.R. Mahesh *et al.* [10]	UCI provided heart disease dataset	AdaBoost (AB)- NB, AB-AltDTree, AB-RF, AB-RedEPTree, AB-CART	AB-NB-80.6 AB-AltDTree-93.56 **AB-RF-95.47** AB-RedEPTree - 82.23 AB-CART-81.67
2021	Talha Karadeniz *et al.* [11]	Statlog heart data set in UCI	NaiveBayes (NB), SVM, ANN, CAFL, RVC, SCC	NB-85.2 SVM–81.5 ANN–81.5 CAFL–88.3 **RVC,SCC-88.8**

(*Continued*)

Table 7.1 Comprehensive view of machine learning with accuracy for heart disease prediction. (*Continued*)

Year	Author	Data set resource	ML techniques with accuracy (in percentage)	
2021	Abid Ishaq *et al.* [12]	Heart-failure-clinical-records-dataset is derived from the UCI repository	DT, AdaBoost, LR, SGD, RF, GBM, ExtraTree Classifier(ETC), GNB, SVM	DT-82.78 AdaBoost-88.52 LR-83.60 SGD-53.09 RF-91.80 GBM-84.42 **ETC-92.62** GNB-74.59 SVM-76.22
2021	Pronab Ghosh *et al.* [13]	Cleveland, Long Beach VA, Switzerland, Hungarian and Statlog	DT, RF, KNN, AB, GB, DTBM, RFBM, KNNBM, ABBM, GBBM	DT-86.97 RF-88.65 KNN-83.61 AB-89.07 GB-86.97 DTBM-87.97 **RFBM-92.65** KNNBM-89.63 ABBM-89.07 GBBM-90.97

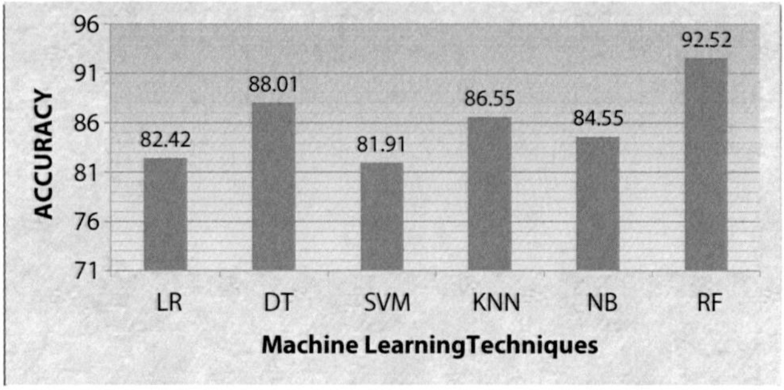

Graph 7.1 Heart disease prediction Models accuracy comparison.

The accuracy comparison of the different ML models for heart disease prediction represented in Graph 7.1. The accuracy graph that follows is a fairly basic model that displays the statistics and accuracy scores of different machine learning models from Table 7.1 describes various survey papers:

7.5 Challenges and Limitations

Ensemble learning techniques have proven effective, but they are not without challenges:

- Computational Complexity: Some ensemble methods, especially those involving deep learning, can be computationally intensive.
- Interpretability of models: the increased complexity of ensemble models can make it difficult to interpret and understand model decisions.
- Data quality: The accuracy and representiveness of the training data are crucial to the effectiveness of ensemble models.

7.6 Future Directions

The field of Heart disease prediction through ensemble learning continues to evolve. Possible future directions include:

- Explainable ensemble models: developing ensemble models with improved interpret ability to help medical professionals understand predictions.

- Personalized medicine: adapting ensemble models to individual patient profiles form or accurate and targeted predictions and interventions.
- Data augmentation: exploring techniques to augment limited cardiac patient data to improve model generalization.

7.7 Conclusion

Ensemble learning techniques have become a powerful tool in heart disease prediction, providing increased accuracy and robustness. The application of ensemble techniques in the prediction of heart disease has proven to be a powerful and promising approach in the field of health care analytics. This review highlights the various strengths and challenges of ensemble methods that have been instrumental in improving the accuracy and robustness of predictive models. As technology advances and health data become more available, ensemble methods will likely continue to evolve. These developments hold promise for improving early detection and intervention for heart disease, ultimately improving patient outcomes and reducing the global burden of cardiovascular disease.

References

1. Deba, D.A. and Sitote, T.M., Chronic kidney disease prediction using machine learning techniques. *J. Big Data*, Springer, 2022, https://doi.org/10.1186/s40537-022-00657-5.
2. Arumugam, K., Naved, M., Shinde, P.P., Leiva-Chauca, O., Huaman-Osorio, A., Gonzales-Yanac, T., Multiple disease prediction using Machine learning algorithms, 2021, https://doi.org/10.1016/j.matpr.2021.07.361.214-7853/ Elsevier Ltd.
3. Gnanavel, V.K., Sukanya, R., Mercy, H., Jayalakshmi, P., Veeramalai, S., GUI Base Prediction of Heart Stroke Stages by Finding the Accuracy using Machine Learning Algorithm. *2022 International Conference on Data Science, Agents & Artificial Intelligence (ICDSAAI)*, IEEE, 2022, 979-8-3503-3384-8/22|DOI: 10.1109/ICDSAAI55433.2022.10028815.
4. Asif, D., Bibi, M., Arif, M.S., Mukheimer, A., Enhancing Heart Disease Prediction through Ensemble Learning Techniques with Hyperparameter Optimization. *Algorithms*, 16, 308, 2023, https://doi.org/10.3390/a16060308.
5. Sugendran, G. and Sujatha, S., Earlier Identification of heart disease using enhanced genetic algorithm and fuzzy weight based support vector machine algorithm. Elsevier: *Meas. Sens.*, https://doi.org/10.1016/j.measen.2023.100814.

6. Ozcan, M. and Perker, S., A classification and regression tree algorithm for heart disease modelling and prediction. *Healthcare Anal.*, 2, 100130, 2023, Elsevier.
7. Liu, J., Dong, X., Zhao, H., Tian, Y., Predictive classifier for Cardiovascular Disease Based on Stacking Model Fusion. MDPI. *Processes*, 10, 749, 2022, https://doi.org/10.3390/pr10040749.
8. Abdollahi, J. and Nouri-Moghaddam, B., A hybrid method for heart disease diagnosis utilizing feature selection based ensemble classifier model generation. *Iran J. Comput. Sci.*, 5, 229–246, 2022, https://doi.org/10.1007/s42044-022-00104-x.Springer.
9. Abdellatif, A., Abdellatif, H., Kanesan, J., Chow, C., Chuah, J.H., Gheni, H.M., An Effective Heart Disease Detection and Severity Level Classification Model using Machine Learning and Hyperparameter Optimization Methods. *IEEE Access*, 2022, DOI: 10.1109/ACCESS.2022.3191669.
10. Mahesh, T.R., Dhilipkumar, V., Vinoth Kumar, V., Asghar, J., Geman, O., Arulkumaran, G., Arun, N., Ada Boost Ensemble method using K-Fold cross validation for Survivability with the early detection of Heart Disease. *Comput. Intell. Neurosci.*, 2022, 11, articleID:9005278, https://doi.org/10.1155/2022/9005278, Hindawi.
11. Karadeniz, T., Tokdemir, G., Maras, H.H., Ensemble methods for Heart Disease Prediction. *New Gener. Comput.*, Springer Japan KK, 2021, https://doi.org/10.1007/s00354-021-00124-4.
12. Ishaq, A., Sadiq, S., Umer, M., Ullah, S., Mirjalili, S., Rupapara, V., Nappi, M., Improving the Prediction of heart failure Patien's survival using SMOTE and Effective data mining techniques. *IEEE Access*, 2021, Digital Object Identifier 10.1109/ACCESS 2021.3064084.
13. Ghosh, P., Azam, S., Jonkman, M., Karim, A., Javed Mehedi Shamrat, F.M., Ignatious, I., Sulthana, S., Beeravolu, A.R., DeBoer, F., Effective Prediction of Cardiovascular Disease Using Machine Learning Algorithms with Relief and LASSO Feature Selecction Techniques. *IEEE Access*, 2021, Digital Object Identifier 10.1109/ACCESS.2021.3053759.
14. Asadi, S., Roshan, S.E., Kattan, M.W., Random Forests warm optimization-based for heart disease diagnosis. *J. Biomed. Inf.*, 115, 103690, 2021, Elsevier.
15. Hu, Z., Qiu, H., Su, Z., Shen, M., Chen, Z., A Stacking ensemble model to predict daily number of hospital admissions for cardiovascular diseases. *IEEE Access*, 2020, Digital Object Identifier 10.1109/ACCESS.2020.3012143.
16. Beulah ChristalinLatha, C. and CarolinJeeva, S., Improving the accuracy of prediction of heart disease risk based on ensemble classification techniques. *Inf. Med. Unlocked*, 16, 100203, 2019, Elsevier.
17. Anuradha, P. and David, V.K., Feature Selection and Prediction of Heart diseases using Gradient Boosting Algorithms. *International Conference on Artificial Intelligence and Smart Systems (ICAIS-2021)*, IEEE Xplore Part Number: CFP21OAB-ART; ISBN: 978-1-7281-9537-7 DOI:10.1109/ICAIS50930.2021.9395819.

18. Deberneh, H.M. and Kim, I., Prediction of Type 2 Diabetes Based on Machine Learning Algorithm. *Int. J. Environ. Res. Public Health*, 18, 3317, 2021, https://doi.org/10.3390/ijerph18063317.
19. Aslam, M.H. and Hussain, S.F., Prediction of Heart Failure by using Machine Learning and Feature Selection. *International Conference on Emerging Technologies (ICET)*, IEEE, 2022, |978-1-6654-5992-1/22/$31.00|DOI:10.1109/ICET56601.2022.10004668.
20. UlHaq, A., Li, J.P., Memon, M.H., Nazir, S., Sun, R., A Hybrid Intelligent System Framework for the prediction of Heart Disease using Machine Learning Algorithms. *Mobile Inf. Syst.*, 2018, Article ID: 3860146, 21, https://doi.org/10.1155/2018/3860146.
21. Ambesange, S., Vijayalaxmi, A., Sridevi, S., Venkateswaran, Yashoda, B.S., Multiple Heart Diseases Prediction using Logistic Regression with Ensemble and Hyper Parameter tuning Techniques, IEEE, 2020, IEEE-978-1-7281-6823-4/20.

8

A Video Surveillance: Crowd Anomaly Detection and Management Alert System

Anitha Ponraj[1]*, Umasree Mariappan[2], M. J. Sai Kiran[3], S. Tejeswar Reddy[3], N. Vinay[3] and P. Bharath[3]

[1]Department of Computer Science and Engineering, Kalasalingam Academy of Research and Education, Kalasalingam University, Krishnan Koil, Tamil Nadu, India
[2]Department of Information Technology, P.S.R. Engineering College, Sivakasi, Tamil Nadu, India
[3]Department of Computer Science and Engineering, Kalasalingam Academy of Research and Education, Krishnan Koil, Tamil Nadu, India

Abstract

As our urban environments change quickly, public safety and security are becoming vital concerns. In order to solve these issues, monitoring equipment has become increasingly prevalent, especially in busy public areas. The goal of this suggested system is to create a face-detecting crowd surveillance system by utilizing deep learning and OpenCV techniques. The suggested system uses deep learning and computer vision techniques to track and examine crowd behavior in real-time. With extensive applications in a variety of fields, including crowd management, event planning, surveillance, and urban planning, video crowd counting has become a critical problem in computer vision. An overview of the methods, difficulties, and uses of video crowd counting is provided in this study. Initially, we explore the various methodologies utilized in video crowd counting, encompassing conventional approaches, deep learning-based strategies, deep sorting, and their combination. While deep learning-based techniques use convolutional neural networks (CNNs) to automatically extract features from raw data, traditional methods frequently rely on handcrafted features and classical machine learning algorithms.

***Keywords*:** Crowd surveillance, crowd monitoring, crowd counting, deep convolutional neural networks (DCNN), deep sorting, crowd behavior

**Corresponding author*: anisainotech@gmail.com

Budati Anil Kumar, Singamaneni Kranthi Kumar and Li Xingwang (eds.) Quantum Computing Models for Cybersecurity and Wireless Communications, (139–152)

8.1 Introduction

Advanced technology solutions called crowd surveillance systems are made to track and examine people's movements, actions, and personal traits in a crowd or public area. These systems use cameras, a variety of sensors, and machine learning algorithms to track, identify, and evaluate people's movements in real time. Accurately counting the number of individuals in a certain area or within a particular crowd is one of the main purposes of a crowd monitoring system. The use of cameras with computer vision technologies is how this is accomplished. By using computer vision algorithms to analyses the photos or videos that these cameras take of the audience, the number of people in attendance may be accurately determined.

There are steps in the counting process where people are found and identified by the system inside the recorded videos and to prevent double counting, the system follows a person's movements throughout time once it has been recognized and counting as new people arrive or depart the area, the system updates the count in real-time, counting the number of distinct persons within the crowd progressively.

Crowd surveillance systems are capable of more than just counting individuals; they can also be used to analyses behavior and activities in order to derive useful insights. Figuring out how packed or busy a place is by measuring the density of people there. observing how people move in the crowd and analyzing that movement to look for unusual or anomalous behaviors, like abrupt direction changes or crowded conditions. observing people's gait patterns to spot potentially dangerous or suspicious activity. keeping an eye out for odd or potentially harmful behaviors, including altercations or violent behavior, in the interactions between people. Crowd surveillance systems help authorities improve public safety, optimize crowd management measures, and efficiently respond to emerging events by integrating sophisticated computer vision techniques with machine learning algorithms to provide real-time insights into crowd dynamics. But in order to make sure that these technologies are used responsibly and in compliance with ethical and legal standards, it's critical to weigh the advantages of crowd monitoring against concerns for civil liberties, privacy, and ethic.

8.2 Related Work

Stott *et al.* [1] proposed and identifying and detecting the crowd is the initial step towards tracking, monitoring, and analyzing that crowd. The current status of crowd behavior can be seen from a variety of angles.

A paradigm for identifying aberrant behavior in crowd scenes was presented, and studies using crowd analysis were reviewed.

Nguyen *et al.* [2] proposed in this project adds surveys and reviews on crowd management to the literature evaluation of this paper since it deals with the managerial side of crowd study. Concerning technical practices and the role of technology in crowd management, this fact includes surveys and reviews. It also covers methodologies for crowd monitoring and density estimation, technological advancements in crowd planning and monitoring techniques, and crowd management and monitoring techniques to address challenges with suggested solutions.

Chen *et al.* [3] proposed the process of analyzing crowds is crucial to comprehending their behavior and offering options for crowd control. Numerous features of crowds have been examined, including crowd behavior, tracking, density estimation, and detection.

Song *et al.* [4] proposed the relationship between oscillation and average trajectory speed was examined in this paper. He came to the conclusion that a higher oscillation would show a shorter trajectory and a lower average speed. This implies that individuals with the freedom to travel will do so at the speed of their choice, creating lengthy, smooth trajectories. Consequently, pedestrian mobility will be restricted in a crowded area, perhaps leading to disputes.

Direkoglu *et al.* [5] proposed a system with two primary components was suggested after these advancements. Two components of the information management system are the fuzzy logic module and the thermal video analyzer. Operability research and expert system are included in the decision support system module, however. It counts people in gatherings, including pilgrims, tracks people in real time, shows closed roads and preferred routes.

Alam *et al.* [6] proposed this project's primary goal is to provide an estimate that illustrates how early social distancing can dramatically lower the number of new infections and financial losses. The primary goal of research during the coronavirus outbreak was to identify and create effective countermeasures to reduce the virus's spread throughout society.

Aros *et al.* [7] proposed the Classification and object detection tasks are becoming more manageable and straightforward due to developments in deep learning and computer vision. These studies made contributions to various fields of vision, including object tracking, neural style transfer, and segmentation, in addition to detection.

Simhastha *et al.* [8] proposed an enormous group of people assembled in one location is referred to as a crowd. These individuals may be acquainted on a casual basis or share similar feelings or interests. Additional research demonstrates that a crowd need not have same objectives or interests to exist, regardless of the reason for the gathering.

Murphey *et al.* [9] In this work, the average trajectory speed and oscillation were investigated. He came to the conclusion that a longer trajectory and lower average speed would be displayed by a higher oscillation. This implies that individuals with unrestricted mobility would go at the speed that suits them best, creating lengthy, seamless trajectories. As a result, restricted pedestrian mobility in a crowded area may lead to confrontations.

Pooja *et al.* [10] The FSCB algorithm, which detects online crowd behavior in real-time, was presented in this study. It consists of segmenting images, detecting crowd behavior, temporal filtering, and feature detection. Similarly, a crowd detection technique for still photos was introduced. Utilizing a statistical Poisson model of quantized Scale-Invariant Feature Transform (SIFT) word occurrences throughout an image, this appearance-based approach works.

Sohail *et al.* [11] proposed a method for handling interactions between pedestrians and environments that are visualized was developed in this study. With the use of GPU shaders, the system computes a mesh for each specified zone in the urban setting. Parts of the scene are added to the simulation, and the computed mesh is converted into an instance of it.

Kahale *et al.* [12] proposed the study suggested using direct tracking techniques like face recognition or mobile sensors in conjunction with an all-encompassing monitoring strategy like a CCTV camera. Regardless of whether they are operational or not, the number of mobile phones in the vicinity can be used by a cell sensor to determine the total population. According to estimates, 85% of people on the planet use mobile phones. They are a common device.

Prem *et al.* [13] proposed to categories picture pixels as either background or pedestrians, an image with only background is used. The determination of crowd density thus involves the manual establishment of a functional link between the number of pedestrian categorized pixels and the total number of individuals.

Shehzed *et al.* [14] in this they in order to count crowds and detect normal or abnormal activities in indoor and outdoor monitoring situations, this research introduces a revolutionary multi-person tracking system. Four components comprise the proposed system: people identification, tracking, head-torso template extraction, and crowd cluster analysis. First, the system uses the median filter and inverse transform to extract human silhouettes, which lowers the computational cost and manages a variety of intricate monitoring scenarios. Second, individuals may be identified by their head and torso since they are less variable and barely obscured.

Thirdly, each individual is followed over a series of frames by means of normalized cross-correlation and Jaccard similarity in Kalman filter approaches. Lastly, the template marking is applied to crowd counting with cue localization and is grouped using Gaussian mapping to recognize normal and abnormal events.

Al-Sa'd *et al.* [15] this research proposes a crowd monitoring and adaptive social distance estimation approach for video surveillance systems that protects privacy. To create a novel pose-based person localization strategy, develop an adaptive smoothing and tracking model that protects privacy from occlusions and noisy/missing measurements, compute inter-personal distances in real-world coordinates, detect infractions of social distance, and identify crowded areas in a scene.

8.3 Dataset Description

Many studies have concentrated on the subject of crowd counting because of its practicality in addressing social and economic concerns brought on by population expansion. The majority of crowd counting initiatives concentrate on counting people using a single photograph as input, which only allows for partial population estimation. In the meanwhile, a single image cannot convey the usefulness of place and time that video input can. Due to the fact that videos offer more information, knowing the overall number of persons in a crowd can help with a variety of real-world applications for crowd counting, including planning management and security monitoring. There are currently only two methods for addressing the crowd count problem in video: counting by region of interest and counting by lines of interest, despite the fact that the output of the problem is substantially bigger. We concluded to restrict the number of persons in a video crowd to a problem that receives an input of a video crowd and outputs the total number of individuals in that video crowd. Given that crowd density is one of the most significant characteristics of a crowd, this problem centers on addressing its challenge.

8.4 Problem Definition

The task at hand involves creating a crowd surveillance system for public areas using Python, primarily concentrating on identifying and detecting faces in the crowd and the challenge for video crowd counting is precisely calculating the number of people in a crowd scene that is recorded on camera. This task involves counting and identifying people in spite of obstacles like crowded backdrops, occlusions, scale differences, and viewpoint alterations. The objective is to create reliable algorithms that can process live video streams and provide precise crowd counts for a range of uses, and behavior of crowd and the abnormality which including public safety, event management, urban planning, and surveillance. Real-time image processing, deep learning models, and computer vision techniques should all be included in this system.

8.5 Proposed Methodology and System

8.5.1 Proposed Methodology

A. *Data Acquisition Module*
   It deals with gathering the crowd scene video files from many sources, including public events, web repositories, and surveillance cameras. It manages activities including processing videos, obtaining data, and extracting frames.
B. *Preprocessing Module*
   It handles preprocessing operations on video frames to improve their quality and make them more appropriate for algorithms that count crowds and analyses the crowd behavior which includes functions for resizing, subtracting background, normalizing, and denoising.
C. *Crowd Detection Module*
   Regions of interest (ROIs) containing crowds within video frames and finds crowd-filled areas of interest in video frames and applies methods such as density-based grouping, object detection, and foreground-background segmentation.
D. *Feature Extraction Module*
   In order to make counting easier, pertinent features are extracted from observed crowd scenes. It combines learned representations (such deep features from convolutional neural networks) with handcrafted characteristics (like color, texture, and shape).
E. *Counting Algorithm Module*
   Crowd counting techniques uses to calculate how many people are in each of the identified crowded areas. It includes

both deep learning-based techniques (such as convolutional neural networks and recurrent neural networks) and conventional techniques (such as density estimation and regression-based approaches).

F. *Post-processing Module*
In this post-processing procedures will enhance accuracy and refine counting findings. It includes methods including error correction, crowd aggregation, and crowd density estimation.

Figure 8.1 shows the workflow for the crowd alert system, detailing the sequential stages involved in detecting and managing crowd anomalies. The process begins with video cameras capturing footage, which is then pre-processed to enhance quality and extract relevant data. Following this, crowd detection algorithms identify the presence and density of people. The system then performs feature extraction to analyze characteristics essential for anomaly detection. The extracted features are used to develop a model capable of distinguishing between normal and abnormal crowd behaviors. Finally, decision-making processes utilize the model to perform crowd counting and detect anomalies, triggering alerts when unusual patterns are observed.

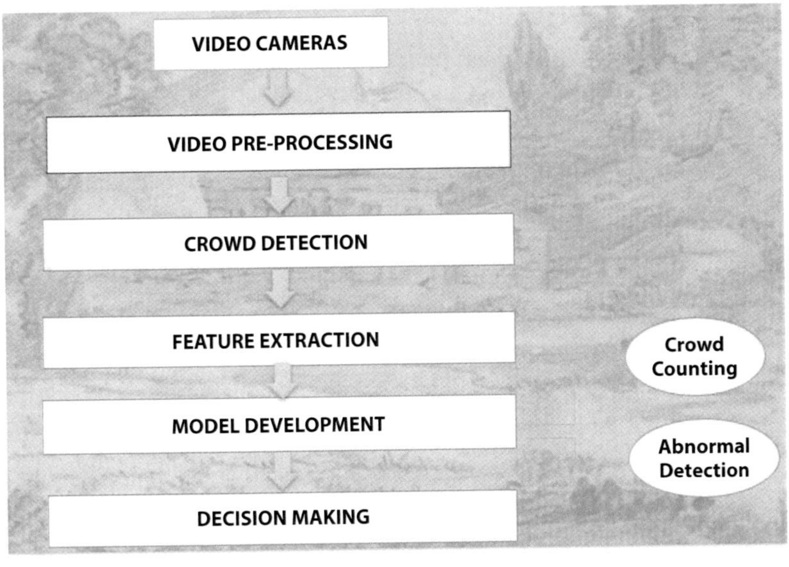

Figure 8.1 Workflow of crowd surveillance system.

8.5.2 Proposed System

The system starts by taking a real time video which has taken from crowd places. As we need to find the number of persons in that video and send the alert message to admin or higher authorities and also to check the crowd behavior and the abnormal activities in the crowd and detect the person who may do the abnormal activities or suspicious behavior will be captured.

It starts by taking the input as real time video and does all the preprocessing techniques such as processing on video frames, resizing, subtracting background, doing normalization, and denoising.

Next comes the model building to count crowd and to analyses the abnormal behavior for this Video process it process the video so that is should be easier to develop the model and tracking the person and detecting purpose Deep sorting is used which traces the person and detects them so that if the person is visible for more number of times also it tracks and detects and gives the correct crowd count.

Figure 8.2 shows that the crowd counting model working as follows:

Input: Video feeds from surveillance cameras.
Process: The model analyzes the video feed to estimate the number of people in the frame.
Output Decision: If the count exceeds a specified threshold, the model flags the situation as abnormal and sends an alert.

If the count is within a normal range, the model continues monitoring without triggering alerts.

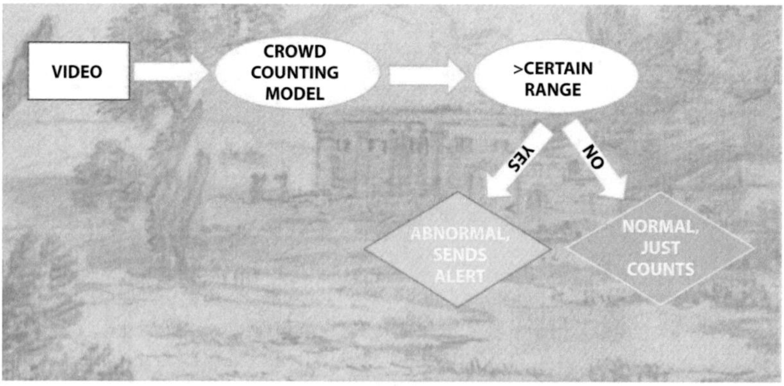

Figure 8.2 Flowchart of crowd counting model.

Modules in Computer Vision Techniques

- Using object detection techniques to find and follow people in a crowd for this Deep sort is used.
- Using face recognition software to recognize people you know or identify people who seem suspect.
- Create algorithms for behavioral analysis to examine patterns of behavior such aggressive gestures, lingering, and abrupt movements.
- Training machine learning models to identify abnormal behavior based on predetermined criteria, including straying from the crowd's flow or making erratic motions or carrying the suspicious things or carrying knife or gun and if the persons are very close to each other, is known as abnormality detection.
- Next comes the Crowd Counting techniques to estimate crowd density and monitor crowd movement over time, use crowd counting techniques built on deep learning models such as convolutional neural networks

Use crowd flow analysis to find locations that are crowded or odd behaviors among the crowd. After building the model we analyses the crowd count and Gives the Guidance Support in which if the crowd is more than specific range the model sends the mail to the admin and he will check and inform to Guidance supporter or security to monitor the crowd.

Figure 8.3 shows that the abnormal activity detection model working as follows:

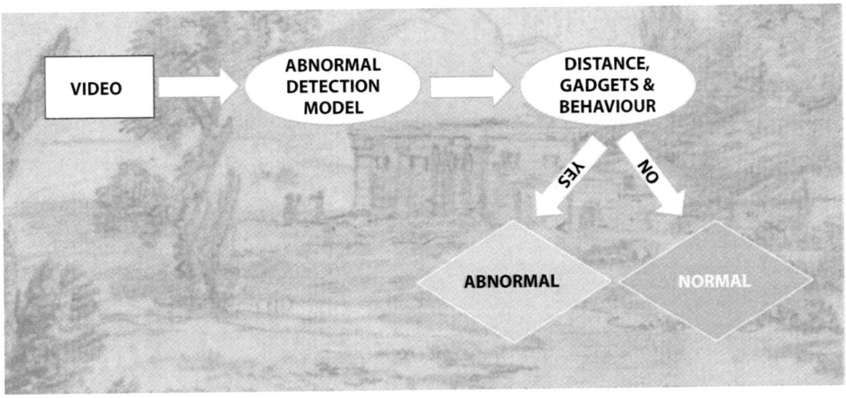

Figure 8.3 Flowchart of abnormal detecting model.

Core Task: The model employs advanced algorithms to detect anomalies based on the individual's behavior, carried gadgets, and their proximity to others or restricted zones.
Key Features:
Behavior Analysis: Utilizes AI techniques, such as pattern recognition and machine learning, to identify unusual behaviors (e.g., running in restricted areas, loitering, or erratic movements).
Gadget Detection: Scans for unusual or prohibited items carried by individuals, such as weapons, bags left unattended, or other suspicious gadgets using object detection technology.
Distance Measurement: Monitors the physical distance between individuals or proximity to critical areas (e.g., security perimeters, high-risk zones) to detect violations of safe or restricted distances.
Adaptability: The model adjusts to various environments, accounting for different crowd densities, lighting conditions, and viewpoints.

It Examine data in real-time to spot unusual patterns of behavior or possible security risks. When anomalous behavior is discovered, generate notifications or alerts for security staff. Giving security staff access to data visualization tools would help them keep an eye on crowd dynamics and react to possible threats in a timely manner.

8.6 Results

The dataset which is real time video which is taken as input is pre-processed and model is developed for crowd surveillance system for counting number of persons and the prediction of abnormal activity by using Deep sorting and Deep convolutional neural networks models where built and trained.

Figure 8.4 Crowd surveillance system crowd count.

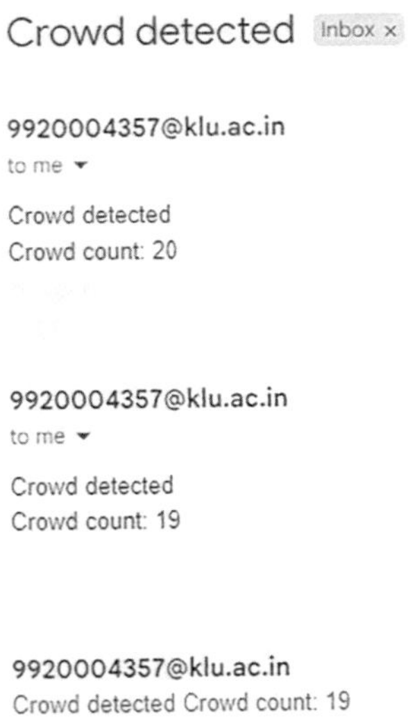

Figure 8.5 Crowd surveillance system alert mail.

Figure 8.4 illustrates the crowd counting process within the crowd surveillance system. This component accurately estimates the number of individuals in a monitored area, utilizing advanced algorithms and data from video feeds. By analyzing patterns and densities, the system can provide real-time crowd counts, which are essential for maintaining safety and managing resources in public spaces. The crowd counting feature plays a critical role in ensuring the effectiveness of the overall crowd alert system by enabling timely responses to potential overcrowding or unusual activities.

Figure 8.6 Crowd surveillance system abnormal activity.

As the model is developed it mainly focuses on Crowd Surveillance in which individual crowd count will be shown as output like number of person in the crowd if the crowd count is more than the certain range then the mail will be sent to the admin with the crowd count so that the security staff or the persons under him will monitor the crowd flow by taking the measures the control the crowd.

As in this we have given limit as 19 persons if the crowd count is 19 or above the alert mail will be sent to the admin as shown in Figure 8.5. So that the admin can guide to his workers or security to monitor the crowd.

It detects the crowd behavior, if any person is suspicious or doing any abnormal activities like roaming here and there, and if the persons are very close to each other, carrying weapons like knife or gun, by facial and body gestures the model will detect the abnormality and on the screen it gives as normal likewise it finds the abnormality in the crowd so the public is safe guided and there will be no rushing and damage to the properties and lives as well.

Figure 8.6 depicts the process of detecting abnormal activity within the crowd surveillance system. This stage is crucial for identifying potential threats or unusual behavior in crowded environments. The system leverages advanced machine learning algorithms to analyze patterns and deviations from normal crowd behavior. By monitoring various parameters such as movement speed, direction, and density, the system can promptly detect anomalies, such as sudden dispersals or unusual gatherings. Once detected, these anomalies trigger alerts, allowing for quick intervention and ensuring public safety.

8.7 Conclusion and Future Scope

8.7.1 Conclusion

In conclusion, the development of a crowd surveillance in public places and detecting faces in which crowd counting system and detecting the abnormal person in public places is an important project that will have a big impact on a lot of different areas, such event management, urban planning, public safety, and retail analytics. With the goal of precisely estimating the number of people and detecting the abnormality in crowd situations recorded in video footage, we have designed, implemented, and assessed a thorough technique for crowd counting algorithms through this project.

We have proposed a modular system architecture that includes important elements like crowd detection, feature extraction, counting algorithms, real-time processing, scalability, and application-specific adaptation. We did this by conducting a thorough review of the literature and utilizing cutting-edge methods from computer vision, machine learning, and deep learning. The suggested system seeks to achieve high accuracy, efficiency, and scalability while addressing the needs and restrictions of various application domains through methodical experimentation and evaluation. With possible applications in surveillance, transit, event management, retail analytics, and other areas, the suggested video crowd counting method has promise for improving crowd control, public safety, and urban planning techniques. We work together to create practical solutions that tackle real-world problems and eventually improve the resilience and well-being of communities all around the world by constant innovation and teamwork.

8.7.2 Future Scope

In real-world applications, the system is expected to handle congested scenarios and massive video datasets with ease due to its efficient scalability. This comprises resource management techniques, effective data structures, and algorithms. Event management, urban planning, retail analytics, and surveillance are just a few of the application domains for which the system may be tailored. This entails designing and implementing the algorithm with domain-specific criteria and constraints.

References

1. Stott, C. and Radburn, M., Understanding crowd conflict: Social context, psychology and policing. *Curr. Opin. Psychol.*, 35, 76–80, Oct. 2020.
2. Nguyen, V. and Ngo, T.D., Single-image crowd counting: A comparative survey on deep learning-based approaches. *Int. J. Multimed. Inf. Retr.*, 9, 2, 63–80, Jun. 2020.
3. Chen, Q. and Shi, L., Mobile crowd sensing technologies: A survey and new perspectives. *Int. J. Sci.*, 7, 6, 329–336, 2020.
4. Li, X., Song, W., Xu, X., Zhang, J., Xia, L., Shi, C., Experimental study on pedestrian contact force under different degrees of crowding. *Saf. Sci.*, 127, Art. no. 104713, Jul. 2020, doi: 10.1016/j.ssci.2020.104713.
5. Direkoglu, C., Abnormal crowd behavior detection using motion information images and convolutional neural networks. *IEEE Access*, 8, 80408–80416, 2020.
6. Alam, T. and Aljohani, M., Decision support system for real-time people counting in a crowded environment. *SSRN Electron. J.*, 12, 1, 34–41, 2020.
7. Aros-Vera, F., Sadeghi, A., Younes Sinaki, R., Sormaz, D., A simulation-based framework for checkpoint design in large-scale crowd management: Case study of the papal mass in philadelphia. *Saf. Sci.*, 127, 104701, Jul. 2020.

8. FPJ Web Desk, What is Simhastha Mahaparv Kumbh All About?, The free press J., Accessed: Jul. 30, 2020.
9. Murphey, D., Steps for a Safe and Effective Crowd Management Strategy, Eventinterface, Accessed: Jun. 21, 2020.
10. Shrivastav, P. and Vakula Rani, J., A Real-Time Crowd Detection and Monitoring System using Machine Learning. *2023 International Conference on Intelligent Data Communication Technologies and Internet of Things (IDCIoT).*
11. Salim, S., O Khalifa, O., Rahman, F.A., Lajis, A., Crowd Detection And Tracking In Surveillance Video Sequences. *2019 IEEE International Conference on Smart Instrumentation, Measurement and Application (ICSIMA).*
12. Kahale, N., On the economic impact of social distancing measures. *SSRN Electron. J.*, 2020. Available at SSRN: https://ssrn.com/abstract=3578415 or http://dx.doi.org/10.2139/ssrn.3578415
13. Prem, K., Liu, Y., Russell, T.W., Davies, N., The effect of control strategies to reduce social mixing on outcomes of the covid19 epidemic in Wuhan, China: a modeling study. *Lancet Public Health*, 5, 5, e261-e270, 2020.
14. Shehzed, A., Jalal, A., Kim, K., Multi-Person Tracking in Smart Surveillance System for Crowd Counting and Normal/Abnormal Events Detection. *2019 International Conference on Applied and Engineering Mathematics (ICAEM)*, Taxila, Pakistan, pp. 163–168, 2021, doi: 10.1109/ICAEM.2019.8853756.
15. Al-Sa'd, M. *et al.*, A social distance estimation and crowd monitoring system for surveillance cameras. *Sensors*, 22, 2, 418, 2022.

9

Revolutionizing Learning with Qubits: A Review of Quantum Machine Learning Advances

Shatakshi Bhusari, Aniket Badakh, Kalyani Daine, Nikita Gagare and Prasad Raghunath Mutkule*

Department of Information Technology, Sanjivani College of Engineering, Maharashtra, India

Abstract

As the synergy between quantum computing and machine learning unfolds, the paradigm shift brought by QML (Quantum Machine Learning) stands at the forefront of transformative advancements. From quantum-enhanced optimization algorithms to innovative approaches in quantum data representation, the breadth of QML techniques. Special attention is devoted to the emerging field of QNN (Quantum Neural Networks), QSVM (Quantum Support Vector Machines), and the application of quantum computing in enhancing classical machine learning workflows. The practical implications and challenges associated with implementing QML on existing quantum hardware are thoroughly examined, shedding light on the current state and future prospects of scalable quantum machine learning solutions. The paper addresses the intricacies of adapting classical machine learning algorithms to the quantum realm and emphasizes the need for error correction in quantum mechanisms to guarantee quantum results reliability also an extensive examination of the current state of Quantum Machine Learning (QML), emphasizing both the remarkable advancements and the persistent challenges within this burgeoning interdisciplinary field. The primary objectives include synthesizing the latest research findings, offering insights into the practical applications and potential impact of QML, and identifying areas requiring further exploration and development.

**Corresponding author*: mutkuleprasad000@gmail.com

Budati Anil Kumar, Singamaneni Kranthi Kumar and Li Xingwang (eds.) Quantum Computing Models for Cybersecurity and Wireless Communications, (153–168) © 2025 Scrivener Publishing LLC

Keywords: Quantum machine learning (QML), synergy of quantum computing and machine learning, transformative advancements in QML, quantum enhanced optimization algorithms, Quantum neural networks (QNN), quantum support vector machines (QSVM), QML on quantum hardware, challenges in implementing QML, scalable quantum machine learning solutions

9.1 Introduction

Quantum Machine Learning (QML) also known as the intersection of quantum computing and machine learning, represents a captivating frontier at the merging of two groundbreaking fields. Quantum computing introduces unique principles rooted qubits that provides superposition as well as entanglement between quantum states [1]. Algorithms of Quantum intended for machine learning tasks include QSVM (Quantum Support Vector Machines) for classification, QNN (Quantum Neural Networks) inspired by classical neural networks, and innovative clustering algorithms harnessing quantum principles. One of the remarkable features of quantum computing is its potential for exponential speedup, attributed to the ability to process multiple states simultaneously. Quantum Fourier Transform and algorithms like Shor's algorithm showcase this advantage in solving specific problems more efficiently than classical counterparts. Quantum data representation involves encoding classical data for quantum processing, employing techniques like amplitude encoding [2, 3]. Hybrid approaches, like the Variational Quantum Eigensolver (VQE) and quantum-classical neural networks, aim to synergize classical and quantum computing resources for enhanced performance. Quantum machine learning also delves into data analysis with algorithms like Quantum Singular Value Decomposition (QSVD) and explores applications in optimization, feature selection, and random walks. Several potential advantages offered by Quantum computing are solving critical machine learning problems, promising breakthroughs in computational efficiency and problem-solving capabilities. The key advantages are given as below:

9.1.1 Parallelism

Superposition: Quantum bits, or qubits, have the capacity to simultaneously exist in multiple states, enabling parallel computations. This characteristic empowers quantum computers to process extensive amounts of information concurrently, offering a substantial advantage over classical computers in tasks that entail the manipulation of large datasets [4].

9.1.2 Quantum Speedup

Speedup: Solving certain mathematical problems or searching unsorted databases using Quantum algorithms. This holds the potential to significantly accelerate machine learning algorithms and computations compared to their classical counterparts.

9.1.3 Quantum Entanglement

Enhanced Correlation: This feature can be harnessed to establish richer relationships between variables in machine learning models, potentially improving the modeling of complex dependencies in data [5–7].

9.1.4 Quantum Fourier Transform

Efficient Signal Processing: The Quantum Fourier Transform (QFT) and related quantum algorithms can efficiently process signals and transform data.

9.1.5 Quantum Machine Learning Algorithms

Specialized Algorithms:, QSVM and QNN are Quantum algorithms designed for machine learning tasks, helps to solve specific problems more efficiently. These algorithms can offer advantages in classification, regression, clustering, and other machine learning tasks.

9.1.6 Quantum Data Representation

Higher Information Density: Quantum data representation, including techniques like amplitude encoding, allows for higher information density and more efficient representation of complex data structures. This can lead to improvements in data processing and analysis.

9.1.7 Quantum Sampling

Improved Sampling Techniques: Quantum computers can potentially provide more efficient sampling techniques, allowing for better exploration of probability distributions. This can be advantageous in various machine learning applications, particularly in probabilistic models.

9.1.8 Quantum Annealing

Optimization Advantages: Quantum annealers, such as those developed by D-Wave, are designed for optimization problems, which are prevalent in machine learning. Quantum annealing can potentially offer advantages in solving complex optimization tasks more quickly than classical methods [8].

9.1.9 Hybrid Quantum-Classical Approaches

Combining Strengths: Hybrid approaches, integrating both quantum and classical components, aim to combine the strengths of both paradigms. For example, the Variational Quantum Eigensolver (VQE) seeks for complex problems by means of optimization by combining classical and quantum computing resources.

9.2 Review of Literature

9.2.1 Overview of Key Quantum Computing Principles

Quantum computing represents a computational paradigm harnessing the principles of quantum mechanics to execute operations on quantum bits, known as qubits [6]. In stark contrast to classical computing, the foundational principles of quantum computing introduce key concepts like

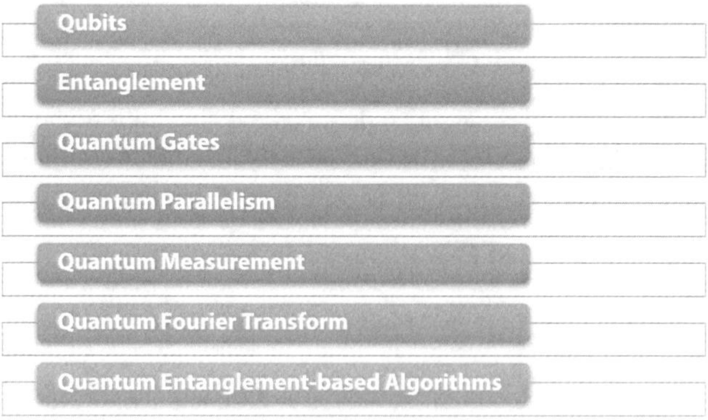

Figure 9.1 Key quantum computing principles.

superposition, entanglement, and quantum gates [7]. A synopsis of the essential principles that define quantum computing is presented as shown in Figure 9.1 above [8].

9.2.1.1 Qubits (Quantum Bits)

A) Classical vs. Quantum Bits
   Classical bits are confined to either a 0 or 1 state, whereas qubits exhibit a phenomenon referred to as superposition that is the ability to exist simultaneously in multiple states.
B) Superposition
   Qubits can represent a combination of 0 and 1 at the same time, enabling parallel computation and the ability to process multiple possibilities simultaneously [9].

9.2.1.2 Quantum Gates

A) Classical Gates vs. Quantum Gates
   Logic gates such as AND, OR, NOT used by classical computers for computations. For manipulation of qubits, Quantum computers use quantum gates [10].
B) Unitary Operations
   Quantum gates are unitary operations, meaning they are reversible. They preserve the probability amplitudes associated with quantum states.

9.2.1.3 Quantum Parallelism

A) Exploiting Superposition
   Quantum computers can perform operations on all possible inputs simultaneously due to superposition. This leads to an exponential increase in computational power for certain algorithms compared to classical counterparts.

9.2.1.4 Quantum Measurement

A) Wavefunction Collapse
   Superposition of qubits collapses when a qubit is measured, into one of the classical states (0 or 1) with a probability determined by the amplitudes of its superposition.

B) Probabilistic Outcomes
Quantum measurement's outcome is probabilistic, introducing a fundamental element of uncertainty [11].

9.2.1.5 Quantum Fourier Transform

A) Efficient Signal Processing
The QFT (Quantum Fourier Transform) is a quantum algorithm that efficiently performs operations analogous to classical Fourier transforms.

9.2.1.6 Quantum Entanglement-Based Algorithms

A) Bell's Inequality
Quantum entanglement is harnessed in algorithms like the Bell test, showcasing non-local correlations that defy classical intuition.
B) Quantum Key Distribution
Utilizes entanglement for secure communication through protocols like the famous BBM92 protocol developed by Bennett, Brassard, Mermin [12].

9.3 Basic Quantum Operations, Qubits, and Quantum Gates

9.3.1 Basic Quantum Operations

Quantum operations involve manipulating qubits using quantum gates to perform specific tasks each associated with a certain probability.

9.3.2 Quantum Bits (Qubits)

In classical computing, bits are the basic units of information, taking values of 0 or 1. This allows qubits to represent a combination of 0 and 1 at the same time. The state of a qubit is described by a quantum state vector. To perform parallel computations on different states at once, the superposition property is used providing a potential for exponential speedup in certain algorithms.

9.3.3 Quantum Gates

Exploring the intricacies of quantum computing and the evolution of quantum algorithms hinges upon grasping the fundamentals of basic quantum operations, qubits, and gates. Quantum circuits, pivotal in this domain, are amalgamations of these gates arranged in precise sequences to execute intricate computations, with their behaviors elucidated by the tenets of quantum mechanics. In the realm of classical computing, logic gates like AND, OR, and NOT are instrumental in manipulating bits and driving computations forward. However, quantum computing diverges significantly by employing quantum gates to manipulate qubits. These gates are epitomized by unitary matrices and are distinguished by their reversibility, facilitating the recovery of the initial quantum state from the output state. Quantum gates serve as linchpins in constructing quantum circuits tailored for specific computations.

Several prevalent quantum gates include:

A) Hadamard Gate (H)
This gate puts qubits into a superposition of $|0\rangle$ and $|1\rangle$ states. It is fundamental for creating superposition.

B) Pauli-X Gate (X)
Similar to a classical NOT gate, it flips the state of a qubit from $|0\rangle$ to $|1\rangle$ or vice versa.

C) Pauli-Y Gate (Y)
This gate introduces a phase shift and a bit flip, creating a rotation around the y-axis on the Bloch sphere representation.

D) Pauli-Z Gate (Z)
This gate introduces a phase shift without changing the basis states. It is often used for specific phase operations.

E) CNOT Gate (Controlled NOT)
This gate performs a NOT operation on a target qubit depending on the state of a control qubit. It is a two-qubit gate, introducing entanglement.

9.4 Quantum Machine Learning Algorithms

Quantum machine learning (QML) algorithms leverage the principles of quantum computing to enhance or solve certain machine learning tasks more efficiently than classical algorithms. All algorithms are shown in Table 9.1 below.

Table 9.1 Advantages, and limitations of quantum machine learning algorithms.

Algorithm	Scope and applications	Advantages	Limitations
QSVM	Binary and multiclass classification	Quadratic speedup, potential for large datasets	Quantum resource demands, problem-dependent benefits
QNN	Various ML tasks (pattern recognition)	Quantum parallelism, potential for specific tasks	Scalability issues, challenging training
Quantum Clustering	Unsupervised clustering	Quantum parallelism, efficient convergence	Performance dependent on dataset, substantial resources
QPCA	Dimensionality reduction	Quadratic speedup for computing principal components	Quantum resource requirements, error correction challenges
Quantum Boltzmann Machines	Probabilistic modeling and sampling	Potential quantum speedup in exploring distributions	Implementation challenges, benefits may vary
QSVC	Clustering based on support vectors	Quantum-classical combination for potential improvements	Effectiveness depends on dataset, practical challenges
QAM	Pattern recall with noisy/partial input	Quantum superposition and entanglement benefits	Precise quantum operations required, scalability issues

(*Continued*)

Table 9.1 Advantages, and limitations of quantum machine learning algorithms. (*Continued*)

Algorithm	Scope and applications	Advantages	Limitations
QLSA	Solving linear systems of equations	Exponential speedup for specific linear problems	Demanding resource requirements, scalability challenges
QkNN	Identifying k-nearest neighbors	Quantum speedup in search for nearest neighbors	Practical implementation challenges, problem-dependent
QGANs	Generating realistic data samples	Quantum parallelism in training process	Limited practical implementations, challenges in training

9.4.1 Quantum Support Vector Machines (QSVM)

Objective: Classification of data points into different classes.
Advantages: QSVM can provide a quadratic speedup compared to classical support vector machines. It employs a quantum-enhanced kernel to map data into a higher-dimensional space.

9.4.2 Quantum Neural Networks (QNN)

Objective: Similar to classical neural networks, QNNs aim to perform tasks such as pattern recognition and classification.
Advantages: QNNs leverage quantum gates and entanglement for parallel processing, potentially providing computational advantages over classical neural networks.

9.4.3 Quantum Clustering Algorithms

Objective: Grouping similar data points into clusters.
Advantages: Quantum clustering algorithms, like the quantum k-Means algorithm, explore quantum parallelism and quantum entanglement to find optimal solutions more efficiently than classical counterparts.

9.4.4 Quantum Principal Component Analysis (QPCA)

Objective: Reducing the dimensionality of data while preserving its variance. Advantages: QPCA can provide a quadratic speedup compared to classical principal component analysis. It utilizes quantum parallelism to calculate principal components more efficiently.

9.4.5 Quantum Boltzmann Machines

Objective: Modeling and sampling from probability distributions. Advantages: Quantum Boltzmann Machines use quantum annealing to explore probability distributions efficiently, potentially providing advantages in probabilistic modeling.

9.4.6 Quantum Support Vector Clustering (QSVC)

Objective: Clustering data points based on support vector clustering. Advantages: QSVC combines quantum algorithms with classical clustering techniques to achieve potentially improved performance for certain datasets.

9.5 Quantum Hardware for Machine Learning

Several platforms have emerged, each with its unique characteristics and advantages. Superconducting qubits, utilized by industry leaders like IBM and Google, exploit the superconducting properties of certain materials to create qubits, demonstrating high coherence times essential for quantum error correction. Trapped ion quantum computers, championed by companies such as IonQ and Honeywell, rely on manipulating individual ions using electromagnetic fields, offering long coherence times and high-fidelity quantum gates. Topological qubits, a theoretical approach championed by Microsoft's StationQ project, explore the use of anions with topological properties as the basis for qubits, providing inherent robustness against specific errors. Photonic quantum processors, as researched by Xanadu Quantum Technologies, leverage photons for qubit representation and manipulation, exhibiting resistance to certain types of noise, making them promising for quantum communication. Quantum dots, semiconductor-based artificial atoms, provide scalability and compatibility with existing technologies, attracting interest from various research institutions and companies. Silicon spin qubits, supported by Intel, leverage the spin states of electrons in silicon devices, offering long coherence times and compatibility with classical

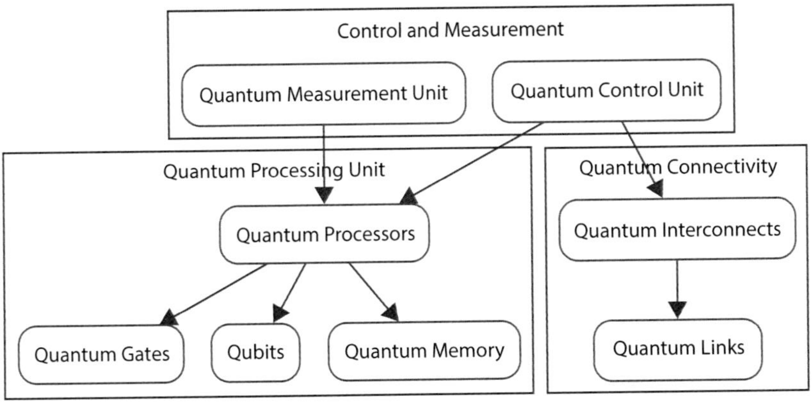

Figure 9.2 Block diagram of quantum hardware for machine learning.

silicon electronics. Diamond NV centers, explored by companies like Rigetti, utilize defects in diamond lattices for qubit representation, demonstrating high coherence times and the ability to optically read and manipulate qubit states as depicted in Figure 9.2 above. Quantum annealers, exemplified by D-Wave, specialize in solving optimization problems through quantum annealing, proving effective for specific optimization tasks. The quantum hardware landscape is dynamic, with ongoing efforts focused on improving performance, scalability, and error correction capabilities.

9.6 Challenges in Building Scalable and Error-Resistant Quantum Hardware

Building scalable and error-resistant quantum hardware poses several formidable challenges:

9.6.1 Decoherence and Quantum Error Correction

Maintaining quantum coherence in the face of environmental interactions and errors during quantum operations is a fundamental challenge. Developing effective quantum error correction codes to mitigate errors without compromising computational efficiency is crucial [13].

9.6.2 Quantum Gate Fidelity

Imperfections in gates, leading to errors, remain a significant challenge, and improving gate fidelity is an ongoing focus of research.

9.6.3 Scalability

Establishing and maintaining qubit connectivity, minimizing crosstalk, and managing quantum error correction become increasingly complex as the system scales [14, 15].

9.6.4 Qubit Connectivity and Crosstalk

Efficiently connecting qubits while minimizing interference or crosstalk is crucial for effective quantum computation. Achieving proper qubit connectivity and minimizing crosstalk challenges are central to building large and reliable quantum processors.

9.6.5 Material Science and Qubit Implementation

Developing qubits with long coherence times and high fidelity requires advancements in materials science. Identifying and fabricating materials with the desired quantum properties for qubit implementation remains a complex task [16].

9.6.6 Quantum Interconnects

Enabling efficient transfer of quantum information between distant qubits is a significant challenge. Developing robust quantum interconnects to facilitate communication within quantum processors and among quantum devices is crucial for scalability.

9.6.7 Thermal Management

Operating quantum hardware at extremely low temperatures for maintaining qubit coherence poses challenges in thermal management. Efficiently managing cryogenic and cooling technologies becomes critical.

9.6.8 Error Mitigation Strategies

Developing effective error mitigation strategies that correct or suppress errors without compromising quantum computational power is an ongoing challenge. Researchers are exploring various techniques, including error-optimized compilation, error-mitigating circuits, and machine learning-based error correction methods.

Overcoming these challenges requires collaborative efforts across disciplines, including quantum physics, materials science, and engineering. Continued research and innovation are essential for achieving scalable and error-resistant quantum hardware.

9.7 Challenges and Limitations in Quantum Machine Learning

9.7.1 Quantum Computational Overheads

The introduction of significant computational overhead in quantum algorithms poses a challenge. This additional computational load, including the need for quantum error correction and complex gate operations, can offset the potential speedup offered by quantum computing, affecting the practical advantages of quantum algorithms.

9.7.2 Hybrid Quantum-Classical System Integration

Efficiently integrating quantum algorithms into classical workflows is a complex task. Achieving seamless interoperability between quantum and classical systems is essential for the practical application of quantum machine learning, requiring careful consideration of communication protocols and data transfer mechanisms.

9.7.3 Limited Quantum Expressibility

Quantum circuits' constraints may limit their expressibility, making it challenging to efficiently represent certain types of classical machine learning models. The ability of quantum circuits to capture complex patterns and relationships in data might be restricted due to these limitations.

9.7.4 Data Preprocessing Challenges

Quantum machine learning algorithms often assume access to quantum-enhanced datasets, presenting challenges in data preparation. The practicality of obtaining or interfacing quantum datasets with classical data sources can be a bottleneck in the application of quantum algorithms.

9.7.5 Quantum Algorithm Verification

Verifying the correctness of quantum algorithms introduces non-trivial challenges. The probabilistic nature of quantum measurements and the absence of straightforward classical verification mechanisms make it difficult to ensure the reliability of quantum machine learning results.

9.7.6 Quantum Resource Requirements

Quantum algorithms may demand substantial resources, both in terms of qubit count and complex quantum circuits. This resource intensity can limit the accessibility and scalability of quantum machine learning implementations, particularly on current quantum hardware.

9.7.7 Adaptation to Quantum Hardware Constraints

Adapting classical machine learning algorithms to run efficiently on limited quantum hardware presents challenges. Achieving optimal performance on existing quantum hardware requires careful consideration of constraints such as qubit connectivity and gate error rates.

9.7.8 Limited Quantum Hardware Availability

Access to large-scale and fault-tolerant quantum computers is currently limited. The availability and accessibility of quantum hardware impact the ability to validate and deploy quantum algorithms for real-world problems, hindering widespread practical application.

9.7.9 Algorithmic Complexity

Quantum algorithms for machine learning tasks may exhibit higher algorithmic complexity compared to their classical counterparts. The intricacies of implementing and optimizing complex quantum algorithms can pose challenges, especially when considering the limited quantum resources available.

9.7.10 Quantum Model Interpretability

The probabilistic nature of quantum measurements introduces uncertainty, complicating the task of understanding and interpreting the results, which is crucial for building trust in quantum models.

9.8 Future Directions

The future of quantum machine learning (QML) involves addressing several key challenges and exploring exciting opportunities. Demonstrating quantum advantage across diverse machine learning tasks remains a challenge, demanding clear benchmarks and criteria for quantum supremacy. Hybrid algorithms that seamlessly integrate quantum and classical processing need development for enhanced performance. Quantum data structures, generative models, and transfer learning methods are avenues for exploration. Challenges also include improving the interpretability of quantum models and integrating quantum computing into natural language processing tasks. Bridging the gap between theoretical advancements and practical implementation in industry is crucial. Advancing quantum hardware capabilities and designing quantum algorithms for optimization tasks are paramount challenges. Standardizing benchmarks for quantum machine learning algorithms is essential for evaluating performance across diverse tasks, driving advancements in the field.

9.9 Conclusion

In summary, the future of quantum machine learning (QML) is characterized by both challenges and promising opportunities. Establishing quantum advantage requires clear benchmarks, while hybrid algorithms blending quantum and classical processing hold potential for enhanced performance. Quantum data structures, generative models, and transfer learning present avenues for exploration, driving innovation. Addressing challenges in interpretability and integration into natural language processing is essential. Bridging the gap between theory and industry implementation is crucial, with advancing quantum hardware capabilities and optimization algorithms shaping the practical impact of QML. Standardized benchmarks and collaborative efforts will play key roles in realizing the full potential of QML across diverse applications. Overall, the landscape of QML is dynamic, with ongoing research and collaboration driving advancements in this intersection of quantum computing and machine learning.

References

1. Lloyd, S., Quantum machine learning. *Nat. Phys.*, 10, 9, 631–633, Sep. 2013, DOI: 10.1038/nphys2474.

2. Babbush, R. *et al.*, Quantum Machine Learning for Electronic Structure Calculations. *J. Phys. Chem. C*, 120, 11, 5821–5833, Mar. 2016, DOI: 10.1021/acs.jpcc.6b01085.
3. Aspuru-Guzik, A. *et al.*, Quantum algorithms and the finite element method. *Phys. Rev. A*, 71, 3, 032324, Mar. 2005, DOI: 10.1103/PhysRevA.71.03232.
4. Biamonte, J. *et al.*, Quantum-enhanced machine learning. *Quantum Sci. Technol.*, 2, 4, 04LT01, Dec. 2017, DOI: 10.1088/2058-9565/aa8072.
5. Rebentrost, P., Mohseni, M., Lloyd, S., Supervised learning with quantum-enhanced feature spaces. *Phys. Rev. Lett.*, 113, 13, 130503, Sep. 2014, DOI: 10.1103/PhysRevLett.113.130503.
6. Jurcevic, P. *et al.*, Quantum machine learning for quantum anomaly detection. *Phys. Rev. Lett.*, 126, 18, 180503, May 2021, DOI: 10.1103/PhysRevLett.126.180503.
7. Cao, Y. *et al.*, Quantum Support Vector Machine for Big Data Classification. *Quantum Inf. Process.*, 14, 12, 4229–4244, Dec. 2015, DOI: 10.1007/s11128-015-0948-5.
8. Biamonte, J. *et al.*, Quantum Neural Networks. *Nat. Commun.*, 8, 15046, Mar. 2017, DOI: 10.1038/ncomms15046.
9. Peruzzo, A. *et al.*, Variational Quantum Eigensolvers for Electronic Structure Calculations on Quantum Processors. *Nat. Commun.*, 5, 4213, Jul. 2014, DOI: 10.1038/ncomms5213.
10. Wang, X., Gao, X., Tao, D., Quantum Generative Adversarial Networks with Rigorous Error Bounds. *Quantum*, 4, 241, Mar. 2020, DOI: 10.22331/q-2020-03-12-241.
11. Bravo-Prieto, C. *et al.*, Quantum Linear Systems Algorithms: A Primer. *Quantum*, 4, 378, Nov. 2020, DOI: 10.22331/q-2020-11-06-378.
12. Killoran, N. *et al.*, Quantum Machine Learning with Pennylane. *SoftwareX*, 12, 100311, Mar. 2020, DOI: 10.1016/j.softx.2019.100311.
13. Anand, L. *et al.*, Development of machine learning and medical enabled multimodal for segmentation and classification of brain tumor using MRI images. *Comput. Intell. Neurosci.*, 2022, 1–8, Aug. 2022, doi: 10.1155/2022/7797094.
14. Kolli, C.S., Raghunath, M.P., Meenakshi, S., Maheswari, K., Britto, C.F., Kushwaha, S., Efficient development of supervised learning algorithm for Kidney Stone Prediction. *2022 International Conference on Inventive Computation Technologies (ICICT)*, 2022, doi:10.1109/icict54344.2022.9850573.
15. Raghunath, M.P. and Ankayarkanni, B., An empirical review on brain tumor classification approaches. *Inf. Syst. Manag. Sci.*, 521, 15–27, 2022, doi: 10.1007/978-3-031-13150-9_2.
16. Bhosale, J.D., Thorat, S.S., Pancholi, P.V., Mutkule, P.R., Machine Learning-Based Algorithms for the Detection of Leaf Disease in Agriculture Crops. *IJRITCC*, 11, 5s, 45–50, May 2023.

10

Multi-Band Self-Grounding Antenna for Wireless Technologies

Ch. Siva Rama Krishna, P. Livingston*, S. Jaya Chandra, J. Hari Babu and K. Sai Babu

Lakireddy Bali Reddy College of Engineering, Mylavaram, India

Abstract

The design and construction of a multi-band self-grounding antenna designed for a range of wireless communication applications are presented in this study. Because of its ability to function in a variety of frequency bands, the antenna is compatible with a wide range of wireless technologies. To achieve optimal radiation efficiency and impedance matching, the suggested antenna architecture combines ground-plane dimensions of x=44 and y=40 with a substrate size of x=44, y=40, and z=0.2. By using its own structure as an efficient ground plane and doing away with the requirement for an external ground plane, the self-grounding function improves the antenna's performance. This design strategy lowers manufacturing costs and complexity while also making it easier to integrate the antenna into a variety of devices. In addition, the antenna's small form factor makes it appropriate for incorporation into wearable technology, IoT devices, and cell phones among other small-sized wireless devices. The antenna's effectiveness in attaining desired radiation characteristics across various frequency bands is demonstrated by the simulation results, which guarantee dependable wireless communication performance. The antenna's viability in practice and ability to satisfy the demands of modern wireless communication standards are validated by experiments.

Keywords: Compact antenna design, wireless communication, self-grounding antenna, multi-band antenna, substrate dimensions

**Corresponding author*: stonliving897@gmail.com

Budati Anil Kumar, Singamaneni Kranthi Kumar and Li Xingwang (eds.) Quantum Computing Models for Cybersecurity and Wireless Communications, (169–182) © 2025 Scrivener Publishing LLC

10.1 Introduction

Antennas that can optimally adapt to different frequency bands are in high demand in a time when seamless connectivity across a wide range of wireless technologies is crucial. We are pleased to present a novel solution: the Multi-Band Self-Grounding Antenna. This innovative device is designed to transform wireless communication in a variety of contexts, including 5G, satellite communication, Wi-Fi, Bluetooth, and Zigbee, as well as military and defense applications. Additionally, it can cover the frequencies of radar systems between 5.94 and 5.99GHz and fixed satellite services (FSS) between 5.09 and 5.16GHz. This unmatched flexibility guarantees optimal performance in an extensive variety of usages, from the defense to the civilian sectors, and also reduces the complexity of adopting various wireless technologies. This antenna is unique in that it has a self-grounding technology that improves stability and lowers interference, ensuring strong and dependable communication in even the most difficult settings. With its smooth integration with a broad range of systems and gadgets, from consumer electronics to vital infrastructure, this antenna ushers in a new era of uncompromising connectivity. The Multi-Band Self-Grounding Antenna, which offers unmatched performance, dependability, and versatility across a wide range of wireless technologies, essentially marks a paradigm change in antenna technology. This discovery has the potential to completely change the wireless communication environment, opening up new options and laying the groundwork for a connected future as the need for seamless connectivity grows.

10.1.1 Literature Review

T. Likitha *et al.* (2018) conducted experiments on a non-symmetric ground plane and gapped CPW-fed square loop antenna printed on FR4 substrate ($\varepsilon r = 4.4$, $\tan \delta = 0.002$). The antenna consists of a rectangular monopole measuring 20 x 30.5 mm that is fed by a 50Ω CPW wire that has two gaps of 0.2 mm and a width of 4.5 mm. To enhance impedance matching and promote circular polarization (CP), an irregular ground plane is employed. To generate an extra CP mode and a bigger bandwidth, the design uses a square ring inside a square loop that is positioned next to the rectangular monopole. At 2.45 GHz, the coupled effect of this ring and monopole produces CP radiation. Modeling and optimization of the antenna were done with Mentor Graphics IE3D version 14.0. A return loss of less than -10 dB from 2.4–2.5 GHz, with a maximum of -27 dB at 2.45 GHz, is one of the important findings. At 2.45 GHz, the VSWR of 1:2 suggests adequate impedance matching to 50Ω in the vicinity of this frequency. At 2.45 GHz, 2D current distributions and 3D radiation patterns show the intended CP operation. At the resonant frequency, the total gain is 3.5 dB, and the radiation and antenna efficiencies are roughly 68%. We find that the simulated E-plane and H-plane radiation patterns coincide fairly well. This design makes use of the linked square ring construction and irregular ground plane to achieve the necessary CP functioning and wide impedance bandwidth [1].

Guo-Ping Gao *et al.* (2019) conducted research and development on the wearable meta surface antenna (MSA) for 5GHz WBAN applications. The MSA is made up of a 3×2 array meta surface (MS) superstrate and a planar inverted-F antenna (PIFA) feeding antenna. While the MS uses nylon conductive textile on wool felt substrate, the PIFA achieves wideband functioning using shorting pins and a slot. When exposed to linearly polarized waves, electromagnetic analysis shows that the MS exhibits an equal relative permittivity of about 15. Due to the downsizing effect, simulations comparing the PIFA alone (Ant 1) and the entire MSA (Ant 2) show that loading the PIFA with the high permittivity MS superstrate significantly reduces resonant frequencies (530-740 MHz lower). Furthermore, with the MSA's input impedance nearer 50Ω in the operational region, impedance matching is enhanced. Similar performance is shown by 3D radiation patterns between Ant 2 and a PIFA on a comparable high permittivity substrate. The MSA is appropriate for wearable WBAN applications due to its good radiation efficiency across 5 GHz, even with a minor reduction in gain. The high effective permittivity of the MS superstrate also helps with antenna downsizing [2].

Jiahao Zhang *et al.* (2017) conducted research on the development and assessment of a flexible wearable antenna with a small feeding network for operation in the 2.45 GHz ISM band. A prototype was created with a shield, its superconductive textile patch and ground, and a nonconductive 3-mm thick felt material used as the antenna substrate. Aperture coupling is used by the compact feeding network topology, which is implemented on a 10x10 mm2 FR-4 PCB, to feed the patch radiator. Excellent agreement between measured results and circuit models in ADS and simulations in CST is observed. Similar to a conventional feed, the constructed antenna achieves a -10 dB impedance bandwidth of 6.6%, spanning 2.33-2.49 GHz. The radiation patterns show a maximum realized gain of 5.6 dB, a front-to-back ratio of over 15 dB, and cross-polarization values below -20 db. The projected radiation effectiveness is approximately 47%, which is reasonable given the textile materials' high loss. Bending experiments show that ISM bands continue to operate for radii as small as 30 mm in both directions.

Measurements conducted on the human subject's physiology reveal a greater bandwidth with some frequency shifting, all within the 2.45 GHz band. A basic human model used in SAR simulations shows conformity at 0.145 W/kg for 0.5 W input power, which is less than the 2 W/kg limit. The prototype of the small fed wearable antenna well satisfies the design goals for flexible, body-worn 2.4 GHz ISM applications [3].

Sam Agneessens *et al.* (2014) conducted experiments to develop a wearable 2.4/5.8 GHz ISM band antenna that is a small, dual-band, half-diamond-shaped HMSIW (half-mode substrate integrated waveguide) antenna made of textile materials. Resonant modes radiating through the open walls and slots of a half-diamond cavity with two slots cut in the top plane are excited by means of the innovative topology. The symmetry plane of the cavity is used as a virtual magnetic wall to promote miniaturization while maintaining performance, dividing the cavity in half. To adjust the dual resonant frequencies, additional size reduction is achieved by optimizing slot diameters and shorting pins in the upper cavity half. Based on the intended resonant frequencies, the design strategy first determines the initial cavity dimensions. Next, using 3D EM simulations, characteristics like cavity width and slot positions/lengths are optimized. Expanded rubber protective foam substrate, conductive textile planes, and brass eyelet vias are used in the manufactured prototype. Simulations are validated by measurements, which reveal -10 dB impedance bandwidths of 5.1% at 5.8 GHz and 4.9% at 2.4 GHz. The radiation patterns show good agreement with the predictions, with radiation efficiency of 72.8%/85.6% in the corresponding bands and maximum actual gains of 4.1/5.8 db. Under bending down to 40mm radii, the antenna retains stable impedance matching and, when worn on a human subject, stable on-body performance with only minor pattern distortion. SAR values that are calculated to be less than 1.6 W/kg across 1g of tissue indicate compliance with safety regulations. This textile HMSIW antenna's dual-band, small, resilient, and efficient on-body radiation qualities make it a great choice for wearable applications [4].

Zhen Yu *et al.* (2021) created a small, multiband microstrip antenna that was modeled after the conventional Chinese window pane design. In order to increase the electrical length and enable four operating bands at 1.6, 2.35, 3.8, and 5.85 GHz for GPS, WLAN, LTE, 5G, and other wireless services, the circular radiating patch comprises carefully arranged slits in this unique shape. The antenna, which is FR-4-fabricated, achieves radiation efficiencies of 45-81%, observed gains of 0.5-5.9 dB, and -10 dB impedance bandwidths of 12-36% across the bands. The suggested design makes use of the conventional window pane structure to provide a wideband, compact, low-profile antenna that is appropriate for portable multi-frequency wireless applications [5].

Hussein Hamed Mahmoud Ghouz *et al.* (2020) created a linear array of two monopole elements (MPA) and a single compact monopole (CMP) as the two compact and broadband microstrip monopole antenna designs. In order to calculate the monopole and substrate dimensions as a function of thickness and dielectric constant, new design equations are presented. The design, simulation, and experimental verification of the CMP and MPA antennas are carried out through the fabrication of prototypes on FR-4 substrate, utilizing CST Studio. The suggested antennas have a broad bandwidth, low VSWR, and omnidirectional (CMP) or directional (MPA) radiation patterns. They also resonate at the frequencies required for Wi-Fi, LTE, and WiMAX applications. While the MPA gives a modest gain of 6 dB and an efficiency of 81% by including a power divider and matching circuit, the CMP designs achieve low gain (2.5-3 dB). The suggested design equations for various substrate materials and antenna characteristics are validated through an extensive parametric investigation. A reasonable degree of consistency is found between the measured and simulated return losses of the manufactured prototypes [6].

Alaa A. Yassin *et al.* (2014) conducted experiments to create a dual-band microstrip patch antenna for WLAN and WiMAX applications, operating at 2.4 GHz and 5.2 GHz. The antenna is made up of a ground plane with a rectangular slit and a rectangular patch with a C-shaped slot. To attain the intended dual-band resonant frequencies, the patch's C-slot and the ground slit are optimized. The IE3D program is used to simulate and design the antenna. To achieve good return loss characteristics at the necessary frequencies, important factors such as patch dimensions, slot dimensions, ground plane size, and slit dimensions are tuned. The simulated findings demonstrate that, at 2.4 GHz and 5.2 GHz, respectively, the suggested antenna achieves impedance bandwidths of 140 MHz (2.38-2.52 GHz) and 640 MHz (5.02-5.66 GHz) with return losses of -23.4 dB and -19.2 db. In the 2.4 GHz and 5.2 GHz bands, the antenna offers good gain and radiation pattern characteristics that are appropriate for WLAN and WiMAX applications [7]. Mohsen Koohestani *et al.* (2023) conducted experiments to create a tiny coplanar-fed planar multiband antenna that rejects the lower WLAN interference band about 5.2 GHz and functions in the Bluetooth (2.4-2.48 GHz) and UWB (3.1-10.6 GHz) frequency bands. Asymmetric coplanar strip (ACS) feedline feeding an inverted right triangular patch monopole with two truncated L-shaped open-ended slits results in a compact size of 20 mm × 10 mm. While the horizontal slit produces a stopband at about 5.2 GHz, the inclined slit introduces a resonance about 2.4 GHz. The working principles of the antenna are revealed by the design evolution process, parametric studies, equivalent circuit model, and characteristic mode analysis. The models are confirmed by experimental results, which show a rejection band from 4.69 to 5.2 GHz and a −10 dB bandwidth from 2.38 to 2.42 GHz and 3.35 to 11 GHz. Throughout the operational bands, the antenna displays virtually omnidirectional radiation patterns, peak achieved gains of 1 to 4.1 dB, and an average efficiency of over 87.3% [8]. Shahidul Islam *et al.* (2019) conducted research on the design of a modified meander line microstrip patch antenna at the 2.4 GHz ISM band with increased bandwidth for Internet of Things (IoT) applications. The antenna is built on a FR-4 substrate and includes a parasitic patch with a shaped ground plane, a connecting patch, and a capacitive load connected to the feed line. Greater gain, bandwidth, and efficiency can be attained with the help of these changes. The ideal dimensions of the ground plane, parasitic patch, connecting patch, and capacitive load are ascertained using parametric research. The constructed antenna displays virtually omnidirectional radiation patterns, a measured realized gain of -0.256 dB, an average efficiency of over 87.3% throughout the operational band, and a measured -10 dB impedance bandwidth of 300 MHz (2.35-2.65 GHz). The antenna's performance is verified using experimental measures, such as power transmission and reception tests and real-time Internet of Things data transmission and reception. The suggested design provides better fractional bandwidth and acceptable gain at a lower cost than current 2.4 GHz microstrip antennas, all the while keeping a small form factor, which makes it a good fit for Internet of Things applications [9].

10.2 Design of Antenna

By using cutting-edge electromagnetic concepts, an antenna can be carefully constructed with the use of High-Frequency Structure Simulator (HFSS) software. Precise modeling, analysis, and optimization are made easier by HFSS, guaranteeing peak performance. Engineers can experiment with different antenna shapes, materials, and configurations using HFSS to satisfy particular needs such radiation pattern, frequency range, and bandwidth. By utilizing its strong simulation capabilities, HFSS makes it possible to adjust antenna parameters for improved radiation characteristics and efficiency. Engineers may speed up the design process and create highly effective antennas for a variety of applications, such as radar systems and wireless communications, by utilizing HFSS's modeling environment.

10.2.1 Design and Results at Primary Level of Antenna

Primary level of antenna design and results is provided in Figure 10.1. Antenna dimensions, substrate qualities, and ground and patch sizes at the initial design phase. The antenna base is defined by the ground dimensions (x=44, y=40), but the radiation characteristics are determined by the patch, which is usually smaller. The thickness of the material is detailed by the substrate dimensions (x=44, y=40, z=0.2), which affect antenna performance. These requirements, which establish parameters such as resonance frequency, impedance matching, and radiation pattern, serve as the basis for the building of antennas. This stage's considerations guarantee effective signal transmission and reception, laying the framework for the phases of testing and optimization that follow.

10.2.2 Design and Results at Secondary Level of Antenna

Secondary level of antenna design and results is provided in Figure 10.2. Substantial consideration is devoted to aspects including substrate material,

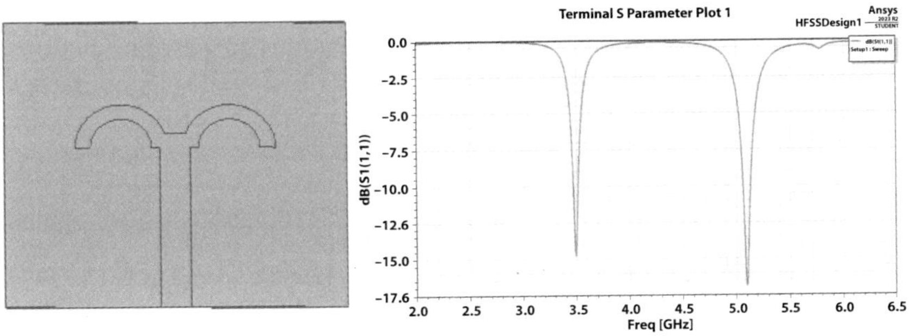

Figure 10.1 Primary level of antenna.

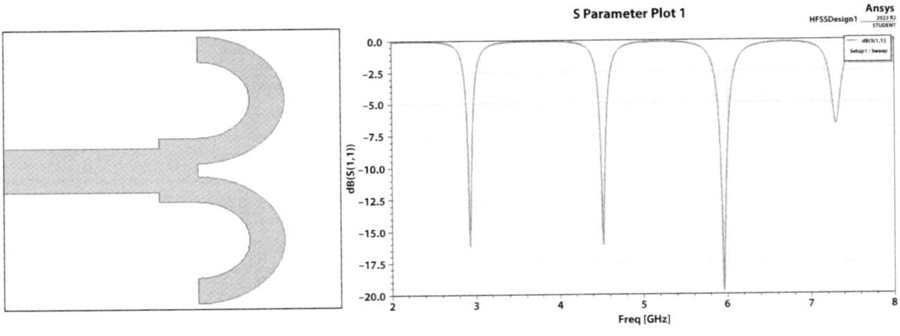

Figure 10.2 Secondary level of antenna.

patch geometry, and ground structure in the secondary stage of antenna design. Following extensive simulation and optimization, Voltage Standing Wave Ratio (VSWR) measurements and S11 polar plots are used to examine the results. These illustrations provide information on the resistance properties and impedance identical of the antenna over its operational frequency range. The antenna's low S11 and VSWR values guarantee effective power transfer and low signal reflections, which improves the antenna's dependability and performance in practical applications.

10.3 Actual Design of Antenna

Actual design of antenna is provided in Figure 10.3. Consider utilizing simulation software like HFSS to construct an antenna with stated dimensions of ground and substrate (x=44, y=40) and (x=44, y=40, z=0.2), respectively. Antenna structural modeling and simulation are made possible by these technologies. Once the antenna is designed, plot the S11 parameter to examine the reflection coefficient and simulate the antenna's performance. S11 shows the amount of power that the antenna reflects back. By analyzing this parameter, antenna performance can be optimized for effective signal transmission and reception. The outcomes of these simulations shed light on antenna behavior and help refine for the required parameters.

10.4 Results of Antenna

Final result of the antennas is provided in Figure 10.4. Performance demonstrates its adaptability to a variety of uses. Wi-Fi, Bluetooth, Zigbee

Figure 10.3 Actual design of antenna.

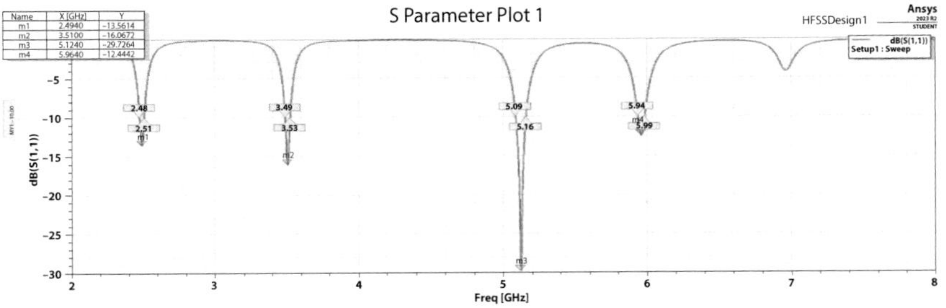

Figure 10.4 Results of antenna through S11 parameter.

(2.48 to 2.51GHz), 5G wireless communication, and satellite connection all function at their best with it. In addition, it can enable WLAN, Wi-Fi, and Fixed Satellite Services (FSS) in the 5.09 to 5.16 GHz band in addition to military and defense communication (3.49 to 3.53 GHz). Furthermore, applications operating in the 5.94 to 5.99 GHz frequency range, such as WLAN, FSS, and radar systems, indicate its efficacy. Its broad interoperability highlights how well-suited it is for many radar and communication applications.

Antenna results VSWR (Voltage Standing Wave Ratio) characteristic is provided in Figure 10.5, which measures the effectiveness of impedance matching, which is essential for the quality of signal transmission. Excellent impedance matching, reduced signal reflections, and maximum power transfer are indicated by a VSWR near 1. Higher VSWR levels, on the other hand, indicate inadequate impedance matching, which can result in signal loss and even device damage. Antenna designers determine performance across operating frequencies by measuring VSWR, which guarantees the best possible communication dependability. Using VSWR data

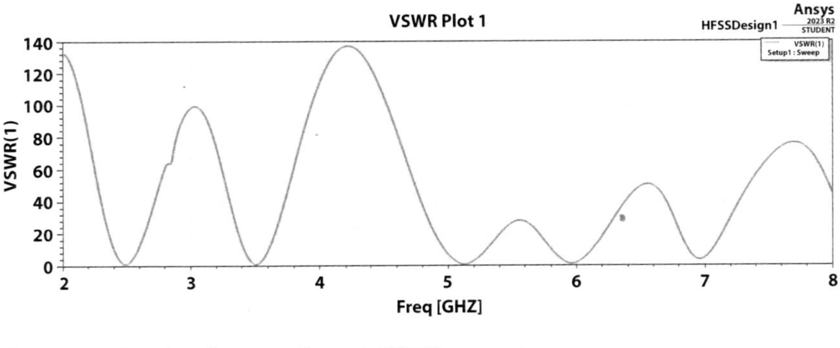

Figure 10.5 Results of antenna through VSWR parameter.

to fine-tune antenna designs and matching networks maximizes efficiency and reduces signal degradation, which is important for wireless networking, radar, and telecommunications applications.

10.4.1 Mathematical Analysis

Understanding factors like reflection coefficient, return loss, and VSWR (Voltage Standing Wave Ratio), which are essential for assessing antenna performance, is part of the mathematical study of antennas. Table 10.1 proposed antenna design parameters.

$$\text{Reflection coefficient } (\Gamma) = \frac{VSWR-1}{VSWR+1}$$

$$\text{Return loss} = \text{-20Log10 } (\Gamma)$$

$$\text{VSWR} = \frac{1+|\Gamma|}{1-|\Gamma|}$$

Whereas, Γ is the Reflection coefficient.

10.4.2 3D Polar Plot

3D polar plot diagrams are provided in Figure 10.6. When designing antennas, a three-dimensional polar plot offers a thorough representation of the radiation pattern. It provides information about the antenna's directional qualities and beam forming capabilities by displaying the radiation characteristics of the antenna across azimuth (horizontal plane) and elevation (vertical plane) angles is shown in Table 10.1. 3D polar plots are used by engineers to evaluate coverage patterns, study antenna performance, and improve designs for particular uses, like satellite systems, radar, and

Table 10.1 Parameters to identify antenna design.

S. no.	Parameter	Values
1.	Reflection coefficient	0.032
2.	Return loss	-29db
3.	VSWR	1.0675

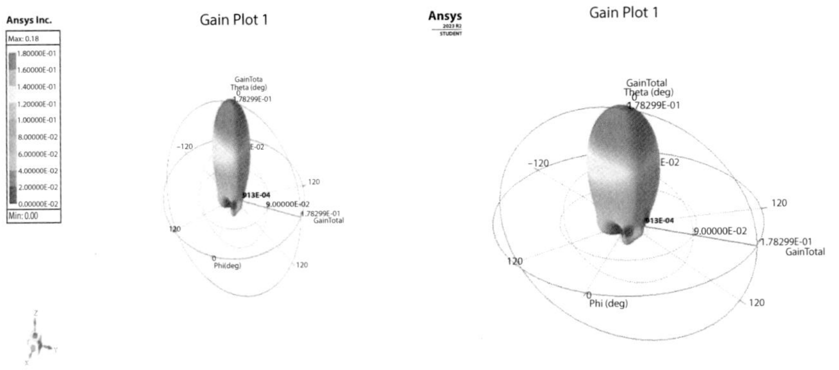

Figure 10.6 3D Polar plot of antenna.

wireless communication. Through the visualization of radiation patterns in three dimensions, antenna designers are able to optimize key characteristics like as gain, directivity, and beam width, which in turn guarantee effective transmission and reception of signals in practical situations.

10.5 Conclusions

- Modern communication systems require a breakthrough in versatility and performance across multiple frequency bands, which the Multi-Band Self-Grounding Antenna for wireless technologies offers. Throughout its operational frequencies, this antenna guarantees excellent impedance matching and little signal loss thanks to its 1.0675 VSWR, 0.032 reflection coefficient, and -29dB return loss.
- It supports Wi-Fi, Bluetooth, and Zigbee applications and spans 2.48 to 2.51 GHz, enabling smooth connectivity in a variety of wireless situations. Furthermore, its coverage includes satellite communication bands that are essential for worldwide connectivity as well as the 5G wireless spectrum, which is essential for next-generation communications.
- This antenna excels with its coverage from 3.49 to 3.53 GHz, ensuring safe and resilient communication channels, which is important in military and defense applications where strong and reliable communication is essential. Moreover, it can enable high-speed data transfer and network connectivity

on Wi-Fi, WLAN, and Fixed Satellite Services (FSS) frequencies ranging from 5.09 to 5.16 GHz.

- Furthermore, the 5.94 to 5.99 GHz frequency range of the antenna is perfect for WLAN, FSS, and radar systems, offering improved radar detection capabilities and enabling vital radar applications.
- Conclusively, the Multi-Band Self-Grounding Antenna provides an all-encompassing resolution for an extensive array of wireless technologies, guaranteeing peak efficiency, dependability, and conformity throughout heterogeneous communication channels, encompassing civilian, business, and military uses. Because of its remarkable features, it is the best option for contemporary communication systems where effectiveness, adaptability, and flexibility are critical.

References

1. Likitha, T., Ashok Kumar, S., Shanmuganantham, T., Design of Circularly Polarized CPW Fed Antenna for ISM band applications, *IEEE Access*, 21, 1–8, 2018, Doi: https://doi.org/10.1109/ICEDSS.2018.8544302.
2. Gao, G.-P., Yang, C., Hu, B., Zhang, R.-F., Wang, S.-F., A Wearable PIFA with an All-Textile Metasurface for 5 GHz WBAN applications. *IEEE Antenn. Wirel. Pr. Lett.*, 18, 2, 288–292 2018, Doi: https://doi.org/10.1109/LAWP.2018.2889117.
3. Zhang, J., Yan, S., Vandenbosch, A.E., A Miniature Feeding Network for Aperture-Coupled Wearable Antennas. *IEEE Trans. Antenn. Propag.*, 65, 5, 2650–2654 2017, Doi: https://doi.org/10.1109/TAP.2017.2677262.
4. Agneesssens, S. and Rogier, H., Compact Half Diamond Dual-Band Textile HMSIW On-Body Antenna. *IEEE Trans. Antenn. Propag.*, 62, 5, 2374–2381, 2014, Doi: https://doi.org/10.1109/TAP.2014.2308526.
5. Yu, Z., Lin, Z., Ran, X., Li, Y., Liang, B., Wang, X., A Novel Pane Structure Multiband Microstrip Antenna for 2G/3G/4G/5G/Wlan/Navigation Applications. *Int. J. Antenn. Propag.*, 2021, 1, 1–15, 2021. Doi: https://doi.org/10.1155/2021/5567417.
6. Ghouz, H.H.M., Sree, M.F.A., Ibrahim, M.A., Novel Wideband Microstrip Monopole Antenna Designs foe Wi-Fi/LTE/WiMAX devices. *IEEE Access*, 9532–9539, 2020, 8, Doi: https://doi.org/10.1109/ACCESS.2019.2963644.
7. Yassin, A.A., Saeed, R.A., Mokhtar, R.A., Dual-Band Microstrip Patch Antenna Design Using C-slot for Wi-Fi and WiMAX Applications, Doi: https://doi.org/10.1109/ICCCE.2014.72.

8. Koohestani, M., Azadi-Tinat, N., Skrivervik, A.K., Compact Slit-Loaded ACS-Fed Monopole Antenna for Bluetooth and UWB Systems with WLAN Band-Stop Capability. IEEE Access, 11, 7540–7550, 2023, Doi: https://doi.org/10.1109/ACCESS.2023.3238577.
9. Islam, M.S., Islam, M.T., Ullah, M.D.A., Beng, G.K., Amin, N., Misran, N., A Modified Meander Line Microstrip Patch Antenna with Enhanced Bandwidth for 2.4Ghz ISM-Band Internet of Things (IOT) Applications. *IEEE Access*, 7, 127850–127861, 2019. Doi: https://doi.org/10.1109/ACCESS.2019.2940049.

11

Navigating Network Security: A Study on Contemporary Anomaly Detection Technologies

Sai Ramya*, **Smera C. and Sandeep J.**

Dept of Computer Science, Christ (Deemed to be University), Bengaluru, India

Abstract

In an era that has been overtaken by digital connectivity, the fact that networks are the center of modern commerce and the operation of life is more than ever evident. And it stands to reason that ensuring proper management of these networks is cardinal especially during the explosion of network attacks and cybersecurity incidents. Security of networks is a high priority, and system intrusion detection is one of the most important tools used for this purpose. The paper discusses various approaches that operate from the classical clustering techniques to the cutting-edge methods integrating blockchain, autoencoders, and graph neural networks. The advised technique supports a holistic and formative model that integrates the contributions of the already accumulated literature. The approach involves combining techniques from various domains such as cloud security, machine learning, and intrusion detection systems. Research is summed up by pinpointing the key emphasis taken to deal with the dynamic nature of network security through cross-functional thinking, offering the prospect of the future in the face of dynamic cyber threats.

Keywords: Blockchain, anomaly detection, cyber security, IDS, technologies in anomaly detection, intrusion detection system, network monitoring system, network security

**Corresponding author*: saiamya816@gmail.com

Budati Anil Kumar, Singamaneni Kranthi Kumar and Li Xingwang (eds.) Quantum Computing Models for Cybersecurity and Wireless Communications, (183–200) © 2025 Scrivener Publishing LLC

11.1 Introduction

In an age defined by digital connectivity, network infrastructure has evolved into the underpinning of modern life and business operations. The dependency on networks to facilitate communication, exchanging data, and various online services and transactions was unknown to the world before. Computer networks are connecting millions of computers and computer users throughout the world [1]. The network has become an infrastructure for many applications that affect our daily lives. It is very important that the computer network needs to be managed properly [1]. In recent years, computer communication networks have grown dramatically both in size and complexity [2]. Moreover, they comprise heterogeneous multi-vendor environments [2]. Network monitoring provides the information necessary for network management. It is important to find network trends and locate network problems quickly [3]. Network monitoring guides network operators in understanding the current behavior of a network [4]. Therefore, accurate and efficient monitoring is vital to ensure that the network operates according to the intended behavior and then to troubleshoot any deviations. However, the practice of network monitoring largely depends on manual operations, and thus, enterprises spend a significant portion of their budgets on the workforce that monitors their networks [4].

Computer security has become a necessity due to the proliferation of information technologies in everyday life. The mass usage of computerized systems has given rise to critical threats [5]. Despite increased research in the security domain, it has yet to be mitigated [5]. The increase in network attacks in terms of coverage, intensity, and aggressiveness is one of the most rapidly increasing challenges [6]. The Centre for Strategic and International Studies published more than 800 major cybersecurity incidents that occurred between 2005 and 2021 [7]. Figure 11.1 provides an overview of the frequency of major incidents, showing that over the period from 2005 to 2021, there were over 800 significant cybersecurity incidents.

In recent years, several significant network security incidents have captured the attention of the cybersecurity community. In 2018, the GitHub DDoS Attack demonstrated a unique threat, exploiting a network amplification technique using open Memcached servers, overwhelming GitHub's network infrastructure [8]. Additionally, the Cloudflare Outage in July 2020 highlighted the consequences of unintentional network anomalies caused by a routing error, disrupting access to numerous websites [9]. The SolarWinds Supply Chain Attack of 2020 stands out as a highly sophisticated supply chain compromise, where threat actors infiltrated SolarWinds'

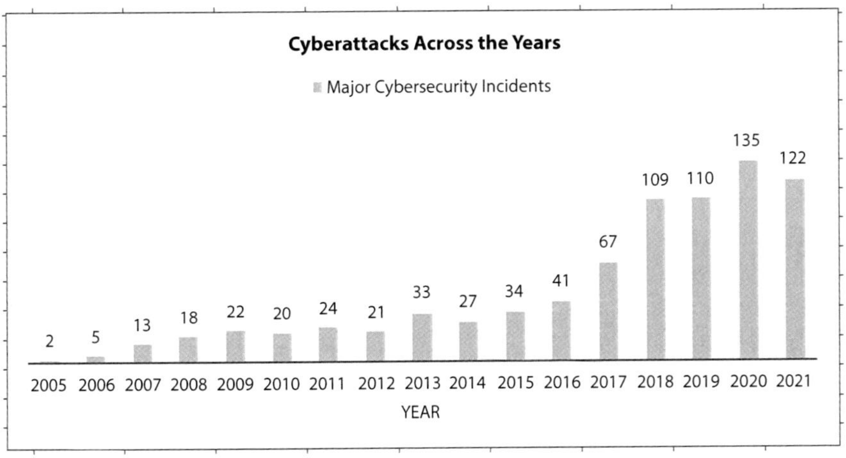

Figure 11.1 Major cybersecurity incidents.

Orion platform updates, compromising the security of numerous organizations, including government agencies and major corporations [10]. The Colonial Pipeline Ransomware Attack in 2021 brought attention to the critical impact of ransomware on essential infrastructure, as Dark Side, a ransomware group, disrupted the fuel supply along the U.S. East Coast, leading to gas shortages [11]. To avoid re-occurrence of incidents such as these, anomaly detection is crucial.

Anomalies are irregular patterns in data that don't match typical patterns. They are generated by a variety of abnormal activities, e.g., credit card fraud, mobile phone fraud, cyber-attacks, etc., which are significant to data analysts. An important aspect of anomaly detection is the nature of the anomaly. The anomalies in data translations are significant and often critical [12]. One of the first tasks envisioned by researchers in creating an anomaly detection model is the correct identification and definition of the problem statement [13]. This means there must be prior knowledge about what type of anomaly researchers would deal with.

Anomalies, meaning departures from regular network functioning patterns, can indicate different cybersecurity threats, data breaches, or operational problems. Through the use of anomaly detection mechanisms, it is possible for organizations to respond to suspicious activities very fast, which would enable them to curb cyber-attacks, protect data which is sensitive and to restore the stability of the network operations. This article will be mainly focusing on the different type of technologies and their techniques used to detect anomaly in the network.

11.2 Related Work

Among Ahmed, Mohiuddin *et al.* different peculiarities in the detection of an assault are the most interesting, where the accuracy of labeled output has been found superior to score-based outputs. This shows that clusters and information theory-based methods also be good in this situation generally; but mostly will have better performance in DoS attack identification as they work well because of their speed. Concerning the calculation complexity, linear methods are possible candidates, especially in dropping a factor of the order of fitting distribution. Both clustering and classifier methods are characterized by the presence of a quadratic complexity, while info theory approaches are mostly associated with exponential ones. The output styles where clustering-based and information theory-based excels, clustering outperforms other DoS detections in terms of time and space complexity. Clustering and classification also are oriented in typical of DoS attacks and statistical methods are having a tendency toward rare when compared to R2L and U2R attacks. Even though statistic techniques have a low complexity, they are applicable for no defense detection task. Clustering is a type of unsupervised learning that doesn't need any pre-labeled data and exhibits superior performance to other techniques in several key aspects [5].

A theoretical understanding and a comparative analysis of various techniques dealing with the problem of anomaly detection presented by Gilberto Fernandes Jr *et al.* put anomalies in two groups including point, collective and contextual based on their nature and then further in groups consisting of operational events (like flash crowd), measurement anomalies, and network attacks depending on their causal aspect. Much of the review goes to show that the detection of anomalies plays very significant role in the evolution of efficient Intrusion Detection Systems (IDS). As for the question, several IDS types are mentioned where anomaly-based detection comes on top as it is the one that can detect both known as well as unknown anomalies dynamically. By thoroughly analyzing present research, the study provides a diverse journey, containing not only simple methods but also complex systems, each offering specific benefits and getting rid of certain issues. The classification methods of sensors are known for their high detection rate, but the constraints imposed by assumptions and resources, on the other hand clustering method, is stable but time-consuming due to the measure of proximity and reliance. The importance of a behavioral science trial among many test approaches for assessing the suitability for solving certain problems is emphasized by the test. Apart from that, the research has pointed out the most imperative knowledge gap in field which is concerning the lack of standard updated labeled datasets. Thus, the experience shows that such kind of future research must be regarded worth doing the investment. The questionnaire bring out the present impediments and the recommendations for making such schemes easy to implement and widespread [13].

Focusing on the study towards Intrusion Detection Systems (IDS) and Blockchain Technology on their Common Ground. Mang *et al.* dig into the various facts of how intrusion detection and blockchain work hand in hand as blockchain's distributed and immutable attributes strengthen identification security. The study goes into considerable detail about the blending blockchain with the intrusion detection frameworks, the cryptographic techniques used, the consensus mechanisms and the resultant problems and implications of the confluence of these technologies. The main concern is about the benefits of blockchain's immutability and distributed ledger, regarding these features as the means to guarantee the trustworthiness of IDS data, thus preventing data manipulation or compromise. In addition to that, the issue of smart contract implementation for automatic mechanism of response within IDS, is also considered in the article [14].

Zhaomin Chen *et al.* provide an exhaustive review paper on autoencoder-procedures which are widely used in the network anomaly domain. Autoencoders, being one of the unsupervised learning models that have earned the top position, are able to detect and describe how data follows a specific pattern thereby making them ideal for spotting network behavior. This research paper is aimed at providing an overview of the existing reconstruction algorithms that autoencoders make use of for detecting the network anomalies, mentioning the topological and architectural frameworks employed. The article expands on pros and cons relevant to autoencoder models, considering for example interpretability vs. scalability, and the influence of hyper parameter choices. The analysis will enhance the knowledge of the benefits of the autoencoder-based method in the detection of anomalies in networks [15].

An attempt to enhance the rapidly growing field of network security by looking into the utilization of Recurrent Neural Networks (RNNs) for the identification of network traffic abnormalities by Benjamin J. Radford and colleagues. The study presented in the paper is supposed to dive deep into the previous research carried out on RNNs used for network traffic abnormalities detection. RNNs, through their unique capacity of modeling sequential dependencies, are suited for expressing the varying nature of network traffic patterns. The paper is based on the application of RNNs and discusses the model design, training methodology, and performance evaluation processes. The research gives the pros and cons of RNN-based techniques in terms of network security. Primarily, it is aimed at giving a detailed insight into how the latest RNNs technology can be employed to detect the network anomalies for the sake of the security measures performing in the network infrastructure [16].

Manisha Rani *et al.* contend to the discussion on cloud security by carrying out a study which apprehends the entire review of the existing researches on Intrusion Detection Systems (IDS) which is specifically suited for the kind of problems presented by cloud computing systems. The multi-tenant cloud infrastructures with dynamic and shared characteristics having motivated them to develop various IDS architecture, algorithms, and deployment strategies with an aim to detect and control security threats in the cloud. This research addresses the key issues of diagnostic systems such as effectiveness of different intrusion detection techniques, scalability, and the cloud technology's evolutionary trends on intrusion detection. It is the objective that it presents a complete review of the cloud-based intrusion detection which also pursues to strengthen the security system in the cloud environments [17].

An attempt to carry out extensive work on the subject of incorporating machine learning techniques into the field of network intrusion detection will be done. Sumaiya Thaseen I and al. extensively analyze different ML algorithms that can be used to find out intrusions and also react appropriately on networked systems. This output is expected to cover a range of machine learning categories, for instance, supervised algorithms like Support Vector Machines and Random Forests are included, as well as unsupervised techniques such as clustering and outliers detection, deep learning methods are also covered. The paper covers the topics on feature selection, model training, and evaluation of the detection performance parameters. The study has covered the in-depth comprehension on utilizing machine learning for network intrusion detection and also shown machine learning various algorithms mitigating and predicting anomalies would be effective. The predicting algorithms for machine learning can fail considering anomalies will not be in operation just within the boundaries of the parameters for the forecasting [18].

A study on the evolving landscape of Generative Adversarial Networks (GANs) by Willone Lim *et al.*, targeted anomaly detection for networking security is soon going to be released [19]. The study reviews and discusses the use of GANs to better detect anomalies in security systems, discussing the state of current research, employed methodologies, and the effectiveness of GANs based approaches. GANs are known as one of the most popular tools when it comes to generating fake data. Therefore, these

AI systems are increasingly identified as the solution to detect new and advanced malicious network security issues. On the other hand, the study discusses the complications and possibilities of using GANs in security networking, which will have model interpretability, scalability, and adaptation to the ever changing threats as its focus points. Additionally, the focus is to give a practical side of future findings with the potential routes for new research along with the insertion of GANs to an excellent anomaly detection building [19].

To elucidate the landscape of anomaly detection techniques in the realm of cloud computing. Katerina Mitropoulou *et al.* undertake a study that explores the integration of Knowledge Graph Embedding, a method capturing semantic relationships, with machine learning mechanisms for enhanced anomaly detection capabilities. have made a study which involved the integration of the Knowledge Graph Embedding, a method capturing semantic relationships with machine learning techniques for the purpose of employing it for anomaly detection. The study also helps in improving the existing anomaly detection systems to deal with those problems related to cloud computing environment which include dynamic scalability and scalability of cloud infrastructure. Furthermore, owing to the synergetic nature of applied knowledge graph embedding and machine learning, cloud computing security systems become enhanced which can be attributed to the augmenting of anomaly detection mechanisms [20].

Waseem Ullah *et al.* have carried out a large study with the objective of defining and explaining the environment/natural setting (ecosystem) where weakly supervised anomaly techniques can be deployed on the graph neural networks (GNNs). The assessment reviews a collection of studies that is dealing with anomaly-finding approaches and techniques, with particular emphasis on the GNNs as they appear especially adequate for picking out small peculiarities in complex multi-relational structures. However, authors focus on feature extractors in weakly supervised environments, which directly relies on the availability of the limited labeled anomaly samples. Therefore, they emphasize the importance of pushing forward the anomaly detection methods specifically in those poorly supervised scenarios. Coming from this literature review, the state-of-the-art methods, obstacles, and development of weak supervision in anomaly detection with the use of graph neural networks is proposed to be fully and comprehensively comprehended which will act as the basis for their AD-Graph model [21].

In the process to navigate through a diverse array of research, encompassing methodologies, algorithms, and frameworks that address the unique challenges associated with public sector networks. Łukasz Wawrowski *et al.*

touch base on topics such as network security, intrusion detection, and anomaly detection techniques, shedding light on approaches that are well-suited for the distinctive characteristics and requirements of public institutions. They also establish a robust foundation for their proposed anomaly detection module. Their study also offers a nuanced understanding of the state-of-the-art in anomaly detection, enabling their work within the broader context of network security in public institutions and contribute to the development of tailored and effective solutions for enhanced network traffic monitoring [22].

have conducted an assiduous research that is intended to elucidate the state-of-the-art progress in anomaly detection using the graph neural networks (GNNs) as its major application. They are devoting to many purposes including cybersecurity, social network analysis, and network traffic monitoring which are just some of the examples. They sweep on the subtlety of GNNs considering their ability of acquiring the complicated association within graph-structured information as it is a crucial part of an executable anomaly detection Their study provides a detailed analysis of the strengths and limitations associated with GNNs, offering insights into their performance in different contexts and shedding light on challenges that may arise. This provide review serves as the groundwork for their proposed approach, positioning their research within the broader landscape of anomaly detection methodologies that leverage the power of graph neural networks [23].

Mahmoud Said Elsayed *et al.* conduct a comprehensive study that delves into the intricate field of network anomaly detection, with a specific emphasis on the integration of Long Short-Term Memory (LSTM) based autoencoders. They navigate through a myriad of studies, investigating the role of recurrent neural networks, particularly LSTMs, in capturing the temporal dependencies inherent in sequential network data. This extensive review scrutinizes various methodological aspects, including architectural configurations, training methodologies, and performance evaluation metrics employed in prior research efforts. They also critically analyze the strengths and potential challenges associated with LSTM-based autoencoders, elucidating their efficacy in discerning anomalies within the dynamic landscape of network behavior. Their study shows a detailed compass, guiding us in positioning their proposed approach for anomaly detection in network security. This nuanced exploration contributes significant depth to the understanding of contemporary techniques, providing a robust foundation for the integration of LSTM-based autoencoders as a sophisticated solution for enhancing the precision and efficiency of network anomaly detection systems [24].

In a comprehensive study to dissect the intricacies of anomaly detection, specifically within the realm of deep weakly-supervised learning. Guansong Pang *et al.* engage to navigate through a diverse array of studies, spanning various methodologies and models employed in the context of anomaly detection, with a pronounced emphasis on leveraging deep learning techniques in scenarios where labeled anomaly data is scarce. It critically analyses the strengths and limitations of existing approaches, shedding light on the challenges inherent in weakly-supervised settings and the strategies devised to overcome them. Additionally, they explore the evolution of deep weakly-supervised anomaly detection, considering the advancements, trends, and emerging paradigms in this dynamic field. Furthermore, the review discusses on the practical applicability of these techniques across diverse domains, highlighting their adaptability to real-world scenarios. Deep weakly-supervised anomaly detection serves as a robust foundation for the methodology, contributing valuable insights and advancements to the ongoing discourse on refining and enhancing anomaly detection systems through the integration of deep learning approaches under weakly-supervised conditions [25].

Meenal Jain *et al.* embark on a meticulous study that traverses the intricate landscape of concept drift detection techniques, with a particular focus on their application in the domain of network anomaly detection. The study conducts extensive array of studies, systematically exploring various methodologies and models employed in concept drift detection, as well as advancements related to network anomaly identification. The study evaluates existing approaches, illuminating the strengths and limitations inherent in individual techniques. Given the hybrid nature of the proposed methodology, integrating K-Means clustering and Support Vector Machines (SVM), the research conducts a thorough examination of prior research that has leveraged these methods for concept drift detection and anomaly detection, respectively. This scrutiny includes an in-depth analysis of the synergy between clustering and SVM-based techniques, aiming to discern their complementarity in addressing the challenges posed by dynamic network environments. Their study not only positions the work within the broader context of anomaly detection but also contributes invaluable insights to the development of adaptive techniques that effectively address the concept drift phenomenon in dynamic network scenarios environments [26].

A study to unravel the intricate landscape of self-supervised learning methodologies, specifically within the dynamic domain of graph anomaly detection. Y. Zheng *et al.* delve to meticulously traverse a diverse array of studies, systematically exploring the rich tapestry of methodologies, models, and advancements that employ self-supervised learning techniques for the detection of anomalies within complex graph structures. The comprehensive review is anticipated to critically assess existing approaches, providing an insightful analysis of the strengths and limitations associated with generative and contrastive self-supervised learning methods in the context of graph-based anomaly detection. The paper proposes generative and contrastive self-supervised learning methodology. This detailed review is expected to shed light on the unique strengths of the collaborative effort, showcasing how the integration of diverse perspectives enriches the proposed approach. This meticulous exploration serves as a robust foundation for their proposed methodology, contributing novel perspectives and strategies to the ongoing discourse on advancing anomaly detection techniques within the intricate context of graph data [27].

For presenting a sophisticated analysis of the landscape surrounding fuzzy logic-based methodologies in the realm of detecting Distributed Denial of Service (DDoS) attacks and anomalies in network traffic. Danial Javaheri *et al.* embark on a meticulous and comprehensive study, adeptly navigate through a diverse array of studies, systematically classifying and evaluating the myriad fuzzy logic-based techniques employed for the classification and mitigation of DDoS attacks, as well as the detection of anomalies in intricate network traffic patterns. This extensive study is anticipated to go beyond a mere categorization of methods, providing a nuanced discussion on the strengths and limitations inherent in the existing approaches. Their paper offers critical insights into the evolving cybersecurity landscape, shedding light on the adaptive nature of DDoS attacks and the challenges associated with anomaly detection in network traffic. Moreover, the review is expected to extend its purview to encompass a forward-looking perspective, elucidating potential future directions and advancements in the realm of fuzzy logic-based methodologies. This approach not only demonstrates the awareness of the dynamic cybersecurity landscape but also positions their work as a catalyst for future research. The fuzzy logic-based detection methods provide a robust foundation for their research paper [28].

Indrajit Mukherjee *et al.* embark on a comprehensive and detailed study, providing a sophisticated analysis of the multifaceted domain of anomaly detection within the context of Internet of Things (IoT) networks. The study navigates through a diverse array of studies, systematically categorizing and evaluating various simulations and modeling approaches employed for anomaly detection in the intricate and dynamic IoT environment. This study delves into the realm of machine learning techniques, exploring how these methodologies are harnessed to discern anomalies amid the heterogeneity of IoT networks. Also critically assess existing methodologies, offering a nuanced understanding of the strengths and limitations inherent

Table 11.1 Key features of anomaly detection study.

Authors	**Technology**	**Output style**
Gilberto Fernandes Jr *et al.* [13]	IDS Categorization	Classif. - High rates, Cluster. - Stability. Open issues: No standard labeled dataset.
Meng *et al.* [14]	Blockchain, IDS Frameworks	Blockchain boosts IDS trust. Smart contracts automate responses.
Zhaomin Chen *et al.* [15]	Autoencoder Techniques	Autoencoders for effective anomaly detection. Issues: Model interpretability, scalability.
Manisha Rani *et al.* [17]	ML Algorithms	ML for efficient anomaly detection, effectiveness tied to parameter bounds.
Willone Lim *et al.* [19]	Generative Adversarial Networks	GANs use synthetic data for novel threat identification. Challenges: Model interpretability, scalability.
Katerina Mitropoulou *et al.* [20]	Knowledge Graph, ML Mechanisms	Synergy of knowledge graph and ML for enhanced cloud anomaly detection.
Waseem Ullah *et al.* [21]	Autoencoder-based GNNs	Autoencoder-based GNNs excel in capturing relationships for weakly supervised anomaly detection.
Mahmoud Said Elsayed *et al.* [24]	LSTM-based Autoencoders	LSTM-based autoencoders capture temporal dependencies for precise anomaly detection.
Lingqiang Xie *et al.* [23]	Graph Neural Networks (GNNs)	GNNs capture relationships for effective anomaly detection. Study on strengths and limitations.
Meenal Jain *et al.* [26]	Concept Drift Detection	Hybrid method (K-Means + SVM) for drift and anomaly detection.

in current approaches. This insightful analysis extends beyond a mere survey, aiming to illuminate the challenges associated with anomaly detection in the unique context of IoT networks. Furthermore, the study explores the interplay between simulation, modeling, and machine learning, shedding light on how these elements synergize to enhance anomaly detection capabilities within the complex IoT landscape [29].

Research on autoencoder technique of network anomaly detection that emphasizes the enhancement of achievement by using NSL-KDD set of data has carried out. W. Xu *et al.* conduct an in-depth array of studies, systematically categorizing and evaluating methodologies and techniques employed in the context of autoencoder-based anomaly detection. The major objective of the study is a multi-layered investigation of the significance of autoencoders in application of security measures in computer networks, with special focus on the NSL-KDD dataset of datasets—a central point of research. The study follows the step-by-step analysis procedures of existing solution., It also offer meaningful ideas into the pros and cons of current methods. It is not only the theory of survey but also aims to penetrate into the substructure of this issue which entails to increase the accuracy in network anomalies detection. The survey also looks into new strategies, developments, and optimizations which have been suggested in earlier research including issues, thus proposing a detailed exploration of this dynamic automated network denial. Not only does the study add weight to their individual research but it also stirs a debate on the general topic of raising the effectiveness of anomaly detection techniques in a real-world scenario especially when assessed against NSL-KDD [30].

In summary, collective body of literature surveyed brings a diverse appreciation of anomaly detection techniques in the space of network security. These studies based on different aspects, including the application of labeled data in attack detection, blockchain and intrusion detection systems integration, are only a part of these studies which provide such insights. Autoencoder-based methods, a widely chosen tool by a few authors, are outlined to be very potent in recreating fine detailed behaviors of networks, refer to Table 11.1. Machine learning in the cloud, RNN techniques, GANs and GNNs are some of the other technologies expand the anomaly detection methodologies.

11.3 Methodology

One of the main features of a successful anomaly detection model is covering the wide range of network behavior's spectrum using a huge and varied dataset. As shown in Figure 11.2, the set of data will go through the

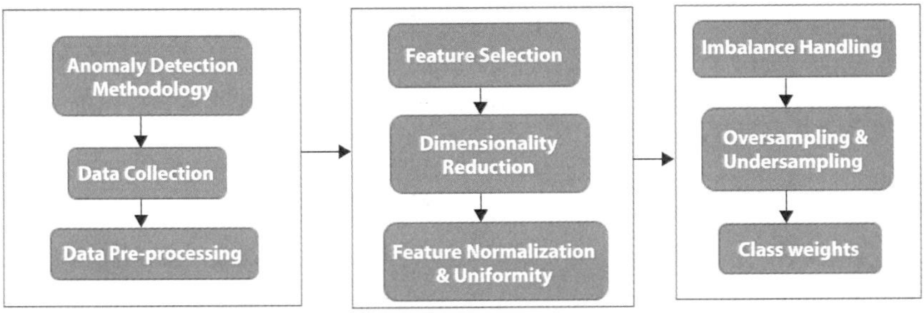

Figure 11.2 Machine learning.

pre-processing stage, which includes handling missing values, normalization of features, and unifying data units to achieve uniform representation. The objective of the anomaly detection models is to find the optimum features that are most sensitive to recognize anomalies. The dimensionality reduction method can implement behaviors like the Principal Component Analysis (PCA) or Information Gain; both can be checked to evaluate their performance. Exploring the over-sampling, under-sampling, or other class weights techniques in the training process would help balance the classification of the network data, which is an innate imbalance of the normal and odd structures.

The model performance is to be optimized by taking a holistic approach towards hyperparameter tuning. Figure 11.3 shows the way extra settings like learning rates, batch sizes, and configurations are set for network architecture by means of cross-validation. The diverse set of anomaly detection methodologies presented in the literature, explore ensemble techniques to combine the strengths of different models. Investigation of ensemble methods like stacking or bagging can be pursued to reinforce the system's stability and overall efficacy in detecting anomalies.

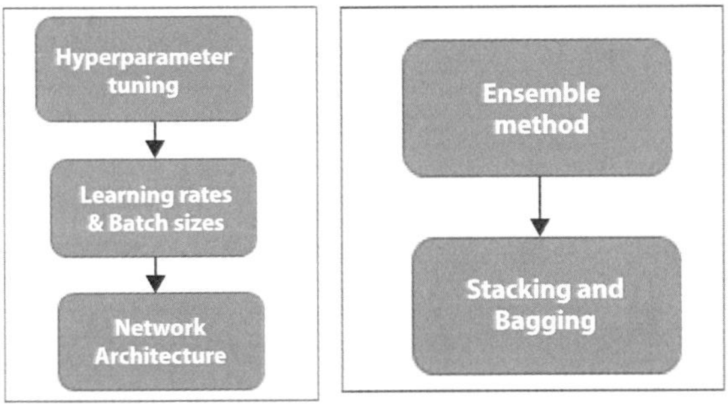

Figure 11.3 Ensemble methods.

Inspired by the intersection of Intrusion Detection Systems (IDS) and Blockchain technology discussed in the literature, explore the potential integration of Blockchain for enhancing the security and trustworthiness of the anomaly detection system. This may involve leveraging the immutability and decentralized nature of Blockchain to secure critical components of the detection infrastructure.

To test the approach appropriately, perform simulations and comparative studies. Figure 11.3 depicts the usual techniques of imitating real-life situations, putting in artificial fluctuations, and evaluating degree of trustworthiness. Performance comparisons will be conducted against state-of-the-art detection methods not only with regard to their accuracy but also false positive rates and the cost of computations. By leveraging autoencoders, recurrent neural networks, graph neural networks, and ensemble techniques, the model aims to address the challenges posed by diverse network behaviors. Besides that, the construction of blockchain methods and solid implementation of simulation tests will guarantee the development of anomaly detection in the emerging zone of network security.

An isolated approach that neglects the use of a diverse dataset and advanced pre-processing techniques may result in a model that lacks the adaptability needed to accurately identify anomalies across various network behaviors.

Overlooking, the integration of Blockchain technology may leave the detection infrastructure vulnerable, lacking the enhanced security and trustworthiness that decentralized and immutable systems can provide. The utilization of a vast and varied dataset, coupled with meticulous pre-processing techniques, establishes a foundation for adaptability to a wide spectrum of network behaviors. The incorporation of dimensionality reduction methods and the proactive management of class imbalance as shown in Figure 11.4 showcase a commitment to feature optimization and model generalization. By including simulations and comparative studies, the proposal ensures thorough testing and validation, solidifying its position as a comprehensive and advanced approach in the evolving landscape of network security.

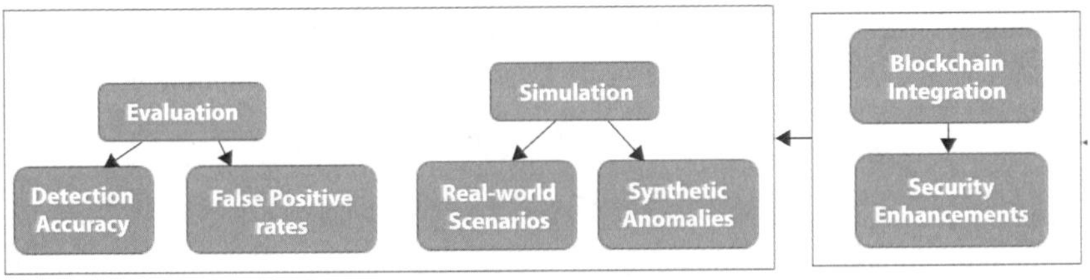

Figure 11.4 Blockchain integration and result analysis.

11.4 Conclusion

This paper provides an extensive exploration of contemporary anomaly detection technologies within the realm of network security, resourcing answers to the present-day pressing challenge of provisions for robust assurances against the ever-changing world of cyber threats. It accurately combines a number of methodologies at the cutting edge of technologies, the majority of which are clustering, classification, blockchain integration techniques, autoencoders, and graph neural networks. A unique classifier is built by integrating multiple techniques that range from linear clustering to cutting-edge approaches like blockchain integration, autoencoders, and graph neural networks. By stressing the fact that adaptation to network behavior fluctuation is so important, the methodology seems to be holding a stand that sits between conventional and contemporary approaches making its framework more holistic and adaptive. Since networks are becoming increasingly more complex and interconnected with time, this study is in agreement that proactive action and adaptive strategy are the most effective anomaly detection strategies. One of the main insights of this research is the importance of the multidisciplinary approach, which is brought in by the application of a variety of research tools. This approach envisions the power of an interdisciplinary approach as well as multiple methods and proposes the use of such perspectives to achieve a comprehensive understanding of the complex challenges in network security.

References

1. Svoboda, J., Ghafir, I., Prenosil, V., Network monitoring approaches: An overview. *Int. J. Adv. Comput. Netw. Secur.- IJCNS*, 5, 88–93, 2015.
2. Abar, S., Konno, S., Kinoshita, T., Autonomous network monitoring system based on agent-mediated network information. *Int. J. Comput. Sci. Netw. Secur.*, 8, 2, 326–333, 2008.
3. Wong, E., Network monitoring fundamentals and standards. *Comput. Sci.*, 29, 3, 43–44, 2000.
4. Lee, S., Levanti, K., Kim, H.S., Network monitoring: Present and future. *Comput. Netw.*, 65, 1–8, 2014.
5. Ahmed, M., Mahmood, A.N., Hu, J., A survey of network anomaly detection techniques. *J. Netw. Comput. Appl.*, 60, 19–31, 2016.
6. Chandola, V., Banerjee, A., Kumar, V., Anomaly detection: A survey. *ACM Comput. Surv. (CSUR)*, 41, 3, 1–58, 2009.

7. Falowo, O.I., Popoola, S., Riep, J., Adewopo, V.A., Koch, J., Threat actors' tenacity to disrupt: Examination of major cybersecurity incidents. *IEEE Access*, 10, 134038–134051, 2022.
8. Chadd, A., DDoS attacks: Past, present and future. *Netw. Secur.*, 2018, 13–15, 2018.
9. John, J., Okonkwo, O., Akawuku, G., Onyagu, C., Detecting and preventing of DDoS attack in cloud computing environment based on hybrid technique (CloudFlare and WAF). *Newport Int. J. Eng. Phys. Sci.*, 3, 28–40, 2023.
10. Yang, J., Lee, Y., McDonald, A., SolarWinds software supply chain security: Better protection with enforced policies and technologies, in: *Software Engineering, Artificial Intelligence, Networking and Parallel/Distributed Computing*. Springer, USA, 2022.
11. Beerman, J., Berent, D., Falter, Z., Bhunia, S., A review of Colonial Pipeline ransomware attack. *IEEE/ACM 23rd International Symposium on Cluster, Cloud and Internet Computing Workshops (CCGRIDW)*, pp. 8–15, 2023.
12. Fischer, F., Mansmann, F., Keim, D.A., Pietzko, S., Waldvogel, M., Large-scale network monitoring for visual analysis of attacks, in: *Visualization for Computer Security*. VizSec 2008. Lecture Notes in Computer Science, vol. 5210, J.R. Goodall, G. Conti, K.L. Ma, (Eds.), Springer, Berlin, Heidelberg, 2008.
13. Fernandes, G., Rodrigues, J.J.P.C., Carvalho, L.F. *et al.*, A comprehensive survey on network anomaly detection. *Telecommun. Syst.*, 70, 447–489, 2019.
14. Meng, W., Tischhauser, E.W., Wang, Q., Wang, Y., Han, J., When intrusion detection meets blockchain technology: A review. *IEEE Access*, 6, 10179–10188, 2018.
15. Chen, Z., Yeo, C.K., Lee, B.S., Lau, C.T., Autoencoder-based network anomaly detection. *2018 Wireless Telecommunications Symposium (WTS)*, pp. 1–5, 2018.
16. Radford, B.J. et al., Network traffic anomaly detection using recurrent neural networks. arXiv preprint arXiv:1803.10769, 2018.
17. Rani, M., A review of intrusion detection system in cloud computing. *Proceedings of International Conference on Sustainable Computing in Science, Technology and Management (SUSCOM)*, Amity University Rajasthan, Jaipur-India, 2019.
18. Sumaiya Thaseen, I., Poorva, B., Ushasree, P.S., Network intrusion detection using machine learning techniques. *2020 International Conference on Emerging Trends in Information Technology and Engineering (IC-ETITE)*, pp. 1–7, 2020.
19. Lim, W., Chek, K.Y.S., Theng, L.B., Lin, C.T.C., Future of generative adversarial networks (GAN) for anomaly detection in network security: A review. *Comput. Secur.*, 139, 103733, 2024.
20. Mitropoulou, K., Kokkinos, P., Soumplis, P., Varvarigos, E., Anomaly detection in cloud computing using knowledge graph embedding and machine learning mechanisms. *J. Grid Comput.*, 22, 1, 6, 2024.

21. Ullah, W., Hussain, T., Min Ullah, F.U., Muhammad, K., Hassaballah, M., Rodrigues, J.J., Albuquerque, V.H.C.D., AD-Graph: Weakly supervised anomaly detection graph neural network. *Int. J. Intell. Syst.*, 2023, 1–12, 2023.
22. Wawrowski, L., Białas, A., Kajzer, A., Kozłowski, A., Kurianowicz, R., Sikora, M., Michalak, M., Anomaly detection module for network traffic monitoring in public institutions. *Sensors*, 23, 6, 2974, 2023.
23. Xie, L., Pi, D., Zhang, X., Chen, J., Luo, Y., Yu, W., Graph neural network approach for anomaly detection. *Measurement*, 180, 109546, 2021.
24. Said Elsayed, M., Le-Khac, N.A., Dev, S., Jurcut, A.D., Network anomaly detection using LSTM based autoencoder. *Proceedings of the 16th ACM Symposium on QoS and Security for Wireless and Mobile Networks*, pp. 37–45, 2020, November.
25. Pang, G., Shen, C., Jin, H., Van Den Hengel, A., Deep weakly-supervised anomaly detection. *Proceedings of the 29th ACM SIGKDD Conference on Knowledge Discovery and Data Mining*, pp. 1795–1807, 2023, August.
26. Jain, M., Kaur, G., Saxena, V., A k-means clustering and SVM based hybrid concept drift detection technique for network anomaly detection. *Expert Syst. Appl.*, 193, 116510, 2022.
27. Zheng, Y., Jin, M., Liu, Y., Chi, L., Phan, K.T., Chen, Y.-P.P., Generative and contrastive self-supervised learning for graph anomaly detection. *IEEE Trans. Knowl. Data Eng.*, 35, 12, 12220–12233, 2023.
28. Javaheri, D., Gorgin, S., Lee, J.-A., Masdari, M., Fuzzy logic-based DDoS attacks and network traffic anomaly detection methods: Classification, overview, and future perspectives. *Inf. Sci.*, 2023.
29. Mukherjee, I., Sahu, N.K., Sahana, S.K., Simulation and modeling for anomaly detection in IoT network using machine learning. *Int. J. Wireless Inf. Netw.*, 30, 173–189, 2023.
30. Xu, W., Jang-Jaccard, W., Singh, A., Wei, Y., Sabrina, F., Improving performance of autoencoder-based network anomaly detection on NSL-KDD dataset. *IEEE Access*, 9, 140136–140146, 2021.

12

File Fragment Classification: A Comprehensive Survey of Research Advances

Teena Mary* **and Sreeja C.S.**

Department of Computer Science, CHRIST (Deemed to be University), Bengaluru, India

Abstract

A crucial task in digital forensics is file fragment classification, which involves classifying file fragments into their respective types based on their content. It is integral to digital forensics and data recovery, where investigators reconstruct and analyze fragmented files to gather evidence in criminal cases, data breaches, or other cybercrimes. This comprehensive survey paper offers insights into the different methodologies used for file fragment classification, including but not restricted to specialized approaches, hierarchical classification, and neural networks. The paper also highlights the challenges in file fragment classification, such as the need for format standardization, limited training data, scalability, and noise and ambiguity. A research gap analysis of the existing literature was conducted, and it was identified that further research could be done to explore the effectiveness of different approaches for file fragment classification, including transfer learning, ensemble methods, and so on.

Keywords: Digital forensics, file fragment classification, content-based analysis, neural network, hierarchical classification

12.1 Introduction

A significant research area in computer forensics and data recovery is file fragment classification. It is the process of categorizing or mapping a

**Corresponding author*: teena.mary@res.christuniversity.in

Budati Anil Kumar, Singamaneni Kranthi Kumar and Li Xingwang (eds.) Quantum Computing Models for Cybersecurity and Wireless Communications, (201–218) © 2025 Scrivener Publishing LLC

portion of data, such as a file fragment or a disk block, to a specific file type or data format. The objective is to determine the file type based on the available data fragments. The classification of file fragments plays a crucial role in the reconstruction and analysis of digital evidence, aiding in the identification, recovery, and organization of fragmented files. It is also used in network security to identify and categorize files or data packets, enabling the detection of malicious or unauthorized content. This survey paper aims to deliver an extensive perspective on the advancements in this domain, from early research to the most recent methodologies employed for file fragment classification.

Classifying file fragments involves developing and implementing techniques to categorize and organize fragmented data based on their salient attributes, including file type, content, and metadata. A deep understanding of file fragments' characteristics and contextual relevance empowers investigators to reconstruct files, extract meaningful information, and attain insights into digital artifacts that substantially contribute to investigations, incident response, and litigation proceedings.

The applications of file fragment classification span diverse domains, encompassing digital forensics, cybersecurity, data recovery, file system analysis, data carving, and information retrieval. In digital forensics, it facilitates the recovery and analysis of evidentiary fragments, enabling investigators to reconstruct files and discern pertinent information. In the context of cybersecurity, it aids in identifying and analyzing fragmented malicious files, thereby facilitating the detection of potential threats and vulnerabilities.

In the early stages of research, the classification of file fragments relied heavily on manual analysis and simple heuristics. Researchers developed techniques to identify and associate file fragments with their respective file types (e.g., JPEG, DOC, PDF) based on specific signatures or patterns. Although effective to some extent, these approaches had to be improved in handling complex fragmentation scenarios and large-scale data sets.

Researchers turned to more sophisticated methods as the field progressed, incorporating machine learning and data mining techniques. These methods use statistical models and algorithms for pattern recognition to automatically categorize file fragments according to their content, metadata, and structural attributes. For instance, some studies have explored the application of support vector machines (SVMs) [1–4], decision trees, and statistical metrics like byte frequency distribution [4], Shannon entropy [5], Hamming weight [1], kurtosis [6], the difference between consecutive byte values (or "rate of change") [7, 8], principal component analysis [9, 10], etc. to achieve higher accuracy in file fragment classification.

Recently, a growing interest has been in leveraging deep learning techniques for file fragment classification. Deep neural networks, such as convolutional neural networks (CNNs) and feed-forward neural networks (FFNNs), have demonstrated remarkable performance in various computer vision and natural language processing tasks [10–19]. Researchers have adapted these architectures to handle file fragment classification by treating fragments as input data and training the networks to learn the underlying patterns and relationships.

Moreover, advancements in data pre-processing techniques have also contributed to the progress in file fragment classification. Researchers have developed efficient algorithms for fragment identification, extraction, and reassembly, enabling more accurate classification and reconstruction of fragmented files. These techniques encompass traditional approaches, such as file carving and data carving, and novel methodologies utilizing advanced clustering and similarity analysis algorithms.

This survey paper will review the existing literature on file fragment classification, including the various techniques proposed over the years. The significant challenges in file fragment classification and future research directions are also discussed. The paper is categorized into five sections. Section 12.2 will overview on the selection criteria and how the paper is organized. Section 12.3 will review the existing literature on file fragment classification followed by a concise summary of the survey findings in Section 12.4. Section 12.5 will discuss the significant challenges in file fragment classification. Ultimately, the paper will draw its conclusions in Section 12.6 and provide directions for future research.

12.2 Methodology

The objective of this section is two-fold. First, it delves deeper into the criteria used for the selection of the papers that are considered as part of the survey. Following that, a brief overview on the organization of the paper is given, which helps understand the logic behind the categorization of the topics.

12.2.1 Selection Criteria

In this survey paper, a diverse search strategy was used to identify relevant research papers from various digital sources. The selection process involved a sampling method, leveraging popular academic databases such as Google Scholar, IEEE Xplore, and reputable journals. The search criteria were deliberately kept broad to encompass a wide spectrum of perspectives, methodologies, and findings within the chosen research domain. Additionally, the inclusion of thesis documents further enriched the dataset, providing insights from academic scholars and graduate researchers. The varied origins of the selected papers contribute to the paper's robustness, encompassing contributions from different research avenues and ensuring a comprehensive analysis of the existing literature in file fragment classification.

12.2.2 Structure of the Paper

The chosen structure for explaining the research in file fragment classification follows a logical progression that facilitates a systematic and thorough investigation of the topic.

The structure begins with signature-based approaches, which serve as a fundamental and widely used technique in file fragment classification. Following signature-based approaches, content-based approaches are introduced, offering insights into analyzing file fragment content, including byte patterns and natural language processing techniques. The subsequent section focuses on deep learning-based approaches, which have gained prominence for their ability to extract complex features and patterns from file fragments. CNNs, transformer models and RNNs have performed exceptionally in various classification tasks. Lastly, the survey paper explores hierarchical classification methods, which provide a structured organization of file fragments into tree structures or taxonomy-based systems. The graphical representation of this concept is illustrated in Figure 12.1.

The logical flow of the survey paper's structure ensures the introduction to foundational concepts before progressing to more advanced and specialized techniques. This method enables a unified comprehension of the different methodologies and their practical applications in file fragment classification.

12.3 Approaches for File Fragment Classification

12.3.1 Signature-Based Approaches

In file fragment classification, signature-based approaches have been one of the earliest methodologies for identifying and categorizing file types based on unique signatures or byte patterns. File signatures are specific

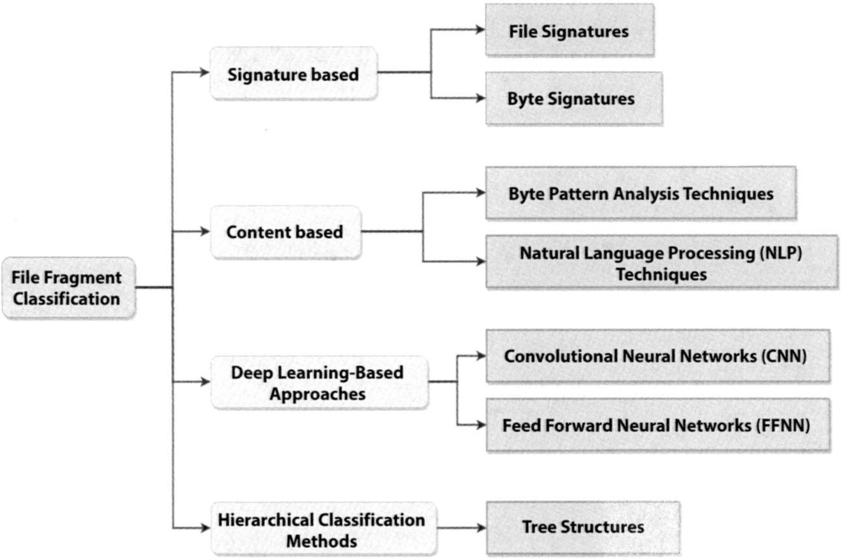

Figure 12.1 Graphical representation of the structure of the paper.

byte patterns or sequences in a file's header or footer that serve as unique identifiers for particular file types. File signatures are used to recognize and classify file types. Headers and footers are special sections or metadata at the beginning and end of a file that provide details regarding the file format, structure, or properties. They contain specific byte patterns or information that can assist in identifying the file type or providing context for file fragment classification. Byte signatures are specific patterns or sequences that can identify particular characteristics or structures within a file fragment. Byte signatures can help recognize specific file formats or detect specific features within a file fragment. Signature-based approaches leverage the distinctive characteristics of file and byte signatures to classify file fragments [20] efficiently. File signatures refer to specific byte sequences located within headers or footers of files, which serve as identifiers for particular file types. On the other hand, byte signatures involve analyzing byte patterns within file fragments to recognize and classify their content.

One of the early papers highlighting the significance of signature-based approaches is [20] by Vassil Roussev. The author emphasizes the limitations of traditional approaches and presents specialized techniques that help improve the accuracy of the classification.

Alongside file and byte signatures, the empirical method for file fragment classification introduced by J. H. Lee *et al.* is detailed in [2]. The authors propose encoding file fragments based on byte signatures and classifying them by comparing their similarity to known file types. This empirical approach demonstrates the practicality of signature-based techniques in achieving accurate file fragment classification.

Early researchers aimed to achieve reliable and efficient identification of file types by utilizing signature-based approaches in file fragment classification. However, these approaches proved inefficient since they heavily relied on header and footer bytes and led to misclassification in fragments where those data were not fully available. With these methods alone, there were challenges in handling fragmented files and improving classification accuracy for complex file types, which motivated further research in this area.

12.3.2 Content-Based Approaches

Content-based approaches in file fragment classification involve analyzing the content of file fragments to determine their type. These approaches typically involve extracting features or analyzing byte patterns, statistical properties, textual information, or visual content within the file fragment. It can be broadly classified into byte pattern analysis techniques and natural language processing (NLP) techniques.

Byte pattern analysis techniques involve analyzing the byte patterns in file fragments to determine their type. Researchers have suggested numerous techniques for format classification relying on statistical attributes, including Shannon entropy, byte frequency distribution, N-gram analysis, and bag-of-visual words (BoVW) [21–23]. One of the early papers that used a content-based approach was [24] by Mason and Heydari. They used a set of three algorithms, byte frequency analysis, file header/trailer analysis and byte frequency cross-correlation analysis, to do the classification. In the paper [25], Karresand and Shahmehri present an algorithm that uses the rate of change of the byte contents to classify the file fragments. The paper [6] uses statistical metrics to identify patterns exhibited by the fragments and classify them into their respective data types.

In recent years, the paper [26] by Mina Erfan and J. Saeed proposes a content-based approach to recognize the file types of file fragments using BoVW. Likewise, the work presented in [21] by Haque and Tozal introduces a novel feature generation model utilizing byte embeddings (Byte2Vec), which translates fragments into dense vector representations. An interesting methodology was adopted in the study [22], which introduces an algorithm capable of identifying six types of useful files (pdf, txt, jpg, doc, html, exe) and distinguishing a type of file fragment with greater accuracy than similar algorithms. The algorithm generates a "fingerprint" of each file based on its content and statistical features and then compares it with known file types to identify the file. In [23], Alsubhi *et al.* propose an approach that initially categorizes file fragments based on their content type rather than the original file's format.

A different approach to the file fragment classification was taken up by Ming Xu *et al.* in the paper [27], where they converted a set of 8 bits into a pixel, reshaped the pixels into 2D to get a grayscale image and then used a classifying algorithm to categorize the images into the relevant data types. In the paper [9], Amirani *et al.* use Principal Component Analysis and neural networks to extract features from the fragments and then apply a classifier to these extracted features to get the data type of the fragment. Zheng *et al.*, in their paper [4], extracted the features of Byte Frequency Distribution and entropy and used them in an SVM algorithm to classify the file fragments. They clearly distinguish between file types (which may include nested files, like PDFs and DOC files) and data types (commonly found embedded within other files, such as JPEG images). However, their focus is primarily on file categories and doesn't involve handling any foreign objects embedded within them.

NLP techniques involve analyzing the content of file fragments to determine their type. For instance, the paper [28] proposes an approach to file fragment classification that involves analyzing the content of file fragments using n-gram analysis. Similarly, the paper [1] proposes employing natural language processing (NLP) techniques in file fragment classification., which involves analyzing the content of file fragments to determine their type using SVMs with the bag of words model. Beebe *et al.*, in their paper [3], used concatenated unigrams and bigrams as input and a linear kernel SVM for classifying the fragments, which reportedly had a significant improvement in accuracy over the existing models. Felix *et al.* used sparse coding methodology to extract the feature vectors from the file fragments and to accurately classify them into their corresponding file type using the SVM classifier in their paper [29].

12.3.3 Deep Learning-Based Approaches

Deep learning-based approaches have gained significant attention in the field of file fragment classification, offering powerful techniques to automatically learn and extract complex features from file fragments and for accurately categorizing file types based on their content. Two prominent deep learning models utilized in this context are Convolutional Neural Networks (CNNs) and Feed Forward Neural Networks (FFNNs). Several research papers have contributed to developing and advancing deep learning-based approaches in file fragment classification, explicitly focusing on CNNs and FFNNs.

12.3.3.1 Convolutional Neural Networks (CNNs)

A powerful deep learning model widely used in file fragment classification tasks, particularly for analyzing visual content, is Convolutional Neural Networks (CNNs). CNNs are designed to capture spatial dependencies within data, making them well-suited for image-based classification tasks. Such networks typically comprise multiple layers, consisting of convolutional, pooling, and fully connected layers. Convolutional layers are tasked with applying filters to extract local features from input images, thereby capturing hierarchical and spatial relationships. Pooling layers down sample the extracted features to retain relevant information, reducing computational complexity. Fully connected layers process the high-level features for classification purposes.

In [11], Gale *et al.* introduce lightweight models for file fragment classification, employing depth-wise separable Convolutional Neural Networks (CNNs). These models demonstrate the capability to identify the type of file fragments independent of metadata reliance.

Mittal *et al.* [12] present a file-type identification tool designed for data carving and memory forensics. This tool utilizes compact neural network architecture, incorporating a trainable embedding space similar to successful natural language processing models. The advantage of this approach is that it can handle large-scale file fragment classification tasks with high accuracy.

The paper [13] studies the classification of file fragments using CNNs, which aims to learn effective feature representations from byte sequences automatically.

In his paper [17], Heister uses recurrent and convolutional neural networks to classify four file types: JPEG, CSV, GIF and XML. However, these file types could be easily classified using existing statistical techniques.

A comparison between convolutional neural networks and feedforward artificial neural networks (FFANN) for file fragment classification is done in the paper [14]. The results show that the FFANN provides better results as compared to CNNs.

A novel scheme based on fragment-to-grayscale image conversion and deep learning to classify file fragments was proposed in the paper [15]. The proposed approach treats a file fragment as a grayscale image and employs image classification methods, utilizing deep Convolutional Neural Networks (CNNs) for fragment classification.

12.3.3.2 Feed Forward Neural Networks (FFNNs)

A feedforward neural network belongs to the category of artificial neural networks, distinguished by its one-way flow of data, starting from the input layer and traversing through one or more hidden layers before culminating in the output layer. The architecture comprises interconnected neurons organized into layers, where each neuron within a layer forms connections with every neuron in the subsequent layer. This allows for the extraction of intricate patterns and relationships within data.

In the context of file fragment classification problems, feedforward neural networks have proven to be highly useful. By training the network on labeled datasets of file fragments, it can effectively learn to recognize and classify different types of fragments based on their content or characteristics. The network's ability to handle complex, non-linear relationships makes it well-suited for capturing and modeling the diverse patterns found in file fragments. Additionally, feedforward neural networks can be scaled up to handle large volumes of file fragments, making them applicable in scenarios that involve processing and classifying extensive datasets. The versatility and accuracy of feedforward neural networks have made them a valuable tool in file fragment classification tasks, facilitating various applications in areas such as digital forensics, malware detection, and data recovery.

The paper [16] proposes a machine learning-based approach for content-based analysis to recognize the file types of file fragments. The method involves training a Feed-Forward Neural Network with a 2-byte sliding window to extract features from the file fragments. This approach offers the advantage of classifying file fragments based on their content instead of relying on specific byte sequences in the file header and footer, which might be altered or absent.

12.3.4 Hierarchical Classification Methods

Hierarchical classification methods have been proposed to improve the accuracy of file fragment classification by considering the internal structure of file types and the relationships between classes and types. In hierarchical classification, data and file types are first classified into classes, and then they are classified into class-based types. This approach can improve classification accuracy by considering the relationships between classes and types. In this topic, we will discuss hierarchical classification methods in file fragment classification and relevant research papers that have proposed these methods.

In their work described in [2], Bhatt *et al.* introduce a hierarchical machine-learning-based approach, utilizing optimized Support Vector Machines (SVMs) as the base classifiers for file fragment classification. The authors also suggest a classification system for file types that can be used for conducting hierarchical classification. The advantage of this approach is that it can improve classification accuracy by considering the internal structure of widely used file types such as PDFs.

In [30], Beebe *et al.* present a hierarchical class-to-type modeling approach for data and file type classification. The method incorporates expectation maximization clustering to derive alternative hierarchical models from the data. Precision, recall, and overall classification accuracy levels are measured to determine the optimal hierarchy. The advantage of this approach is that it can improve classification accuracy by considering the relationships between classes and types.

A comparative analysis of the prominent papers in the area has been added in Table 12.1.

12.4 Survey Findings

Over 90% of the papers that were examined use Govdocs1 as their data source for the process of file fragment classification. The data is organized into 1,000 directories, each comprising 1,000 files of diverse types. Additionally, 10 randomly designated streams are specifically allocated for development and testing purposes. A recent dataset, FFT-75, was published, and it has a uniform distribution of 75 different file types. Some papers have also used some private datasets for their research.

From the review of the relevant papers in file fragment classification, it can be inferred that content-based analysis is the most used methodology for the classification. This pattern can mainly be attributed to its ability to capture intrinsic characteristics and patterns within the data. Unlike methods reliant on external information or metadata, content-based analysis directly examines the contents of file fragments, allowing the classification model to discern patterns, features, and relationships inherent to the fragment's content.

In the early years, the researchers mostly adopted a method where they extracted features from the file fragments and used machine learning-based classification models like KNNs, SVMs, etc., to classify the fragment into

Table 12.1 Comparison of file fragment classification approaches in different papers.

Ref no	Year	No. of file types	Algorithm	Dataset	Result
[11]	2023	75	Depth-wise separable CNNs	FFT-75	The model achieved 79% accuracy on the dataset.
[21]	2022	63	Byte2vec model for feature extraction and KNN for classifying the fragments	Govdocs1	The model achieved 72% accuracy on the dataset.
[26]	2021	31	Mapped the fragment into an 8-bit grayscale image and used texture analysis for classification	Govdocs1	The model achieved an accuracy of 74.9% for the classification of 512-byte fragments and 87.3% in the case of 4096-byte fragments.
[22]	2021	6	Sequential Forward Selection algorithm (SFS) and Sequential Floating Forward Selection algorithm (SFFS) are used for feature reduction, and three multiclassifier algorithms are used for classification.	Govdocs1	The KNN algorithm with the SFFS feature reduction technique gave a classification accuracy of 98%.
[12]	2021	75	CNNs	FFT-75	The FiFTy model has an average classification accuracy of 77.5%.

(Continued)

Table 12.1 Comparison of file fragment classification approaches in different papers. (*Continued*)

Ref no	Year	No. of file types	Algorithm	Dataset	Result
[16]	2021	13	For each fragment, a feature vector based on 2-byte sequence histograms is computed, which is subsequently employed to train a Feedforward neural network.	Govdocs1	The model achieved 89% - 90% accuracy with multiple architectures.
[23]	2020	18	The model categorizes file fragments by content, not file format, and then refines them into narrower file type categories.	Private dataset	The model attained an overall average accuracy of 81.6%.
[2]	2020	14	A hierarchical machine learning approach utilizing optimized Support Vector Machines (SVM) as the underlying classifiers.	Govdocs1	The model attained an average accuracy of 67.78%.
[14]	2019	9	Byte histograms and byte-pair histograms trained feedforward neural networks.	Govdocs1	Model has an F1 score of 0.8772.
[13]	2018	20	CNNs	Govdocs1	The CNN models outperformed the existing models like SVM, KNNs and XGboost.

(*Continued*)

Table 12.1 Comparison of file fragment classification approaches in different papers. (*Continued*)

Ref no	Year	No. of file types	Algorithm	Dataset	Result
[15]	2018	16	Conversion of fragments to grayscale image followed by using deep CNNs for classification	Govdocs1	The model attained an accuracy of 70.9%.
[29]	2017	15	Sparse coding, N-grams and SVM model	Govdocs1	The model obtained an average prediction accuracy of 53.59% for when the SVM parameter, C = 1.
[27]	2014	29	Fragment to grayscale image conversion, image classification	Govdocs1	The file-unbiased model achieved an average classification accuracy of 39.7%, whereas the type-unbiased model attained 54.7%.
[1]	2012	24	File fragments are treated as "bags of bytes," and their feature vectors are constructed using counts of unigrams and bigrams.	Govdocs1	The model attained an average accuracy of 49.1%.
[28]	2005	6	Byte frequency distribution, histogram	Private dataset	Model has an accuracy of 85% to 100%, but it is heavily reliant on header data.

the relevant file type. As research in deep learning continues to expand, researchers are exploring the application of deep learning techniques in file fragment classification, including the incorporation of image classification methods into the process.

12.5 Challenges and Future Directions

File fragment classification is a challenging problem in digital forensics due to the diversity of file types and the complexity of file formats. Several research papers have proposed different methodologies for file fragment classification, but some challenges still need to be addressed. Here are some of the major research challenges in file fragment classification:

1. Lack of standardization: There is a lack of standardization in file formats, making it challenging to develop a universal approach for file fragment classification. Different file formats have different internal structures, requiring specialized classification approaches [2].
2. Limited training data: File fragment classification requires much training data to achieve high accuracy. However, obtaining labeled training data is challenging, especially for rare file types.
3. Scalability: As the number of file types and file fragments increases, the scalability of file fragment classification methods becomes challenging. The classification accuracy may decrease as the number of file types and file fragments increases [23].
4. Noise and ambiguity: File fragments may contain noise and ambiguity, affecting classification accuracy. Noise and ambiguity can be introduced during the data acquisition process or due to the complexity of file formats [13].

Despite these challenges, there are still areas where there is a scope for further research to help develop the field. Here are some future research directions in file fragment classification:

1. Hierarchical classification: Hierarchical classification approaches have been suggested to enhance the accuracy of file fragment classification by accounting for the internal structure of file types and the interrelations between classes and types. Further

investigation could explore the efficacy of hierarchical classification methods in the area of file fragment classification.
2. Deep learning: Deep learning techniques have shown promising results in file fragment classification. With newer and larger datasets available for file fragment classification, the effectiveness of deep learning for solving file fragment classification can be explored, especially for rare file types.
3. Transfer learning: The method uses pre-trained models for classification tasks. The use of transfer learning for file fragment classification is a less explored area of research, and further research can help understand if developments in this area can help get better results for the classification problem, especially for file types with limited training data.
4. Ensemble methods: Ensemble methods involve combining multiple classifiers to improve classification accuracy. Further research can also be done in this area.

In summary, file fragment classification is a challenging problem in digital forensics, and some challenges still need to be addressed. However, there are still areas with scope for further research that will help develop the field.

12.6 Conclusion

The classification of file fragments is a critical issue in digital forensics, and it involves classifying file fragments into different types based on their content. Researchers have proposed various methodologies to address this problem. Signature-based approaches involve using predefined signatures to identify file types. Content-based approaches involve using the content of file fragments to identify file types. Deep learning-based approaches involve using neural networks to learn effective feature representations from file fragments. Hierarchical classification methods involve classifying data and file types into classes and class-based types.

Despite the progress made in file fragment classification, challenges still need to be addressed. These challenges include more standardization in file formats, limited training data, scalability, and noise and ambiguity.

Further research can be done to explore the effectiveness of hierarchical classification, deep learning, transfer learning, and ensemble methods for file fragment classification. These methods can improve classification accuracy and help develop the field.

In conclusion, file fragment classification is a challenging problem in digital forensics, and various methodologies are available to solve this problem. However, challenges still need to be addressed, and there is a scope for further research in this area. Hierarchical classification, deep learning, transfer learning, and ensemble methods are future research directions in file fragment classification that can improve classification accuracy and help develop the field.

References

1. Fitzgerald, S., Mathews, G., Morris, C., Zhulyn, O., Using NLP techniques for file fragment classification. *Digital Invest.*, 9, S44–S49, 2012.
2. Roussev, V. and Candice, Q., File fragment encoding classification—an empirical approach. *Digital Invest.*, 10, S69–S77, 2013.
3. Beebe, N.L., Maddox, L.A., Liu, L., Sun, M., Sceadan: Using concatenated n-gram vectors for improved file and data type classification. *IEEE Trans. Inf. Forensics Secur.*, 8, 9, 1519–1530, 2013.
4. Zheng, N., Wang, J., Wu, T., Xu, M., A fragment classification method depending on data type. *IEEE International Conference on Computer and Information Technology; Ubiquitous Computing and Communications; Dependable, Autonomic and Secure Computing; Pervasive Intelligence and Computing*, pp. 1948–1953, 2015.
5. Conti, G., Bratus, S., Shubina, A., Sangster, B., Ragsdale, R., Supan, M., Perez-Alemany, R., Automated mapping of large binary objects using primitive fragment type classification. *Digital Invest.*, 7, S3–S12, 2010.
6. Moody, S.J. and Erbacher, R.F., SÁDI – statistical analysis for data type identification. *Third international workshop on systematic approaches to digital forensic engineering*, pp. 41–54, 2008.
7. Sportiello, L. and Zanero, S., File block classification by support vector machine. *IEEE Sixth international conference on availability, reliability and security*, pp. 307–312, 2011.
8. Sportiello, L. and Zanero, S., Context-based file block classification. *Advances in Digital Forensics VIII: 8th IFIP WG 11.9 International Conference on Digital Forensics, Pretoria, South Africa, January 3-5, 2012, Revised Selected Papers*, vol. 8, pp. 67–82, 2012.
9. Amirani, M.C., Toorani, M., Mihandoost, S., Feature-based type identification of file fragments. *Secur. Commun. Netw.*, 6, 1, 115–128, 2013.
10. Sitompul, O.S. and Rahmat, R.F., Distributed autonomous neuro-gen learning engine for content-based document file type identification. *International conference on cyber and IT service management (CITSM)*, pp. 63–68, 2014.
11. Ghaleb, M., Saaim, K., Felemban, M., Al-Saleh, S., Al-Mulhem, A., File fragment classification using light-weight convolutional neural networks," arXiv preprint, vol. arXiv:2305.00656, 2023.

12. Mittal, G., Korus, P., Memon, N., FiFTy: large-scale file fragment type identification using convolutional neural networks. *IEEE Trans. Inf. Forensics Secur.*, 16, 28–41, 2020.
13. Wang, Y., Su, Z., Song, D., File fragment type identification with convolutional neural networks. *Proceedings of the 2018 International Conference on Machine Learning Technologies*, pp. 41–47, 2018.
14. Vulinović, K., Ivković, L., Petrović, J., Skračić, K., Pale, P., Neural networks for file fragment classification. *42nd International Convention on Information and Communication Technology, Electronics and Microelectronics (MIPRO)*, pp. 1194–1198, 2019.
15. Chen, Q., Liao, Q., Jiang, Z., Fang, J., Yiu, S., Xi, G., Li, R., Yi, Z., Wang, X., Hui, L., Liu, D., File fragment classification using grayscale image conversion and deep learning in digital forensics. *IEEE Security and Privacy Workshops (SPW)*, pp. 140–147, 2018.
16. Bhat, A., Likhite, A., Chavan, S., Ragha, L., File fragment classification using content based analysis. *ITM Web Conf.*, 40, 03025, 2021.
17. Hiester, L., File fragment classification using neural networks with lossless representations, 2018.
18. Harris, R.M., Using artificial neural networks for forensic file type identification, Master's thesis, Purdue University, West Lafayette, 2007.
19. Penrose, P., Macfarlane, R., Buchanan, W.J., Approaches to the classification of high entropy file fragments. *Digital Invest.*, 10, 4, 372–384, 2013.
20. Roussev, V. and Simson L, G., File fragment classification-the case for specialized approaches. *Fourth international IEEE workshop on systematic approaches to digital forensic engineering*, 2009.
21. Haque, M.E. and Tozal, M.E., Byte embeddings for file fragment classification. *Future Gener. Comput. Syst.*, 127, 448–461, 2022.
22. Masoumi, M., Keshavarz, A., Fotohi, R., File fragment recognition based on content and statistical features. *Multimed. Tools Appl.*, 80, 18859–18874, 2021.
23. Alsubhi, M.A., Moussa, A.N., Alfaqiri, A.S., Khaleel, F.L., GenSpec: A file fragment classification approach. *International Conference on Computing and Information Technology (ICCIT)*, pp. 1–5, 2020.
24. McDaniel, M. and Heydari, M.H., Content based file type detection algorithms. *36th Annual Hawaii International Conference on System Sciences*, p. 10, 2003.
25. Karresand, S., File type identification of data fragments by their binary structure. *IEEE Information Assurance Workshop*, pp. 140–147, 2006.
26. Erfan, M. and Saeed, J., File fragment type classification by bag-of-visual-words. *ISC Int. J. Inf. Secur.*, 13, 101–116, 2021.
27. Xu, T., Xu, M., Ren, Y., Xu, J., Zhang, H., Zheng, N., A file fragment classification method based on grayscale image. *J. Comput.*, 9, 8, 1863–1870, 2014.
28. Li, W.-J., Wang, K., Stolfo, S.J., Herzog, B., Fileprints: identifying file types by n-gram analysis. *Proceedings from the Sixth Annual IEEE SMC Information Assurance Workshop*, pp. 64–71, 2005.

29. Wang, F., Quach, T.T., Wheeler, J., Aimone, J.B., James, C.D., Sparse coding for n-gram feature extraction and training for file fragment classification. *IEEE Trans. Inf. Forensics Secur.*, 13, 10, 2553–2562, 2018.
30. Beebe, N., Liu, L., Sun, M., Data type classification: hierarchical class-to-type modeling. *Advances in Digital Forensics XII: 12th IFIP WG 11.9 International Conference, New Delhi, January 4-6, 2016, Revised Selected Papers*, vol. 12, pp. 325–343, 2016.

13

Deepfake Detection and Forensic Precision for Online Harassment

K. Gouthami, K. Sunitha*, D.U. Durgarani and M. Prathyusha

MLEW, Guntur, A.P., India

Abstract

In an era marked by the pervasive threat of online harassment and the alarming rise of deepfake technology, this research introduces a groundbreaking solution—Blockchain-based Deepfake Detection and Forensic Precision—that promises unmatched defense against the insidious proliferation of manipulated digital content. Leveraging the decentralized and tamper- resistant nature of blockchain, the proposed system not only detects deepfakes with unprecedented accuracy but also ensures forensic precision in identifying their origins. The integration of blockchain technology establishes a transparent and immutable ledger, recording the entire lifecycle of digital media, thereby creating an indelible chain of custody. Through the implementation of advanced machine learning algorithms and neural networks, the system can adeptly discern subtle nuances indicative of deepfake content, mitigating the potential harm caused by malicious actors seeking to exploit individuals through fabricated digital personas.

The synergy between blockchain and deep learning not only fortifies the defense against online harassment but also empowers forensic experts with an unassailable toolset for attributing and tracking the source of malicious content. The decentralized architecture not only enhances security by eliminating single points of failure but also ensures the integrity of the detection process, rendering it impervious to manipulation or evasion attempts. Furthermore, the system's real-time detection capabilities serve as a proactive shield, promptly identifying and neutralizing emerging threats in the ever-evolving landscape of digital deception. As online platforms grapple with the challenges posed by deepfakes, this research provides a robust and comprehensive solution that transcends the limitations of existing detection mechanisms. The fusion of blockchain and deep learning not only elevates the precision of identification but also establishes a resilient framework for the ongoing

**Corresponding author*: sunitha.kandepu@gmail.com

Budati Anil Kumar, Singamaneni Kranthi Kumar and Li Xingwang (eds.) Quantum Computing Models for Cybersecurity and Wireless Communications, (219–226) © 2025 Scrivener Publishing LLC

battle against online harassment. The implications of this research extend beyond individual defense, permeating into the realms of journalism, national security, and the preservation of trust in digital media. By ensuring the accountability of digital content through blockchain's incorruptible ledger, society is endowed with a powerful deterrent against the proliferation of misinformation and targeted harassment campaigns. This research not only confronts the immediate threats posed by deepfakes but also contributes to the broader discourse on the responsible and ethical use of emerging technologies. As the digital landscape continues to evolve, the proposed Blockchain-based Deepfake Detection and Forensic Precision system stands as a beacon of innovation, providing a robust defense against online harassment and fortifying the foundations of trust in the digital realm.

***Keywords*:** Blockchain, deepfake, detection, forensic precision, defense

13.1 Introduction

In the relentless battle against the escalating menace of online harassment and the formidable challenge posed by the proliferation of deepfake technology, this pioneering research unveils a revolutionary solution: Blockchain-based Deepfake Detection and Forensic Precision. This innovative system not only promises an unmatched defense against the insidious spread of manipulated digital content but also introduces a new paradigm for the identification and attribution of malicious actors. By harnessing the intrinsic characteristics of blockchain, a decentralized and tamper-resistant ledger [5] the proposed framework establishes an impregnable foundation for detecting deepfakes with unparalleled accuracy. The integration of blockchain technology provides a transparent and immutable record of the entire lifecycle of digital media, creating an indelible chain of custody. This not only bolsters the resilience of the detection process but also ensures forensic precision in pinpointing the origins of deceptive content.

Advanced machine learning algorithms and neural networks are seamlessly woven into the fabric of the system, enabling it to discern subtle intricacies indicative of deepfake manipulations. This adept technological synergy empowers the system to mitigate potential harm inflicted by malicious actors who exploit individuals through fabricated digital personas, thereby safeguarding the integrity of online spaces. The decentralized architecture not only fortifies the defense against online harassment by eliminating single points of failure but also engenders an ecosystem of trust and accountability. In real-time, the system acts as a vigilant guardian, promptly identifying and neutralizing emerging threats in the constantly evolving landscape of digital deception. As digital platforms grapple with the challenges posed by deepfakes, this research contribution transcends the limitations of existing detection mechanisms, offering a comprehensive solution that redefines the boundaries of online security. The fusion of blockchain and deep learning not only elevates the precision of identification but also establishes a resilient framework for the ongoing battle against online harassment. Beyond individual defense, the implications of this research extend into critical domains such as journalism, national security, and the preservation of trust in digital media. The immutable ledger created by blockchain technology serves as a powerful deterrent against the insidious spread of misinformation and targeted harassment campaigns, thereby reshaping the contours of ethical digital engagement. This research not only confronts the immediate threats posed by deepfakes but also contributes significantly to the broader discourse on the responsible and ethical use of emerging technologies. In the ever-evolving digital landscape, the proposed Blockchain-based Deepfake Detection and Forensic Precision system stands as a beacon of innovation, providing not only a robust defense against online harassment but also fortifying the foundations of trust in the digital realm.

13.2 Literature

The genesis of the proposal for "Blockchain-based Deepfake Detection and Forensic Precision for Unmatched Defense against Online Harassment" emerged from the pressing need to address the escalating threats posed by the convergence of deepfake technology and online harassment.

Recognizing the growing sophistication of malicious actors in exploiting digital mediums to perpetrate harm, the research team sought to devise an innovative solution that transcended the limitations of conventional detection mechanisms. The idea was conceived against the backdrop of an increasingly interconnected and vulnerable digital landscape, where the manipulation of audio-visual content [1] through deepfake technology posed a severe threat to individual privacy, public discourse, and societal trust. The decision to integrate blockchain technology into the framework stemmed from the desire to establish an incorruptible and decentralized foundation that could fortify the defense against deep fake proliferation. Blockchain's inherent characteristics of transparency, immutability, and tamper resistance provided a robust infrastructure for recording and verifying the entire lifecycle of digital media, thus ensuring forensic precision in the identification of deepfake origins. The interdisciplinary nature of the proposal was driven by the recognition that addressing the complex challenges of online harassment required a convergence of expertise in blockchain technology, deep learning [2], and forensic analysis. The team aimed to create a holistic system that not only detected deepfakes with unmatched accuracy but also empowered forensic experts with the tools to attribute and trace the source of malicious content. The urgency of the proposal was further underscored by the societal implications of unchecked online harassment, necessitating a proactive and innovative approach to safeguard digital spaces. In essence, the origin of this proposal lies in the proactive response to a critical societal challenge, driven by the imperative to harness cutting-edge technologies in a synergistic manner to protect individuals and uphold the integrity of digital interactions in an era fraught with evolving threats and challenges.

13.3 Theoretical Analysis and Software Simulation

13.3.1 Theoretical Analysis

The theoretical underpinnings of "Blockchain-based Deepfake Detection and Forensic Precision for Unmatched Defense against Online Harassment" rest on the integration of two cutting-edge technologies—blockchain and deep learning. At its core, blockchain's decentralized and tamper-resistant ledger provides an immutable record of digital content, establishing an unassailable chain of custody. This characteristic not only ensures transparency but also safeguards the integrity of the detection process, as any attempt to manipulate or alter information is immediately detectable. Moreover, the decentralized architecture eliminates single points of failure, enhancing the security and resilience of the overall system. On the other hand, the theoretical foundation extends to the realm of deep learning, where advanced machine learning algorithms [4] and neural networks are employed to scrutinize digital content for subtle indicators of deepfake manipulation. The system's ability to discern nuanced patterns, anomalies, and inconsistencies within multimedia content contributes to its unmatched accuracy in deepfake detection. The synergy between blockchain and deep learning is crucial in addressing the multifaceted challenges posed by online harassment. The incorporation of forensic precision into the theoretical framework ensures not only the identification of deepfakes but also the attribution of their origins. This theoretical analysis positions the proposed project at the forefront of technological innovation [2], providing a holistic defense mechanism that leverages the strengths of blockchain and deep learning to combat the evolving landscape of digital deception and harassment.

For theoretical alignment of Digital calculations we can use the alignment score functions (Internet).

Name	Digital content alignment score function
Content base attention	Score (S_t,h_i) =Cosine$[S_t,h_i]$
Additive (*)	Score $(S_t,h_i) = V_a \tanh (W_a[S_t,h_i])$
Location-base	α_{ti}=softmax $(W_a[S_t,h_i]$ (soft max alignment depend on Target Position
General	Score $(S_t,h_i) = S^T_t W_a h_i$ Where W_a is the triangle weight matrix in the attention Layer
Dot product	Score $(S_t,h_i) = S^T_t h_i$
Scaled dot product(^)	Score $(S_t,h_i) = S^T_t h_{i/} \sqrt{n}$

13.3.2 Software Simulation

The software simulation for "Blockchain-based Deepfake Detection and Forensic Precision for Unmatched Defense Against Online Harassment" intricately replicates the proposed system's multifaceted approach to fortifying digital spaces. The simulation commences by emulating the decentralized and tamper-resistant nature of blockchain technology, establishing a virtual ledger that records and verifies the entire lifecycle of digital media. This simulated blockchain ensures transparency and immutability, creating an indelible chain of custody crucial for forensic precision in identifying deepfake origins. The integration of advanced machine learning algorithms and neural networks into the simulation enables the system to analyze digital content [3] with unparalleled accuracy, mimicking the nuanced scrutiny required for detecting subtle indicators of deepfake manipulation. As simulated malicious actors attempt to exploit individuals through fabricated digital personas, the system's real-time detection capabilities act as a proactive shield, promptly identifying and neutralizing emerging threats.

The decentralized architecture within the simulation not only eliminates single points of failure but also replicates the robust security mechanisms inherent in blockchain, rendering the detection process impervious to manipulation or evasion attempts [5]. Throughout the simulation, the software showcases the seamless synergy between blockchain and deep learning, underscoring the theoretical underpinnings of the proposed project. The simulated software not only provides a dynamic testing ground for the detection and attribution of deepfakes but also offers a glimpse into the transformative potential of the proposed system, heralding a new era in the defense against online harassment through innovative technological integration.

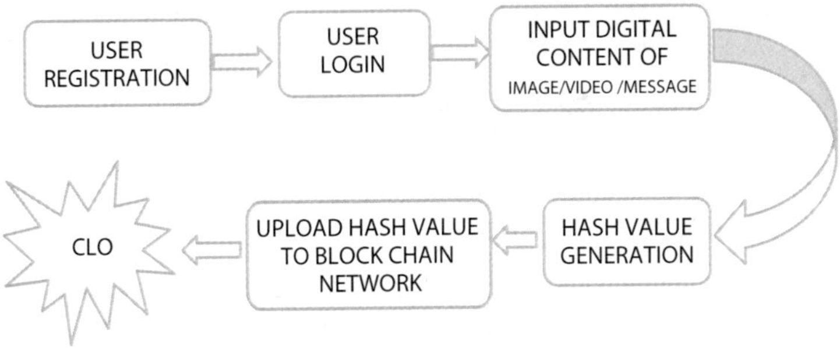

13.3.3 Testing and Optimization

The comprehensive testing and optimization strategy for "Blockchain-based Deepfake Detection and Forensic Precision for Unmatched Defense against Online Harassment" is paramount to ensure the robustness, reliability, and effectiveness of the proposed system. The testing phase begins with meticulous unit testing, scrutinizing each component, from the decentralized blockchain ledger to the advanced deep learning algorithms, to validate their individual functionalities. This process establishes a solid foundation, addressing potential bugs or inconsistencies early in the development cycle. Integration testing follows suit, assessing the seamless collaboration and interoperability of the blockchain and deep learning components to ascertain their collective performance.

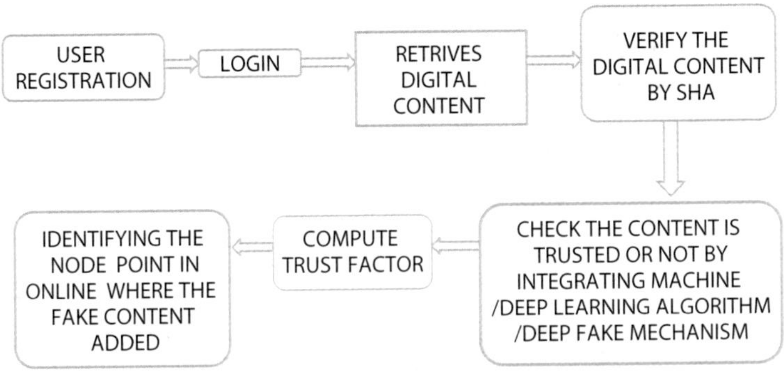

Results

- Unprecedented reduction in the spread of deepfake content on digital platforms.
- Enhanced trust and accountability in online interactions through tamper-resistant forensic tracking.
- Timely prevention of online harassment incidents with real-time detection capabilities.
- Clear attribution and traceability of malicious content, aiding law enforcement in investigations.
- Strengthened security against manipulation attempts through decentralized architecture.
- Substantial decrease in the effectiveness of deepfake-based harassment campaigns.
- Increased user confidence in online spaces, fostering a safer digital environment.
- Ethical and responsible technology use in addressing the challenges of digital deception.
- A paradigm shifts in the fight against online harassment, setting new standards for defense mechanisms.

References

1. How Faking Videos Became Easy — And Why That's SoScary[Online], Available: https://fortune.com/2018/09/11/deep-fakes-obama-video/.
2. Li, Y. and Lyu, S., Exposing DeepFake Videos By Detecting Face Warping Artifacts. ArXiv abs/1811.00656. *IEEE Conference on Computer Vision and Pattern Recognition Workshops (CVPRW)*, University at Albany, State University of New York, USA, 2019, https://arxiv.org/abs/1811.00656.
3. Li, Y., Chang, M., Lyu, S., In Ictu Oculi: Exposing AI Created Fake Videos by Detecting Eye Blinking. *2018 IEEE International Workshop on Information Forensics and Security (WIFS)*, Hong Kong, China, pp. 1–7, 2018, https://www.researchgate.net/publication/330797421_In_Ictu_Oculi_Exposing_AI_Created_Fake_Videos_by_Detecting_Eye_Blinking.
4. Yang, X., Li, Y., Lyu, S., Exposing Deep Fakes Using Inconsistent Head Poses. *ICASSP 2019 - 2019 IEEE International Conference on Acoustics, Speech and Signal Processing (ICASSP)*, pp. 8261–8265, 2019, https://www.researchgate.net/publication/332791104_Exposing_Deep_Fakes_Using_Inconsistent_Head_Poses.

5. Gipp, B., Kosti, J., Breitinger, C., Securing Video Integrity Using Decentralized Trusted Timestamping on the Bitcoin Blockchain. *MCIS 2016 Proceedings. 51. Tenth Mediterranean Conference on Information Systems (MCIS) at AIS Electronic Library (AISeL), Paphos, Cyprus, September 2016 Proceedings by an authorized administrator of AIS Electronic Library (AISeL)*, 2016, https://aisel.aisnet.org/mcis2016/51\.

14

Design of Automatic Seed Sowing Machine

Chiluka Ramesh*, K. Sarada, V. Ajay Shankar and K. Ravi Kumar

Dept of ECE, Malineni Lakshmaiah Women's Engineering College, Guntur A.P., India

Abstract

Automation in the agricultural sector has the potential to revolutionize farming practices and address various challenges faced by farmers, including productivity and time constraints. Automating seed sowing can significantly enhance productivity by speeding up the process which is a potential implication in the field of farming, particularly in India. Automation in agriculture can help overcome the problem of insufficient skilled manpower and improve the overall growth of developing countries. By implementing automation, tedious manual work can be eliminated, and production processes can be accelerated. This, in turn, can lead to increased agricultural output and improved social welfare, especially in rural areas. Seed sowing is a crucial step in agriculture, and automating this process can reduce human effort and increase yields. The evolution of this system is driven by a DC motor controlled by an Arduino control kit, can help simplify the work for farmers. Manual seed planting often results in issues such as improper seed placement, inefficiencies in spacing, and physical strain on farmers, which can limit the dimensions of grass land. By optimizing the design of the agriculture machine and carefully selecting components, these limitations can be addressed, leading to better performance and improved results in seed planting. Overall, the automation of agricultural processes, including seed sowing, has the potential to significantly benefit the agricultural sector by increasing productivity, reducing manual labor, and improving the livelihoods of farmers.

Keywords: IoT, agriculture, farming, arduino uno, servo motor, automation, DC motor, sensors

**Corresponding author*: drchilukaramesh@gmail.com

Budati Anil Kumar, Singamaneni Kranthi Kumar and Li Xingwang (eds.) Quantum Computing Models for Cybersecurity and Wireless Communications, (227–236) © 2025 Scrivener Publishing LLC

14.1 Introduction

Indian economy heavily relies on the agriculture sector. As the population grows and food consumption increases, there is a constant and substantial demand for food production. However, addressing this issue goes beyond simply providing more land for agricultural use; it also involves maximizing crop yield on existing agricultural land.

One of the challenges faced by many countries, including India, is the lack of skilled manpower in the agricultural sector. This shortage of skilled labor significantly affects the growth and overall development of the agricultural industry. To overcome this challenge, it is crucial to introduce technology and automation into agriculture. By incorporating technology, the need for manpower can be reduced, leading to increased productivity.

India has made tremendous advancement in farming sector since several years. The emphasis shifted from expanding agricultural land to increasing production through various means, such as improved farming techniques, better irrigation systems, and the use of advanced agricultural machinery. This shift has allowed for greater efficiency and productivity in the sector [11].

The introduction of technology in agriculture has a great potential to revolutionize the industry, leading to increased productivity, reduced labor requirements, and improved overall development. By adopting modern farming practices, leveraging data-driven insights, and implementing advanced technologies, India can further enhance its agricultural sector and meet the growing demand for food production.

The objective of Automation [7] is to reduce usage of manpower in manufacturing companies and helps in overcoming exhaustive physical work. Automating the seed sowing process in the agricultural sector can indeed help reduce human effort and increase yield, which is particularly relevant in a country like India where a significant portion of the population depends on agriculture. Using a DC motor for the automated plantation of seeds is one approach to achieve this automation. DC motors are commonly used in various agricultural applications, including seed drills and precision planters.

By leveraging advanced technology and mechanized systems, this innovation aims to achieve the following key goals:

Enhanced Efficiency: To significantly reduce the time and labor required for sowing, enabling farmers to cover larger areas efficiently.

Precise Seed Placement: To ensure accurate seed placement at optimal intervals and depths, promoting uniform germination and healthy crop growth.
Customization and Adaptability: To provide the capability to adjust settings based on varying crop types, soil conditions, and field specifications, thereby maximizing adaptability.
Resource Conservation: To minimize seed wastage by precisely controlling seed dispensing, leading to more sustainable and cost-effective farming practices.
Increased Crop Yields: To contribute to higher agricultural productivity through consistent and optimized seed distribution, ultimately leading to greater crop yields.
Technological Advancement: To integrate cutting-edge controls, sensors, and actuators for seamless operation and to stay at the forefront of agricultural innovation.
Reduced Physical Strain: To alleviate the physical burden on farmers by automating the labor-intensive task of seed sowing, improving overall well-being.
Contribution to Sustainable Agriculture: To support environmentally-conscious farming practices by minimizing environmental impact and conserving natural resources

Overall, the objective of an automatic seed sowing machine is to transform conventional agricultural practices, fostering a more efficient, productive, and sustainable approach to seed planting.

14.2 Literature Survey

The authors [1] describe design and development of automatic seed drill device using Arduino. The basic purpose of this project is to decrease the expenses and also to save the time. To achieve this, the agribot utilizes solar energy. The system comprises of photovoltaic cell for capturing solar energy, and converting into power which drives DC motor. This electrical energy is used to charge a battery, which provides the necessary power to a shunt wound DC motor. The motor is responsible for driving the agribot and enabling its movement in the field.

In addition to the solar-powered motor, the agribot is equipped with sensors. These sensors work in conjunction with a Wi-Fi interface that is operated through an Android application. The sensors and Wi-Fi interface allow for precise maneuvering of the robot in the field. This helps reduce the dependency on manual labor.

The agribot is designed to navigate various ground contours efficiently. It performs the digging operation, it sows the seeds. This automation of seed sowing and digging tasks eliminates the need for manual labor and increases efficiency in the agricultural process.

Overall, the use of solar energy, along with the integration of sensors and a Wi-Fi interface, makes the automatic seed sowing agribot a cost-effective and time-saving solution for agriculture.

The article [2] demonstrates the overall sketch of mechanized seed drilling system that offers improved velocity of functioning and also improves drilling capability for advanced agricultural processes, including robotic-based cultivation.

The seed sowing machine is equipped with DC motor and cell operated wheels. The machine identifies the amount of seed depository and provides an alert if the seeds are empty. It also incorporates obstacle detection capabilities, allowing it to easily identify any obstacles that come in its path or divert its course.

During all cycles seeds are dispensed from the container by ensuring a smooth, efficient nut planting without any wastage [9]. By utilizing battery-powered wheels and a DC motor, this automatic seed sowing machine offers enhanced operational efficiency. It ensures accurate seed placement and minimizes seed wastage. The inclusion of obstacle detection capabilities allows for safe navigation in the field, preventing any potential damage to the machine or hindrance in the seed sowing process.

In conclusion, the machine described by the author provides a reliable and efficient solution for seed sowing in agricultural applications. Its features, such as battery-powered wheels, obstacle detection, and alarm generation, contribute to improved productivity and reduced seed wastage in the field.

The research paper [3] focuses on the outline and expansion of non-automatic machine. The objective is to perform the sowing operation by accurately placing seeds and fertilizers with desired spacing and depth. Additionally, the machine ensures that the seeds are properly covered with soil and compacted for optimal growth.

The recommended nut to nut distance and penetration of nuts can differ depending on the field during specific environment. These variations are necessary to achieve optimum yields in different agricultural contexts.

The manually operated seed planter machine is designed to address these specific requirements for each crop and agro-climatic condition [10].

It provides a means to achieve precise seed placement and spacing, ensuring uniform distribution of seeds in the field. By carefully controlling the depth of seed placement, the machine helps optimize the germination and growth of the seeds.

The ability of the machine to envelope the nuts with clay which is also crucial. It ensures that the seeds are adequately protected and in close contact with the soil, promoting healthy growth and development.

Overall, the manually operated seed planter machine described in the research paper offers a practical solution for achieving accurate seed placement, spacing, and coverage. By addressing these critical aspects of the sowing operation, the machine contributes to maximizing yields and optimizing agricultural productivity.

The author [4] describes a novel seed sowing processes using robotic technology. The objective of the system includes insertion of nuts at specific positions during the drilling process.

The system incorporates a wheel attached to the base of machine. This wheel facilitates the motion of the machine across the field.

The metering mechanism is responsible for dropping the seeds from the hopper. It consists of a set of scoops or compartments that release the seeds at precise intervals. The seeds are then distributed through distributor pipes, which ensure proper distribution across the field.

By employing robotics technology, the seed sowing system described in the research paper offers a precise and efficient method for seed placement. The use of a metering mechanism with scoops and seed distributor pipes ensures accurate seed spacing and distribution. Additionally, the inclusion of a tiller helps create an ideal seedbed for optimal growth.

Overall, this seed sowing system demonstrates the potential of robotics technology in improving the precision and efficiency of agricultural operations. By achieving accurate seed placement and spacing, the system contributes to maximizing crop yields and enhancing agricultural productivity.

The author [5] describes the outline and development of a machine for sowing seeds. The objective include perform planting, pollinating, monitoring various sensor parameters.

The machine is designed to be directed remotely, successfully navigating the machine at the desired location while carrying out aforementioned tasks. For navigation, the system utilizes six DC motors. These motors provide the required movement and maneuverability for the machine. The velocity of the motors is managed by a processor, allowing for precise control over the robot's motion [6].

Seeding and fertilizing operations are controlled using a solenoid. The solenoid enables the release of seeds and fertilizers at the desired locations [9]. This mechanism ensures accurate seeding and fertilizing, contributing to the overall efficiency of the agricultural process.

Additionally, the robot is equipped with sensors to monitor soil parameters such as pH, temperature, moisture, and humidity. These sensors provide valuable information about the soil conditions, allowing for informed decision-making in terms of seeding, fertilizing, and overall crop management.

By combining remote control capabilities, navigation systems, and monitoring sensors, the seeding and fertilizing agriculture robot described in the research paper offers an automated and efficient solution for precision agriculture. It reduces the need for manual labor, improves accuracy in seed and fertilizer placement, and provides real-time data for better crop management.

14.3 Proposed System

The functional schematic representation of proposed work is as shown in Figure 14.1. The following are the various components required for experimental setup of automatic seed sowing machine:

- Arduino Board
- L293D Motor Driver

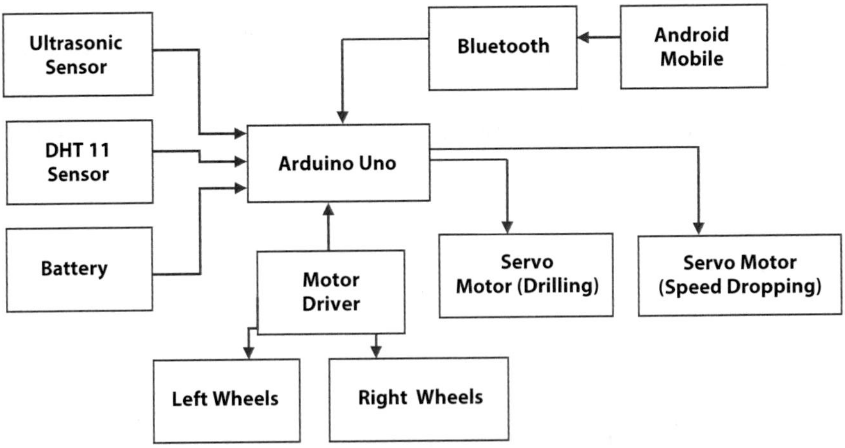

Figure 14.1 Functional schematic representation of proposed work.

- Micro Servo Motor
- HC – 05 Bluetooth Module
- Battery
- LM2596 Buck converter

The automatic seed drilling robot is implemented to operate using electricity obtained from photo voltaic cell. It needs two forms of feeding defining the spacing across seeds drilled in the field.

It is equipped with various sensors to aid in its operation. These sensors can include proximity sensors, GPS, and cameras. They serve different purposes such as guiding the machine, ensuring proper seed placement, and detecting soil conditions.

The control unit of the machine, typically an Arduino MEGA, acts as the brain of the system. It processes data from the sensors in real-time and makes decisions regarding seed placement, depth, and spacing.

The power source for the machine can vary depending on its scale and type. It could be powered by electricity, diesel engines, or even solar power, as mentioned in this case.

The block diagram provided shows the components involved in the robot's movement, sowing, flow, barrier identification etc. The key operating unit is the Arduino MEGA [8] energized with 9-V cell. UV sensors detect obstacles, and the Arduino MEGA analyzes the sensor inputs to manage the output to the lifting servos. DC motors, powered by a 12 V battery, are used for the robot's movement, with the Arduino MEGA controlling the motor direction and speed using an L293D module. Soil moisture and DHT22 sensors provide input to an Arduino UNO regarding the soil moisture level, temperature, and humidity.

Figure 14.2 Arduino control kit.

Figure 14.2 shows the Arduino control kit.

Overall, the proposed work is designed for traverse field in parallel rows, dig up the earth, and plant seeds simultaneously, significantly reducing the time required for planting. The combination of sensors, control unit, and power source enables efficient and accurate seed sowing in agriculture. Figure 14.3 shows the DC motor and Figure 14.4 shows the automated seed showing machine for real time setup.

Figure 14.3 DC motor.

Figure 14.4 Automatic seed sowing machine.

14.4 Conclusions

When comparing seed sowing machines to traditional methods of seed planting, several advantages can be observed:

Maintaining Row Spacing and Seed Rate Control: Automatic seed sowing machines are designed to maintain consistent row spacing, ensuring uniform plant distribution. This is achieved through the use of sensors and control units that precisely regulate the distance between seeds. Traditional methods, on the other hand, rely on manual labor, which may result in uneven spacing and inconsistent seed rates.

Controlling Seed Depth and Minimizing Seed Loss: Automatic seed sowing machines allow for precise control over seed depth, ensuring optimal planting conditions for germination. This helps to minimize seed loss and achieve better seed-to-soil contact, which can lead to improved crop establishment. In contrast, traditional methods often involve manual seed placement, which may result in uneven depth and potential seed loss.

By utilizing advanced technologies such as sensors, control units, and automation, automatic seed sowing machines offer more accurate and efficient seed placement compared to traditional methods. The machines can maintain consistent row spacing, control seed rates, and regulate seed depth, leading to improved crop performance and reduced seed wastage.

References

1. Umarkar, S. and Karwankar, A., Automated Seed Sowing Agribot Using Arduino. *International Conference on Communication and Signal Processing*, India, April 6-8, 2016.
2. Shinde, T.A. and Awati, J.S., Design and Development of Automatic Seed Sowing Machine. *SSRG Int. J. Electron. Commun. Eng. - (ICRTESTM)*, 40–44, ISSN: 2348-8549, Special Issue – April 2017.
3. Kyada, A.R., Design And Development of Manually Operated Seed Planter Machine. *Lecture 5th International & 26th All India Manufacturing Technology, Design and Research Conference (AIMTDR 2014)*, vol. 2, IIT Guwahati, Assam, India.
4. Sambare, S.D. and Belsare, S.S., Seed Sowing Using Robotics Technology. *Int. J. Sci. Res. Manage. (IJSRM)*, 3, 5, 2889–2892, 2015, ISSN: 2321-3418.
5. Shivprasad, B.S., Ravishankara, M.N., Shoba, B.N., Design And Implementation Of Seeding And Fertilizing Agriculture Robot. *Int. J. Appl. Innovation Eng. Manage. (IJAIEM)*, 3, 6, 251–255, June 2014.

6. Swetha, S., Solar Operated Automatic Seed Sowing Machine. Cloud Publications *Int. J. Adv. Agric. Sci. Technol.*, 4, 1, 67–71, 26 February 2015, Article ID Sci-223.
7. Vijaya Saradhi, D., Katragadda, S., Valiveti, Hybrid filter detection network model for secondary user transmission in cognitive radio networks. *H.B. Int. J. Intell. Unmanned Syst.*, *11*, *1*, 61–74, 2023.
8. Premalatha, P. and Sigh, S., Design and Development of Automatic Seed Sowing Machine. *Asian J. Electr. Sci.*, 8, 2, 51–54, 2019.
9. Mujawar, M., Vijaya Saradhi, D., Ajmal Naz, M., Muduli, Design and performance comparison of arrays of circular, square and hexagonal meta-material structures for wearable applications. *J. Magn. Magn. Mater.*, *553*, 169235, 2022.
10. Mujawar, M., Saradhi, V., Lenin Desai, D., Venkateswararao, S., Performance Analysis of Dipole and Bow-Tie Antenna for Underwater Communication Using FEKO. *2021 IEEE International Conference on Emerging Trends in Industry 4.0, ETI 4.0 2021*, 2021.
11. Ramesh, C., Venkata Rao, D., Murthy, K.S.N., Image Restoration using Patch based Gaussian Distribution Distance analysis with PCA correlation factor. *J. Adv. Res. Dyn. Control Syst. (JARDCS)*, *10*, *6*, 843–851, 2018, ISSN No. 1943-023X.

15

In Motion: Exploring Urban Rides Through Data Analytics

Rajkumar Sai Varun, Nimmagadda Narayana, Dudam Vipassana* and Mohan Dholvan

Department of ECM, Sreenidhi Institute of Science and Technology, Hyderabad, India

Abstract

In this Fast-Growing Generation, Data Analytics provides a lot of support to the companies as to optimize their strategies to compete with their competitors. The rapid urbanization of modern cities has brought a lot of changes in the Transportation. Through this project, our aim is to extract the valuable information from the large dataset related to the urban rides including the trip duration, amount transactions, pick up/drop off times, location and other required attributes. Using the Exploratory Data Analysis, we understand the patterns, trends and the anomalies within the data without emerging with the Machine Learning algorithms. The Novelty of this project is to understand the behavior of the driver and the customer for the detection and prevention from the Fraudulent activities. Our findings will give actionable insights to the Transportation companies like Ola, Uber, Rapido etc. to improve their service efficiency and bring the trustworthiness between the Company and the Customer.

***Keywords*:** Data analytics, exploratory data analysis, metric logic calculations, fraud detection

15.1 Introduction

From a business perspective, data is essential for decision-making about how well the company is performing. Companies that successfully use data analytics have a higher chance of success. Several important metrics and

**Corresponding author*: vipassanadudam@gmail.com

Budati Anil Kumar, Singamaneni Kranthi Kumar and Li Xingwang (eds.) Quantum Computing Models for Cybersecurity and Wireless Communications, (237–250) © 2025 Scrivener Publishing LLC

methods are frequently taken into consideration in business analytics to obtain various business insights. Considering various metrics over the past years there was significant growth in the data analysis of Urban rides analytics using various methods [1].

Exploratory Data Analysis (EDA) is a statistical method for summarizing the information and the characteristics of the data sets. This method usually uses statistics, graphics, and other data visualization methods. The Exploratory Data Analysis method usually includes a few key steps like Data collection, Data Cleaning, Data Visualization. EDA is very useful in providing a systematic approach to uncover the insights buried within the large datasets of ride-analysis data. This Technique allows us to peel off the layers of complexity present in urban transportation systems, by revealing the valuable insights present in the data and revolutionize the way cities move. Few approaches for this method are univariate, bivariate or multivariate [4].

EDA maximizes the insight into the database to understand the database structure, it also visualizes the potential relationships between variables, it is used to extract relevant variables from the dataset, and it is also used to detect outliers and anomalies from the dataset. Therefore, analyzing datasets with EDA allows for a deeper understanding of their features and potential issues [5, 6].

Fraud Detection involves systematic identification and prevention of fraudulent activities in various domains. Advances in GPS tracking technology have revolutionized fraud detection in the taxi industry. By leveraging data analytics techniques, we can efficiently identify suspicious behaviors and irregularities of driver activities, which helps us to understand the underlying dynamics driving these fraudulent activities [9, 10].

The project's ultimate objective is to analyze the data using the data analytics rather than using the machine learning algorithms, so as to reduce the time taken by the algorithms and its complexity. In this project we mainly focus on the insights driven from the data and understand the loops within an organization, so as to optimize the company's Business strategy. We use the EDA method which mainly enables us to collect the data, clean the data, and then visualize the data. It mainly deals with the real time tracking of the data.

15.2 Literature Survey

Data is crucial from a business standpoint because of the various ways in which it can be applied. This can be used to extract important information using a variety of approaches. Machine learning is often used to extract predictions and information from data. The forecasts will also be adjusted in accordance with a variety of important performance factors. Depending on the kind of data provided to the system, several model types can be created. When it comes to representing data and making predictions based on patterns found in the data, machine learning will be quite helpful. Numerous other methods exist for processing data in order to extract specific information from the raw data and validate it. To make it simple for the firm to comprehend and obtain comprehensive business insights.

This document discusses the Uber ride data analytics in New York City utilizing machine learning. Uber's dataset was classified using K-means clustering, which made it possible to determine the demand for Uber rides in the various regions of New York City. Gaining an understanding of the spatial distribution and patterns of taxi pickups in New York City is the paper's main goal. Another goal of the research is to create a predictive model that can estimate demand for pickups, which could enhance the effectiveness of taxi dispatching and service [1].

This study highlights the transformative potential of Big Data Analytics (BDA) in health care, emphasizing its role in revolutionizing patient treatment and health management. Through critical analysis of existing literature, findings underscore the increasing adoption of data-driven approaches in various domains, as evidenced by the utilization of structured and unstructured data sources [7].

Since its founding in March 2009, Uber Technologies has experienced rapid expansion. Understanding consumer behavior is the primary goal of the study, which also aims to determine Uber's market value in New York City. Utilizing R programming and several graphical representations, the trip trend on the Uber platform is displayed. For intricate and interactive graphical representations, Ggplot2 is utilized. This study aids in the identification of consumer segments, the optimization of the business's operating costs, and the forecasting of prospective demand growth [2].

This study provides an in-depth analysis of exploratory data analytics, emphasizing its techniques and resources. It primarily focuses on the properties of the data and obtaining insights by comprehending the underlying structures and patterns in the data. The combined use of correlation analysis, data transformation methods, visualizations, and statistics is summed up by EDA. methods and techniques used in the EDA process, including graphical and non-graphical, univariate and multivariate approaches depending on the data [4, 8].

This work presents a novel way to machine learning-based data analysis of Uber ride data by Jonnadula Narasimharao, Marri Johnwesley, Akula Prasanth Kumar, and Kanchi Aashritha. Real-time data is crucial for businesses like Uber to maximize their efficiency. The two main goals are to estimate taxi fares using machine learning methodologies like linear regression and random forest regression, to identify trends in taxi ride data using data analytics. These can aid in forecasting demand. Bar graphs are used to illustrate all of these observations, which will help the reader easily understand the data. The steps involved in outlier detection, correlation analysis, model selection, and data preprocessing are described in the study. To ensure accurate forecasts and prepare the data for machine learning models, it goes over the importance of each stage [3].

15.3 Proposed Methodology

For a business, machine learning algorithms are neither effective nor efficient when it comes to interpretation, resource utilization, market segmentation, customer engagement, and retention. So, in order to resolve this issue, we will analyze the business performance and provide predictions using data analytics. Over the past few years there has been significant growth in Big Data and Data Analytics using various methods. In this study, we will analyze and predict the behavior of a business organization in the urban transportation sector of New York City. Exploratory analysis is one of the methods for analyzing and understanding the data.

Exploratory data analysis (EDA) is the method of studying and understanding data to discover patterns, locate outliers, and identify relationships between variables. We will apply EDA to raw datasets and then take into account the statistical analysis to arrive at predictions. The proposed method has following steps involved:

A. Proposed Architecture
B. Raw Data (Dataset)
C. Data Importing
D. Exploratory Data Analysis(EDA)
E. Statistical Analysis
F. Data Visualization
G. Fraud Detection

A. Proposed Architecture
Figure 15.1 shows the project architecture.

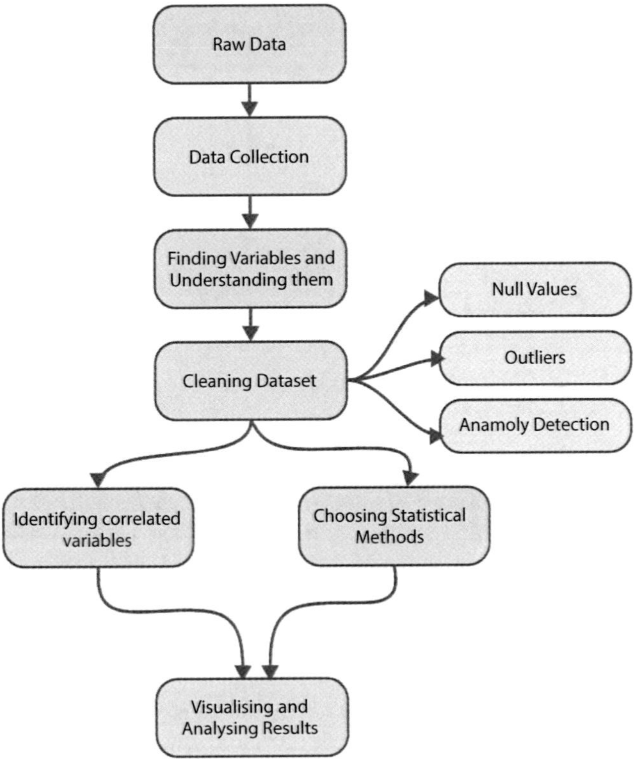

Figure 15.1 Proposed architecture.

B. Raw Data (Dataset)

Raw data is defined as the data generated by a system or specifically a business organization which is not processed in any way. As shown in Figure 15.2, raw data comprising CSV files containing information about taxi zones in New York City and the history of rides.

Unnamed: 0	VendorID	lpep_pickup_datetime	lpep_dropoff_datetime	store_and_fwd_flag	RatecodeID	PULocationID	DOLocationID	passenger_count
0	2.0	2020-01-01 06:47:28.000	2020-01-01 06:52:54.000	N	1.0	74	75	1.0
1	2.0	2020-01-01 13:25:34.000	2020-01-01 13:30:43.000	N	1.0	74	75	1.0
2	2.0	2020-01-01 14:20:35.000	2020-01-01 14:26:25.000	N	1.0	74	75	1.0
3	2.0	2020-01-02 06:56:47.000	2020-01-02 07:03:03.000	N	1.0	74	75	1.0
4	2.0	2020-01-02 09:34:46.000	2020-01-02 09:41:02.000	N	1.0	74	75	1.0

Figure 15.2 Raw data – sample (CSV file).

Unnamed: 0	lpep_pickup_datetime	lpep_dropoff_datetime	PULocationID	DOLocationID	passenger_count
10930477	2017-12-31 22:16:34	2017-12-31 22:20:20	116	244	1.0
11401428	2017-12-31 22:26:33	2017-12-31 22:30:13	244	244	1.0
11076590	2017-12-31 23:00:25	2017-12-31 23:15:57	116	235	1.0
11746896	2017-12-31 23:00:50	2017-12-31 23:09:17	116	166	1.0
10933387	2017-12-31 21:51:45	2017-12-31 21:56:19	41	41	1.0
11919594	2017-12-31 21:13:36	2017-12-31 21:20:41	166	41	1.0

Figure 15.3 Data importing.

C. Data Importing

Real-time data (raw data) is collected in large quantities from the business organization. The raw data includes information of rides and zones. As shown in Figure 15.3, the data is then imported into a data frame and the columns and information present within the dataset are analyzed.

D. Exploratory Data Analysis (EDA)

EDA is the process of analyzing datasets to understand the patterns, locate outliers using statistical and other data visualization methods. Refer to Figures 15.4 and 15.5 for a detailed illustration of Bar plot & Scatter plot. Exploratory Data analysis can be divided into four types:

- Univariate non-graphical. A single variable is used in this form of data analysis. As it is a single variable, causes and relationships are not addressed.
- Univariate graphical. Due to the inability of non-graphical methods to provide complete insights of the data, graphical methods are required. Some types of univariate graphical methods are histograms, box plots.
- Multivariate non-graphical. Multiple variables are used in this form of data analysis. By using statistics, this type demonstrates how two or more variables are related.
- Multivariate graphical. This form of data analysis uses graphs to show the relationships between two or more sets of data. Some types of multivariate graphical methods are scatter plot, run chart, bubble chart, heat map, and multivariate charts. We are following the multivariate graphical approach for this study.

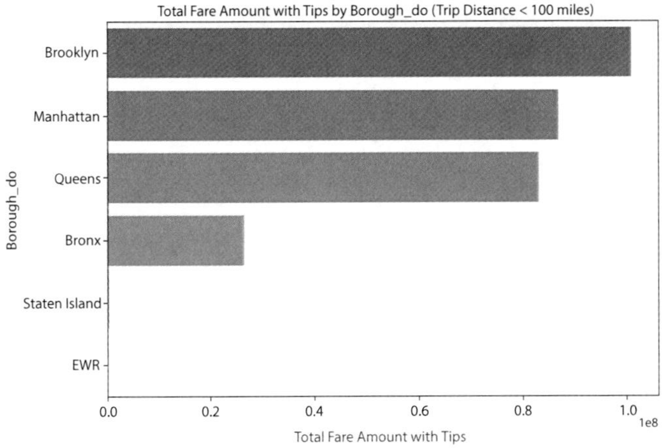

Figure 15.4 Bar plot representing the total fare amount with tip amount by borough location.

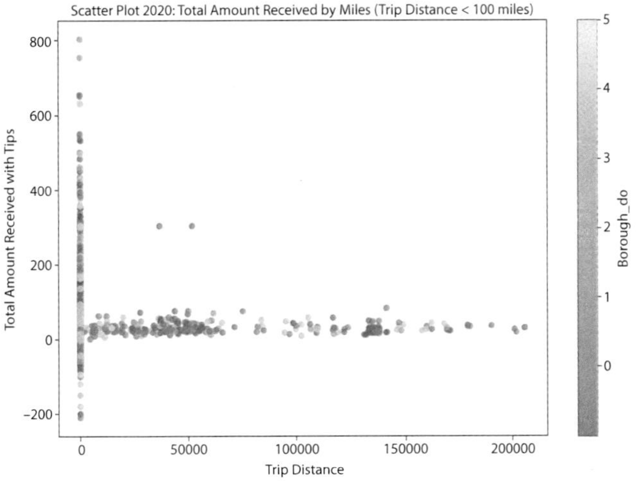

Figure 15.5 Scatter plot and color bar representing the total amount received by trip distance.

E. Statistical Analysis

Statistical Analysis provides a more detailed view of operational landscapes and provides business organizations insights required to make strategic and evidence-based decisions. It helps organizations make educated decisions by providing insights from data. In order to comprehend, interpret and utilize large datasets statistical analysis provides a systematic approach that encompasses everything from data extraction to development of actionable recommendations. Businesses can discover hidden patterns in their data and extract important insights by navigating these complex processes

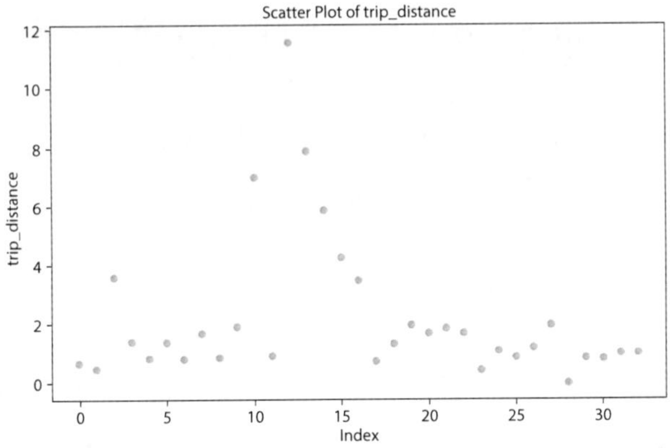

Figure 15.6 Scatter plot representing the data of the column trip_distance.

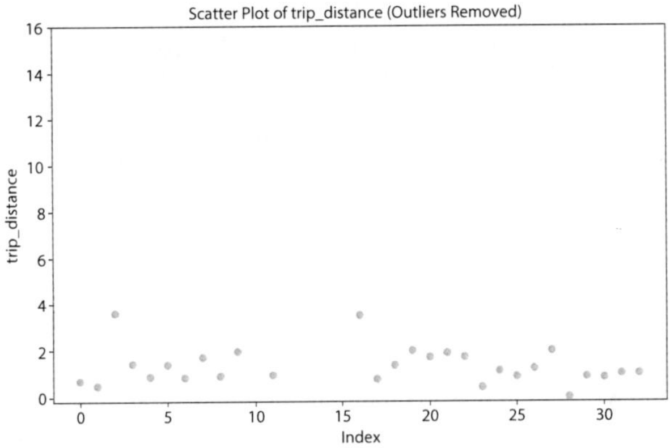

Figure 15.7 Scatter plot representing the data after the removal of outliers from the column trip_distance.

in order to take strategic decisions based on their data. Refer to Figures 15.6 and 15.7 for a detailed illustration of scatter plots representing the data before and after removal of outliers.

We have used IQR (Interquartile Range) methods to find and replace the outliers in the data. IQR is calculated by the difference between 75th and 25th percentiles of the data. The data which fall below Q1-1.5IQR or above Q3+1.5IQR are considered as outliers.

F. Data Visualization

Data visualization is defined as graphical representation of data. This also helps to understand trends, patterns, and outliers in data. In Figure 15.8, we can observe the visualisation of the heat map.

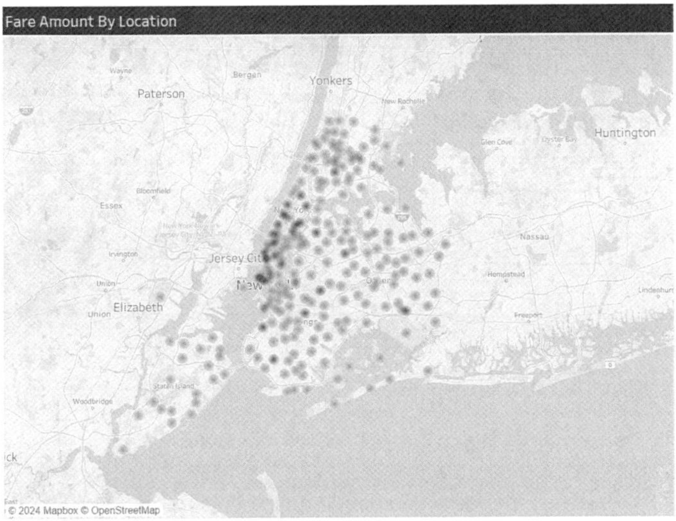

Figure 15.8 Heat map for fare amount by location.

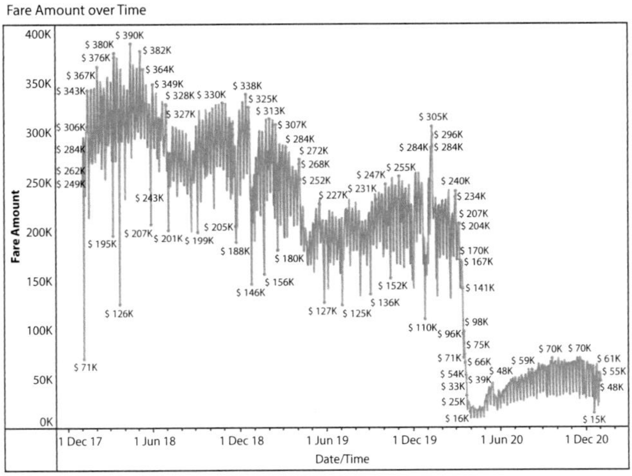

Figure 15.9 Visualization representing fare amount over time.

Similarly Figure 15.9 illustrates the line graph. Data visualization provides strategic decision-making, improved customer service and increased employee management.

G. Fraud Detection

Fraud Detection is defined as the process of detecting scams and fraudsters who try to obtain property or money through false means. For any business fraud detection is one of the top priorities to prevent financial losses, maintain trust, and ensure regulatory compliance. Figures 15.10 and 15.11 gives insights about the frequency of pick-ups and the patterns of trips, which helps in understanding of the fraud occurrence.

While Machine Learning or AI has their place in fraud detection, data analytics offers a complementary and practical approach that prioritizes interpretability, flexibility, and business understanding.

	Borough_loc	pickup_count
0	Bronx	85124
1	Brooklyn	227959
2	EWR	343
3	Manhattan	584838
4	Queens	296230
5	Staten Island	1143

Figure 15.10 Analyzing the frequency of pick-ups at various locations in each borough.

	Borough_do	trip_count	total_amount	tolls_amount	avg_trip_distance	profit_amount	profit_percentage
0	None	3378	50.3	0.0	2.575077	50.3	100.0
1	Bronx	139172	42.3	0.0	5.629261	42.3	100.0
2	Brooklyn	745479	48.8	0.0	4.320474	48.8	100.0
3	EWR	24	3.3	0.0	1.012083	3.3	100.0
4	Manhattan	757405	6.8	0.0	3.296901	6.8	100.0
5	Queens	690875	38.8	0.0	3.816826	38.8	100.0
6	Staten Island	383	3.8	0.0	11.418799	3.8	100.0

Figure 15.11 Understanding the patterns of trips in each borough.

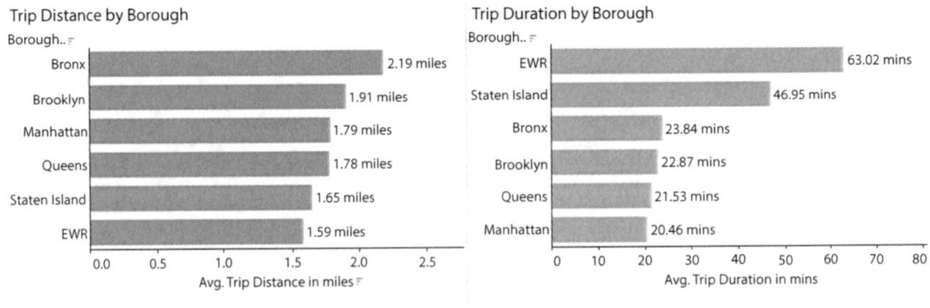

Figure 15.12 Understanding one of the key performance indicators - trips by location (operational analytics).

15.4 Result Analysis

The study sets out to use EDA process and extensive Data Visualization methods to achieve optimization in decision making process and organization's

Pickup Locations:

	PULocationID	Borough_loc	Zone_loc	pickup_count
0	74	Manhattan	East Harlem South	3795
1	75	Manhattan	East Harlem North	3496
2	74	Manhattan	East Harlem North	2174
3	75	Manhattan	East Harlem South	2000

Figure 15.13 Analyzing pick up locations for understanding the patterns of fraud detection.

Drop-off Locations:

	DOLocationID	Borough_loc	Zone_loc
0	74	Manhattan	East Harlem North
1	75	Manhattan	East Harlem South
2	42	Manhattan	Central Harlem North
3	41	Manhattan	Central Harlem
4	236	Manhattan	Upper East Side North

Figure 15.14 Analyzing drop off locations for understanding the patterns of fraud detection.

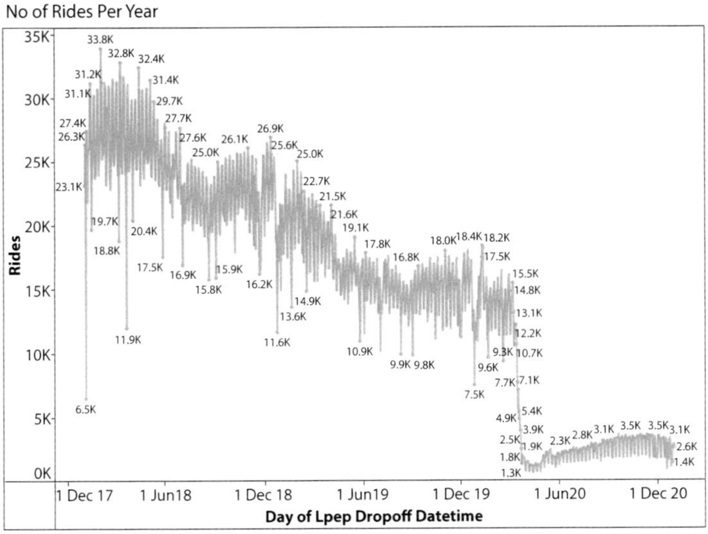

Figure 15.15 Understanding the trends of rides (operational analytics).

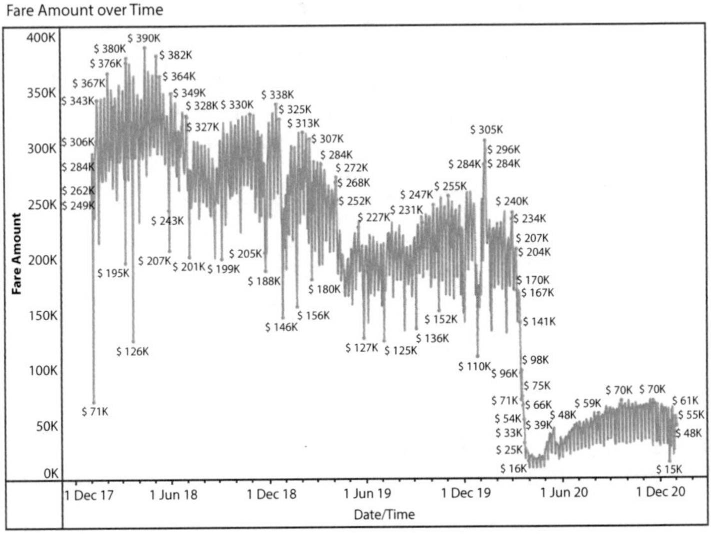

Figure 15.16 Understanding the trends of fare amount (financial analytics).

business strategy in the market. As discussed, in contrast to the machine learning approach, the proposed methodology provides higher interpretability and flexibility in getting insights which are valuable for organization goals. Following are the results as discussed: Figure 15.12 explains one of the KPI's. The detailed analysis of pick up locations & drop off locations and patterns for fraud is depicted in Figures 15.13 and 15.14. In Figures 15.15 and 15.16, we can observe operational and financial analytics.

15.5 Conclusion

In conclusion, our project adopts a data centric approach, prioritizing the utilization of data analytics techniques, specifically Exploratory Data Analysis (EDA) to gain valuable insights and optimize the organization's business strategy. By focusing on real-time data tracking, cleaning, and visualization, we aim to streamline operations, uncover hidden patterns within the organization, and perform decision making processes. Through this method, we aspire to not only reduce the time and complexity associated with traditional machine learning algorithms but also to promote a culture of data-driven optimization, ultimately positioning the company for sustained success and competitive advantage in the market.

References

1. Srinivas, R., Ankayarkanni, B., Sathya Bama Krishna, R., Uber Related Data Analysis Using Machine Learning. *Proceedings of the Fifth International Conference on Intelligent Computing and Control Systems (ICICCS 2021)*, IEEE Xplore Part Number: CFP21K74-ART; ISBN: 978-0-7381-1327-2.
2. Patil, M., Kumari, V., Patil, A., Ahire, L., Mandawkar, U., UBER DATA ANALYSIS USING GGPLOT. *J. Eng. Sci.*, 12, 7, July/ 2021, ISSN NO: 0377-9254.
3. Kumar, A.P., Aashritha, K., Johnwesly, M., Narasimharao, J., A novel approach to analyze uber data using machine learning. *IJARST*, 13, 03, Mar 2023, ISSN: 2457-036.
4. Rao, A.S., Vardhan, B.V., Shaik, H., Role of Exploratory Data Analysis in Data Science. *2021 6th International Conference on Communication and Electronics Systems (ICCES)*, Coimbatore, pp. 1457–1461, India, 2021, doi: 10.1109/ICCES51350.2021.9488986.
5. Komorowski, M., Marshall, D., Salciccioli, J., Crutain, Y., Exploratory Data Analysis, 2016, 10.1007/978-3-319-43742-2_15.
6. Camizuli, E. and Carranza, E.J., *Exploratory Data Analysis (EDA)*, The Encyclopedia of Archaeological Sciences, pp. 1–7, 2018, 10.1002/97811 19188230.saseas0271.
7. Batko, K. and Ślęzak, A., The use of Big Data Analytics in healthcare. *J. Big Data*, 9, 3, 2022.
8. Nandeshvar, K., Joseph, A., Sakthivel, K., Shiyam, S., New York City Taxi Trip Duration Prediction Using Machine Learning. *Int. J. Res. Appl. Sci. Eng. Technol.*, 11, 5107–5112, 2023, 10.22214/ijraset.2023.52768.
9. Liu, S., Ni, L., Krishnan, R., Fraud Detection From Taxis' Driving Behaviors. *IEEE Trans. Veh. Technol.*, 63, 464–472, 2014, 10.1109/TVT.2013.2272792.
10. Ge, Y., Xiong, H., Liu, C., Zhou, Z.-H., A Taxi Driving Fraud Detection System. *Proceedings - IEEE International Conference on Data Mining, ICDM*, pp. 181–190, 2011, 10.1109/ICDM.2011.1.

16

Design of Novel Chatbot Using Generative Artificial Intelligence

Sk. Khader Zelani*, Sk. Gousiya Begum, M. Chandana and N. Lakshmi Tirupatamma

Dept of ECE, Malineni Lakshmaiah Women's Engineering College, Guntur A.P, India

Abstract
Chatbots have emerged as versatile tools for human-computer interaction, offering automated conversational experiences across diverse domains. The integration of Generative Artificial Intelligence (AI) techniques has revolutionized chatbot design, enabling machines to generate human-like responses and adapt to complex user queries dynamically. This paper explores the design principles, methodologies, and innovations associated with developing chatbots using Generative AI. We review the underlying technologies, including deep learning architectures, natural language processing (NLP) techniques, and conversational modeling approaches. Additionally, we discuss the challenges and ethical considerations inherent in chatbot design, such as data privacy, bias mitigation, and user trust. Through case studies and practical examples, we highlight best practices and emerging trends in the field, emphasizing the potential of Generative AI-powered chatbots to enhance user engagement, streamline customer support processes, and facilitate personalized interactions across various domains.

Keywords: Chatbot design, generative AI, natural language processing, machine learning, conversational agents, AI chatbots, generative models, human-computer interaction

**Corresponding author*: zelani786@gmail.com

Budati Anil Kumar, Singamaneni Kranthi Kumar and Li Xingwang (eds.) Quantum Computing Models for Cybersecurity and Wireless Communications, (251–258) © 2025 Scrivener Publishing LLC

16.1 Introduction

A chatbot is a computer program designed to simulate conversation with human users, typically through textual or auditory channels. By leveraging natural language processing (NLP) and machine learning algorithms, chatbots can interpret user queries, generate responses, and engage in meaningful dialogues across various platforms and applications. The introduction highlights the diverse range of applications where chatbots are employed. This may include customer service, e-commerce, healthcare, education, finance, and entertainment industries, among others. Chatbots serve as virtual assistants [1], providing information, answering questions, guiding users through processes, and facilitating transactions, thereby enhancing user experiences and streamlining workflows. The introduction briefly traces the evolution of chatbots, from early rule-based systems to advanced AI-driven models [2]. Early chatbots relied on predefined rules and pattern matching techniques to respond to user inputs. However, with the advent of machine learning and deep learning technologies, chatbots have become more sophisticated, capable of learning from data and adapting their responses based on contextual cues and user interactions. The introduction acknowledges the emergence of Generative AI as a transformative paradigm in chatbot design [3]. Generative AI enables chatbots to go beyond simple rule-based responses and generate human-like text dynamically. By employing techniques such as recurrent neural networks (RNNs), transformers, and attention mechanisms, chatbots powered by Generative AI can understand the nuances of language, maintain context over extended conversations, and produce coherent and contextually relevant responses.

PCOD (Polycystic Ovary Syndrome) can be reduced in large part by using AI (Artificial Intelligence) to improve management techniques, individualized treatment plans, and diagnostic precision. Recent researchers have focus on the development of AI helps medical personnel analyze large patient data sets, including test results, symptoms, and medical histories, to find trends and more accurately predict PCOD. It does this by using machine learning algorithms [4]. AI-powered imaging tools, such MRIs and ultrasounds, make it easier to identify ovarian cysts and evaluate the morphology of the ovaries. Additionally, AI-driven decision support systems let medical professionals create individualized treatment programs based on the traits of each patient as well as lifestyle choices and genetic predispositions [5]. Healthcare professionals can enhance PCOD management, improve patient outcomes, and reduce long-term health consequences by utilizing AI for early identification and targeted interventions.

A medical condition known as polycystic ovarian syndrome (PCOS) affects women who are fertile and has an impact on hormones. Hormonal imbalance causes a monthly cycle to be delayed or even absent [6]. For PCOS, there is no known etiology. It might be challenging to conceive if a woman has PCOS, which is characterized by significant weight gain, facial hair growth, acne, hair loss, skin pigmentation, and irregular cycles.

With weight control, early detection, and treatment, the risk of long-term conditions including diabetes type 2 and heart problems may be decreased. The existing methods and therapies are insufficient for early-stage detection and prediction [7]. In order to address this problem, we offer a technique that can forecast PCOS therapeutic efficacy based

Objectives and Scope of the Paper: Finally, the introduction outlines the key objectives and scope of the paper. It sets the stage for exploring the design principles, methodologies, innovations, challenges, and ethical considerations associated with developing chatbots using Generative AI. The paper aims to provide Telegram bots accessible insights into best practices, emerging trends, and practical application in our mobile of Generative AI-powered chatbots across various domains [8], contributing to the broader discourse on AI-driven human-computer interaction.

Overall, the evolution of chatbots reflects the ongoing advancements in AI technologies, user experience design [9], and the growing demand for intelligent and conversational interfaces across various domains and applications.

Design Methodologies Step Wise

Let us begin by providing an overview of BotFather. This service assists users in managing and creating Telegram bots. The Telegram bot is not a private bot; it is a public bot. This is a public Telegram bot that is accessible to everyone.

STEP-1: Enter your account information and visit the web.telegram.organd.website

STEP-2: To find BotFather, search now

STEP-3: You may now see the START button.

STEP-4: The BotFather Services will be displayed after pressing the START button.

STEP-5: To create a chatbot, type the command "/newbot" and hit Enter.

STEP-6: It will now ask for the bot's name.

STEP-7: It will now prompt you to select or provide a username in a specific format.

To prevent inconvenience, adhere to the format below.

(Suggestion: collegename_rollno.last 3digits_bot)
For example: I'm giving as drive_514_bot
! If you received a "congratulations," you should know that your bot has been created.

STEP-8: We are going to incorporate ChatGpt (which requires an account) and Botfather.
Consequently, you will receive a special token (Do Not Share) upon chatbot creation.
Now create a folder on your desktop and launch VScode inside of it. The folder is called Telegram-chatBot-ChatGpt.
(Pythaon script will connect both telegram and ChatGpt)

STEP-9: Now that the CMD prompt is open, install some libraries.
pip install pytelegrambotapi
(By installing, you can access telegramBot by using python Script)
Next, we also need to install the ChatGpt library. By utilizing the Cmd
pip install openai

STEP-10: Now let's create a python file naming it as app.py
→Now copy your unique token (that u have got on telegram).
→Note in VScode as
botToken='6914568825:AAETeAFnlB2_U1YvhpYfPxk6 NBsHt3DLzlo'

STEP-11: Now visit to the following Website https://platform.openai.com/

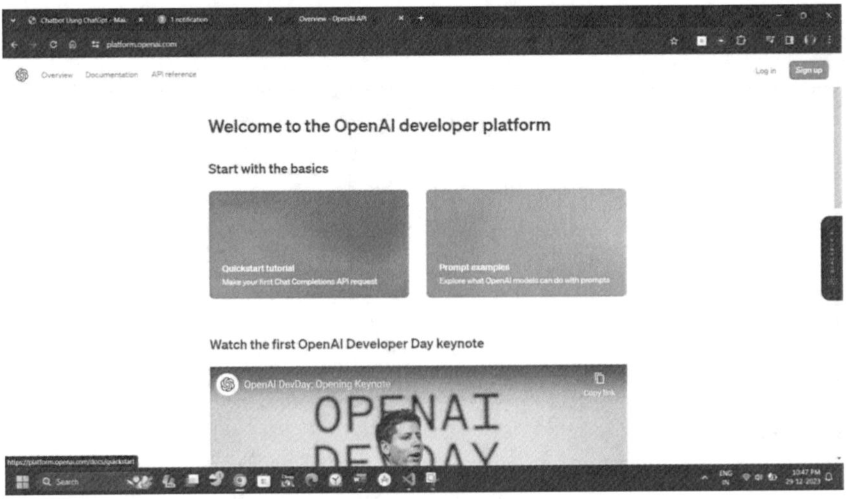

STEP-12: Give a name; for example, my name is the Telegram Bot key. It will then confirm if you are a robot or a person after that.

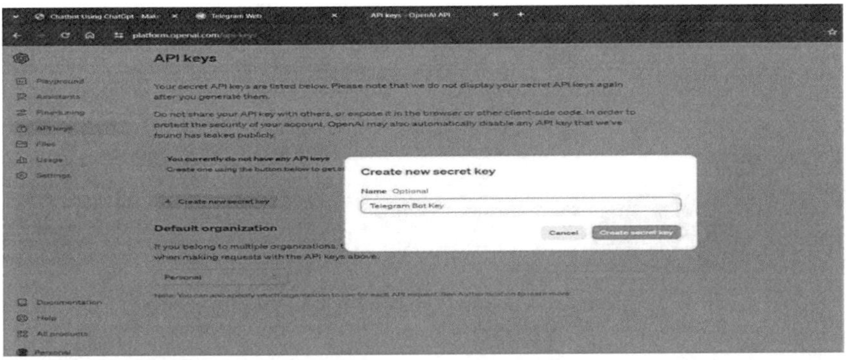

You'll receive a unique key following verification; make a copy of it. NOTE: Avoid clicking "Done." You must first copy the API key

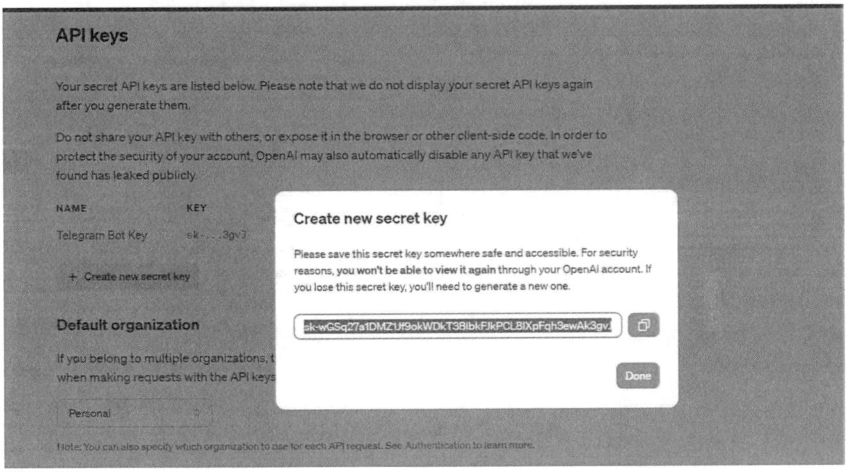

directly, as you won't be able to view it again.

STEP-13: Now the copied API key, is to be pasted on VScode as followed,

Open API key='sk-wGSq27a1DMZ1Jf9okWDkT3BlbkFJk-PCL8IXpFqh3ewAk3gvJ'

STEP-14: Now u have to write the Code in python

-After writing, click on run button OR run it on terminal as python app.py

-After running, it will don't print any output, Don't worry, it just waits for the input.

STEP-15: After running, open telegram and click on the 1st link you got in the Congratulations message, i.e. my link is t.me/drive_514_bot

STEP-16: Now u will see the following interface, click on START

STEP-17: Now u will see the following interface.
(Before giving input run the prog. once)
I have given the input as to create an article

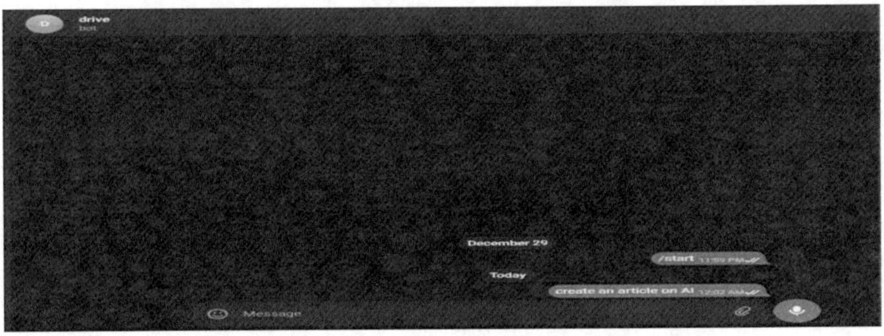

Results:

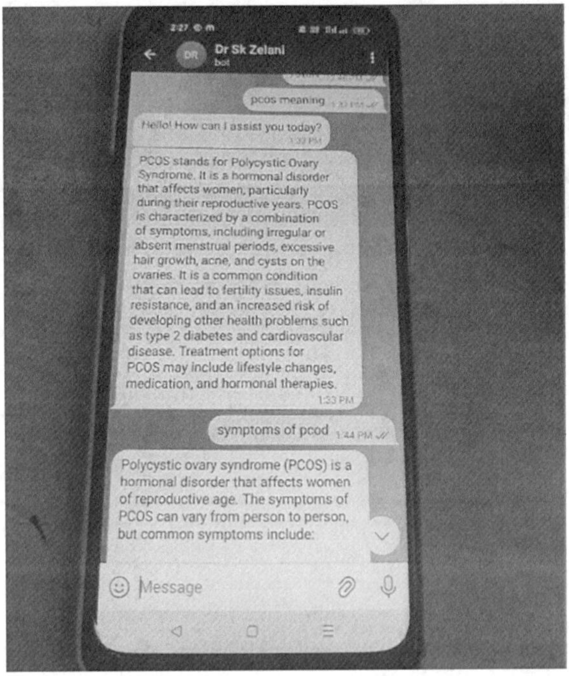

16.2 Conclusion and Future Scope

An extensive research has been carried out to develop a low profile and optimized chatbot is designed which can be used in mobile using telegram app and it is most flexible, handy and secure. Virtual assistants powered by artificial intelligence (AI) include Google Assistant, Amazon Alexa, and Microsoft Cortana. A new frontier in conversational AI is generative AI-driven chatbots, particularly those built on deep learning architectures like transformers and recurrent neural networks (RNNs). These interfaces let users conduct hands-free discussions and carry out activities by speaking commands.

References

1. Siddaiah, N., Zelani, K., Bhavanam, S.N., Modelling of Capacitive Pressure Sensor for Medical Applications. *Int. J. Pharm. Res. (09752366)*, 2, 1018–1025, 2020.
2. Schmidt, P.G. and Meir, A.J., Using Generative AI for Literature Searches and Scholarly Writing: Is the Integrity of the Scientific Discourse in Jeopardy? *Not. Am. Math. Soc.*, *71*, 1, 93–104, 2023.
3. Shaik, K.Z., P, S., Prasad, K.S., Design and implementation of artificial magnetic conductor surface as decoupling structure in microstrip antenna arrays. *Circuit World*, *47*, 3, 290–300, 2021.
4. Haase, J. and Hanel, P.H., Artificial muses: Generative artificial intelligence chatbots have risen to human-level creativity. *J. Creat.*, *33*, 3, 100066, 2023.
5. Shaik, K.Z., Siddaiah, P., Prasad, K.S., A novel miniaturized, multiband, AMC-integrated CPW-fed antenna operating at millimetric wave frequencies suitable for IoT applications. *Int. J. Intell. Unmanned Syst.*, *11*, 1, 182–193, 2022.
6. Zelani, S.K., Siddaiah, P., Prasad, K.S., A Novel AMC Loaded CPW Fed Wide Band Antenna for 5G Applications. 6, 7, 235–245, 2018.
7. Saritha, V., Kumar Karra, A., Zelani, S.K., Prasanth, C., Cloud-Connected Smart Energy Meter with Remote Monitoring and Control, in: *Smart and Intelligent Systems: Proceedings of SIS 2021*, pp. 297–305, Springer, Singapore, 2022.
8. Shaik, K.Z., CPW-Fed Microstrip Patch Antenna for Millimeter Wave Applications. *Int. J. Integr. Eng.*, *14*, 7, 69–83, 2022.
9. Vijaya Saradhi, D., Katragadda, S., Valiveti, H.B., Hybrid filter detection network model for secondary user transmission in cognitive radio networks. *Int. J. Intell. Unmanned Syst.*, *11*, 1, 61–74, 2023.

17

The Smart Nebulizer Cap for Enhanced Asthma Management

Rossly Netala*, **Aadi Praharsha and Mohan Dholvan**

Department of ECM, Sreenidhi Institute of Science and Technology, Hyderabad, India

Abstract
This Asthma, a prevalent chronic respiratory condition worldwide, continues to pose substantial challenges to public health. Despite advancements in medical treatments, the effective management of asthma attacks remains a pressing concern. This research introduces an innovative solution: the Smart Nebulizer Cap, a wearable device engineered to enhance asthma management by providing prompt and convenient relief during asthma exacerbation. The Smart Nebulizer Cap represents a significant breakthrough in asthma management, addressing the critical need for a portable and efficient solution to alleviate asthma attack.

***Keywords*:** Portability, convenience, user-friendly design, compact, effective medication delivery

17.1 Introduction

Traditional methods of managing asthma attacks often rely on cumbersome nebulizers, which, while effective, are not always conducive to the demands of modern lifestyles. Recognizing this gap, our research endeavors to introduce a transformative solution: the Smart Nebulizer Cap. This innovative wearable device represents a paradigm shift in asthma management, offering a portable, user-friendly, and efficient means of delivering medication during asthma exacerbation. By seamlessly integrating into the daily lives of

**Corresponding author*: rosslynetala@gmail.com

Budati Anil Kumar, Singamaneni Kranthi Kumar and Li Xingwang (eds.) Quantum Computing Models for Cybersecurity and Wireless Communications, (259–266) © 2025 Scrivener Publishing LLC

individuals with asthma, the Smart Nebulizer Cap seeks to redefine how we approach and respond to asthma, COPD, and Bronchitis.

Nebulizer technology as shown in Figure 17.1 plays a vital role in the delivery of medication directly to the lungs for the treatment of various respiratory illnesses [4]. Mesh nebulizers, a specific type that utilizes a vibrating mesh to generate a fine mist, offer several advantages including portability, efficiency, and quiet operation compared to traditional jet nebulizers [3, 6]. However, optimizing the performance of mesh nebulizers requires careful consideration of various factors, one of which being acoustic coupling [1].

Acoustic coupling refers to the interaction between the vibrating mesh and the surrounding air or liquid within the nebulizer chamber. This interaction can significantly impact the overall performance of the device in terms of factors such as: Efficiency: Acoustic coupling can influence the efficiency of energy transfer from the piezoelectric actuator to the mesh, ultimately affecting the rate of medication nebulization [1]. Medication Delivery: The characteristics of the aerosol mist generated by the nebulizer, such as particle size and deposition pattern within the lungs, can be influenced by acoustic coupling [2].

Understanding and optimizing acoustic coupling in silicon-based vibrating mesh nebulizers is therefore crucial for achieving optimal performance and ensuring effective drug delivery to the lungs.

This paper will delve into the impact of acoustic coupling on mesh nebulizer performance. We will explore the design considerations related to the mesh itself and how they influence acoustic coupling [1]. Additionally, we will compare acoustic coupling in mesh nebulizers to other nebulizer

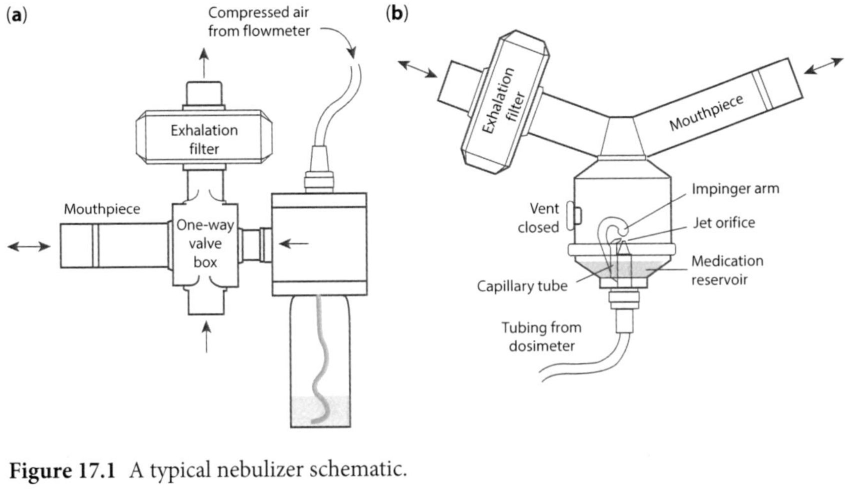

Figure 17.1 A typical nebulizer schematic.

technologies such as jet and ultrasonic nebulizers, highlighting the strengths and weaknesses of each approach [2, 6].

This study will delve into the impact of nebulizer performances However, there is still room for improvement regarding user experience and ease of use, especially for those who require frequent nebulization treatments. Even with a more compact design compared to jet nebulizers, mesh nebulizers can still be cumbersome to carry around, especially for those who need frequent treatments throughout the day. Nebulization times can vary depending on the medication and device, but they can sometimes feel lengthy for patients, especially children. The face mask or mouthpiece used with nebulizers can feel uncomfortable, particularly for long term use.

17.2 Literature Survey

Use of Nebulizer Development: A Brief Review [1] L Castañeda. Ultrasonic Spray Pyrolysis; Thin Solid Films; Nebulizers Process. Biomed J Sci & Tech Res 40(5)-2021. BJSTR. MS.ID.006505. Year-2022 Journal/conference Details Biomedical Journal of Scientific and technical research. Methodology –analyzed exiting methods of nebulization In Vitro Comparison of Nebulized Budesonide Deposition Patterns from Different Nebulizer Technologies in a Multicompartmental Lung Model (2023). Respiratory Care (https://www.aarc.org/resource/respiratory-care/) Methodology – The study compared the deposition patterns of nebulized budesonide from three different nebulizer technologies (jet, mesh, and ultrasonic) using a multicompartmental lung model. Development and Characterization of Novel Nebulized Liposomes for Co-Delivery of Hydrophobic and Hydrophilic Drugs for Treatment of Respiratory Infections (2021). Journal-American Association of Pharmaceutical Scientists (AAPS) (https://www.aaps.org/pharmsci/annual-meeting). Methodology – development and characterization of novel liposomal formulations for nebulized co-delivery of hydrophobic and hydrophilic drugs for respiratory infections. The Impact of Different Nebulization Techniques on Drug Delivery to the Lungs (2019). Journal of Aerosol Medicine and Pulmonary Drug Delivery (https://home.liebertpub.com/publications/journal-of-aerosol-medicine-and-pulmonary-drug-delivery/24/for-authors). Methodology – study investigated the impact of different nebulization techniques on drug delivery to the lungs. Machine Learning for Nebulized Drug Delivery Optimization (2023) Conference: International Conference on Machine Learning for Health (MLHC). Journal-International Conference on Machine Learning for Health (MLHC) Proceedings. Methodology – The researchers propose a model that can predict factors influencing drug deposition and suggest strategies for improving treatment efficacy. The Use of Telemonitoring with Nebulized Medication for Patients with Exacerbations of Chronic Obstructive Pulmonary Disease: A Systematic Review (2022). Journal of Telemedicine and Telecare (https://journals.sagepub.com/home/jtt). Methodology – This systematic review analyzed existing research on the use of telemonitoring with nebulized medication for COPD patients.

17.3 Methodology

We chose the preferred reporting items for systematic reviews and meta-analyses (PRISMA) as the systematic review methodology. A total of four databases were searched, including PubMed, Scopus, SpringerLink and the IEEE Xplore Digital Library. All databases were searched using keywords Wearable Systems^ and Hospital Care, Asthma, Wearable Patient Monitoring, Existing nebulizer methods, as mentioned below in Table 17.1,

Table 17.1 Comparison of methods.

	Existing Methods		
Type	**Methodology**	**Objective**	**Reference**
Mesh	Vibrating mesh with microscopic holes generates mist. Piezoelectric actuator creates vibrations.	Portability and efficiency	[1, 2]
Jet	Compressed air forces medication through orifice. - Traditionally bulky and loud.	Lower cost option.	[3, 4]
Ultrasonic	High-frequency sound waves vibrate crystal, creating mist. - May be quieter than jet nebulizers.	Portable but may require frequent cleaning.	[5, 6]
Electrospray	Electric field creates charged aerosol mist – Relatively new technology.	Potential advantages in particle size control and efficiency.	[7, 8]

while effective in delivering medication to the lungs, often come with drawbacks that limit user experience and adherence to treatment. Traditional jet nebulizers, though widely available, can be bulky, loud, and require a significant medication volume. Ultrasonic nebulizers offer some portability but may require frequent cleaning and potentially generate a less optimal mist. Mesh nebulizers, a more recent development, address some of these issues with their compact size and efficiency, but they can still be tethered to a power source and lack the ultimate discretion some users desire. These limitations highlight the need for innovative nebulizer designs that prioritize portability, user comfort, and ease of use.

Our proposed method can impact those with immediate and often attention.

Jet Nebulizers: These workhorses of inhalation therapy utilize the Venturi effect. Compressed air, often generated by an external compressor, is forced through a narrow orifice at high velocity. This creates a region of low pressure around the orifice. Liquid medication drawn from a reservoir is then sheared into a mist by the combination of the high-speed airflow and the low-pressure zone. While effective, jet nebulizers can be bulky and noisy due to the external compressor as shown in Figure 17.2. Additionally, the forceful airflow can generate some larger droplets that may not reach the deep lung regions [4].

Ultrasonic Nebulizers: These offer a quieter and more compact alternative. The schematic for the ultrasonic nebulizer is shown in Figure 17.3. They employ piezoelectric crystals. When exposed to electrical current, these crystals vibrate at ultrasonic frequencies (typically above 1 million cycles per second). These high-frequency vibrations are transmitted to the liquid medication in a dedicated chamber, causing it to break down into a fine mist with much smaller droplets compared to jet nebulizers. However, ultrasonic

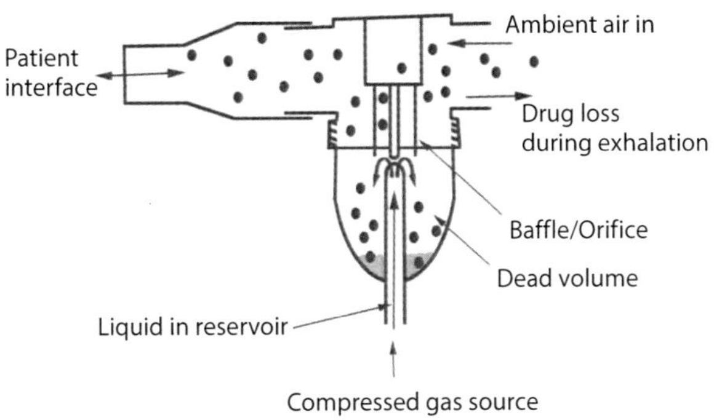

Figure 17.2 Typical jet nebulizer.

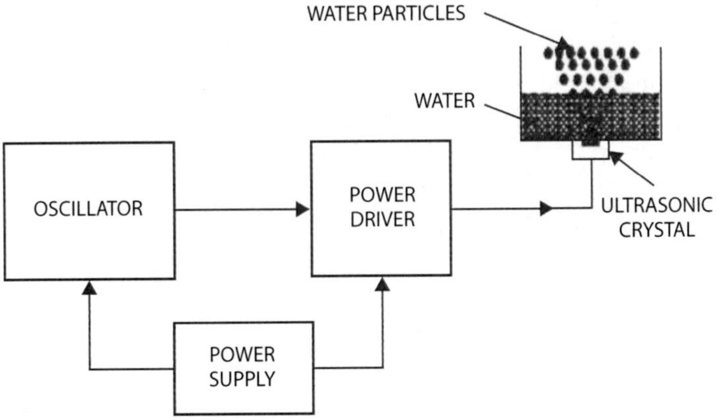

Figure 17.3 Ultrasonic nebulizer schematic.

technology may not be suitable for all medications as the high-frequency vibrations can sometimes degrade heat-sensitive drugs [2].

Our Proposed System:

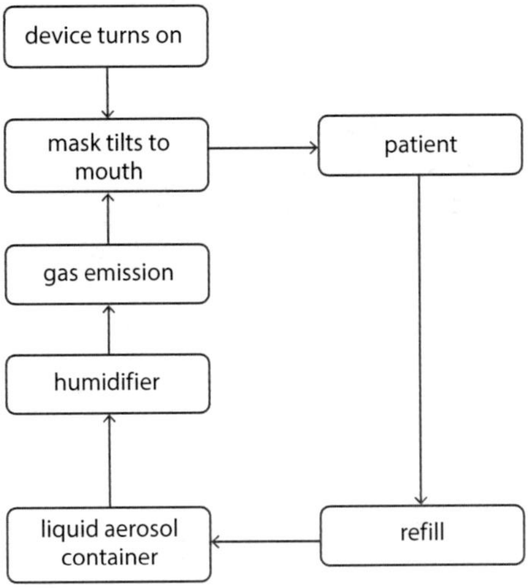

This represents a significant advancement in inhalation therapy, offering a more efficient and user-centric approach to medication delivery for respiratory illnesses. Unlike traditional nebulizers that can be bulky and inconvenient, the compact design and intuitive operation enhance treatment adherence, particularly for patients who struggle with conventional methods.

The core functionality revolves around a two-stage process. Activation triggers a miniaturized compressor that generates pressurized air. This airflow shears the liquid medication within a dedicated chamber, transforming it into a fine mist with significantly increased surface area.

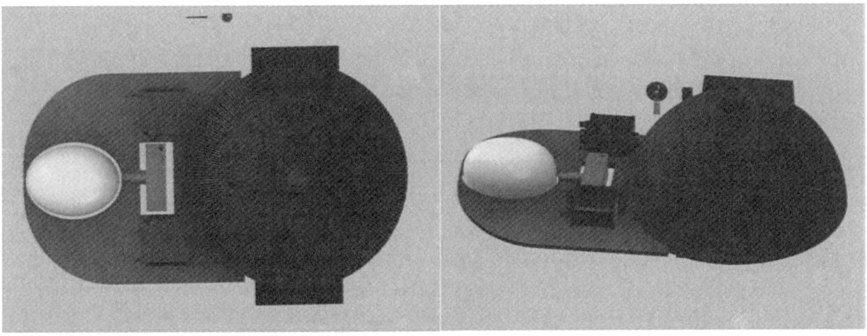

17.4 Conclusions

In conclusion our project adopts a user friendly approach. The integration of state-of-the-art technology into a wearable form factor signifies a paradigm shift in asthma care. This represents a significant advancement in inhalation therapy, offering a more efficient and user-centric approach to medication delivery for respiratory illnesses. This innovative wearable device represents a paradigm shift in asthma management, offering a portable, user-friendly, and efficient means of delivering medication during asthma exacerbations. Through this Smart Nebulizer Cap, we not only aspire technological advancement but also positive shift in lives of those managing asthma.

References

1. Houlihan, R., Timothy, M., Duffy, C., MacLoughlin, R., Olszewski, O., Acoustic Structural Coupling In A Silicon Based Vibrating Mesh Nebulizer, in: *2021 21st International Conference on Solid-State Sensors, Actuators and Microsystems (Transducers)*, pp. 615–618, IEEE, 2021, June.
2. Tsai, C.S., Ye, M., Liao, C.C., Pocket-sized ultrasonic nebulizer for inhalation drug delivery, in: *2013 IEEE International Ultrasonics Symposium (IUS)*, pp. 1190–1192, IEEE, 2013, October.

3. Omron Healthcare, Mesh nebulizer V/S Compressor nebulizer, Retrieved March 18, 2024, from https://www.omronhealthcare-ap.com/healthblog/en/article/detail/45-how-to- choose-a-nebulizer.
4. Healthline, What is a Nebulizer? Types, Uses, Cleaning, and More, 2022, August 24, Retrieved March 18, 2024, from https://medlineplus.gov/ency/patientinstructions/000006.htm.
5. Patel, R., Bhavsar, M., Amiya, R., A Review of Nebulizer Technologies and Their Applications in Drug Delivery. *J. Aerosol Med. Pulm. Drug Delivery*, 36, 1, 1–22, 2023.
6. Naidu, H., Kahraman, O., & Feng, H., Novel applications of ultrasonic atomization in the manufacturing of fine chemicals, pharmaceuticals, and medical devices. *Ultrason. Sonochem.*, 86, 1, 105984, 2022. doi: https://doi.org/10.1016/j.ultsonch.2022.105984.
7. Liu, S., Wang, Z., Wang, C., Sun, Y., Sun, J., A Wearable Electrospray Nebulizer for Continuous Inhalation Therapy. *Microsyst. Nanomach.*, 15, 1, 111–118, 2019, https://www.ncbi.nlm.nih.gov/pmc/articles/PM C6803223/.
8. Li, Y., Sun, J., Liu, S., Zhang, Y., Sun, Y., A Microfluidic Electrospray Chip for Nebulization with Enhanced Efficiency and Controllable Particle Size. *Microfluid. Nanofluid.*, 26, 8, 1–13, 2022.

18

Design of a Digital VLSI Parallel Morphological Reconfigurable Processing Module for Binary and Grayscale Image Processing

Y. Bhaskara Rao*, K. Rajitha, D. Vijay Harsha Vardhan, N. Naga Raja Kumari and D. Vijaya Saradhi

Department of ECE, MLWEC, Pulldigunta, Guntur, A.P., India

Abstract

An efficient processing element was used to design the data/image processing. The mesh-connected and ring-connected systolic arrays are created by the detailed communication networks, circuit blocks and instruction sets are created for the retrieving and learning phases of the neural network operations. Therefore, a parallel Morphological Image Processor (MIP) has been developed onto a full-custom optoelectronic Very Large Scale Integration (VLSI) designed by combining an on-chip focal-plane photo detectors and transmitters with 2-dimensional fine-grain parallel array architectures. The opto-detected binary image is processed by the optical I/O array processor to perform morphological functions using the programmable structuring element of size. MIPL is a specific language and defined for parallel morphological image processing, this is fully supported by MIP hardware. Grayscale images and binary images play a main role in the image processing field for the applications of machine intelligence, object recognition, authentication, tracking, and document analysis. This paper proposed, the image processing functions and algorithms can be implemented in a reconfigurable processing module for an image processor using application-specific integrated circuits (ASICs) for each algorithm. The reconfigurable module performs basic morphological mathematical operations on grayscale and binary images, as well as certain image processing algorithms. Field programmable gate arrays used to implement the reconfiguration module and compared to existing systems. Delay,

**Corresponding author*: bhaskararao.yenugula@gmail.com

Budati Anil Kumar, Singamaneni Kranthi Kumar and Li Xingwang (eds.) Quantum Computing Models for Cybersecurity and Wireless Communications, (267–278) © 2025 Scrivener Publishing LLC

speed, power consumption, and memory space were the performance parameters used to examine the model's performance.

Keywords: Morphological image processor (MIP), ASIC, VLSI, binary and grayscale images

18.1 Introduction

In the area of images and video applications, binary image processing is one of the prevailing tools. Binary image processing is implemented by processors like CPU or Digital signal processing (DSP). In many applications, efficiency of these processors is below par. Application specific integrated circuits are dedicated processor chips which can implements binary operations. But these chips have limited range of applications. So these chips are developed. Dedicated chips provide high efficiency, but they cannot be tailored. Complementary Metal-Oxide-Semiconductor (CMOS) technology requires flexibility nowadays, which device size is constantly decreases. The reconfigurable technique can be filled with gap and to provide the flexible processor and high performance.

General purpose processors require large Chips and application specific chips have a small range of applications, these chips were developed to generalize binary image operations based on reconfiguration. To perform basic binary operations chips are designed like opening, closing, erosion, and dilation. The combination of digital and analog circuits is used in chips designing [1]. Low robustness, scalability, and accuracy are shown in the analog parts [2]. General purpose processors contain a digital array architecture; here every array can handle one pixel only. The processor proposed, the ability to handle certain basic algorithms and binary images. There are more than binary images in image processing. Grayscale images must be handled by image processing system, in real-time applications these grayscale images are usually obtained.

This paper proposed the reconfigurable image processing module that can handle both grayscale images and binary images. The control units for the input and output logic can be changed to replace the module for binary image processing was proposed [3]. The processor's high speed and simple structure capable to handle wide range of applications. In recent years, the design of novel VLSI architectures has been carried out from considerable research for DSP applications. Many DSP functions are highly structured nature; this nature makes to derive regular circuit architectures, such as systolic arrays, which are perfect for VLSI implementation. Architectures may be tailored to particular sample rate, power and area requirements by exploitation of algorithm parallelism and using techniques like pipelining.

Chien, S. and Chen, L., [20] Morphological processing has been shown that an image can be edit based on shape and size of the interest objects, as well as removes noise and clutter. Additionally, only local connections between pixels are used in the computation of morphological operations and is simple to implement in parallel opto-electronic architecture. On general-purpose computers, morphological image processing algorithms at a 1000-frame video rate are computationally very intensive and difficult to perform. To solve the problem, on-chip focal-plane photo detectors and transmitters and a full 2-dimensional fine-grain parallel array architectures are combined to develop high-speed morphological image processor. The focal-plane morphological image processor, which forms the core of the optical image analysis workstation's preprocessing stage. The workstation develops a highly parallel system capable of target recognition automatically and high speed identification using electronics and optics.

The VLSI neuroprocessor has been designed by two techniques that are mixed signal design and digital design. Comparing these two techniques, digital design could provide better programmability, which is used to implementing different networks. Moreover, Digital signal provides better expandability to solve the large-scale scientific problems. Systolic systems are easy to implement in digital design because of its regularity and due to modularity it is easy to modify. The system throughput in terms of data pipelining can be greatly increased by configuration of the connectionist networks in a systolic. The feedback learning phase and the feed-forward propagation phase share the same architecture between them, which suggests re-configurability is not required. To achieve the fault tolerant design a redundant path is attached.

This paper is organized as follows. Section 18.2 presents a Survey of the literature, and Section 18.3 describes the Digital VLSI Parallel Morphological Reconfigurable Processing Module is designed For Grayscale and binary Image Processing. The results of the image operations are presented in Section 18.4 and comparison with the presented processors is made. The Section 18.5 provides the conclusion.

18.2 Literature Survey

Ammar *et al.* [4] In the encrypting scheme, pixel intensities represents with their residues was proposed. It was proposed that the residues may be reverse converted into binary using a modified version for selecting optimum moduli based on the Chinese Remainder Theorem (CRT).

Yong Liu; Lai, E.M. *et al.* [5] There was discussed two RNS based encoding schemes. The first scheme generated the encoding key using a nonlinear chaotic map and, while CRT used by second scheme. A processor for image coding was designed using the Residue Number System (RNS), and the encoded image data for wireless transfer was established.

Wei *et al.* [6] By transforming between the bases an arithmetic parallelism is easy to achieve, the Rivest Shamir Adleman (RSA) hardware implementation uses the RNS Montgomery modular multiplication algorithm. RSA is first practically used public-key cryptosystems generally for secure data transfer. Montgomery modular multiplication is a method for performing fast modular multiplication in the modular arithmetic computation. In this literature, Transport Triggered Architecture (TTA) is used to design the cipher chip. When performing encryption or decryption, a cipher is a cryptography algorithm which has well defined series steps may be follows the process. TTA is one type of CPU designs used in computer architecture where programs were directly controls a processor's internal transport buses.

Youssef *et al.* [7] Initially, the image was transformed into residues in the image encryption scheme, that residues placed into reference DNA sequence secretly. Different keys were subjected to encryption in this sequence.

Rejeb *et al.* [8] Real-time fractal coding self-similarity search hardware architecture utilizing RNS was presented. A lossy compression method for digital image is called fractal compression that is based on fractals. The method based on the fact that parts of an image frequently resemble one another, textures and natural images are the best suited applications for it. These parts are converted by fractal algorithms into mathematical data which is referred as 'fractal codes' and used to encoded images and recreate them.

A. Tatsaki *et al.* [10] Lattice Vector Quantizer (LVQ) and Discrete Cosine Transform (DCT) based on RNS is used for adaptive lossy compression of images. Investigated the floating point arithmetic, 2-D Lifting-based Discrete Wavelet transform (DWT) architecture and the scope of the residue arithmetic in JPEG2000 compression. RNS was used for image compression when computing finite field wavelet transform.

Yong Liu; Lai, E.M. *et al.* [5] It was established based on RNS, a 2-dimensional biorthogonal DWT processor is designed. To reduce the distortion at the borders of the image, a symmetric extension scheme was used. In this literature, a Field Programmable Gate Array (FPGA) development board is used to designed and simulated such as memory interface, controllers and the RNS-based FIR filter bank's data path.

D. Younes and P. Steffan *et al.* [7] It was demonstrated, Using the RNS a spatial sharpening filter was realized on a grayscale image in this method. Look-Up Tables (LUTs) helps to conversion of the image from binary representation into RNS. Three parallel Residue Arithmetic Units (RAUs), which correspond to the moduli of three, were additions and multiplications required for convoluting the image and the filter mask. LUTs are helps in converting the sharpened images back into binary based representations. The Virtex4 FPGA device had been implements the structure. The computation in the standard binary number system, power consumption and timing-performance were reported and compared.

P. Steffan and D. Younes [11]. To calculate the low pass filtered version of the image, the difference between the original image and the sharpened image is employed. The sharpened image is used to compute the original image and RNS is used to convolution the sharpening masks with the image. The application of RNS-based arithmetic in special filtering was examined. In order to implement OHR based spatial filter kernels, the construction of adders and multipliers as well as an image coding technique based on the One Hot Residue (OHR) number system was presented.

Atta-ur-Rahman; Naseem, M.T.; Qureshi, I.M.; Muzaffar, M.Z., *et al.* [12] For medical images a special domain reversible watermarking was proposed. Pixel locations are selected at randomly, the water mark was represented by a single bit that was embedded. In order to increase the amount of bits at each pixel location from the residue pixels, which consist of 9 bits per pixel in an uint8 image, to 10, one parity bit was concatenated with both the residue pixels and the watermark. In order to ensure that the decoding is 'no reference' the receiver was made with location of the pixel where the watermark is embedded and acts as a reference or key. Based on CRT, the residuals are used to reconstruct the original intensity.

18.3 Design of a Digital VLSI Parallel Morphological Reconfigurable Processing Module for Binary and Grayscale Image Processing

Figure 18.1 demonstrates the framework for a Digital VLSI Parallel Morphological Reconfigurable Processing Module was designed for Grayscale and binary Image Processing.

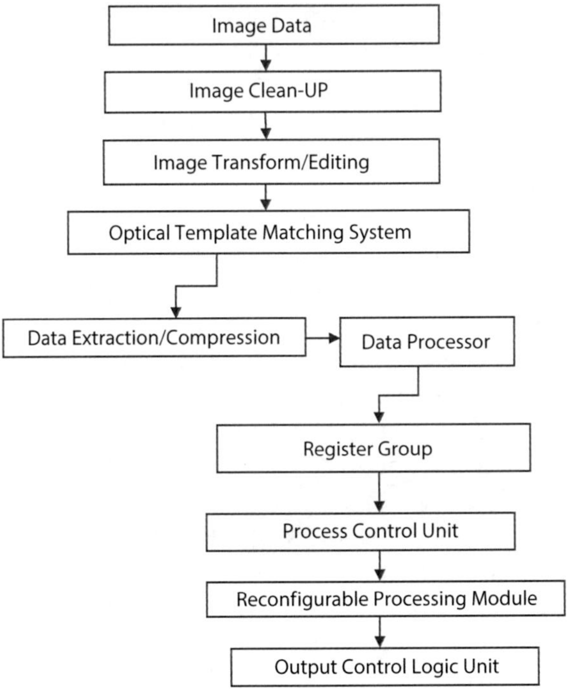

Figure 18.1 Reconfigurable processing module for binary and grayscale image processing.

The capable of binary image processor proposed, this is used for variety of applications such as video processing applications, computer VLSI On systems, authentication systems machine intelligence, identification and also in several image applications. Figure 18.1 shows the binary image processor of the architecture.

For visuals perception the images captured in real-time are not always appreciable. The illumination condition affects the quality of the image. To improve the visual quality of the image, contrast enhancement is required. In this article, the image enhancement techniques are applied to real-time images are considered. Further, the image processing algorithms in very large-scale integration (VLSI) hardware an investigation is done on implementing. The computational complexity and the memory requirement are more due to the image data are comparatively larger. From this study, the need for image processing algorithms computation efficiently is realized. The image processing algorithms efficient computation on hardware platforms, in particular field programmable gate arrays (FPGA), is considered. [9] The prototype of the gamma-transformation technique used for image enhancement is modeled initially in MATLAB, and then it is implemented using an FPGA as an experiment.

One of the simplest morphological algorithms is Noise filtering Kou, F., Chen, W., Wen, C., Li, Z., [13]. The image data is distorted when noise in an image leads. Therefore, an important operation is noise filtering to get distortion free and error processed images Li, Z., Zheng, J., Zhu, Z., Yao, W., Wu, S., [14]. Given equation describes the noise filtering.

$$\{[(A\Theta\mathcal{B} \oplus \mathrm{B}] \mid \oplus \mathrm{B}\}\} = (\mathrm{A} \cdot B) \circ B \tag{18.1}$$

Banerjee, S., Chakraborty, S., Dey, N., Pal, A.K., Ray, R., [15] The process of obtaining an object's boundaries of an image this is called 'Boundary extraction'. The boundary extraction expression is:

$$\mathrm{A} - (\mathrm{A}\Theta\mathrm{B}) \tag{18.2}$$

This 'template matching' for optical character recognition is a technique that comparing with input templates to a set of system templates to identify the character. Computing the similarity between the templates and the covered window after moving the template over the entire image is the process of "Template matching". The implementation of template matching through the two dimensional convolution. The pixel output value in convolution is computed by multiplying two matrices elements and adding the results values. The image represents one of the matrices itself, while the template represents other matrix, which is called as a convolution kernel. Naseem, M.T., Qureshi, I.M., Cheema, T.A., Atta-ur Rahman [16] The original image represents as $f(x, y)$, the template represents as $t(x, \mathrm{y})$ and the enhanced image represents as $g(x, y)$ this is using after convolution. The convolution can be abbreviated by:

$$g_{xy} = f_{xy} \, ^{\circ} \, t_{xy} \tag{18.3}$$

Here indicates the convolution of two function.

Grayscale opening and closing, grayscale erosion, grayscale images as grayscale dilation and all can be extended to the above mentioned operations. Data compression might be as simple as Data runs are stored as a single data value rather than the original data run and count when using run length coding (RLE). Binary images are made with the long runs of zeros and ones and RLE is easily adaptable to these binary images. Binary data contain input of the processor, then compressed data of the input the output is obtained. In the reconfigurable module, number of binary image processing algorithms were implemented. By using shifted locations, motion detection of the objects is estimated. The locations were identified based on image differencing operation [17].

The output control logic is part of the reconfigurable processing module and computing units, is the heart of the processor. The register group which is configurable, process control unit, two bus interfaces, and input and output logic controllers are also included in the processor Guo, W., Liu, Y., Bai, S., Wei, J., Sun, D., [18]. The binary processor's core is formed by the reconfigurable processing module (RPM). The output control logic and the compute units are its two basic components. In order to select the outputs from the compute unit, the output control logic converts serial data into parallel data based on a set of parameters. The compute units allocate and execute the logic and image operations at high speed. The binary computation units can executes the algorithms for image processing with the help of connections pattern between them. The binary operations can be carried out by the compute units in parallel or pipelined fashion. Block diagram is shows the reconfigurable processing module in Figure 18.1. The suggested module can do more binary operations when compared to the previous proposed processor.

[19] The binary compute units use Pipelining or parallelism to execute number of binary operations. The computation units executes the operations is determined by parameters and reconfigurable registers such as image resolution parameters, logical operation parameters, auxiliary parameters, input and output selection parameters and mask image sizes . Low hardware utilization makes the pipe lined architecture is effective when single image needs single operation. The number of pipelined stages increases the processing time. The time is directly affected by the number of pipelined stages. A factor of 'n' reduces the processing time, where the number of pipelined stages 'n' and high hardware utilization are both advantages of parallel processing over a pipelined structures. The binary compute units use pipelined or parallelism [21].

18.4 Result Analysis

In this paper, the Digital VLSI Parallel Morphological Reconfigurable Of Processing Module was designed For processing Binary And Grayscale Image is discussed. In terms of the morphological operations, the comparison is done such boundary extraction for grayscale and binary images, misses operation and binary hit, dilation, erosion, opening, closing, and run length encoding algorithm. Modifying the input and output control logics

Table 18.1 Performance metrics evaluation.

Parameters	RNS	RPM
Memory (MB)	3345.23	2984
Power Consumption (mW)	140	123
Delay (ns)	7.74	4.32
Speed	150	180

slightly, the processor architecture may integrates this module and that may be used for video processing and wide range of image applications. The Table 18.1 shows that the performance analysis of proposed method is evaluated with parameters, delay, power consumption, speed, accuracy, and Memory.

The Figure 18.2 shows the Memory comparison between standard RNS based approach and RPM approach.

The Figure 18.3 shows the Power Consumption comparison between standard RNS based approach and RPM approach.

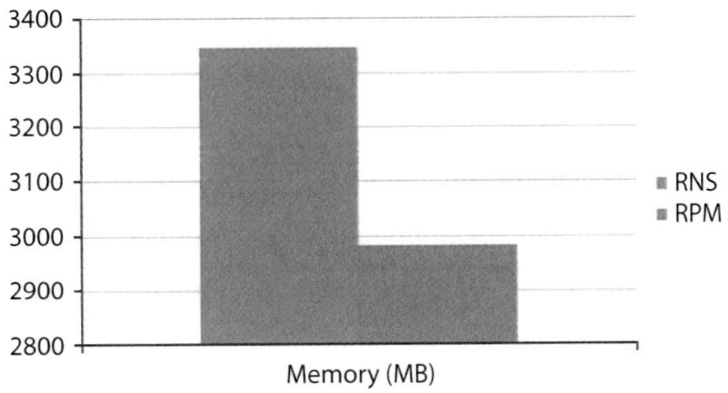

Figure 18.2 Memory (MB) comparison graph.

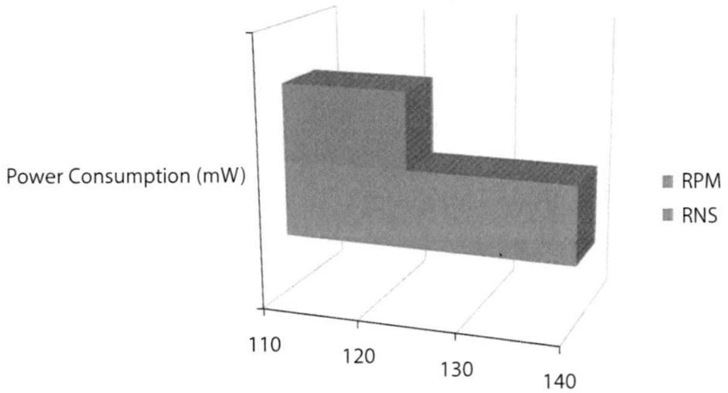

Figure 18.3 Power consumption comparison graph.

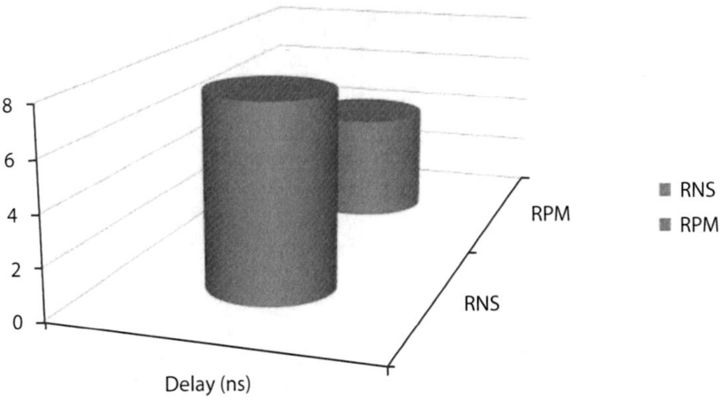

Figure 18.4 Delay comparison graph.

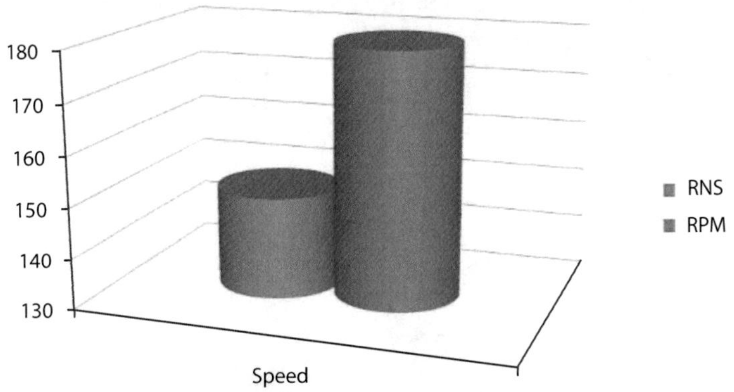

Figure 18.5 Speed comparison graph.

Figure 18.4 shows the Delay comparison between standard RNS based approach and RPM approach.

Figure 18.5 shows the speed comparison between standard RNS based approach and RPM approach.

18.5 Conclusion

In this paper, the Digital VLSI of Parallel Morphologically Reconfigurable Of Processing Module was designed For processing Grayscale and binary image is discussed. Therefore, A fully-custom optoelectronic VLSI design of parallel morphological image processor (MIP) is created by combination of the 2-dimensional fine-grain parallel array architectures with on-chip focal-plane the context detectors and transmitters. A programmable structuring element with opto-detected binary image of random size is processed by an optical I/O array processor to perform out morphological operations Dailey, D., Cathey, F.W., Pumrin, S., [22]. For parallel morphological image processing, a special language called MIPL has been developed and is completely supported by MIP hardware. In this paper, the image processor was proposed by the reconfigurable module. Morphological image operations handled by the module for grayscale and binary images that operations are erosion, dilation, opening, closing, run length encoding for binary data and boundary extract. It is identified by simple structure, high speed and applications for document authentication and object detection to image analysis. Compared to other based models, the presented RPM model has better performance in terms of delay, power consumption, speed, memory.

References

1. Miao, W., Lin, Q., Zhang, W. *et al.*, A programmable SIMD vision chip for real-time vision applications. *IEEE Solid-State Circuits, 43, 6*, 1470–1479, Jun.2008.
2. Lopich, A. and Dudek, P., A SIMD Cellular processor array vision chip with asynchronous processing capabilities. *IEEE Trans. Circuits Syst. I, 58, 10*, 2420–2431, oct 20 11.
3. Zhang, B., Mei, K., Zheng, N., Reconfigurable Processor for Binary Image Processing. *IEEE Trans. Circuits Syst. Video Technol., 23, 5*, 823–831, May 2013.
4. Ammar, A., Al Kabbany, A., Youssef, M., Amam, A., A secure image coding scheme using residue number system. *Radio Science Conference, 2001. NRSC 2001. Proceedings of the Eighteenth National*, vol. 2, pp. 399–405, 2001, doi: 10.1109/NRSC.2001.929397.
5. Liu, Y. and Lai, E.M., Design and implementation of an RNS-based 2-D DWT processor. *IEEE Trans. Consum. Electron., 50, 1*, 376–385, Feb 2004, doi: 10.1109/TCE.2004.1277887.
6. Youssef, M.I., Emam, A.E., Saafan, S.M., AbdElghany, M., Secured Image Encryption Scheme Using both Residue Number System and DNA Sequence. *Int. J. Emerg. Sci. Eng. (IJESE), 1, 12*, 22–27, October 2013, ISSN: 2319–6378.
7. Younes, D. and Steffan, P., Efficient image processing application using residue number system. *Mixed Design of Integrated Circuits and Systems (MIXDES), 2013 Proceedings of the 20th International Conference*, 20-22 June 2013, pp. 468–472.
8. Rejeb, B., Henkelmann, H., Anheier, W., *Real- time implementation of fractal image encoder using residue number system*, 2012, doi=10.1.1.112.288.
9. Mujawar, M., Vijaya Saradhi, D., Ajmal Naz, M., Muduli, A., Design and performance comparison of arrays of circular, square and hexagonal meta-material structures for wearable applications. *J. Magn. Magn. Mater., 553*, 169235, 2022.

10. Tatsaki, A., An adaptive image coder based on residue number system," Electronics, Circuits, and Systems. *ICECS '96., Proceedings of the Third IEEE International Conference on*, 13-16 Oct 1996, vol. 2, pp. 700–703, 1996, doi: 10.1109/ICECS.1996.584458.
11. Younes, D. and Steffan, P., Fast and Power Reduced RNS- Based Image Filtering in Spatial Domain. *Electroscope, 40, 5*, 1278–1563, 2010.
12. Atta-ur-Rahman, Naseem, M.T., Qureshi, I.M., Muzaffar, M.Z., Reversible watermarking using Residue Number System. Information Assurance and Security (IAS). *2011 7th International Conference on*, pp. 162–166, 5-8 Dec. 2011, doi: 10.1109/ISIAS.2011.6122813.
13. Kou, F., Chen, W., Wen, C., Li, Z., Gradient domain guided image filtering. *IEEE Trans. Image Process.*, 24, 11, 4528–4539, Nov 2015.
14. Li, Z., Zheng, J., Zhu, Z., Yao, W., Wu, S., Weighted guided image filtering. *IEEE Trans. Image Process., 24, 1*, 120–129, Jan 2015.
15. Banerjee, S., Chakraborty, S., Dey, N., Pal, A.K., Ray, R., High Payload Watermarking using Residue Number System. *Int. J. Image Graph. Signal Process. (IJIGSP), 7, 3*, 1–8, February 2015, DOI: 10.5815/ijigsp.
16. Naseem, M.T., Qureshi, I.M., Cheema, T.A., Atta-ur Rahman, Spread Spectrum based Invertible Watermarking for Medical Images using RNS & Chaos. *Int. Arab J. Inf. Technol.*, 223–231, 2014.
17. Shaik, K.Z., P, S., Prasad, K.S., Design and implementation of artificial magnetic conductor surface as decoupling structure in microstrip antenna arrays. *Circuit World, 47*, 3, 290–300, 2021.
18. Guo, W., Liu, Y., Bai, S., Wei, J., Sun, D., Hardware Architecture for RSA Cryptography Based on Residue Number System. *Trans. Tianjin Univ., 18, 4*, 237–242, August 2012.
19. Moharrami, S. and Taleshmekaeil, D.K., The Application of the Residue Number System in Digital Image Processing: Propose a Scheme of Filtering in Spatial Domain. *Res. J. Appl. Sci., 7, 6*, 286–292, 2012, DOI: 10.3923/rjasci.2012.286.292.
20. Chien, S. and Chen, L., Reconfigurable morphological image processing accelerator for video object segmentation. *Signal Process. Syst., 62, I*, 77–96, 2011.
21. Yang, J.-H., Chang, C.-C., Lin, C.-H., Residue number system oriented image encoding schemes. *Imaging Sci. J., 58, 1*, 3–11, 2010, DOI: 10.1179/136821909X12490326247489.
22. Dailey, D., Cathey, F.W., Pumrin, S., An Algorithm to Estimate Mean Traffic Speed Using Uncalibrated Cameras. *IEEE Trans. Intell. Transp. Syst., I, 2*, 98–107, june 2000.

19

Intrusion Detection System Using Machine Learning

Ballikura Dhanunjay[1*], Earla Sanjay[1], Aakaram Karthik Raj[1] and Mohan Dholvan[2]

[1]*Department of ECM, Sreenidhi Institute of Science and Technology, Hyderabad, India*

[2]*Department of ECM, Sreenidhi Institute of Science and Technology, Hyderabad, India*

Abstract

Advancements in technology over the years have led to a massive increase in the number of data that is being recycled on the internet every day. But also, this huge amount of data exchanged through the internet has a flip side where it needs to be protected and kept secure, hence the need for an intrusion detection system (IDS). Intrusion Detection System (IDS) refers to a system that keeps surveillance and analysis of data and identifies any form of attack. Intruders who know many different ways to break into a network are the primary reason for security breaches. The IDS is implemented using technologies such as machine learning algorithms for attack classification and detection whenever an attack occurs, as well as determining suitable algorithms of machine learning appropriate for attack identification. The role played by the Intrusion Detection System (IDS) cannot be overemphasized in dissuading attacks. However, emerging technologies like cloud computing and, the Internet of Things, among others bring about high traffic volumes with irrelevant attributes that do not count when it comes to attack discovery. To address these problems feature selection approaches (FSA) have been used which eliminate irrelevant features and find relevant ones.

Keywords: Intrusion detection system, host, detection techniques, machinelearning, support vector machine, NSL-KDD

**Corresponding author*: ballikuradhanunjay@gmail.com

Budati Anil Kumar, Singamaneni Kranthi Kumar and Li Xingwang (eds.) Quantum Computing Models for Cybersecurity and Wireless Communications, (279–292) © 2025 Scrivener Publishing LLC

19.1 Introduction

A modern cyber security infrastructure is unthinkable without network intrusion detection systems (NIDS) [3]. They are purposed to continuously monitor network traffic for any signs of potential security violations and alert the administrator once such violations have been identified [2, 7]. Such measures are crucial to avoid data hacks or other activities that may destroy the system. Machine learning falls under artificial intelligence, which involves training algorithms on large datasets to identify patterns and make projections [1, 4]. For NIDS, machine learning algorithms can be trained using data sets of normal and malicious network traffic to acquire insights into the characteristics that differentiate the two types of traffic, such as normal and abnormal traffic [2, 6]. This allows it to be used in classifying new, unseen network traffic as either normal or abnormal. Any violation or intrusion in a system calls for a report to the administrator or sent to the security information and events management (SIEM) center. Multiple outputs fed into SIEM systems help differentiate between false alarms and actual threats by using filtering techniques[1, 3, 4]. This project seeks to identify network intrusions that are caused by unauthorized users with the help of machine learning algorithms [5, 9]. "Intrusion" or "attack" detection can be done by training the machine learning algorithms with correlated data for an intrusion [1, 8]. MLP, KNN, and SVM machine learning algorithms are used in this project to create machine learning models [1, 11, 13].

19.2 Literature Survey

In our everyday lives and businesses, the internet has become part and parcel of it. World business is associated with the Internet. Many companies use the Internet for e-business purposes every day. Therefore, it makes sense to increase the way modern companies are interconnected. The Internet has proved to be immensely profitable for firms and individuals as they have been able to connect to a large population in one go, however, it does have a downside in that the company's digital infrastructure (databases, network devices, etc.) are at risk from data breaches [9], unauthorized access by malicious programs or hackers (or) "intruders" [5, 10]. This leads to lawsuits against these firms by their customers because they do not adequately secure their databases so that user information is kept private. Without having an IDS also means that other forms of malicious activity like network attacks and malware infection can occur [14]. Network attacks usually attempt to disable or shut down a network or system [12], they can be harmful, including financial losses thereby damaging the reputation of an organization while malware infections happen when a system gets infiltrated with viruses/trojans which can also cause serious consequences.

19.3 Methodology

A. Existing System

To inhibit the dangerous activities happening inside the network system, intrusion detection systems (IDS) provide defensive measures against different rapid network attacks like distributed denial of service (DDoS), ransomware, botnet, etc. Figure 19.1 shows existing system framework model. In particular, this study applied three disparate machine learning algorithms for classification which include Naïve Bayes (NB), Support Vector

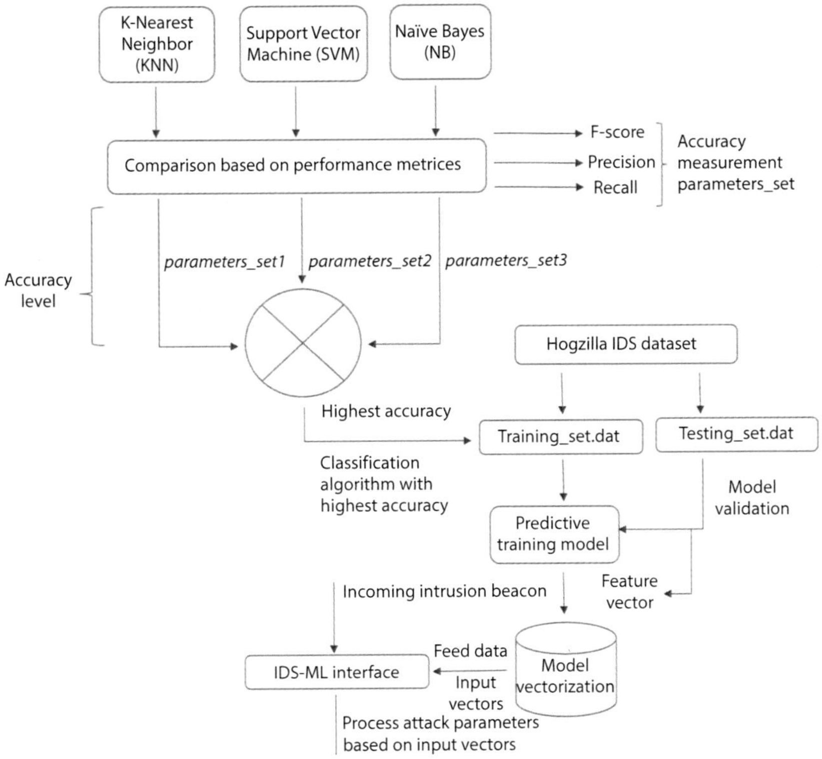

Figure 19.1 Existing system framework model.

Machine (SVM), and K-nearest neighbor (KNN) to check their accuracy and reduce processing time on an algorithm using UNSW-NB15 dataset to find out the best suitable one that can effectively learn about the pattern of malicious network activities.

The best-fit algorithm chosen from among these three algorithms after measuring its performance metrics was used in IDS as input data feeds along with the feature set comparison results collected for future intrusion prediction and behavior analysis purposes. Additionally, during the testing phase of the model's support-validation status classification reports such as precision, recall, and f1-score were produced as well as confusion matrix compared to deciding using this approach. Classification models were three compared to establish the best algorithm in terms of accuracy, classification report, and confusion matrix. The dataset will be preprocessed for classifying purposes. Consequently, it will be expected to provide a model that could predict intrusion attacks and classify them into their respective classes.

B. Proposed System

We used machine learning algorithms to design a model in the Proposed Intrusion Detection System (IDS) by training it on the NSL-KDD dataset sourced from the Canadian Institute for Cybersecurity. The data set consists of 125,974 samples of both normal and abnormal network behavior. In the proposed system we use Support Vector Machine(SVM), K-Nearest Neighbors(KNN), and Multi-Layer Perceptron(MLP) machine learning algorithms to train our detection model over the NSL-KDD dataset. To improve the true positive rate of the detection system, we trained the datasets on three types of machine-learning models. The purpose of this assignment is to develop machine-learning algorithms that can accurately identify intrusions as well as the kind of intrusion that has occurred into a given network at the earliest stage possible. Quick identification of intruders will help minimize the extent of damage incurred by a network and ease its recovery. Furthermore, it should create a model that can distinguish between regular and irregular activities with little False Positive Rate (FPR).

C. System Architecture

A system architecture is a conceptual model which gives the structure, behavior, and other views of a system. An architectural description is a formal representation for describing systems in such a way that they can be reasoned about in terms of their structures and behaviors. A system architecture comprises system components as well as sub-systems developed, which will collectively make up the complete system, Figure 19.2 shows proposed system. Attempts have been made to standardize languages for specifying

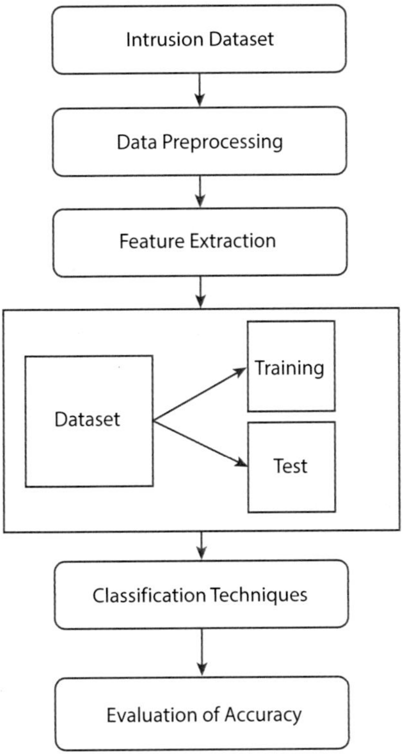

Figure 19.2 Proposed architecture.

architectural designs; this group is commonly referred to as architecture description languages (ADLs).

D. Dataset
The Canadian Institute for Cybersecurity's NSL-KDD dataset encompasses 125,974 data samples of both normal and abnormal network statuses. It is made up of 158 attributes. These include protocol type, number of failed login attempts, type of service, root access, source error rate, and priority of the data packets.

19.4 Algorithm

In our Intrusion Detection System (IDS), one of the algorithms we use is a Support Vector Machine algorithm with linear kernel type while classification. The SVM algorithm tries to locate a hyperplane in the n-dimensional plane and separate the data points of the dataset into classes. The number of dimensions depends on the attributes given as input to the algorithm. The second algorithm used is K-Nearest Neighbor (KNN) which, in general, is designed for classification tasks. KNN does not make any changes to the dataset during its training phase; it just stores it. When an input to classify is provided, it categorizes that input data into similar data. A deep learning algorithm, the Multi-Layer Perceptron (MLP) sequential model is employed as a third method. In MLP there are neurons connected to other neurons that have been assigned weights indicating how important they are. Activation of neurons results from reaching an input's activation function threshold. MLP learns through backpropagation in which each weight is adjusted till it reaches its target attribute. Our final dataset for these algorithms contains 93 attributes but only those attributes having Pearson Correlation Co-efficient above 0.5 are selected concerning intrusions.

Pearson Correlation Coefficient is calculated as:

$$r = \frac{\Sigma(x_i - \overline{x})\Sigma(y_i - \overline{y})}{\sqrt{\Sigma(x_i - \overline{x})^2 \Sigma(y_i - \overline{y})^2}}$$

Table 19.1 shows attribute correlation. The attributes having a correlation greater than 0.5 with the attribute 'intrusion' are:

Table 19.1 Attribute correlation.

count	0.613251
logged_in	0.693770
srv_serror_rate	0.710852
serror_rate	0.712861
dst_host_serror_rate	0.714247
dst_host_same_srv_rate	0.716820
dst_host_srv_serror_rate	0.717387
dst_host_srv_count	0.718579
same_srv_rate	0.798358
intrusion	1.000000

19.5 Implementation

A. Use case diagrams(UML)

The Network Intrusion Detection use case diagram shows the interaction between users and the system, as well as how one module communicates with others and relates to each other. Figure 19.3 shows use-case diagram.

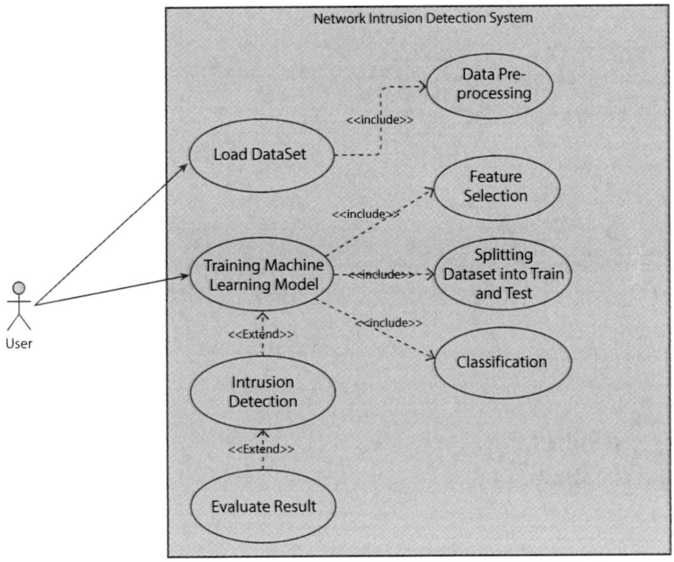

Figure 19.3 Use case diagram.

B. Sequence diagram

Figure 19.4 shows sequence diagram. The Network Intrusion Detection sequence diagram shows the sequence in which each process occurs:

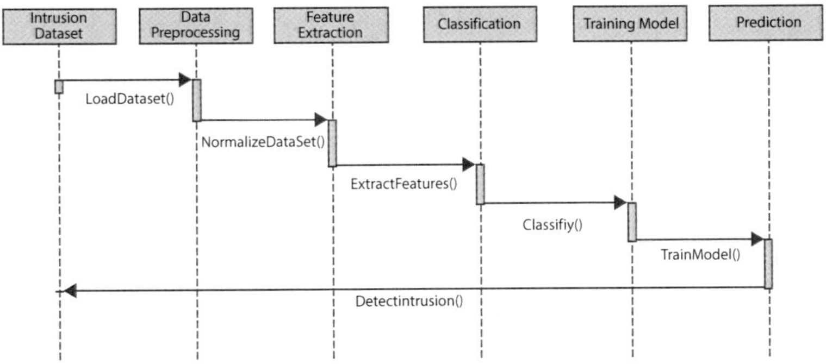

Figure 19.4 Sequence diagram.

C. Training module:
Data Pre-processing

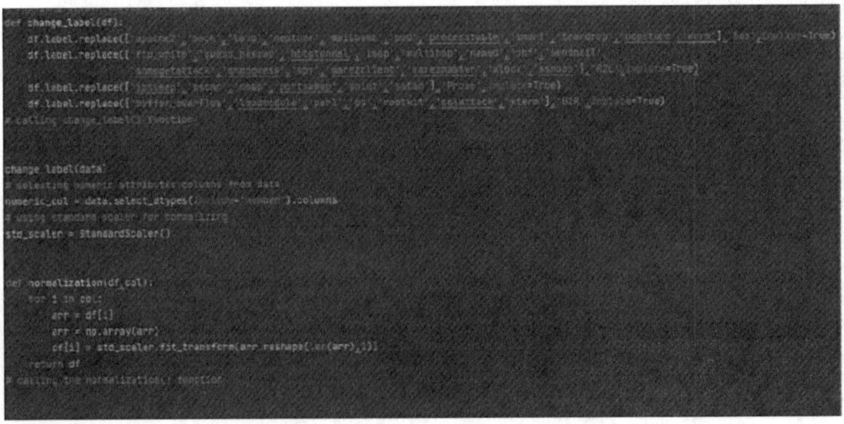

Figure 19.5 Data pre-processing.

Finding attributes with correlation >0.5 with target attribute and saving the final dataset multi_data to csv file, Figure 19.5 shows data preprocessing.

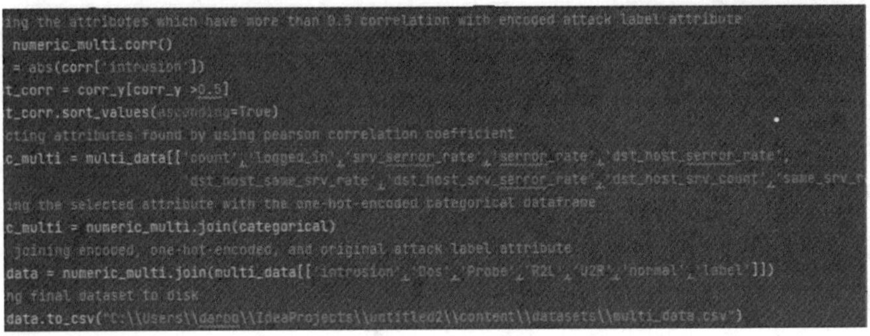

Figure 19.6 Feature extraction.

Creating a machine learning model using SVM with kernel mode as linear and saving the created model, Figure 19.6 shows feature extraction.

```
def lsvm_implemtation():
    X = multi_data.iloc[:,0:93].to_numpy() # dataset excluding target attribute (encoded, one-hot-encoded, original)
    Y = multi_data['intrusion'] # target attribute
    # splitting the dataset 75% for training and 25% testing
    X_train, X_test, y_train, y_test = train_test_split(X,Y, test_size=0.25, random_state=42)
    lsvm = SVC(kernel='linear',gamma='auto')
    lsvm.fit(X_train,y_train) # training model on training dataset
    # saving trained model to disk
    pkl_filename = "C:\\Users\\daroo\\IdeaProjects\\untitled2\\content\\models\\lsvm_multi.pkl"
    if not path.isfile(pkl_filename):
        with open(pkl_filename, 'wb') as file:
            pickle.dump(lsvm, file)
        print("Saved model to disk")

        # loading trained model from disk
    with open(pkl_filename, 'rb') as file:
        lsvm = pickle.load(file)
    print("Loaded model from disk")
    y_pred=lsvm.predict(X_test) # predicting target attribute on testing dataset
    ac=accuracy_score(y_test, y_pred)*100  # calculating accuracy of predicted data
    print("LSVM-Classifier Multi-class Set-Accuracy is ", ac)
    # classification report
    print(classification_report(y_test, y_pred,target_names=le2.classes_))
```

Figure 19.7 Creating and training ML model with SVM.

One way to create an MLP is by making use of the sequential model, Adam optimizer, and saving the model

```
def mlp_implementations():
    X = multi_data.iloc[:,0:93]  # dataset excluding target attribute (encoded, one-hot-encoded,original)
    Y = multi_data[['Dos','normal','Probe','R2L','U2R']] # target attributes
    # splitting the dataset 75% for training and 25% testing
    X_train, X_test, y_train, y_test = train_test_split(X,Y, test_size=0.25, random_state=42)
    mlp = Sequential() # initializing model
    # input layer and first layer with 50 neurons
    mlp.add(Dense(units=50, input_dim=X_train.shape[1], activation='relu'))
    # output layer with softmax activation
    mlp.add(Dense(units=5,activation='softmax'))
    # defining loss function, optimizer, metrics and then compiling model
    mlp.compile(loss='categorical_crossentropy', optimizer='adam', metrics=['accuracy'])
    # training the model on training dataset
    history = mlp.fit(X_train, y_train, epochs=100, batch_size=5000,validation_split=0.2)
    filepath = 'C:\\Users\\daroo\\IdeaProjects\\untitled2\\content\\models\\mlp_multi.json'
    weightspath = 'C:\\Users\\daroo\\IdeaProjects\\untitled2\\content\\weights\\mlp_multi.h5'
    if not path.isfile(filepath):
        # serialize model to JSON
        mlp_json = mlp.to_json()
        with open(filepath, "w") as json_file:
            json_file.write(mlp_json)

        # serialize weights to HDF5
        mlp.save_weights(weightspath)
        print("Saved model to disk")

        # load json and create model
        json_file = open(filepath, 'r')
        loaded_model_json = json_file.read()
        json_file.close()
        mlp = model_from_json(loaded_model_json)
```

Figure 19.8 Creating and training sequential model.

Creating a machine learning model using K-NN with number of neighbors = 5 and saving the created model.

```
knn_implementation():
X = multi_data.iloc[:,0:93].to_numpy() # dataset excluding target attribute (encoded, one-hot-encoded, orig
Y = multi_data['intrusion'] # target attribute
# splitting the dataset 75% for training and 25% testing
X_train, X_test, y_train, y_test = train_test_split(X,Y, test_size=0.25, random_state=42)
knn=KNeighborsClassifier(n_neighbors=5)
knn.fit(X_train,y_train) # training model on training dataset
pkl_filename = "C:\\Users\\garoo\\IdeaProjects\\untitled2\\content\\models\\knn_multi.pkl"
if not path.isfile(pkl_filename):
    # saving trained model to disk
    with open(pkl_filename, 'wb') as file:
        pickle.dump(knn, file)
    print("Saved model to disk")
    # loading trained model from disk
    with open(pkl_filename, 'rb') as file:
        knn = pickle.load(file)
    print("Loaded model from disk")
y_pred = knn.predict(X_test)  # predicting target attribute on testing dataset
ac=accuracy_score(y_test, y_pred)*100  # calculating accuracy of predicted data
print("KNN-Classifier Multi-class Set-Accuracy is ", ac)
```

Figure 19.9 Creating and training ML model with K-NN.

User Interface Module

Using streamlit create an interface to upload network status information as a csv file.

```
f main():
    predict_res = ''
    res = ''
    fin_stat = ''
    filename = st.file_uploader(label="Upload the CSV: ", type='csv')
    data = pd.read_csv(filename)
    data.drop(['Unnamed: 0'], axis=1, inplace=True)
    x_fin = data.iloc[:, 0:93].to_numpy()
    option = st.selectbox('Which model do you want to use?', ('MLP', 'SVM', 'KNN'
    if option == 'MLP':
        predict_res = mlp_prediction(x_fin)
    elif option == 'SVM':
        predict_res = lsvm_prediction(x_fin)
    else:
        predict_res = knn_prediction(x_fin)
    res = attack_dict[predict_res]
    if res == 'Normal':
        fin_stat = 'Status of the system is normal'
    else:
        fin_stat = f'Intrusion Detected of type: {res}'
    st.write(fin_stat)
```

Figure 19.10 User Interface using streamlit.

19.6 Results and Outputs

Classification Report for SVM model

	Precision	Recall	F1-score	support
Accuracy			**0.96**	**31493**
macro avg	**0.68**	**0.67**	**0.67**	**31493**
Weighted avg	**0.95**	**0.95**	**0.95**	**31493**

Figure 19.11 SVM classification report.

Classification Report for KNN model

	Precision	Recall	F1-score	support
Accuracy			**0.98**	**31493**
macro avg	**0.85**	**0.79**	**0.81**	**31493**
Weighted avg	**0.97**	**0.97**	**0.97**	**31493**

Figure 19.12 K-NN classification report.

Classification Report for MLP (Sequential)

	Precision	Recall	F1-score
Accuracy	**0.98**	**0.96**	**0.97**

Figure 19.13 MLP (sequential) classification report.

19.6.1 User Interface

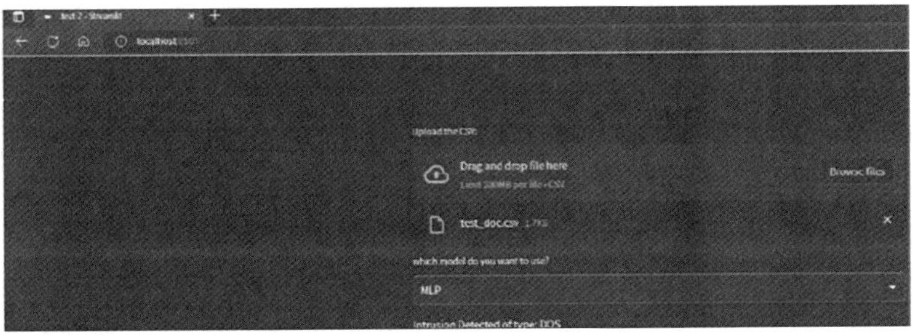

Figure 19.14 Working demo of user interface.

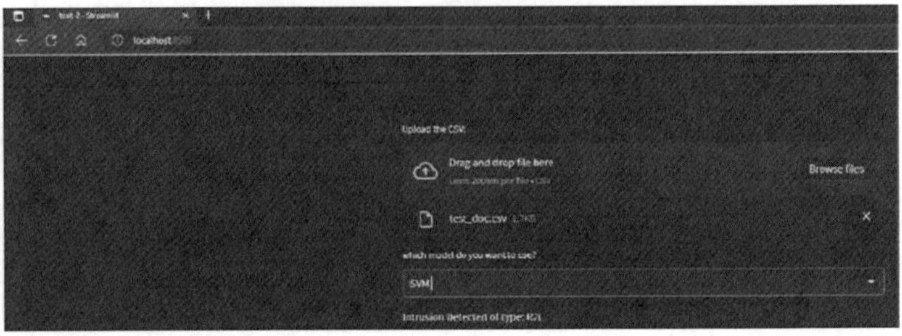

Figure 19.15 Working demo of user interface.

Figure 19.16 Working demo of user interface.

19.7 Conclusion and Future Scope

After such algorithms and procedures have been undergone, we can conclude that it is possible to create a machine-learning model that will predict and detect intrusions in networks. Better security of user data for an organization including early detection of unauthorized network intrusion and tracing how much data was compromised in the invasion can be achieved by precise and timely detection of intruders. The models and the data are not heavily loaded, needing minimal overheads and little or no preprocessing which makes it lightweight; once the model is trained, it does not require much processing power.

Every company concerned with its security should have NIDS. The proposed network detection system, based on machine learning (ML), can discover intruders in the network. Most significantly, the proposed system offers a higher accuracy in its detection rate and can detect types of intrusions that are still unfamiliar to other standard systems at an increased precision. The truth is that this system may not prevent all breaches but it helps organizations rapidly recover from them as it enables early detection.

The proposed network detection system, based on machine learning (ML), can discover intruders in the network. Most significantly, the proposed system offers a higher accuracy in its detection rate and can detect types of intrusions that are still unfamiliar to other standard systems at an increased precision. The truth is that this system may not prevent all breaches but it helps organizations rapidly recover from them as it enables early detection. In the future combining the Intrusion Detection System with a Network Intrusion Prevention System which allows to actively prevent an on-going intrusion can bolster network security even more.

References

1. Agarwal, A., Sharma, P., Alshehri, M., Mohamed, A.A., Alfarraj, O., Classification model for accuracy and intrusion detection using machine learning approach. *PeerJ Comput. Sci.*, 7, e437, 2021, https://doi.org/10.7717/peerj-cs.437.
2. Alikhanov, J., Jang, R., Abuhamad, M., Mohaisen, D., Nyang, D., Noh, Y., Investigating the Effect of Traffic Sampling on Machine Learning-Based Network Intrusion Detection Approaches. *IEEE Access*, 10, 5801–5823, 2022, doi:10.1109/ACCESS.2021.3137318.
3. Mosaiyebzadeh, F., Araujo Rodriguez, L.G., Macêdo Batista, D., Hirata, R., A Network Intrusion Detection System using Deep Learning against MQTT Attacks in IoT. *2021 IEEE Latin-American Conference on Communications (LATINCOM)*, pp. 1–6, 2021, doi: 10.1109/LATINCOM53176.2021.9647850.
4. Magán-Carrión, R., Urda, D., Díaz-Cano, I., Dorronsoro, B., Towards a Reliable Comparison and Evaluation of Network Intrusion Detection Systems Based on Machine Learning Approaches. *Appl. Sci.*, 10, 1775, 2020, https://doi.org/10.3390/app10051775.
5. Raviteja, P. *et al.*, Implementation of machine learning algorithms for detection of network intrusion. *Int. J. Comput. Sci. Trends Technol. (IJCST)*, 8, 2, 163–169, 2020.
6. Li, Z., Rios, A.L.G., Xu, G., Trajković, L., Machine Learning Techniques for Classifying Network Anomalies and Intrusions, in: *Proceedings of the 2019 IEEE International Symposium on Circuits and Systems (ISCAS)*, Sapporo, Japan, 26–29 May 2019, pp. 1–5, [Google Scholar].
7. Ashraf, N., Ahmad, W., Ashraf, R., A comparative study of data mining algorithms for high detection rate in intrusion detection system. *Ann. Emerg. Technol. Comput.*, 2, 1, 49–57, 2018.
8. Bhattacharya, S., Kaluri, R., Singh, S., Alazab, M., Tariq, U., A novel PCA-firefly based XGBoost classification model for intrusion detection in networks using GpU. *Electronics*, 9, 2, 219, 2020.

9. Ring, M., Wunderlich, S., Scheuring, D., Landes, D., Hotho, A., A survey of network-based intrusion detection data sets. *Comput. Secur.*, *86*, 147–167, 2019, https://doi.org/10.1016/j.cose.2019.06.005 [Google Scholar].
10. Musa, U.S., Chhabra, M., Ali, A., Kaur, M., Intrusion Detection System using Machine Learning Techniques: A Review. *2020 International Conference on Smart Electronics and Communication (ICOSEC), Trichy, India*, pp. 149–155, 2020, doi: 10.1109/ICOSEC49089.2020.9215333.
11. Thaseen, I.S., Poorva, B., Ushasree, P.S., Network intrusion detection using machine learning techniques, in: *2020 International conference on emerging trends in information technology and engineering (IC-ETITE)*, pp. 1–7, IEEE, 2020, February.
12. Chowdhury, M.N., Ferens, K., Ferens, M., Network intrusion detection using machine learning, in: *Proceedings of the International Conference on Security and Management (SAM)*, The Steering Committee of The World Congress in Computer Science, Computer Engineering and Applied Computing (WorldComp), pp. 30, 2016.
13. Taher, K.A., Jisan, B.M.Y., Rahman, M.M., Network intrusion detection using supervised machine learning technique with feature selection, in: *2019 International conference on robotics, electrical and signal processing techniques (ICREST)*, pp. 643–646, IEEE, 2019, January.
14. Kumar, K. and Batth, J.S., Network intrusion detection with feature selection techniques using machine-learning algorithms. *Int. J. Comput. Appl.*, 150, 12, 1–13, 2016.

20

Prediction of Arrival Delay Time in Freightage Rails

Bobbala Shriya, Gudishetty Shrita, Vanga Pragnya Reddy and Nanda Kumar M.*

Dept. of ECM, Sreenidhi Institute of Science and Technology, Yamnampet, Hyderabad India

Abstract

This work addresses the challenge of optimizing rail infrastructure use by focusing on short-term arrival delay prediction in freight rail operations. Leveraging data from the National Railway Company of Luxembourg on routes connecting Bettembourg to nine terminal stations across the EU, we compare various machine learning models, including LightGBM, Linear Regression, Random Forest, KNN, XGBoost, and a Voting Regressor ensemble. The LightGBM model outperforms others, demonstrating its efficacy in predicting arrival delay times. Departure delay time, trip distance, and train composition emerge as crucial features influencing short-term arrival delays. Our findings offer valuable insights for the National Railway Company of Luxembourg, proposing the developed short-term prediction model as a decision-support system. The model enables estimation of future operational times, empowering operators to proactively manage disruptions. Additionally, the study extends the analysis by introducing a Voting Regressor ensemble, further enhancing predictive accuracy of 94%. This research contributes to advancing rail disruption prediction models, fostering improved operational efficiency and reduced delays in freight rail transportation.

Keywords: Data-driven models, delays forecasting, freight transport, gradient boosting, rail operation delays

**Corresponding author*: nanda.mkumar12@gmail.com

Budati Anil Kumar, Singamaneni Kranthi Kumar and Li Xingwang (eds.) Quantum Computing Models for Cybersecurity and Wireless Communications, (293–310) © 2025 Scrivener Publishing LLC

20.1 Introduction

In the dynamic landscape of freight transportation, rail operations have gained prominence for their economic advantages, operational efficiency, reliability, environmental benefits, and safety. This shift towards rail has been encouraged by public agencies, emphasizing its role in intermodal transportation [1]. As rail intermodal operations become increasingly pivotal for the overall efficiency and dependability of the freight transport industry, the optimization of rail infrastructure emerges as a critical aspect. This optimization involves the meticulous management, maintenance, and utilization of technology and data analytics to enhance performance [2, 3].

However, the complexity of rail networks, coupled with a substantial volume of rolling stock, gives rise to a significant challenge – train delays. These delays can stem from the unpredictable preparation time before departure and variations in a train's performance during its journey [4–6]. Arrival delay prediction, crucial for rail risk management, entails calculating the deviation between actual and scheduled arrival times for trips between stations. In the face of disruptions, train dispatchers must swiftly assess the impact on schedules, strategically adjusting operations to mitigate losses and prevent a cascading chain of delays that could disrupt the entire system [7, 8].

In this context, the integration of data-driven models for short-term arrival delay prediction becomes imperative, offering a proactive approach to addressing challenges within the dynamic rail environment. The objective of this study is to comprehensively analyze and propose strategies for optimizing rail infrastructure within the freight transportation industry. Emphasizing the increasing prominence of rail in intermodal operations, our aim is to investigate the key factors contributing to operational efficiency, reliability, and safety. Through a combination of maintenance protocols, effective management practices, and the integration of cutting-edge technology and data analytics, we seek to enhance the overall performance of rail transportation. The study aims to provide actionable insights that facilitate the adaptation and improvement of rail infrastructure to meet the evolving demands of the contemporary transportation system [9, 10].

Despite the growing importance of rail transportation in intermodal operations, challenges persist in optimizing rail infrastructure. Issues such as inadequate maintenance, suboptimal management practices, and a lack of technology integration hinder the industry's ability to meet evolving demands. The current state of rail infrastructure may compromise efficiency, reliability, and safety, impacting the overall performance of the freight transport sector. The absence of a holistic approach that combines maintenance, management, and technology solutions poses a significant hurdle. Addressing these challenges is crucial to ensuring the seamless integration of rail into intermodal transportation, thereby enhancing the industry's efficiency and dependability.

This paper discusses about the prediction of arrival delay time of freightage rails and the section 20.2 gives the detail overview of literature. The section 20.3 discuss about the methodology which has proposed work, system architecture, data set, data processing, training and testing, algorithms etc.,. the section 20.4 belongs to experimental results of the work implemented and the section 20.5 gives the clear overview of conclusion followed by the references.

20.2 Literature Survey

The system addresses the challenge of scheduling extra freight trains in railway networks with fixed passenger timetables. It utilizes an integer linear programming formulation for optimal timetabling and introduces a Lagrangian heuristic for real-world instances, offering a flexible solution. By offering the best itineraries that facilitate the addition of new freight trains, the suggested method effectively maximizes closely correspond to the choices of operators. It promises flexible in managing safety-related operational constraints, enhancing the railway's overall efficacy network [1].

The system's dependence on mathematical formulae, particularly integer linear programming, may cause issues and complexity in the operations of extensive railway networks. The recommended method gives a practical blueprint for mixed traffic rail - road network freight train scheduling. Although it increases productiveness, it requires careful considering the computational requirement and the operational difficulties that come from straying from ideal timetables potentially lead to issues during the procedure. A practical solution for scheduling freight trains in railway networks with mixed traffic is supplied by the presented strategy. Even while it boosts productivities, it requires careful considerations of computing requirements and connected operational difficulties.

Using big data analytics and technology for railways whole data collection is required for asset management administration and use that compares to blockchain. Through the application of advanced analytical methods such as by using machine learning, the system enhances decision-making, effectively acknowledging issues, and increasing the efficacy of railway asset management. The supplement of big data analytics to railroad asset management enhances decision-making abilities by using state-of-the-art analysis tools and methodologies [2]. It allows for further effective data collection, administration, and application, which ultimately improves overall efficacy of asset management in the railroad industry. There are many obstacles to overcome while implementing big data analytics for railway asset management, such as the need for considerable upfront investments, integration issues, and data security worries. Overcoming these difficulties needed for the proposed system to operate to its full potential, making use of extensive data.

Next generations of railway communication system will include enhanced physical layer upgrades, adjustable intelligent surfaces, relays, and multiplexing techniques. It addresses difficulties with HST communication, such as adapting to harsh environments, latency limitations, and frequency band scarcity, and investigate AI/ML-assisted systems [3]. The suggested system improves HST communication and optimizes performance for challenging railway situations through the utilization of adaptive physical layer technology. It integrates complex MIMO algorithms, relays, and modifiable intelligent surfaces for specific rail applications, which may add to spectrum efficiency, latency, and dependability. Even with these advancements, there might still be challenges for implementing the recommended system, such as potential complexity of implementing adjustable intelligent surfaces and ensuring a seamless AI/ML integration. In order to completely profit from the upgraded physical layer for the upcoming railway.

As part of this proposed system, train routes are optimized to reduce energy consumption and operating delays [4]. It refines system efficiency and passenger comfort by managing the trade-off between energy savings and late fees through the use of genetic algorithms, ant colony optimization, and improved brute force approach. The system optimizes train paths in order to reduce energy consumption, delays, and train-to-train encounters. Sophisticated optimization methods are used in railway operations to increase efficiency, safeness, and passenger comfort. Algorithm implementation could present challenges, potentially for robust real-time adaptation to shifting operational conditions. Furthermore, the system's efficacy might be determined by how well train behaviours and network dynamics are predicted. The study demonstrates that optimizing train paths with complex algorithms may successfully minimizes train

The proposed method uses Markov chains to estimate the progress of train delays in railway networks using actual operational data. The Dutch train system serves as an example of how both homogeneous and non-homogeneous Markov models are developed, offering simple yet effective tool for assessing the stability of timetables and projecting delays [5]. Using Markov chains, this proposed method provides a practical mean of modeling and predicting the progress of train delay. When real operational data is added to models, the models become more accurate and timetable robustness can be assessed in a real-world environment. The proposed models may not function well for various railway networks, requires adjustments to account for unique operational characteristics. Additionally, level of detail and quality of the operational data that is currently accessible.

20.3 Methodology

Using data from the National Railway Company of Luxembourg, the primary goal of the article is to investigate the short-term forecast of arrival delay time in freight rail operations between Bettembourg and nine terminal stations in the EU. Many data-driven models, such as LightGBM, Linear Regression, Random Forest, KNN, XGBoost, and a Voting Regressor, are used in the analysis. Notably, when it comes to short-term arrival delay durations, the lightGBM model performs better than the others. The length of trip, train composition, and departure delay time are important factors that affect forecasts. Predictions from many models are combined using an ensemble technique, or more specifically a Voting Regressor, to increase forecast accuracy. The proposed system aims to improve the accuracy of arrival delay prediction while highlighting the necessity to explore state-of-the-art techniques such as the Voting Regressor for additional performance improvement. This research provides valuable information for optimizing freight rail operations and relieving the impact of disruptions in the dynamic European rail network.

A. System Architecture:

The gathering of different data from railway operations, including train schedules, delays, weather, and pertinent variables, is the initial stage in the system architecture. Subsequently, large stage of preparation is executed, encompassing the management of missing values, data cleansing, and feature engineering to generate significant variables. The updated data is then put into a number of data-driven models, including extension voting classifier, KNN, random forest, lightGBM, linear regression, and extension-XGBoost. These models use complex algorithms to accurately predict arrival delay durations.

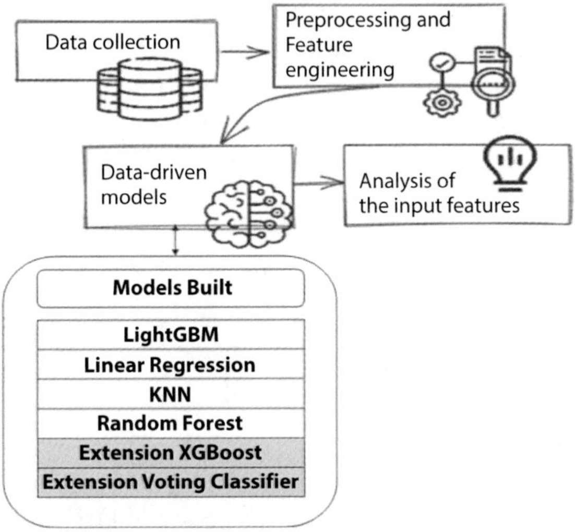

Figure 20.1 System architecture with models.

The data-driven models thoroughly analyze important input features, like departure delay durations, journey distances, and train compositions, to determine how these affect arrival delay predictions. The culmination of this analysis identifies the best-performing model, which is then deployed using the Flask framework. Flask facilitates the development of a robust and scalable web service, allowing real-time access to the predictive model's insights. Figure 20.1 illustrates the operational process of the proposed model flowchart which ensures a seamless integration of data collection, preprocessing, modeling, and deployment, offering a versatile solution for accurate and efficient arrival delay predictions in railway operations.

B. Dataset:

Figure 20.2 illustrates the dataset for delay prediction encompasses 3000 rows and 8 columns, providing a comprehensive snapshot of critical factors influencing railway operations. Teu, representing Twenty-Foot Equivalent Unit, quantifies container capacity, while Train Length and Wagon_Quantity offer insights into the physical dimensions of trains. Train_Weight indicates the total weight, while Distance_Station shows how close the station is Arrival_Delay logs departure delays, while Total_Distance measures the total journey distance. The target variable - delay is essential for projecting arrival delays.

This dataset holds a range of information required to describe and understand the dynamics of train delays. Using these correlations between Teu,

	Teu	Train_Length	Wagon_Quantity	Train_Weight	Distance_Station	Total_Distance	Departure_Delay	Delay
0	98	5	-11.0	194.0	1448	430	408.0	-22.0
1	2336	10	-8.0	279.0	2330	750	741.0	-9.0
2	840	20	-2.0	293.0	2296	806	811.0	5.0
3	258	20	-5.0	281.0	2342	805	756.0	-9.0
4	135	25	-1.0	215.0	1448	320	259.0	-21.0
...	...	...	...	...	...	...	...	...
2995	1982	940	-4.0	126.0	728	1150	1142.0	-8.0
2996	2051	940	-9.0	170.0	1013	1238	1221.0	-17.0
2997	427	940	-5.0	237.0	1452	1146	1132.0	-14.0
2998	707	940	22.0	130.0	696	1100	1112.0	12.0
2999	3837	940	1.0	152.0	861	1120	1113.0	-7.0

3000 rows × 8 columns

Figure 20.2 Dataset freight rail.

Train_Length, Wagon_Quantity, Train_Weight, Distance_Station, Total_Distance, and Departure_Delay, it creates predictive models that can effectively forecast delays. These factors guarantee a comprehensive and subtle approach, allowing for a solid analysis that helps in the optimization of freight- rail operations. Because of its multidimensional properties, this dataset is an ultimate resource for researchers and business experts who want to reduce the adverse effects of delays on overall operational performances and increase the efficacy of rail transport.

C. Data Preprocessing:

The pandas data frame and numpy are necessary libraries for handling and arranging the delay prediction dataset during the processing phase. Effective tabular management of data is made possible by the pandas data frame, which offers multipurpose tools for tabular data conversion, cleaning, and assessment of data. Numpy is helpful for reshaping data since it provides the array operations required to increase the dataset's compatibility and analytical efficacy. The columns which are not useful are deleted in order to streamline the dataset and get rid of duplicate or unneeded data.

Normalization is an important first step in preparing the dataset for modeling. This process prevents the likelihood such that the unequal magnitudes of any one feature will dominate the study by guaranteeing that numerical features are on a uniform scale. Normalization improves the performance of machine learning models, particularly when the algorithms in this model are sensitive to the scale of features.

For visualizing on the dataset's characteristics, seaborn and matplotlib are used. These libraries facilitate the creation of pleasing graphs that reveal patterns and trends within the data. Additionally, LightGBM, a powerful gradient boosting framework, is used to depict the relevance of many features in the dataset. Understanding feature importance informs the modeling process and aids to pinpoint the crucial components influencing arrival delays. The entire data processing technique ensures that the dataset is standardized, cleaned, and visually inspected in order to get it ready for the development of different machine learning models

D. Training and Testing:

The next step in the workflow is to separate the dataset into training and testing sets to evaluate the prediction performance of the developed models. This process is crucial for assessing how well the model generalize the new data. Using programs like scikit-learn, the dataset is partitioned so a portion is used to train the model and other part is set aside to assess its predictive power. A standard technique that ensures a balance between robust model training and extensive testing using an 80-20 or 70-30 split.

After the data has been split, a metric score calculation function is essential for evaluating the performance of the model. Common measurements include R-squared, Mean Square Error (MSE), and Mean Absolute Error (MAE). The function assesses the difference between predicted and actual delay values, providing numerical metrics of the model's precision and accuracy.

During the training phase, the selected machine learning models like LightGBM, linear regression, random forest, KNN, and extension XGBoost fit to the training set. These models find patterns and relationships in the data for generating accurate predictions. The models are then evaluated with the reserved dataset i.e. the other portion in order to assess how predictive they are. The best algorithm for short-term arrival delay time prediction in freight rail operations is chosen using the computed metric scores, which provide information about each model's efficacy. This iterative procedure helps to create a prediction system that is accurate and dependable by guaranteeing thorough testing and strong model training.

E. Algorithm:

i. LightGBM: LightGBM, which stands for Light Gradient Boosting Machine, improves prediction accuracy by building decision trees consecutively to determine and correct the errors. The unique leaf-wise growth and regularization methods provide faster and more effective memory performance. LightGBM quickly manages categorical characteristics, allows parallel and distributed computing, and aids to create accurate predictive models for train arrival delays in railway operations.

ii. Linear Regression: Modeling the relationship between dependent and independent variables is done statistically using linear regression. The capacity to predict arrival delays in freight train operations is useful for this activity. Precise arrival timing forecasts are obtained by detail examining the factors including train composition, travel distance, and departure delay time.

iii. K-Nearest Neighbors (KNN): A machine learning approach called K-Nearest Neighbors (KNN) uses a multidimensional space to classify data points according to how near they are to each other. By examining the train occurrences which are prior to these, based on departure delays, journey distance, and train composition, this study uses KNN to anticipate arrival delays in freight rail operations. This method gives rail operators critical decision support while improving delay estimations.

iv. Random Forest: The use of Random Forest is required in this study, by using arbitrary data samples it constructs decision trees and aggregates their predictions. This strategy lowers overfitting and improves precision. In railway operations, this ml model is helpful in precisely estimating arrival delays. It is specifically good at estimating arrival times more accurately, streamlining operational management, and handling complexes in rail transportation. To guarantee a more trustworthy and precise final anticipation, we make improvements to this project. We investigate using Voting Classifier and XGBoost. Here, XGBoost generated less mistakes.

v. XGBoost: Extreme Gradient Boosting, or XGBoost, is a potent machine learning model that builds robust prediction models from data which is low standard ones. XGBoost is essential to this research since it aids to estimate freight train arrival delays with high accuracy. It produces precise and trustworthy forecasts by capturing complex relationships between factors including departure delay time, trip distance, and train composition. Enhancing railway operation efficacy and reducing delays is made possible by XGBoost's extraordinary predictive performance, feature selection, and ability to manage missing data.

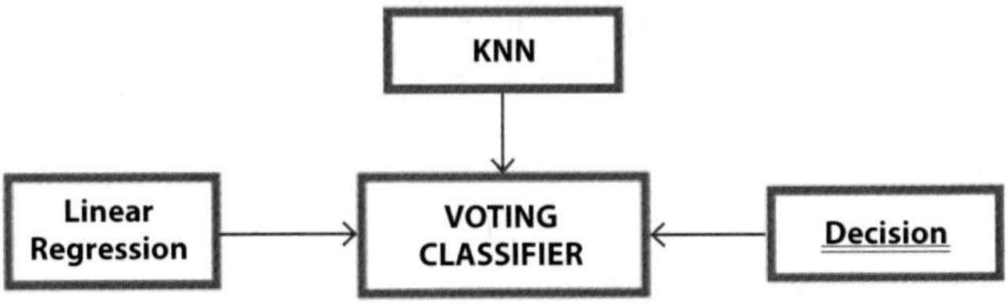

Figure 20.3 Voting Classifier.

vi. Voting Classifier: As shown in Figure 20.3, the Voting Regressor method builds a more reliable and trustworthy regression model by combining predictions from the Linear Regression, Decision Tree Regressor, and K-Neighbors Regressor. It is appropriate for the work since it improves prediction accuracy in a variety of patterns by using the advantages of many regressors.

20.4 Experimental Results

The experimental results of performance measures such as Mean Absolute Percentage Error (MAPE), R- Squared error (R2 Score), Mean Absolute Error (MAE), and Root Mean Square Error (RSME) are discussed in this section.

A. ***MAPE:***

A metric used to quantify a forecasting model's accuracy as a percentage is called Mean Absolute Percentage Error, or MAPE. For every observation, it shows the mean absolute percent difference between the values that were anticipated and those that were observed.

The average of the absolute percentage mistakes between the values that were predicted and those that were observed is called MAPE. The formula for calculating MAPE is given in Equation 20.1 and Figure 20.4 illustrates about the classification performance of MAPE in different techniques

$$MAPE = \frac{1}{n}\sum_{i=1}^{n}\left|\frac{\hat{y}_i - y_i}{y_i}\right| \times 100 \tag{20.1}$$

Where $\hat{y}_i$ = predicted value for ith data point
y_i = actual value for ith data point
n=number of observations

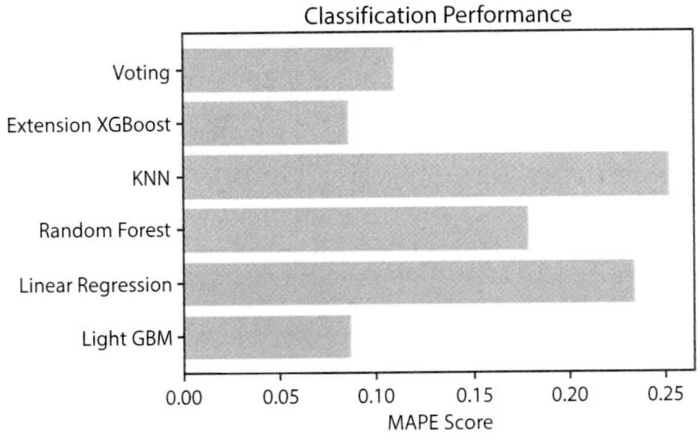

Figure 20.4 MAPE graph.

B. *R2 SCORE:*

Another name for the R-squared value is the coefficient of determination. It is a statistical measure that shows how much of the variance in the dependent variable in a regression model can be accounted for by the independent variables. R-squared is the ratio of the overall variance in the data to the variation explained by the model. The formula to calculate Squared-R Performance metrics is given in Equations 20.2–20.4 and Figure 20.5 illustrates about the classification performance of R2SCORE in different techniques

$$R^2 = 1 - \frac{SS_{res}}{SS_{tot}} \tag{20.2}$$

$$SS_{res} = \Sigma_{i=1}^{n} (y_i - \hat{y}_i)^2 \tag{20.3}$$

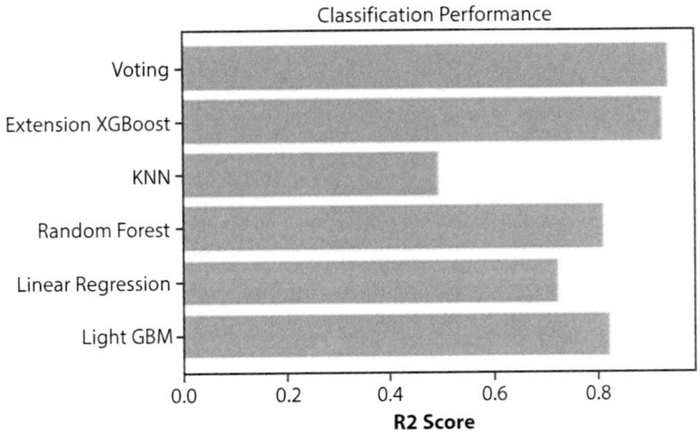

Figure 20.5 R2SCORE graph.

$$SS_{tot} = \Sigma_{i=1}^{n}(y_i - \overline{y})^2 \tag{20.4}$$

Where

SS_{res} = the sum of squares of the residual errors, representing the variation that the model fails to explain

SS_{tot} = the total sum of squares representing total variations in the data

$\overline{y}$ = mean value of the dependent variable

C. MAE:

Without accounting for direction, the mean absolute error, or MAE, is a measurement of the average size of errors in a set of predictions. It is used to evaluate the efficacy of a regression model and is expressed as the average absolute difference between the predicted and actual values. The MAE loss function formula is given as Equation 20.5 and Figure 20.6 illustrates about the classification performance of MAE in different techniques

$$MAE = \frac{1}{n}\Sigma_{i=1}^{n}(\hat{y}_i - y_i)^2 \tag{20.5}$$

D. RMSE:

Another name for Root Mean Squared Deviation (RMSD) is Root Mean Squared Error (MSE). The Root Mean Squared Error (RMSE), which is based on MSE, is a commonly used metric to assess how inaccurate a model is at forecasting quantitative data. It expresses the error's size in the same unit as the output variable and is the square root of the Mean Squared Error (MSE).

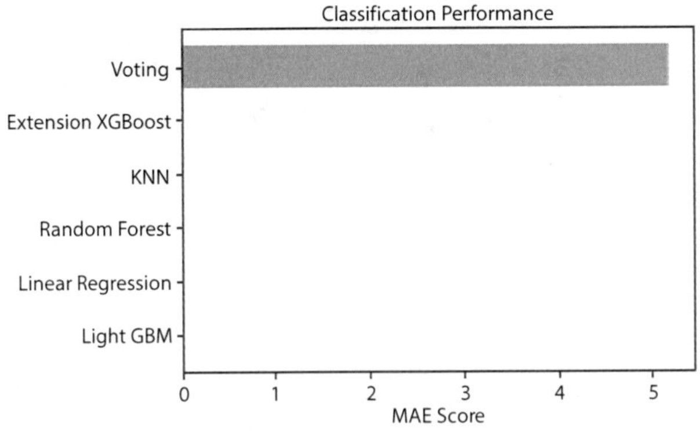

Figure 20.6 MAE graph.

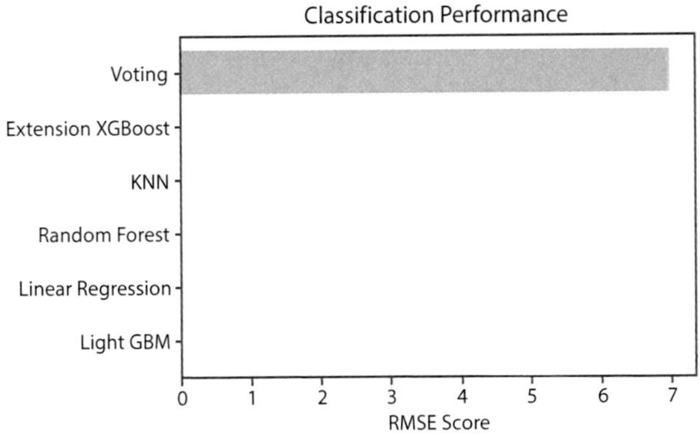

Figure 20.7 RMSE graph.

The square root of the mean of the squared discrepancies between the expected and actual values is how RMSE is computed using the following formula is given as Equation 20.6 and Figure 20.7 illustrates about the classification performance of RMSE in techniques

$$RMSE = \sqrt{\frac{1}{n}\sum_{i=1}^{n}(\hat{y}_i - y_i)^2} \tag{20.6}$$

Table 20.1 shows the ML models and the performance metrics like RMSE, MAPE, MAE, R2 Score using LightGBM, Linear Regression, Random Forest, KNN, XGBoost, voting classifier in which the R2 score has given high performance for voting classifier.

Table 20.1 Performance evaluation table.

S. no.	ML model	MAE	RSME	MAPE	R2 score
1	LightGBM	0.012	0.020	0.087	0.825
2	Linear regression	0.022	0.029	0.234	0.726
3	Random forest	0.016	0.022	0.179	0.815
4	KNN	0.023	0.032	0.252	0.496
5	XGboost	0.010	0.015	0.086	0.929
6	Voting	5.192	6.979	0.110	0.941

In this work, Figure 20.8 illustrates about the home page of system and Figure 20.9 illustrates about the sign up page of system here we enter our details required for signing up (for new users) and Figure 20.10 illustrates about the sign up page of system here we enter our details required for signing in (for existing users) and Figure 20.11 illustrates to upload the required values as input to predict delay and Figure 20.12 illustrates the final result of our system that shows the delay.

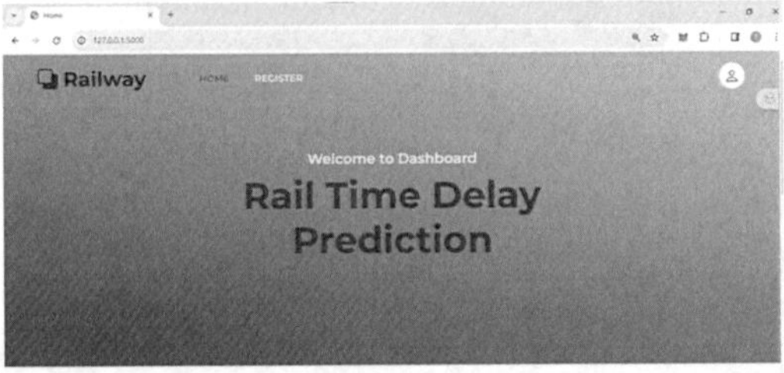

Figure 20.8 Home page.

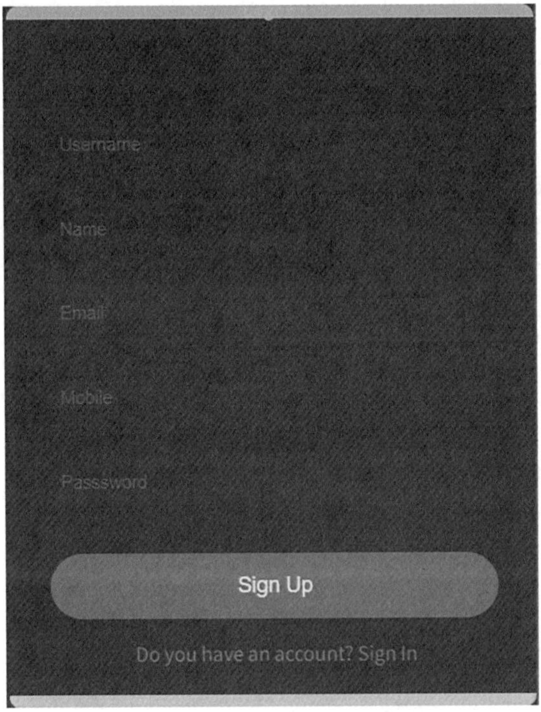

Figure 20.9 Sign-up page.

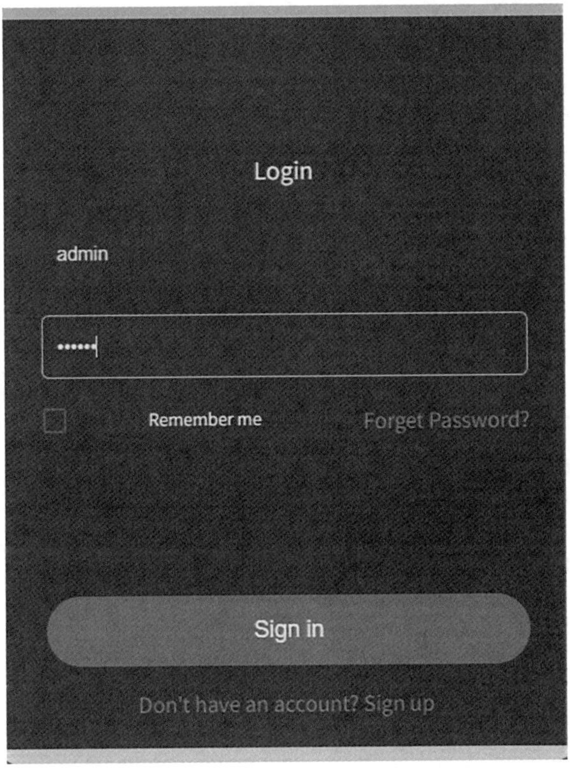

Figure 20.10 Sign in page.

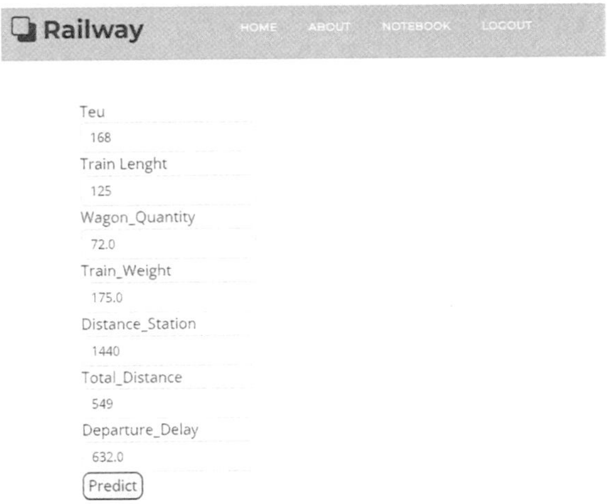

Figure 20.11 Upload input values.

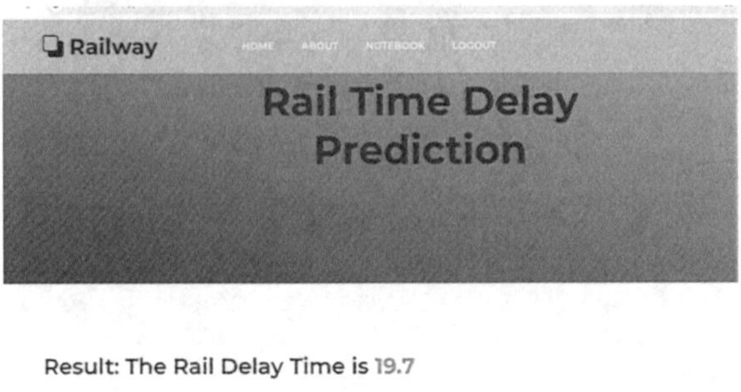

Figure 20.12 Predict result for given input values.

20.5 Conclusions

This paper validates our theory that choosing slices might enhance machine learning efficiency, and that choosing Here, addresses the critical demand for real-time operational insights by offering a comprehensive and creative method of forecasting freight train arrival delay times. Regression algorithms are used to evaluate five data-driven models: Light GBM, Linear Regression, Random Forest, KNN, and XGBoost. Of these, XGBoost performs the best, having the highest R2 and the lowest values of RMSE and MAPE.

One notable element that allows stakeholders to determine which characteristics are most responsible for strong R2 scores is the addition of SHAPLEY to improve model interpretability. Decision-makers are empowered to comprehend and take appropriate action based on the factors impacting arrival delay estimations due to the transparency in feature importance.

The study has significant practical ramifications for a range of freight transport industry stakeholders. Anticipated results include better resource allocation, cost savings, and more dependable delivery schedules, all of which will contribute to the overall effectiveness and efficiency of freight rail operations. Additionally, the study closes a significant gap in the body of knowledge by emphasizing short-term delay estimates for freight trains rather than the more conventional focus on network delays and passenger trains. Consequently, this study makes a substantial contribution to improving operational interventions and reliability in the freight rail industry, offering insightful information for next planning and decision-making processes.

Subsequent investigations into freight rail operations may focus on determining the best routes for trains, utilizing intelligent scheduling and navigation methods to minimize journey durations and delays. By using machines to do repetitive tasks, the entire process—from data collection to model building and utilization—can be automated, offering a way to save time and boost productivity. Furthermore, more research into the SHAP approach can yield a through comprehension of the reasons behind delays, supplying knowledge to improve real-time operations and overall rail efficiency.

References

1. Cacchiani, V., Caprara, A., Toth, P., Scheduling extra freight trains on railway networks. *Transp. Res. B, Methodol.*, 44, 2, 215–231, 2010.
2. Mcmahon, P., Zhang, T., Dwight, R., Requirements for big data adoption for railway asset management. *IEEE Access*, 8, 15543–15564, 2020.
3. Li, Q., Sibel, J.C., Berbineau, M., Dayoub, I., Gallee, F., Bonneville, H., Physical layer enhancement for next-generation railway communication systems. *IEEE Access*, 10, 83152–83175, 2022.
4. Zhao, N., Roberts, C., Hillmansen, S., Nicholson, G., A multiple train trajectory optimization to minimize energy consumption and delay. *IEEE Trans. Intell. Transp. Syst.*, 16, 5, 2363–2372, 2015.
5. Artan, M.S. and Sahin, I., Exploring patterns of train delay evolution and timetable robustness. *IEEE Trans. Intell. Transp. Syst.*, 23, 8, 1205–11214, 2022.
6. Bešinović, N., Goverde, R.M.P., Quaglietta, E., Roberti, R., An integrated micro–macro approach to robust railway timetabling. *Transp. Res. B, Methodol.*, 87, 14–32, 2016.
7. Corman, F. and Meng, L., A review of online dynamic models and algorithms for railway traffic management. *IEEE Trans. Intell. Transp. Syst.*, 16, 3, 1274–1284, 2015.
8. Bhavsar, P., Safro, I., Bouaynaya, N., Polikar, R., Dera, R., Machine learning in transportation data analytics, in: *Data Analytics for Intelligent Transportation Systems*, pp. 283–307, 2017.
9. Pineda-Jaramillo, J.D., Insa, R., Martínez, R., Modeling the energy consumption of trains by applying neural networks. *Proc. Inst. Mech. Eng., F, J. Rail Rapid Transit*, 232, 816–823, 2018.
10. Srujan, N., Mohd, A., Yuva, K., Nanda, K.M., Advanced Graduate Graduate Admission Prediction. *IEEE 8th International Conference for Convergence in Technology (I2CT)*, Mumbai, 2023.

21

Predicting Flight Delays with Error Calculation Using Machine Learned Classifiers

L. Sai Nageswara Raju, T. Naman Krishn Raj, Raipole Manihas Goud* **and Mohan Dholvan**

Department of ECM, Sreenidhi Institute of Science and Technology, Hyderabad, India

Abstract
Flight delays are a constant problem in the airline business, which is made worse by the fact that air travel is more crowded now than it was 20 years ago. There are big financial costs for planes because of these delays, and they also hurt the environment. To deal with this important problem, airlines are constantly looking for different ways to cut down on delays and cancellations. We use many different types of machine learning models in this research, such as Neural Network, Ridge Classification, Logistic Regression, Support Vector Machine, Voting Classifier, Gaussian Naïve Bayes, KNN, Multilayer Perceptron, Decision Tree, and Random Forest. Our goal is to correctly guess how likely it is that a flight will be delayed. By using these advanced computer methods, we hope to be able to give accurate predictions about when certain flights will arrive. This ability to predict the future holds a lot of potential for making the aircraft industry more efficient and improving customer happiness. In the end, our work helps lessen the bad effects of flight delays, which makes the air travel system more reliable and sustainable.

Keywords: Flight delay, flight data, prediction, machine learning classifiers

21.1 Introduction

Flight delays are a constant problem in the aviation business, which has been dealing with them for a long time. This problem has been made

**Corresponding author*: manihasgoud@gmail.com

Budati Anil Kumar, Singamaneni Kranthi Kumar and Li Xingwang (eds.) Quantum Computing Models for Cybersecurity and Wireless Communications, (311–324) © 2025 Scrivener Publishing LLC

worse by the steady rise in air traffic over the past 20 years [1]. Airlines lose a lot of money because of these delays, and they're also bad for the environment because longer planes and processes on the ground use more fuel and release more pollution [2]. In order to solve this complex problem effectively, we need new ideas that can accurately predict and reduce delays.

Airlines are using more and more advanced computer methods, especially machine learning models, to predict how likely it is that a flight will be late [3]. This is because they know they need to be proactive right away. We are going to look at many different machine learning algorithms in this study. These include Neural Networks, Ridge Classification, Logistic Regression, Support Vector Machines, Voting Classifiers, Gaussian Naïve Bayes, K-Nearest Neighbors (KNN), Multilayer Perceptrons, Decision Trees, and Random Forests [4].

We try to give accurate statements about the arrival status of specific planes by using the strengths of these different models. This way, airlines can make smart choices and act ahead of time to avoid problems. This study is important for more than just improving working efficiency; it could have a huge effect on the airline business and all the people who work in it [5].

By using machine learning to make predictions, airlines can improve their operating flexibility, make better use of their resources, and eventually make customers happier by lowering the number of flight delays and cancellations [6]. Additionally, these kinds of improvements have wider positive effects on the environment, since fewer delays mean less fuel use, pollution, and the general environmental impact of air travel [7].

In a nutshell, our study is a coordinated attempt to use cutting-edge computer methods to make the airline industry better. By using machine learning's ability to predict the future, we hope to give planes useful information that will not only make their operations run more smoothly but also help make the air transportation system more durable and long-lasting [8]. By taking this action, we hope to bring about positive change that will lessen the bad effects of flight delays and help create a future where air travel is reliable, efficient, and good for the environment [9].

21.2 Literature Survey

Flight delays are a big problem in the flight industry that affects companies, customers, and many other people. The goal of this literature review is to give a full picture of all the research that has already been done on what causes flight delays and how to identify them. It will do this by looking at university studies and business journals.

In 2007, Rupp did a study at East Carolina University that looked into why flights are late. This study made it clear that more research needs to be done to find out what causes delays. It set the stage for future studies that will go into more detail about this complicated problem [1].

Cinar *et al.* (2013) used simulations to look into capacity and delay studies for airport moving areas. Their study, which was released in the journals Aircraft Engineering and Aerospace Technology, showed how important it is to improve speed and cut down on delays at airports [4].

Navoneel *et al.* (2019) did a study on using gradient boosting algorithm to predict flight arrival delays. This study, which was published in the results of the Emerging Technologies in Data Mining and Information Security conference, showed that machine learning algorithms can accurately predict flight delays. This helps create predictive models for how airlines run their businesses [5].

Kim *et al.* (2016) used machine learning methods to look into how to predict flight delays caused by bad weather. Their study, which they shared at the 35th Digital Avionics Systems Conference, was mostly about using advanced computer methods to predict and lessen the effects of bad weather on air traffic [6].

Based on Bayesian Network, Cao and Lin (2011) looked at flight return time and predicted delays. Their study, which was published in Computer Engineering and Design, stressed how important it is to have quick return times and forecast models to cut down on delays and boost operating efficiency [7].

Robollo *et al.* (publication year not given) looked into how to describe and predict delays in plane travel. Some specifics about this study are not given, but it is likely that it helped us understand what causes air traffic delays and create prediction models that can lessen their effects [8].

Noriko Etani (2019) made a model that can predict when planes will arrive on time by finding links between flight and weather data. This research showed how important it is to include weather data in forecast models in order to make arrival times more accurate and cut down on delays [11].

The literature we looked at here shows that flight delays are caused by many things, and it's important to use advanced computer methods like machine learning and modeling to solve this complicated problem. Researchers want to help airlines make better choices, run their businesses more efficiently, and make air travel more reliable and cost-effective by finding out what causes delays and making models that can predict them.

21.3 Proposed Methodology

The suggested work includes creating a complex system that combines different machine learning methods, such as Neural Networks [9], Logistic Regression [12], Support Vector Machines, and others, to correctly predict when flights will be late in the airline business. These programs can predict the future, which is how the system tries to improve business efficiency and customer happiness.

Neural networks can learn complicated trends in data, which makes them good for using past data to guess when flights will be late. For easy but useful binary classification tasks, like figuring out if a flight will be late or not, logistic regression is a good choice. Support Vector Machines [11] are great at working with large amounts of data and links that don't follow a straight line. This makes them useful for figuring out when flights will be late in complicated situations.

Also, ensemble methods like Random Forest and Gradient Boosting can be used to mix the forecasts of several models, which makes the system even more accurate and reliable. By using these advanced computer methods, the proposed system aims to give accurate predictions of specific flight arrival times. This will help reduce the costs and damage to the environment caused by delays, ultimately making the aviation industry more reliable and improving performance as a whole.

A. Proposed Architecture:

The architecture for the project is as follows.

The design of the system starts with adding the necessary packages. Next comes data analysis, cleaning, and display. The goal of this step is to understand the information and get it ready for research. The next step is to use experimental data analysis (EDA) techniques to learn more about the data. Then, methods for feature selection are used to find factors that are useful for models.

To guess when flights will be late, different machine learning (ML) and deep learning (DL) methods are used in the modeling process. These include Random Forest [11], Decision Tree [8], Multilayer Perceptron, Naive Bayes [2], KNN Neighbour, and TensorFlow. Metrics for comparing models, such as accuracy, precision, and sensitivity, are used to find and choose the best model.

To make an online app that runs on localhost, the Flask framework is used. Users enter information about the flight, such as its starting point, ending point, and exit time. TensorFlow then processes this information to make predictions. The result tells you how likely it is that the flight will be late. Figure 21.1 shows the proposed system architecture. This design makes

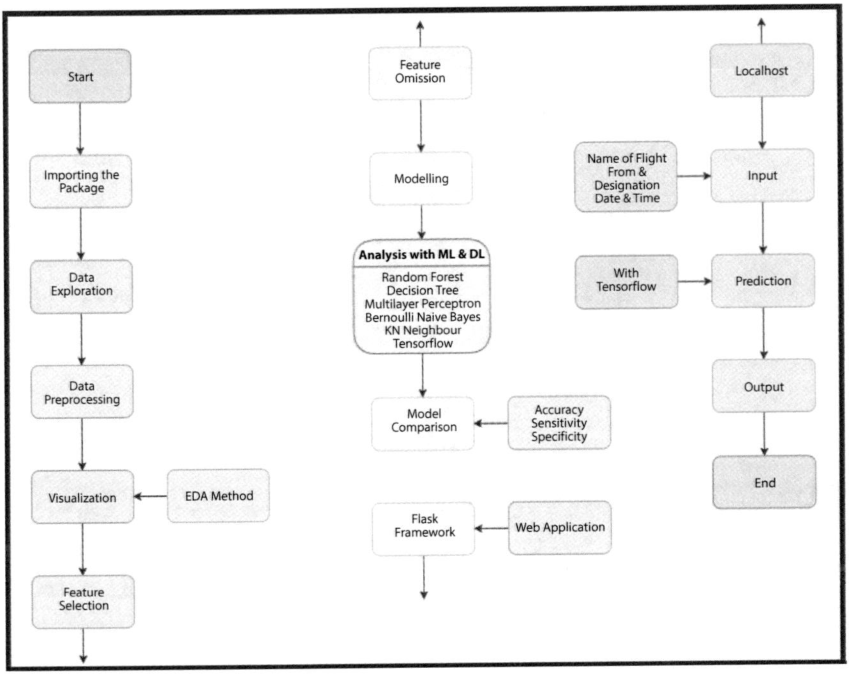

Figure 21.1 Proposed system architecture.

sure that the process is simplified from preparing the data to making the prediction. This makes flight delay predictions more accurate and efficient.

B. Dataset Collection:

The sample has 10,000 items spread out over 22 columns. Each item is a flight record, with information like the year, month, carrier code, carrier name, airport code, airport name, and different flight-related measures. These numbers show how many planes arrive, how many are delayed by 15 minutes or more (arr_del15), what causes the delays (like weather, airline, or NAS), and how many are cancelled or diverted. Plus, the information has overall wait times broken down by things like ship, weather, NAS, security, and late planes. There are some fields that don't have any numbers, which are shown by "NaN." There are three types of data: numbers, floats, and objects (strings). The dataset gives a lot of information about flight operations, delays, and other factors that are related to them. This makes it useful for modeling and analyzing in the aviation field. Figure 21.2 presents the accuracy comparison graphs.

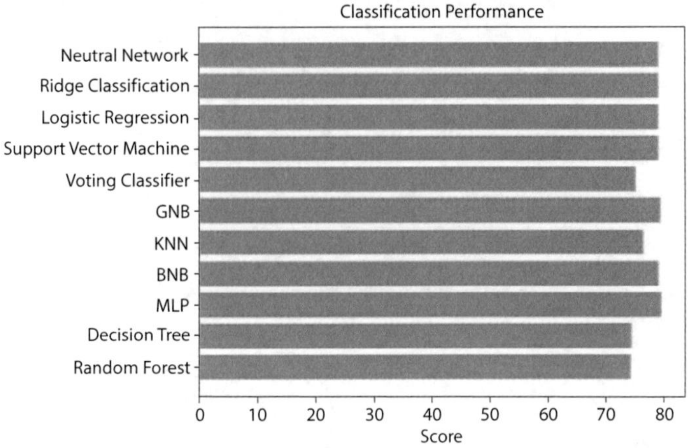

Figure 21.2 Accuracy comparison graphs.

C. Data Processing:

During the data processing part, we will first use the pandas library to work with the data. This library has a lot of useful tools for working with and analyzing data. The dataset will be put into a pandas dataframe, which will make it easy to look through and prepare the data.

Next, we'll change the pandas dataframe into a format that can be used with the Keras library. This library is often used to train and build neural networks. For this process, the dataframe needs to be changed into a shape that Keras can understand, like numpy arrays or tensors.

As part of the data preparation step, we will get rid of any columns that aren't needed for our analysis or prediction job. This step helps make the dataset more manageable by getting rid of traits that aren't needed and could add noise or bias to the model.

After getting rid of columns that aren't needed, we'll do some more preparation, like dealing with missing values, storing category variables, and scaling numerical features if needed. These steps are very important for making sure that the data we use to teach our machine learning models is accurate and of good quality.

Overall, the data preparation step changes the raw information into a clean and organized version that can be used to train machine learning models. This makes it possible to make accurate and reliable estimates about flight delays.

D. Feature Selection:
Feature selection is an important part of machine learning because it helps find the most useful features that help with prediction and gets rid of the ones that aren't needed or aren't relevant. Figure 21.3 displays the home page of the application.

When trying to guess when a flight will be late, feature selection means looking at different things like the airline, the airport, the weather, and past performance measures to see how they affect flight delays. The choice process can be guided by methods such as feature value ranking, association analysis, and subject knowledge.

We can make the model work better, be easier to understand, and require less computing power by choosing only the most useful traits. Another way this process helps lower the risk of over fitting is by focusing on the most important data when making predictions. Additionally, choosing the right features can help us understand the core causes of flight delays, which can help the airline business make decisions and plan how to use its resources.

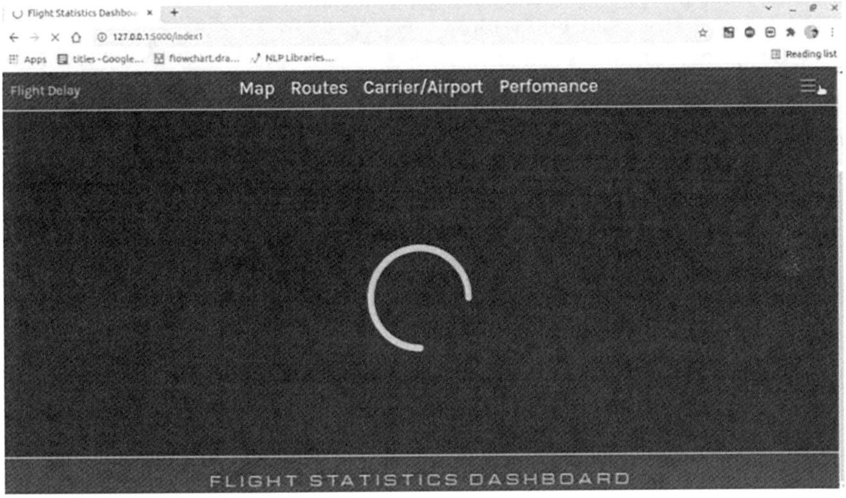

Figure 21.3 Home page.

E. Training & Testing:
We split our information into two parts during the training and testing process. These are the training set and the testing set. The testing set is used to see how well our machine learning models are doing, and the training set is used to teach them. Figure 21.4 demonstrates the action of clicking on the prediction button.

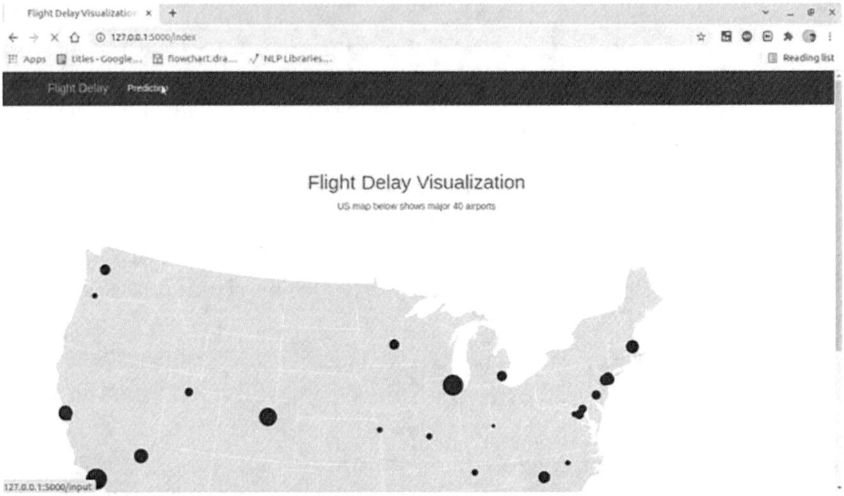

Figure 21.4 Click on prediction.

The training set is shown to the models during training. This is where they learn to find trends and connections in the data. Changing the model's settings over and over again to get the difference between what was expected and what actually happened to be as small as possible.

The trial set, which has data the models have never seen before, is used to judge how well the models did after they were trained. We check how well the models work with new data by looking at things like accuracy, precision, recall, and F1-score.

We can test the models' accuracy in making predictions on new data by dividing the information into training and testing sets. This shows how well they work and how well they can generalize. This repeated process helps make the models better and better prepared for use in the real world. Figure 21.5 shows the flight delay prediction screen.

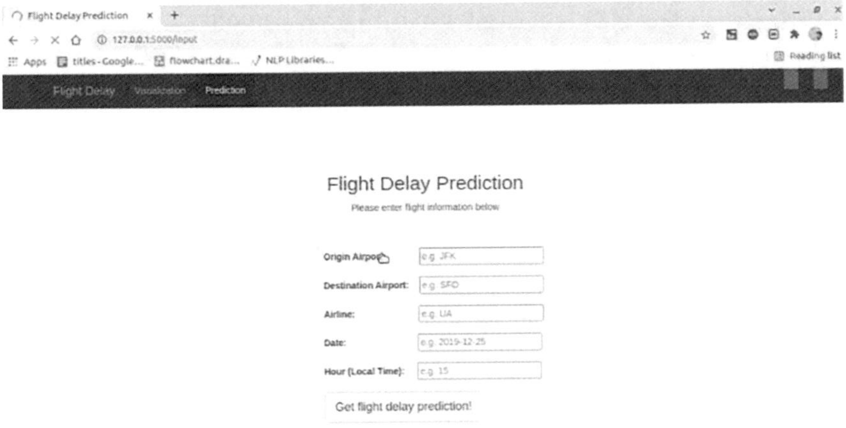

Figure 21.5 Flight delay prediction screen.

F. Algorithms:

Neural Network: Pattern recognition, classification, and regression are just a few of the many uses for neural networks. Their job is to describe complicated connections in data so that predictions and decisions can be made. Neural networks are very good at dealing with big datasets and connections that don't follow a straight line because they work like the brain's linked network of neurons. They work especially well for jobs like recognizing sounds and images, making predictions based on time series, and understanding natural language.

Ridge Classification: Ridge Classification is a type of linear classification that uses regularization to stop problems with multicollinearity and overfitting. It is often used when there are more features than data or when features are strongly linked to each other. Ridge Classification [10] is meant to make linear models more stable by punishing big coefficients. This makes results more stable and generalizable, especially in datasets with a lot of dimensions.

Logistic Regression: In logistic regression, the result variable is a categorical variable with two possible outcomes. This is a statistical method used for binary classification jobs. Its job is to figure out how likely it is that a certain event will happen based on one or more prediction factors.

Logistic Regression [12] is used a lot in medicine, banking, and marketing to do things like guessing how likely it is that someone will get a disease, not pay back a loan, or leave a business, among other things.

SVM: Support Vector Machine, or SVM, is a powerful guided learning method that can be used to do jobs like regression and classification. Its job is to find the best hyperplane that divides the raw data space into classes while leaving the most room between them. SVM [11] works best when there are a lot of dimensions in the data and the decision boundaries are not straight lines. Because it's flexible and reliable, it's used a lot in biology, picture classification, text classification, and other fields.

Voting Classifier: The Voting Classifier is an ensemble learning method that takes results from several separate classifiers and puts them all together to make a single forecast. Among other methods, it brings together the outcomes of decision trees, support vector machines, and logistic regression. The goal of the Voting Classifier [1] is to make predictions more accurate and reliable by using the combined knowledge of several models. It's often used in classification jobs where better results come from having all the models agree. Figure 21.6 presents the final outcome of the prediction.

Gaussian Naïve Bayes: This is a type of the Naïve Bayes algorithm that works with the idea that the features have a Gaussian distribution. It's often used for sorting things into groups, especially when the traits are ongoing. The program figures out the chances of each class based on the Gaussian distribution of feature values and guesses which class is most likely for a given case. Gaussian Naïve Bayes [2] works well, is easy to set up, and works well with big datasets that have traits that change over time.

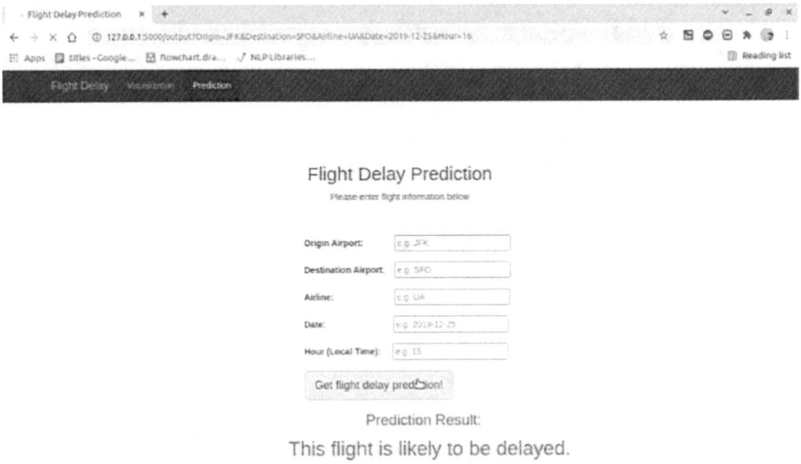

Figure 21.6 Final outcome.

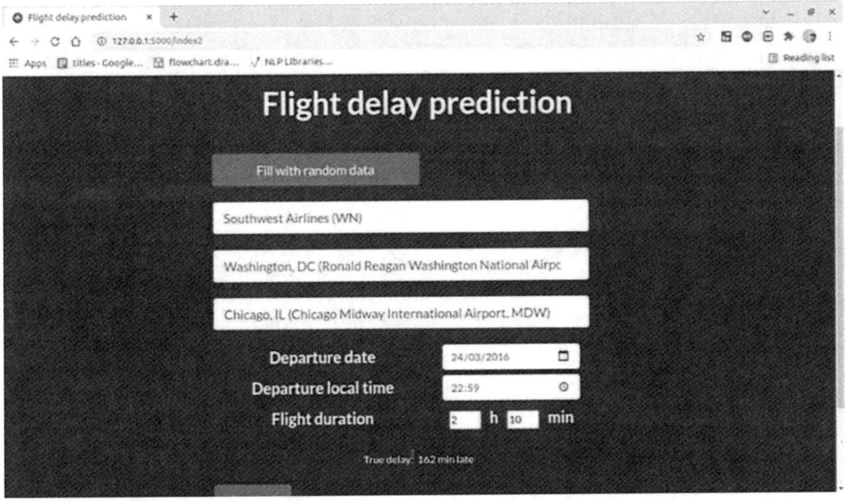

Figure 21.7 Visualization page.

K-Nearest Neighbors: K-Nearest Neighbors (KNN) is a classification method that doesn't use parameters and is used to find patterns and make predictions. Its job is to put new data points into groups based on the group that most of their neighbors are in. KNN [13] thinks that data points that are alike are likely to be in the same class. It's easy to use and can be used for many things, like ranking systems, finding strange things, and picture recognition, especially with small to medium-sized datasets. Figure 21.7 illustrates the visualization page.

Multilayer Perceptron: MLP stands for "multilayer perceptron." It is a type of artificial neural network made up of many layers of nodes, such as an input layer, one or more hidden layers, and an output layer. It's mostly used for jobs that need to be watched, like classification and regression. During training, MLP changes the weights between nodes to learn complex patterns in the data. It works well with relationships that aren't straight and is used a lot in areas like financial predictions, picture recognition, and natural language processing.

Decision Tree: The Decision Tree method is flexible and is often used for jobs like regression and classification. Its goal is to make a forecast model that looks like a tree, with each core node representing a choice based on a trait and each leaf node representing a class name or a number value. Decision trees [8] are useful in many fields, such as banking, healthcare, and marketing, because they are straightforward, easy to understand, and can work with both categories and number data.

Random Forest: Random Forest is a type of ensemble learning that builds many decision trees during training and then gives you the mode of the classes (classification) or the mean forecast (regression) of each tree. By mixing the results of several trees, it aims to improve forecast accuracy and reduce overfitting. Random Forest [11] is strong, flexible, and able to deal with large amounts of data. This means it can be used for many different classification and regression jobs in areas like healthcare, banking, and remote sensing.

21.4 Result Analysis

Accuracy: The accuracy of a test is its ability to differentiate the patient and healthy cases correctly. To estimate the accuracy of a test, we should calculate the proportion of true positive and true negative in all evaluated cases. Mathematically, this can be stated as:

Algorithms	**Accuracy %**
Random Forest	74.1%
Decision Tree	74.4%
MLP	79.6%
BNB	79.05%
KNN	76.4%
GNB	79.4%
Voting Classifier	75.0%
SVM	79.05%
Logistic Regression	79.05%
Ridge Classifier	79.05%
Neural Network	79.05%

21.5 Conclusion

In conclusion, the aviation industry grapples with persistent challenges due to flight delays, worsened by escalating air traffic congestion from sector growth. These delays result in significant financial losses and environmental repercussions. Airlines are deploying various strategies to mitigate delays and cancellations. This study contributes by utilizing diverse machine learning models, including Neural Network [9], Ridge Classification [10], Logistic Regression [12], Support Vector Machine [11], Voting Classifier [1], Gaussian Naïve Bayes [2], KNN [13], Multilayer Perceptron, Decision Tree [8], and Random Forest [11], to predict flight delays accurately. By furnishing reliable forecasts, we aim to enhance operational efficiency and customer satisfaction. Moreover, mitigating the adverse impacts of flight delays, such as financial losses and environmental consequences, promotes a sustainable aviation ecosystem. Integrating data-driven approaches into aviation operations is crucial for proactively addressing delays. By leveraging machine learning, airlines can make informed decisions on scheduling, resource allocation, and contingency planning, improving overall performance and passenger reliability. Continued investment in advanced analytics and predictive modeling is vital for fostering innovation and continual improvement within the aviation sector. This research underscores the imperative of leveraging technology to navigate challenges and drive progress in aviation operations.

The future scope for this research lies in further advancing predictive modeling techniques to enhance the accuracy and efficiency of flight delay predictions. Incorporating real-time data streams, such as weather updates, air traffic information, and aircraft performance data, can significantly improve the robustness of predictive models. Additionally, exploring novel machine learning algorithms and deep learning architectures tailored specifically for aviation data could yield more accurate and reliable predictions.

Furthermore, there is potential for integrating predictive analytics into airline operations management systems to enable real-time decision-making and proactive mitigation of delays. This could involve developing decision support tools that provide actionable insights to airlines, air traffic controllers, and airport authorities.

Moreover, extending the scope of this research to address other aspects of aviation operations, such as aircraft maintenance scheduling, crew rostering, and route optimization, could further optimize overall efficiency and cost-effectiveness in the industry.

Overall, the future scope entails continued innovation and collaboration among researchers, airlines, regulatory bodies, and technology providers to harness the full potential of predictive analytics in revolutionizing the aviation industry.

References

1. Rupp, N.G., *Further Investigation into the Causes of Flight Delays*, Department of Economics, East Carolina University, Greenville, 2007, May 20.

2. Bureau of Transportation Statistics (BTS), Databases and Statistics, [Online]. Available: http://www.transtats.bts.gov.
3. Airports Council International, World Airport Traffic Report, 2015, 2016.
4. Cinar, E., Aybek, F., Caycar, A., Cetek, C., Capacity and delay analysis for airport manoeuvring areas using simulation. *Aircr. Eng. Aerosp. Technol.*, 86, 1, 43–55, 2013.
5. Chakrabarty, N. *et al.*, Flight Arrival Delay Prediction Using Gradient Boosting Classifier, in: *Emerging Technologies in Data Mining and Information Security*, Singapore, 2019.
6. Kim, Y.J., Briceno, S., Mavris, D., Choi, S., Prediction of weatherinduced airline delays based on machine learning algorithms, in: *35th Digital Avionics Systems Conference (DASC)*, 2016.
7. Cao, W.-D. and Lin, A.X.-Y., Flight turnaround time analysis and delay prediction based on Bayesian Network. *Comput. Eng. Des.*, 5, 1770–1772, 2011.
8. Robollo, J.J. and Balakrishnan, H., Characterization and Prediction of Air Traffic Delays. *Trans. Res. Part C Emerg. Technol.*, 44, 231–241, 2014.
9. Sharma, S., Sangoi, H., Raut, R., Kotak, V.C., Oza, S., Flight Delay Prediction System Using Weighted Multiple Linear Regression. *Int. J. Eng. Comput. Sci.*, 4, 4, 11668–11677, April 2015.
10. Kalliguddi, A.M. and Area, K., Leboulluec, Predictive Modelling of Aircraft Flight Delay. *Univers. J. Manag.*, 5, 10, 485–491, 2017.
11. Noriko, E., Development of a predictive model for on-time arrival fight of airliner by discovering correlation between fight and weather data, 2, 1–17, 2019.
12. [Online]. Available: https://towardsdatascience.com/metrics-toevaluate-your-machine-learning-algorithm-f10ba6e38234.
13. Kim, Y.J., Briceno, S., Mavris, D., Choi, S., Prediction of weather-induced airline delays based on machine learning algorithms. *35th Digital Avionics Systems Conference (DASC)*, 2016.

22

Design and Implementation of 8-Bit Ripple Carry Adder and Carry Select Adder at 32-nm CNTFET Technology: A Comparative Study

Venkata Rao Tirumalasetty*, **K. Babulu and G. Appala Naidu**

Dept. of ECE, JNTUGV, Vizianagaram, Andhra Pradesh, India

Abstract

As the CMOS technology nears its limits, there is a growing demand to discover circuit applications in emerging technologies to facilitate swift commercialization. Among the promising device for future electronic devices, Carbon Nanotube Field-Effect Transistors (CNTFETs) stand out, offering potential benefits in low-power and low-voltage digital or analog circuit applications. The paper introduces an implementation of 8-Bit Ripple Carry Adder (RCA) and Carry Select Adder (CSA) by leveraging a 1-bit hybrid full adder. This hybrid full adder combines pass transistor (PT) and transmission gate (TG) logics, offering a balance between performance and power consumption. By incorporating this hybrid full adder into the RCA & CSA architectures, the power consumption is 0.268 μW & 0.563 μW and the delay is 18.648 Ps & 12.584 Ps. The integration of the pass transistor and transmission gate logics provides an effective solution for optimizing the performance of the RCA & CSA, making it suitable for applications that require both speed and energy efficiency. The performance analysis of the proposed 8-bit RCA and 8-bit CSA circuits was conducted using 32-nm CNTFET technology. The evaluation was carried out at a single-ended supply voltage of 0.9 V, utilizing the Mentor Graphics Schematic Design Composer CAD tool.

Keywords: RCA, CSA, CNTFET, hybrid adder, pass transistor logic, transmission gate logic, power consumption, delay, PDP

**Corresponding author*: venkatarao.srp@gmail.com

Budati Anil Kumar, Singamaneni Kranthi Kumar and Li Xingwang (eds.) Quantum Computing Models for Cybersecurity and Wireless Communications, (325–336)

22.1 Introduction

Metal oxide semiconductor (MOS) transistors have faced multiple challenges and issues because of their continuous scaling. As a result, designers have been compelled to explore alternative methods beyond traditional silicon MOSFETs. This transition is essential to accommodate the integration of a larger number of transistors on a single chip, enabling complex applications [1]. These applications require high-speed operation, low energy consumption, high chip density, and overall efficiency. Scaling down the circuits seemed to be the most viable solution in line with Moore's law [2]. However, this approach also presents challenges, such as reduced gate controllability, the short channel effect, and the hot electron effect [3]. The development of low-power, low-delay designs has been fueled by the MOSFET technology, which has spurred the advancement of additional technologies [4, 5].

CNTFETs can be classified based on the number of carbon nanotubes involved. In CNTFETs, each carbon nanotube acts as an individual channel, in contrast to MOSFETs where the entire silicon region serves as the channel.

In terms of mobility, both n-type and p-type CNFETs exhibit the equal mobility, and equally can bring the same dynamic current. The I_{DS}-V_{DS} distinctiveness of CNTFETs and MOSFETs are analogous, providing comparable performance in terms of current flow [6]. Similar to MOSFETs, CNTFETs are also four-terminal devices. They have two input terminals (gate and source) and two output terminals (drain and body) [7].

Operationally, CNTFETs can be categorized into two main types: Schottky Barrier CNTFETs (SB-CNTFET) and MOSFET-like CNTFETs (MOS-CNTFET), as illustrated in Figure 22.1. Schottky Barrier CNTFETs rely on a Schottky barrier at the source-channel junction, while MOSFET-like CNTFETs resemble traditional MOSFETs with a gate-controlled channel [8].

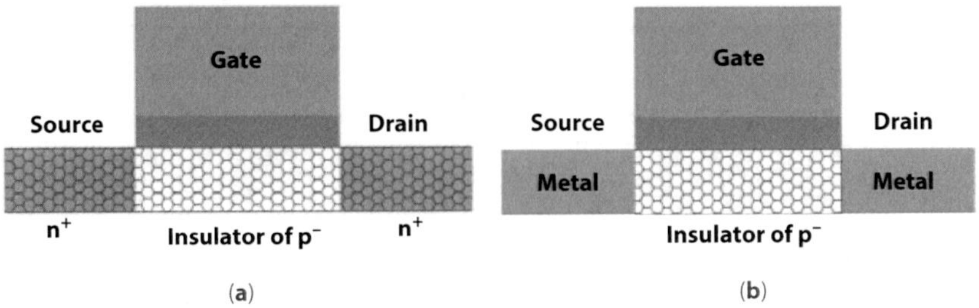

Figure 22.1 (a) SB-CNFET. (b) MOS-CNFET.

These operational categories offer different design options and characteristics, each suited for specific applications and performance requirements.

In this study, a CNTFET with the chiral numbers (n1, n2) = (19, 0) is investigated. The diameter of the carbon nanotube (D_{CNT}) is measured to be 1.487nm, leading to a threshold voltage of 0.289V, calculated using equations (22.1) & (22.2) [9].

$$D_{CNT} = \frac{a \times \sqrt{n_1^2 + n_2^2 + n_1 n_2}}{\Pi} \approx 0.0783 \times \sqrt{n_1^2 + n_2^2 + n_1 n_2} \quad (22.1)$$

$$V_{th} \approx \frac{E_g}{2.e} = \frac{\sqrt{3}}{3} \frac{a.V_{\Pi}}{e.D_{CNT}} \approx \frac{0.43}{D_{CNT}} \quad (22.2)$$

Here, E_g represents the band gap of the CNTFET, while e denotes the charge of an electron. The diameter of nanotubes is determined by D_{CNT} [10].

The speed of large digital circuits is a critical factor in determining their overall performance. Within these circuits, adders play a vital role in digital integrated circuit and system design. In data paths, such as microprocessors and digital signal processors, high-speed adders are fundamental components. These adders facilitate efficient arithmetic operations and enable fast computation, ensuring optimal performance in various computational tasks [11, 12].

Among the available parallel adders, the ripple carry adder (RCA) is the simplest form, employing a series of one-bit full adders in a chain to produce the output. While the RCA is compact in design, it suffers from longer computation times due to its sequential nature. In time-critical applications, the carry look-ahead (CLA) scheme is employed to achieve faster results; however, this comes at the cost of increased area requirements [13–15]. To strike stability among area and delay considerations, the CSA emerges as a favorable solution. The CSA offers a compromise by combining the smaller area of the RCA with the shorter delay of the CLA, making it a viable option for achieving optimal trade-offs between area utilization and computation speed. The subsequent sections of this paper are organized as follows: Section 22.2 outlines the implementations of 8-bit RCA and CSA. Section 22.3 provides a detailed explanation of simulation results. At last, Section 22.4 concludes the paper.

22.2 Implementation of RCA & CSA

A digital circuit called the Full Adder is designed to add three inputs and produce two outputs. The inputs are commonly identified as A, B, and Cin, which represent the two binary numbers that need to be added (A and B) and the input carry (Cin). Sum and C_{out} are the outputs, and the relations between A, B, and Cin with Sum and C_{out} are

$$Sum = ABCin + \bar{A}\bar{B}Cin + \bar{A}B\overline{Cin} + A\bar{B}\overline{Cin} \tag{22.3}$$

$$Cout = AB + BCin + ACin \tag{22.4}$$

Figure 22.2 depicts a 1-bit full adder circuit employing 16 transistors to produce both the sum and carry outputs. Indeed, when designing a circuit

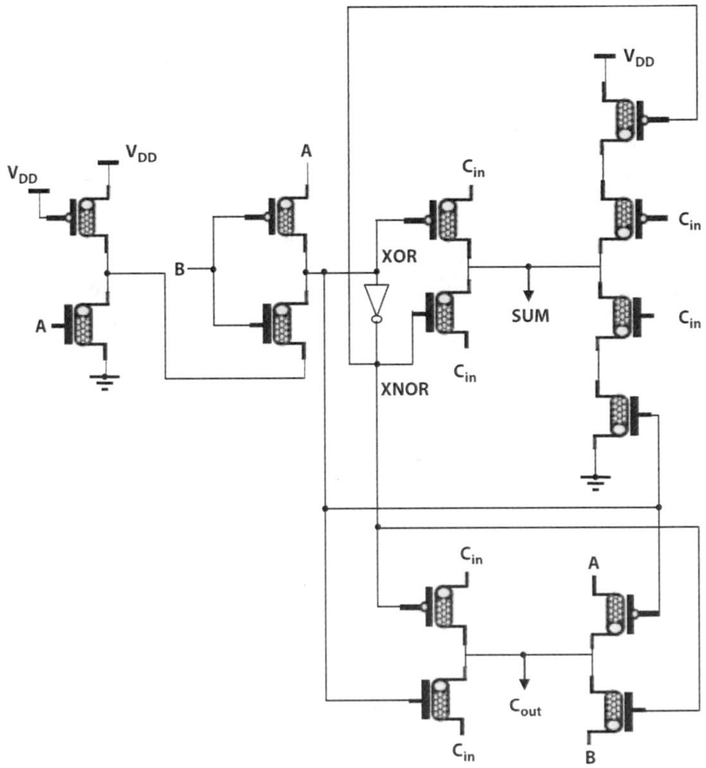

Figure 22.2 Proposed circuit for a 1-bit full adder that uses 16 CNTFETs.

with power constraints, reducing the number of transistors and critical path is a common way to achieve effectiveness. With regards to the proposed 1-bit full adder, this principle is applied to achieve efficient design. The proposed circuit utilizes PTL & TGL for realization, specifically tailored for CNTFET technology. By leveraging these logic styles and optimizing them for CNFET technology, the design aims to achieve improved power efficiency and performance.

It's important to note that CNFET technology offers unique advantages, such as lower power consumption, improved performance, and reduced leakage current compared to traditional CMOS technology. The proposed design leverages these benefits by utilizing PTL and TGL approaches optimized for CNFET technology.

Figure 22.3 represents the block diagram of an 8-bit Ripple Carry Adder (8B-RCA). This diagram illustrates the interconnection of multiple instances of the 1-bit Full Adder to form the complete 8B-RCA circuit. Each 1-bit Full Adder contributes to the addition of one bit from the input numbers, and the carry output of each stage is propagated to the next stage, resulting in the final sum and carry outputs [16–18].

A CSA is a type of parallel adder that is designed to perform fast addition of multi-bit numbers. It utilizes a block carry generation and carry propagation approach to accomplish quick operation. The CSA consists of two main stages: the carry generation stage and the carry propagation stage.

In the carry generation stage, the input numbers are divided into smaller groups, and for each group, the carry bits are generated independently. This is done by using separate ripple carry adders or other carry generation techniques. The carry bits produced in this stage are referred to as "block carries."

In the carry propagation stage, the block carries are selected based on the value of a control signal. The control signal determines which block

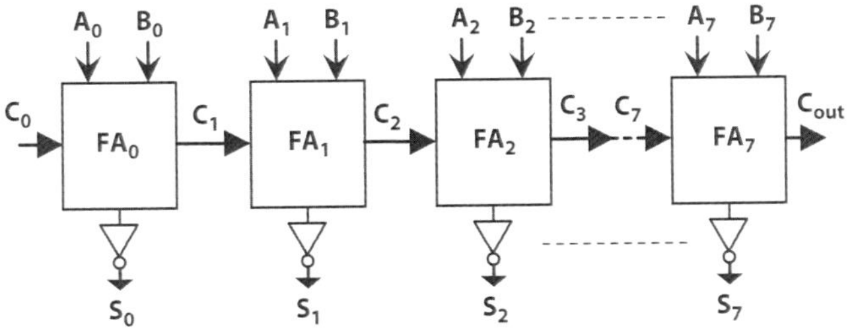

Figure 22.3 8-Bit parallel adder implementation using proposed 1-bit full adder.

carries are propagated and which are blocked. By selectively propagating the appropriate block carries, the CSA can bypass the carry propagation delay for certain groups of bits and reduce the overall propagation delay.

The final sum output is obtained by combining the partial sum bits from each group along with the final carry-out generated in the carry propagation stage. The carry-select adder offers a trade-off between speed and area. While it achieves fast addition by reducing the carry propagation delay, it requires additional circuitry for the carry generation stage, which increases the overall area of the adder.

Overall, the carry-select adder is a popular choice for high-speed arithmetic operations in applications where speed is a critical factor, such as digital signal processing and high-performance computing. The block diagram of the CSA (4-Bit) is presented in Figure 22.4.

CSA Internal Elements:

A carry-select adder consists of several key internal elements that work together to perform efficient addition. The main internal elements of a carry-select adder include:

Full Adders: The carry-select adder is built on full adders as its basic building blocks. They perform addition of three input bits (two operands and a C_{in}) and generate two outputs: a sum bit and a C_{out}. Multiple full adders are used in parallel to process the individual bits of the input numbers.

Multiplexers (MUX): Multiplexers are used in the CSA to select the appropriate carry bits for propagation. They take input signals and a control

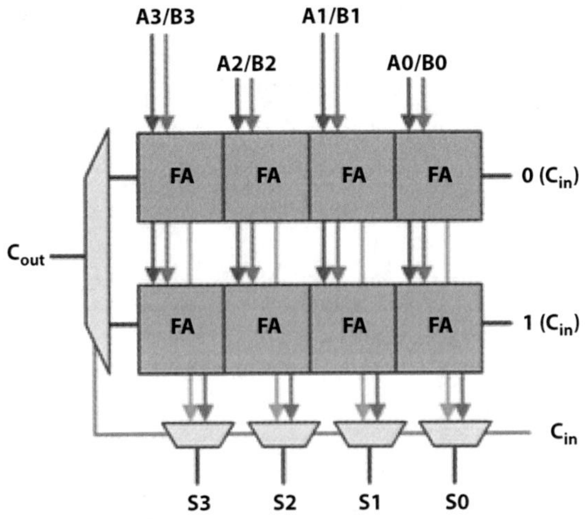

Figure 22.4 Block diagram of Carry Select adder (4-Bit).

signal as inputs and output the selected signal based on the control signal value. In the carry-select adder, multiplexers are used to choose between the generated block carries for each group.

Block Carry Generators: The block carry generators are responsible for generating the block carries for each group of bits. These generators can be implemented using various techniques, such as RCAs, look ahead carry generators, or carry-skip adders. The block carry generators operate in parallel to generate the carry bits for each group independently.

Control Logic: The control logic determines which block carries are selected and propagated based on a control signal. It orchestrates the operation of the multiplexers to choose the appropriate carries for each group. The control logic is typically implemented using combinational logic circuits, such as logic gates or programmable logic devices.

Sum Generation: The sum generation circuitry combines the partial sum bits from each group along with the final C_{out} generated in the carry propagation stage to produce the final sum output. This circuitry typically involves additional logic gates to perform the required combination and generate the correct sum output.

These internal elements work together to enable the efficient operation of the carry-select adder. The block carry generators generate carry bits in parallel for each group, the multiplexers select the appropriate carries for propagation, and the sum generation circuitry combines the partial sums to obtain the final sum output. The control logic coordinates the selection and propagation of the carries, ensuring accurate and efficient addition.

The sum generation circuitry in a CSA combines the partial sums from each group along with the final C_{out} generated in the carry propagation stage to produce the final sum output. Here's how it works:

1. Partial Sum Bits:
   - In a CSA, the addition operation is separated into smaller groups of bits.
   - Each group has its own full adder that generates a partial sum bit and a C_{out} bit.
   - The partial sum bits represent the sum of the corresponding bits from the input operands.
2. Block Carry Propagation:
   - In the carry propagation stage, block carries are selected and propagated based on a control signal.
   - The control signal determines which block carries are chosen for propagation and which are blocked.

- The selected block carries propagate through multiplexers and reach the corresponding full adders in each group.

3. Final Carry-Out:
    - The carry propagation stage also generates a final carry-out bit, which represents the carry-out from the most significant bit (MSB) group.
    - This final carry-out bit is the carry generated when adding the MSB group, taking into account the selected block carries.
4. Sum Generation:
    - The sum generation circuitry combines the partial sum bits and the final Cout bit to produce the final sum output.
    - To generate the sum output, the partial sum bits from each group are connected to a series of logic gates, such as XOR gates.
    - The final Cout bit is connected to the Cin input of the MSB group's full adder.
    - The logic gates perform the required combination of the partial sum bits and the final C_{out} bit, resulting in the final sum output.

By combining the partial sum bits and the final C_{out} bit using appropriate logic gates, the sum generation circuitry generates the correct sum output of the CSA. The final sum output represents the sum of the input operands, considering both the partial sums and the carry generated during the addition process.

A carry-select adder offers several advantages compared to other types of parallel adders. Here are some key points of comparison:

Advantages:

1. Improved speed: The CSA reduces the carry propagation delay by independently generating and selecting block carries, resulting in faster addition compared to ripple-carry adders.
2. Parallel structure: Carry-select adders perform addition in parallel, allowing for efficient computation of multi-bit numbers in a single operation.
3. Scalability: The structure of a CSA can be easily scaled up to accommodate larger bit widths without significant impact on performance.

22.3 Simulation Results

The 32 nm Stanford CNTFET Model technology was used for the simulation of the proposed 1-bit full adder [19]. Using the Mentor Graphics Schematic Design Composer tool, the simulation was executed with 0.7 V supply voltage, 0.289 V threshold voltage, and (19, 0) chirality vector. The simulation of the proposed 1-bit full adder's input and output waveforms is shown in Figure 22.5. The simulation of waveforms tested all possible combinations for inputs (A, B, and C) with values between 000 and 111.

The main goal of this paper is to design and implement 8-bit RCA and CSA with 32-nm CNTFET technology. The RCA is a straightforward and commonly used adder architecture that uses a sequential sequence of adders to perform addition. We explore the design considerations and optimization techniques specific to implementing an 8-bit RCA using CNTFET technology. This includes addressing challenges such as power consumption, delay, and area utilization while ensuring accurate and reliable computation.

Additionally, we explore into the design and implementation of the Carry Select Adder, which offers a compromise between the compactness of the RCA and the shorter delay of other adder architectures like the CLA. We investigate the integration of the CSA with CNTFET technology at the 32-nm node, exploring its benefits, trade-offs, and performance

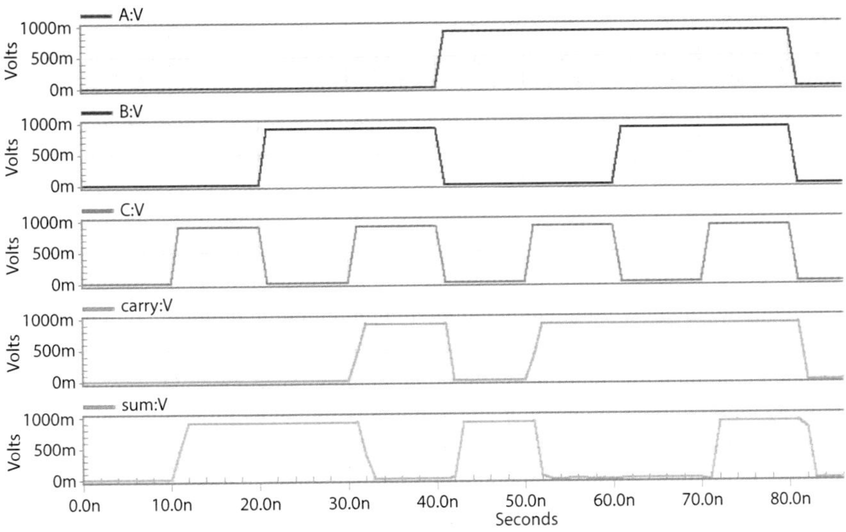

Figure 22.5 Simulated input and output waveforms of 1-bit Full Adder circuit.

characteristics. Table 22.1 shows the performance comparisons between the proposed and alternative 8-bit RCA and 8-bit CSA implementations.

CSA Disadvantages:

1. Increased area: The CSA requires additional circuitry for the carry generation stage, which increases the overall area compared to ripple-carry adders.
2. Additional power consumption: The extra circuitry in the CSA leads to increased power consumption compared to ripple-carry adders.
3. Complexity: The design and realization of a CSA are more complex compared to simpler adders like RCA or CLA adders.

In summary, while the RCA is simple and compact, it suffers from longer computation times. The CSA addresses this issue by parallelizing the computation, resulting in faster addition at the expense of increased area utilization.

Table 22.1 Performance comparisons of the proposed & different implementations of 8-bit RCA & 8-bit CSA with $V_{dd} = 0.9$ V at 32-nm CNTFET technology.

	8-Bit RCA			**8-Bit CSA**		
Design	**Power (μW)**	**Delay (Ps)**	**PDP (aJ)**	**Power (μW)**	**Delay (Ps)**	**PDP (aJ)**
CMOS [6]	0.587	38.245	22.449	1.287	25.452	32.756
CPL [6, 7]	3.567	33.428	119.237	5.493	22.684	124.603
BBL-PT [17]	1.127	45.854	51.677	3.675	33.554	123.310
TGA [8]	2.895	31.257	90.489	4.582	20.869	95.621
TFA [10]	2.567	44.872	115.186	4.369	34.561	150.997
1-Bit Adder [13]	2.954	47.824	141.272	5.382	34.562	186.012
CNTAFS [15]	3.413	28.148	96.069	5.946	17.428	103.626
Proposed Full Adder	**0.268**	**18.648**	**4.997**	**0.563**	**12.584**	**7.084**

22.4 Conclusion

This paper presents a novel and efficient approach for an 8-bit RCA and CSA. The selection of the RCA and CSA is based on accurate resource estimation, providing specific specifications for the design. The incorporation of a hybrid full adder into the RCA and CSA architectures enables high-speed binary addition, which is essential in FPGA applications. The power consumption for the proposed RCA and CSA is measured at 0.268 μW and 0.563 μW, respectively, with corresponding delays of 18.648 Ps and 12.584 Ps. The findings show substantial enhancements in power and delay when compared to conservative designs. Consequently, the proposed RCA and CSA architectures shows potential solution for developing low power and high speed devices.

References

1. Hasan, M., Hossein, M.J., Hossain, M., Zaman, H.U., Islam, S., Design of a scalable low-power 1-Bit hybrid full adder for fast computation. *IEEE Trans. Circuits Syst. II: Express Briefs*, 67, 8, 1464–1468, Aug. 2020.
2. Singh, S. and Kumar, D., Design of Area and Power Efficient Modified Carry Select Adder. *Int. J. Comput. Appl.*, 33, 3, 14–18, November 2011.
3. Rao Tirumalasetty, V., Mohan Krishna, C.V., Sai Sree Tanmaie, K., Lakshmi Naveena, T., Jonathon, C., A novel design of high performance1-bit adder circuit at deep sub micron technology. *Int. J. Eng. Technol.*, 7, 1.1, 660–663, 2018.
4. Misra, A., Birla, S., Singh, N., Dargar, S.K., Highperformance 10-transistor adder cell for low-power applications. *IETE J. Res.*, 1–19, March 2022.
5. Tirumalasetty, V.R. and Srinivasulu, A., Modified level restorers using current sink and current source inverter structures for BBL-PT full adder. *Radioengineering*, 21, 4, 1279–1286, 2012.
6. Xu, Qlu, C., Zhao, C., Zhang, Z., Peng, L., Insight ballisticity of room temperature carrier transport in carbon nanotube field effect transistors. *IEEE Trans. Electron Devices*, 66, 8, 3535–3540, 2019.
7. Shirinabadi Farahani, S. and Reshadinezhad, M.R., A new twelve-transistor approximate 4:2 compressor in CNTFET technology. *Int. J. Electron.*, 106, 691–706, 2019.
8. Bagherizadeh, M., Moaiyeri, M.H., Eshghi, M., A high-performance 5-to-2 compressor cell based on carbon nanotube FETs. *Int. J. Electron.*, 912–927, 2019.
9. Deng, J. and Wong, H.S.P., A compact SPICE model for carbon-nanotube field-effect transistors including non-idealities and its application-Part II:

Full device model and circuit performance benchmarking. *IEEE Trans. Electron Devices*, 54, 12, 3195–3205, 2007.
10. McEuen, P.L., Fuhrer, M.S., Park, H., Single-walled carbon nanotube electronics. *IEEE Trans. Nanotechnol.*, 99, 78–85, 2002.
11. Mujawar, M., Vijaya Saradhi, D., Ajmal Naz, M., Muduli, A., Design and performance comparison of arrays of circular, square and hexagonal meta-material structures for wearable applications. *J. Magn. Magn. Mater.*, 553, 169235, 2022.
12. Vijaya Saradhi, D. and Katragadda, S., Hybrid filter detection network model for secondary user transmission in cognitive radio networks. *Int. J. Intell. Unmanned Syst.*, 11, 1, 61–74, 2023.
13. Tirumalasetty, V.R. and Machupalli, M.R., Design and analysis of low power high-speed 1-bit full adder cells for VLSI applications. *Int. J. Electron.*, 106, 4, 521–536, 2019.
14. Farahani, M. and Moradi, M., Two low power and high efficient full adder cells based on CNTFET technology. *Int. J. Nanoelectron. Mater.*, 11, 321–331, 2018.
15. Tari, H.T., Zarandi, A.D., Reshadinezhad, M.R., Design of a high performance CNTFET-based full adder cell applicable in: Carry ripple, carry select and carry skip adders. *Microelectron. Eng.*, 215, 1–8, 2019.
16. Tirumalasetty, V.R. and Srinivasulu, A., 16-BIT RCA Implementation Using Current Sink Restorer Structure. *Int. J. Des. Anal. Tools Integr. Circuits Syst.*, 4, 9–14, December 2013.
17. Hassoune, I., Flandre, D., O'Connor, I., Legat, J.-D., ULPFA: A New Efficient Design of a Power-Aware Full adder. *IEEE Trans. Circuits Syst. I Regul. Pap.*, 57, 8, 2066–2074, 2010.
18. Tirumalasetty, V.R., Balakrishna, P., Suman, M.C., Prasad, N., Prathyusha, K., Suman, M., Low Static Power Consumption and High Performance 16-Bit Ripple Carry Adder Implementation by Using BBL-PT Logic style. *Int. J. Appl. Eng. Res.*, 9, 23, 22727–22741, 2014.
19. Standford CNTFET Model, https://nano.stanford.edu/downloads/stanford-cnfet-model.

23

XGBoost Classifier Based Water Quality Classification Using Machine Learning

Nagidi Nikhitha, Sudini Poojitha, Vooturi Arjun, K. Sateesh Kumar* and D. Mohan

Dept. of ECM, Sreenidhi Institute of Science and Technology, Telangana, India

Abstract
Water is a main resource for every livelihood on the planet. Water quality is constantly threatened by pollution, despite the fact that public health demands that everyone have access to safe drinking water. Water pollution mitigation thus depends on precise water quality forecast and modeling. While machine learning techniques like Support Vector Machines (SVM), k-Nearest Neighbors (KNN), and Artificial Neural Networks (ANN) have been used with accuracies average around 85%, traditional approaches remain dependent on expensive and time-consuming laboratory and statistical investigations. In this paper, a tree-based classification strategy, more precisely the XGBoost classifier based algorithm is proposed for water quality classification. In order to classify water quality, this approach makes use of seven parameters from the dataset. The XGBoost classifier model is better than other approaches, with an amazing accuracy rate of 96%, according to the study's findings. XGBoost classifier is a very good tool for classifying water quality because of its quick out-of-core compute execution. In this proposed water quality is classified into five different levels based on the quality features. This is where its superiority rests.

Keywords: Water quality prediction, XGBoost classification, pollutants, accuracy, out-of-core compute execution, parameters

**Corresponding author*: sateeshkumarkanagala@gmail.com

Budati Anil Kumar, Singamaneni Kranthi Kumar and Li Xingwang (eds.) Quantum Computing Models for Cybersecurity and Wireless Communications, (337–346) © 2025 Scrivener Publishing LLC

23.1 Introduction

Water quality is a demanding topic that requires careful consideration for many uses [1]. Excess use of water, both beneath and on the surface, and other causes contribute to deterioration of water quantity along with quality [2, 3]. Natural processes cause variations in water's pH and alkalinity, as well as phosphate loading, a rise in fluoride content, and high sulphate concentrations [4]. Water contamination can be effectively addressed if data is studied and water quality is forecasted in advance. This issue has been addressed in numerous past studies; nevertheless, further study is needed to determine the effectiveness, reliability, accuracy, and applicability of current water quality management approaches [5]. The Water Quality Index (WQI) must be monitored on a regular basis to guarantee that the water is safe and clean. However, manual monitoring work is time-consuming, needs a large number of people, and requires a high level of knowledge in judging the cleanliness of water. Because of these limitations, the goal of this research is to create a more accurate, rapid, and simple automatic technique for determining whether water is potable or non-potable for drinking purposes using various Machine Learning Techniques like Support Vector Machines (SVM), k-Nearest Neighbors (KNN), and Artificial Neural Networks (ANN) etc. [9, 10]. Furthermore, when solving complex models, ML techniques can significantly at lower computational costs, allowing decision-makers to shift from physical-based to ML models for difficult situations. As a result, the new emergent hydrological crises, such as droughts and floods, may now be efficiently researched and alleviated thanks to advances in ML algorithms [6, 11].

23.2 Related Work

Many investigations on the classification of water quality have been carried out before to ours. k-Nearest Neighbors (KNN) water quality prediction [1] was proposed simple and flexible, making it appropriate for small range of applications since suffers from memory utilization and computational complexity especially when dealing with large datasets. Further affecting its performance are sensitivity to feature scaling and the requirement for ideal k selection and impacted by noisy data [5, 6]. This problem was overcome by the using the Bayesian algorithm [7]. It used probabilistic reasoning to detect and categorize water quality. Based on observed data and past knowledge, Bayesian algorithms determine the likelihood that a sample belongs to each class. Using previous knowledge to feed the categorization process and managing uncertainty were made possible by this methodical framework. When domain knowledge is present and the dataset is tiny, Bayesian approaches proved especially helpful. They did precise characterization of past distributions and might have trouble with intricate interactions [2]. The initial assessment step is based on the partitioning of neural network connection weights, which determines the relevance of every input parameter in the network [13, 14]. Notwithstanding these difficulties, Bayesian methods offer insightful analyses of water quality, supporting the management of resources and preservation of the environment through decision-making. The research has continued and again it was implemented by the Random Forest [3]. Implementing random forests and carrying out more study produced higher accuracy. But it became complicated because it was tested only 4 to 5 features [7]. The trade-off between accuracy and model simplicity in the classification of water quality was highlighted by the difficulty in controlling the complexity despite the improved performance. Later the SVM model was proposed and it has implemented with the five parameters. Those parameters are considered to predict they include BOD, DO, Nitrate, Ph value, turbidity. This model was implemented in an efficient way and got an accuracy of 95%. Support Vector Machine (SVM), in particular, demonstrated outstanding generalization performance and high prediction accuracy, particularly when predicting Dissolved Oxygen [8, 9, 11]. Its non-parametric characteristics and adaptability make addressing non-linear interactions and implementation simple. After SVM one of the authorized all the algorithms and compared [12]. The investigation looks into a variety of variables, including turbidity, pH, and dissolved oxygen. With the use of machine learning techniques, the research hopes to create models that can predict water quality with accuracy.

This paper advances our understanding of the dynamics affecting water quality and encourages the development of practical solutions to guarantee the availability of sustainable and clean water supplies for a range of uses [5, 12].

23.3 Proposed Methodology

The primary goal of this method is to evaluate the quality of water and to determine whether the water is safe to drink by using XG Boost classifier system using machine learning. It is the one of the prominent machine learning package for classification, regression, and clustering problems

[11]. It is a supervised learning technique used to train the model to find the patterns in a dataset using the features and labels. A Gradient Boosting Decision Trees (GBDT) [8] is a decision tree that helps to predict the label by evaluating condition based feature for making a correct decision. XG boost classifier method is a boosting technique which helps to boost a weak model by combining it with other models to generate a robust model. The existing systems use only limited features for examining the quality whereas the proposed system has taken a greater number of features into the consideration to measure the water quality.

Figure 23.1 shows flow chart of the proposed method. In which step by step process is explained in next sections.

The implementation of proposed methodology involves various steps:

- Data Collection: Gathering pertinent data is the initial stage in creating the model. Numerous water quality measures are

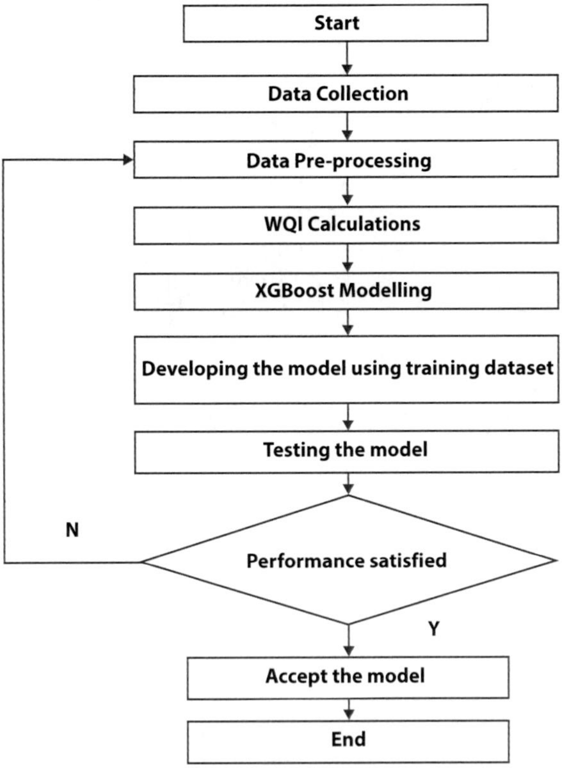

Figure 23.1 Flowchart of the proposed system.

included in this data, including total dissolved solids (TDS), turbidity, pH, dissolved oxygen (DO), chemical oxygen demand (COD), and biochemical oxygen demand (BOD). The information may be gathered from a variety of sources, such as internet databases, labs, and water quality monitoring stations as represented in Figure 23.2.

- Data Pre-processing: One of the key steps in cleaning and preparing data for modeling is data preparation. In this stage, duplicates are eliminated, missing values are handled, and outliers are handled. To guarantee that all features have comparable scales, data may be converted or normalized as needed, which can enhance the model's performance.
- Water Quality Index Calculation: Once the data is pre-processed, the next step is to calculate the water quality index for each observation in the dataset. The WQI [15] is a single value that represents the overall water quality based on multiple parameters. The specific formula for calculating the WQI may depend on the standards or guidelines used in a particular region or country. It usually involves aggregating the individual parameter values using appropriate weighting factors and normalization techniques.
- Training Model: After calculating the WQI for the data points, the dataset is divided into two subsets: training set and a testing set.
- Testing Model: The testing set is used to evaluate the model's performance on unseen data. The model makes predictions on the testing set, and the predicted WQI values are compared to the actual WQI values. This evaluation helps assess how well the model generalizes to new, unseen data and gives an indication of its accuracy.
- Final Classification of Model: Based on the evaluation results, the model's performance is assessed. If the model meets the desired accuracy and performance criteria, it can be considered for deployment to predict the water quality index for new, incoming data. If the model falls short, further optimization or tuning of hyper parameters may be done to improve its performance.

```
DO                                31
PH                                 8
CONDUCTIVITY                      25
BOD                               43
NITRATENAN_N_NITRITENANN         225
FECAL_COLIFORM                   316
TOTAL_COLIFORM                   132
dtype: int64
```

Figure 23.2 List of extracted parameters for estimation of water quality.

23.4 Results and Discussion

Results of the proposed model are presented and discussed in this section. As mentioned in the previous section water quality classification was done using XG Boost classifier algorithm into five different levels like Poor, Good, Very Good and Excellent on the basis of drinking suitability. We conducted a complete water quality assessment across multiple localities, collecting samples from over 1500 places. Each sample's water quality was rigorously evaluated, with measurements of seven critical parameters: dissolved oxygen (DO), pH, conductivity, biochemical oxygen demand (BOD), nitrate and nitrite levels, fecal coliform count, and total coliform count. These metrics serve as critical indications of the overall health and safety of the water. Our technology effectively classifies the quality of water samples using machine learning algorithms, offering useful information for informed decision-making in water resource management and public health across several geographical regions. This was developed and implemented a webpage using Django for better user interaction and feasibility. When we run the code, we got some more accurate results than previous machine learning techniques. We have an approximate accuracy of 96.6% and used seven input factors to classify water quality.

Correlation matrix in the context of XGBoost would specifically analyze the relationships between the features we have mentioned: dissolved oxygen (DO), pH, conductivity, biochemical oxygen demand (BOD), nitrate and nitrite levels, fecal coliform count, and total coliform count.

A strong positive association between two features, such as pH and Nitrate levels, may indicate that as pH rises, Nitrate levels rise as well. A large negative correlation between DO and BOD, on the other hand, may indicate an inverse relationship in which higher levels of dissolved oxygen correlate to lower levels of biochemical oxygen demand.

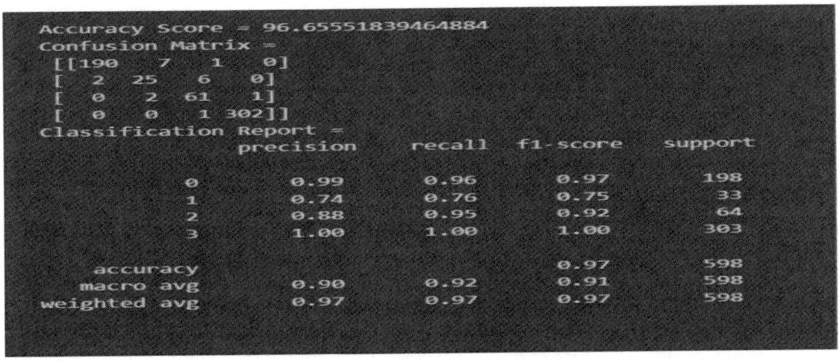

```
Accuracy Score = 96.65551839464884
Confusion Matrix =
 [[190   7   1   0]
 [  2  25   6   0]
 [  0   2  61   1]
 [  0   0   1 302]]
Classification Report =
              precision    recall  f1-score   support

           0       0.99      0.96      0.97       198
           1       0.74      0.76      0.75        33
           2       0.88      0.95      0.92        64
           3       1.00      1.00      1.00       303

    accuracy                           0.97       598
   macro avg       0.90      0.92      0.91       598
weighted avg       0.97      0.97      0.97       598
```

Figure 23.3 Accuracy score of XG Boost classifier method and existing models.

XGBoost's high accuracy rate in water quality classification when compared to other algorithms such as Support Vector Machines (SVM) and Bayesian Trees demonstrates its robustness and effectiveness in dealing with complicated datasets as mentioned in the Figure 23.3. XGBoost's ability to group weak learners and improve the boosting process makes it particularly good at identifying intricate patterns and relationships in data, resulting in superior predicting performance. Its innate ability to handle high-dimensional feature spaces and nonlinear interactions allows it to beat classic algorithms such as SVM and Decision Trees, making it a top choice for difficult classification problems like water quality evaluation.

The incorporation of Django into our water quality prediction system permitted the development of an intuitive shown in Figure 23.4 user-friendly online interface, allowing users to easily input water quality data and quickly obtain accurate forecasts. Using Django's powerful framework, smoothly integrated our XGBoost model's predictive capabilities to

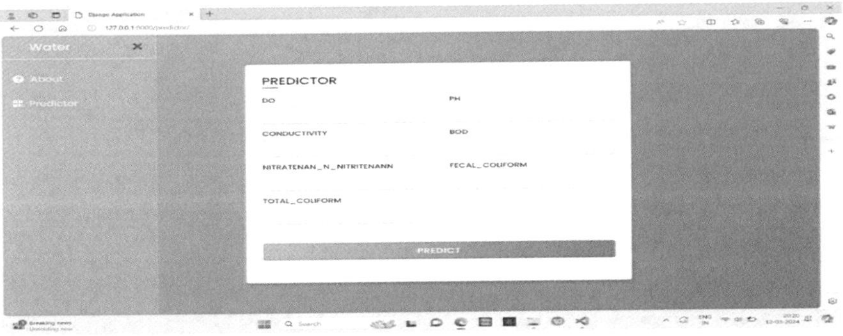

Figure 23.4 Predictor page.

Figure 23.5 Upload input parameters.

the web, allowing customers to obtain cutting-edge water quality categorization from any internet-connected device as presented in Figure 23.5. This seamless connection not only improves the user experience but also increases access to vital water quality insights, promoting informed decision-making and proactive environmental stewardship. The outcome of the proposed model is shown in Figure 23.6 in which water is classified as either Good, Normal or Bad.

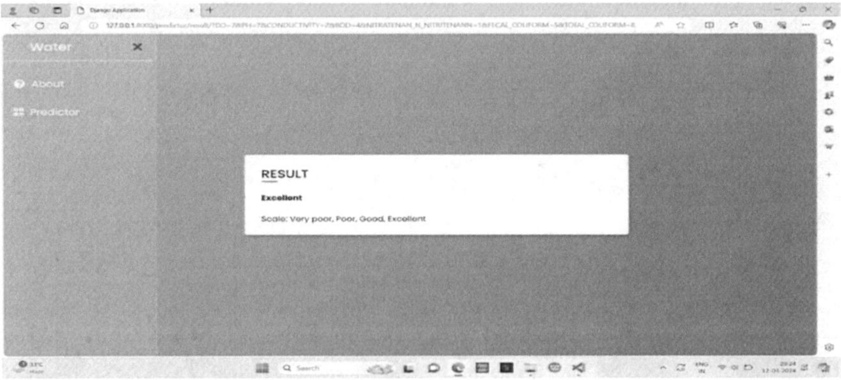

Figure 23.6 Water classification.

23.5 Conclusion

With this study it is concluded that the proposed XGBoost classifier model is far better than other approaches, with an amazing accuracy rate of 96%, according to the study's findings.. In this proposed water quality is classified into five different levels based on the quality features. This is where its superiority rests. Using Django webpage developed and integrated to the proposed XGBoost Classifier. By incorporating additional parameters the quality can be improved.

References

1. Khan, Y. and See, C.S., Predicting and analyzing water quality using Machine Learning: A comprehensive model. *2016 IEEE Long Island Systems, Applications and Technology Conference (LISAT)*, Farmingdale, NY, USA, pp. 1–6, 2016, doi: 10.1109/LISAT.2016.7494106.
2. Jia, X., Detecting Water Quality Using KNN, Bayesian and Decision Tree. *2022 Asia Conference on Algorithms, Computing and Machine Learning (CACML)*, Hangzhou, China, pp. 323–327, 2022, doi: 10.1109/CACML55074.2022.00061.
3. Alomani, S.M., Alhawiti, N.I., Alhakamy, A., Prediction of Quality of Water According to a Random Forest Classifier. *Int. J. Adv. Comput. Sci. Appl.(IJACSA)*, 13, 6, 1–6, 2022, http://dx.doi.org/10.14569/IJACSA.2022.01306105.
4. Muhammad, Z., Jailani, N.A.J., Leh, N.A.M., Hamid, S.A., Classification of Drinking Water Quality using Support Vector Machine (SVM) Algorithm. *2022 IEEE 12th International Conference on Control System, Computing and Engineering (ICCSCE)*, Penang, Malaysia, pp. 75–80, 2022, doi: 10.1109/ICCSCE54767.2022.9935657.
5. Satyanarayan, S., Moon, R., Umer, M., Raju, S., Bhaskar, N., Okali, R., A Prediction of Water Quality Analysis Using Machine Learning, pp. 1–6, 2023, 10.1109/ICDCECE57866.2023.10150940.
6. Liu, X., Zhang, Y., Wang, X. *et al.*, Water Quality Classification Using Machine Learning and Feature Selection Methods. *Water*, 12, 6, 1752, 2020.
7. Sahoo, B. and Gupta, V., Comparative Analysis of Machine Learning Algorithms for Water Quality Prediction. *Water Sci. Technol.*, 83, 3, 596–609, 2021.
8. Zhang, S., Zhu, C., Sin, J.K.O., Mok, P.K.T., A novel ultrathin elevated channel low-temperature poly-Si TFT. *IEEE Electron Device Lett.*, 20, 569–571, Nov. 1999.

9. Huang, Y., Li, M., Fu, L. *et al.*, Water Quality Prediction Model Using Machine Learning Algorithms: A Comparative Study. *Water*, 12, 11, 3201, 2020.
10. Gogoi, S., Baruah, A., Kalita, H.K. *et al.*, Comparative Assessment of Machine Learning Algorithms for Prediction of Water Quality Parameters. *Environ. Monit. Assess.*, 192, 505, 2020.
11. Li, Q., Li, J., Du, Y. *et al.*, Application of Machine Learning Techniques in Water Quality Prediction and Classification: A Review. *Water*, 11, 11, 2364, 2019.
12. Cui, H., Li, Z., Cao, F., Application of XGBoost algorithm in water quality prediction model. *Water Resour. Prot.*, 37, 3, 133–136, 2021.
13. Dharma, V., Nurtanio, N., Nugroho, F., Anggreainy, M., Kurniawan, A., A Review on Machine Learning Methods for Water Quality Prediction, pp. 131–138, 2023, 10.1109/AiDAS60501.2023.10284659.
14. Ragi, N., Holla, R., Manju, G., Predicting Water Quality Parameters Using Machine Learning, pp. 1109–1112, 2019, 10.1109/RTEICT46194.2019.9016825.
15. Yaghoubzadeh, A., Rajabi, M., Nozari, H., Ahmad, S., Support Vector Machine Applications in Water and Environmental Sciences. *Computational Intelligence for Water and Environmental Sciences,* pp. 291–310, 2022, 10.1007/978-981-19-2519-1_14.

Index

Also of Interest

Check out these published and forthcoming titles in the "Sustainable Computing and Optimization" series from Scrivener Publishing

Optimization in Sustainable Energy
Methods and Applications
Edited by Prasenjit Chatterjee, Anita Khosla, Ashwani Kumar and Gülay Demir
Forthcoming 2025. ISBN 978-1-394-24210-8

Bibliometric Analyses in Data-Driven Decision-Making
Edited by Prasenjit Chatterjee, Abhijit Saha, Seifedine Kadry and Gülay Demir
Forthcoming 2025. ISBN 978-1-394-30252-9

Quantum Computing Models for Cybersecurity and Wireless Communications
Edited by Budati Anil Kumar, Singamaneni Kranthi Kumar and Li Xingwang
Published 2025. ISBN 978-1-394-27139-9

Intelligent Data Analytics for Bioinformatics and Biomedical Systems
Edited By Neha Sharma, Korhan Cengiz and Prasenjit Chatterjee
Published 2024. ISBN 978-1-394-27088-0

Optimization Techniques in Engineering
Advances and Applications
Edited by Anita Khosla, Prasenjit Chatterjee, Ikbal Ali and Dheeraj Joshi
Published 2023. ISBN 978-1-119-90627-8

Computational Intelligence in Sustainable Reliability Engineering
Edited by S. C. Malik, Deepak Sinwar, Ashish Kumar, S. R. Gadde, Prasenjit Chatterjee and Bui Thanh Hung
Published 2023. ISBN 978-1-119-86501-8

Decision Support Systems for Smart City Applications
Edited by: Loveleen Gaur, Vernika Agarwal and Prasenjit Chatterjee
Published 2023. ISBN 978-1-119-89643-2

Fuzzy Computing in Data Science
Applications and Challenges
Editors: Sachi Nandan Mohanty, Prasenjit Chatterjee and Bui Thanh Hung
Published 2022. ISBN: 978-1-119-86492-9

Handbook of Intelligent Computing and Optimization for Sustainable Development
Edited by: Mukhdeep Singh Manshahia, Valeriy Kharchenko, Elias Munapo, J. Joshua Thomas and Pandian Vasant
Published 2022. ISBN 978-1-119-79182-9

Machine Learning Algorithms and Applications
Edited by Mettu Srinivas, G. Sucharitha and Anjanna Matta
Published 2021. ISBN 978-1-119-76885-2

Smart Sustainable Intelligent Systems
Edited by Namita Gupta, Prasenjit Chatterjee and Tanupriya Choudhury
Published 2021. ISBN 978-1-119-75058-1

www.scrivenerpublishing.com

Printed in the USA/Agawam, MA
September 28, 2026

910661.113